The Data Compression Book

The Data Compression Book

Featuring fast, efficient data
compression techniques in C

Mark Nelson

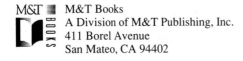 M&T Books
A Division of M&T Publishing, Inc.
411 Borel Avenue
San Mateo, CA 94402

Limits of Liability and Disclaimer of Warranty
The Author and Publisher of this book have used their best efforts in preparing the book and the programs contained in it. These efforts include the development, research, and testing of the theories and programs to determine their effectiveness.

The Author and Publisher make no warranty of any kind, expressed or implied, with regard to these programs or the documentation contained in this book. The Author and Publisher shall not be liable in any event for incidental or consequential damages in connection with, or arising out of, the furnishing, performance, or use of these programs.

Library of Congress Cataloging-in-Publication Data

Nelson, Mark, 1958 -
    The Data Compression Book/by Mark Nelson
        p. cm.
        Includes index.
        ISBN 1-55851-214-4: $29.95   ISBN 1-55851-216-0 (book/disk set): $39.95
        1. Data Compression (Computer Science)   I. Title
        QA76.9.D33N46   1991   91-23080
        005.74'6--dc20   CIP

Project Editor: Tova Fliegel   **Cover Design:** Lauren Smith Design
Copy Editor: Shayne Bell   **Layout:** Marni Tapscott
Technical Reviewer: Robert Jung

95   94   93 92   4 3 2 1

Contents

Acknowledgments

I would like to take this opportunity to thank all the people who made this book possible: Denise, Joseph, and Kaitlin, for their patience and support; Tova and Robert, for keeping me honest and on time (sort of); and Robert X. Cringely, for supplying the secret formula to writing a book. Most importantly, I want to thank Jon Erickson, who made it all possible.

Mark Nelson

I concluded, we kinotropists must be numbered among Britain's most adept programmers of Enginery of any sort, and virtually all advances in the compression of data have originated as kinotropic applications.

At this point, he interrupted again, asking if I had indeed said "the compression of data," and was I familiar with the term "algorithmic compression"? I assured him I was.

The Difference Engine
William Gibson and Bruce Sterling

Why This Book Is for You

If you want to learn how programs like PKZIP and LHarc work, this book is for you. The compression techniques used in these programs are described in detail, accompanied by working code. After reading this book, even the novice C programmer will be able to write a complete compression/archiving program that can be ported to virtually any operating system or hardware platform.

If you want to include data compression in other programs you write, this book will become an invaluable tool. It contains dozens of working programs with C code that can easily be added to your applications. In-depth discussions of various compression methods will help you make intelligent decisions when creating programs that use data compression.

If you want to learn why lossy compression of graphics is the key factor in enabling the multimedia revolution, you need this book. DCT-based compression like that used by the JPEG algorithm is described in detail. Working programs let you experiment with this fascinating new technology.

The Data Compression Book provides you with a comprehensive reference to this important field. No other book available has the detailed description of compression algorithms or working C implementations for those algorithms. If you are planning to work in this field, *The Data Compression Book* is indispensable.

Data Compression Book Source Code Disk

Why bother manually typing in the book's source code when all the information you need is ready to use on disk? Code examples are used throughout the text, and this book's optional disk (PC/MS-DOS format) contains the source code for all the programming examples listed. Only $20 postage-paid!

To order with your credit card, call TOLL FREE 1-800-533-4372
(in CA 1-800-356-2002). Or mail your order with payment to
M&T Books, 411 Borel Avenue, Suite 100, San Mateo, CA 94402
California residents please add applicable sales tax.

CHAPTER 1

Introduction to Data Compression

The primary purpose of this book is to explain various data-compression techniques using the C programming language. Data compression seeks to reduce the number of bits used to store or transmit information. It encompasses a wide variety of software and hardware compression techniques which can be so unlike one another that they have little in common except that they compress data. The LZW algorithm used in the Compuserve GIF specification, for example, has virtually nothing in common with the CCITT G.721 specification used to compress digitized voice over phone lines.

This book will not take a comprehensive look at every variety of data compression. The field has grown in the last 25 years to a point where this is simply not possible. What this book will cover are the various types of data compression commonly used on personal and midsized computers, including compression of binary programs, data, sound, and graphics.

Furthermore, this book will either ignore or only lightly cover data-compression techniques that rely on hardware for practical use or that require hardware applications. Many of today's voice-compression schemes were designed for the worldwide fixed-bandwidth digital telecommunications networks. These compression schemes are intellectually interesting, but they require a specific type of hardware tuned to the fixed bandwidth of the communications channel. Different algorithms that don't have to meet this requirement are used to compress digitized voice on a PC, and these algorithms generally offer better performance.

Some of the most interesting areas in data compression today, however, do concern compression techniques just becoming possible with new and more powerful hardware. Lossy image compression, like that used in multimedia systems, for example, can now be implemented on standard desktop platforms. This book will cover practical ways to both experiment with and implement some of the algorithms used in these techniques.

The Audience

You will need basic programming skills to adequately discuss data-compression code. The ability to follow block-structured code, such as C or Pascal, is a requirement. In addition, understanding computer architecture well enough to follow bit-oriented operations, such as shifting, logical ORing and ANDing, and so on, will be essential.

This does not mean that you need to be a C guru for this book to be worthwhile. You don't even have to be a programmer. But the ability to follow code will be essential, because the concepts discussed here will be illustrated with portable C programs. The C code in this book has been written with an eye toward simplicity in the hopes that C novices will still be able to follow the programs. We will avoid the more esoteric constructs of C, but the code will be C, not pseudocode or English.

Why C?

The use of C to illustrate data-compression algorithms may raise some hackles. A more traditional way to write this book would have been to use pseudocode to sketch out the algorithms. But the lack of rigor in a pseudocode "program" often leads to hazy or incomplete definitions full of lines like "PROCESS FILE UNTIL OUT OF DATA." The result is that pseudocode is easy to read, but not so easy to translate into a working program.

If pseudocode is unsatisfactory, the next best choice is to use a conventional programming language. Though hundreds of choices are available, C seems the best choice for this type of book for several good reasons. First, in many respects C has become the lingua franca of programmers. That C compilers support computers ranging from a lowly 8051 microcontroller to supercomputers capable of 100 million instructions per second (MIPS) has had much to do with this. It doesn't mean that C is the language of choice for all programmers. What it does mean is that most programmers should have a C compiler available for their machines, and most are probably regularly exposed to C code. Because of this, many programmers who use other languages can still manage to code in C, and even more can at least read C.

A second reason for using C is that it is a language without too many surprises. The few constructs it uses as basic language elements are easily translated to other languages. So a data-compression program that is illustrated using C can be converted to a working Pascal program through a relatively straightforward translation procedure. Even assembly-language programmers should find the process relatively painless.

Perhaps the most important reason for using C is simply one of efficiency. C is often thought of as a high-level assembly language, since it allows programmers to get close to the hardware. Despite the increasing optimization found in recent C compilers, it is not likely that C will ever exceed the speed or size possible in hand-coded assembly language. That flaw is offset, however, by the ability to easily port C code to other machines. So for a book of this type, C is probably the most efficient choice.

Which C?

Despite being advertised as a "portable" language, a C program that compiles and executes on a given machine is not guaranteed to run on any other. It may not even compile using a different compiler on the same machine. The important thing to remember is not that C is portable, but that it *can* be portable. The code for this book has been written to be portable, and it compiles and runs cleanly using several compilers and environments. The compilers/environments used here include:

- Microsoft C 6.0, MS-DOS 3.3/5.0
- Borland C++ 2.0, MS-DOS 3.3/5.0
- Zortech C++, MS-DOS 3.3/5.0, with 286 and 386 DOS Extenders
- Interactive Unix System 3.2 with the portable C compiler

One important portability issue is library function calls. Though the C programming language was fairly well defined by the original K&R book (Brian W. Kernighan and Dennis M. Ritchie, *The C Programming Language* [Englewood Cliffs, N.J.: Prentice-Hall, 1978]), the run-time library implementation was left totally up to the whims of the implementor. Fortunately, the American National Standards Institute was able to complete the C language specification in 1990, and the result was published as ANSI standard XJ11.34. This standard not only expanded and pinned down the original K&R language specification, but it also took on the definition of a standard C run-time library. This makes it much easier to write code that works the same way from machine to machine. The code in this book will be written with the intention of using only ANSI C library calls. Compiler-dependent extensions to either the language or the library will be avoided wherever possible.

Given the standardization of the libraries, the remaining portability issues center around two things: sizes of the basic data types and dealing with noncompliant compilers. The majority of data-type conflicts arise when switching between 16- and 32-bit machines.

Fortunately, it is fairly easy to manage the change between 16- and 32-bit machines. Though the basic integer data type switches between 16- and 32-bits, both machines have a 16-bit "short int" data type. Once again, a "long int" is generally 32 bits on both machines. So in cases where the size of an integer clearly matters, it can be pinned down to either 16- or 32-bits with the appropriate declaration.

On the vast majority of machines used in the world today, the C compiler implementation of the "char" data type is 8 bits wide. In this book, we will gloss over the possibility that any other size exists and stick with 8-bit characters. In general, porting a program shown here to a machine with an unusual char size is not too difficult, but spending too much time on it will obscure the important point of the programs here, which is data compression.

The final issue to deal with when writing portable code is the problem of noncompliant compilers. In the MS-DOS world, most C compilers undergo major releases and upgrades every two years or so. This means that most compiler vendors have been able to release new versions of their compilers that now conform closely to the ANSI C standard. But this is not the case for users of many other operating systems. In particular, UNIX users will frequently be using a C compiler which came with their system and which conforms to the older K&R language definition. While the ANSI C committee went to great lengths to make ANSI C upwardly compatible from K&R C, we need to watch out for a few problems.

The first problem lies in the use of function prototypes. Under K&R C, function prototypes were generally used only when necessary. The compiler assumed that any unseen function returned an integer, and it accepted this without complaint. If a function returned something unusual—a pointer or a long, for instance—the programmer would write a function prototype to inform the compiler:

```
long locate_string();
```

Here, the prototype told the compiler to generate code that assumes that the function returned a long instead of an int. Function prototypes didn't have much more use than that. Because of this, many C programmers working under a K&R regime made little or no use of function prototypes, and their appearance in a program was something of an oddity.

While the ANSI C committee tried not to alter the basic nature of C, they were unable to pass up the potential improvements to the language that were possible through the expansion of the prototyping facility. Under ANSI C, a function prototype defines not only the return type of a function, but also the type of all the arguments as well. The function shown earlier, for example, might have the following prototype with an ANSI C compiler:

```
long locate_string( FILE *input_file, char *string );
```

This lets the compiler generate the correct code for the return type and check for the correct type and number of arguments as well. Since passing the wrong type or number of arguments to a function is a major source of programmer error in C, the committee correctly assumed that allowing this form of type checking constituted a step forward for C.

7

Under many ANSI C compilers, use of full ANSI function prototypes is strongly encouraged. In fact, many compilers will generate warning messages when a function is used without previously encountering a prototype. This is well and good, but the same function prototypes will not work on a trusty portable C compiler under UNIX.

The solution to this dilemma is not pretty, but it works. Under ANSI C, the predefined macro __STDC__ is always defined to indicate that the code is being compiled through a presumably ANSI-compliant compiler. We can let the preprocessor turn certain sections of our header files on or off, depending on whether we are using a noncompliant compiler or not. A header file containing the prototypes for a bit-oriented package, for example, might look something like this:

```
#ifdef __STDC__

FILE *open_bitstream( char *file_name, char *mode );
void close_bitstream( FILE *bitstream );
int read_bit( FILE*bitstream );
int write_bit( FILE *bitstream, int bit );

#else

FILE *open_bitstream();
void close_bitstream();
int read_bit();
int write_bit();

#endif
```

The preprocessor directives don't contribute much to the look of the code, but they are a necessary part of writing portable programs. Since the programs in this book are supposed to be compiled with the compiler set to its maximum possible warning level, a few "#ifdef" statements will be part of the package.

A second problem with the K&R family of C compilers lies in the actual function body. Under K&R C, a particular function might have a definition like the one on the next page.

```
int foo( c )
char c;
{
/* Function body */
}
```

The same function written using an ANSI C function body would look like this:

```
int foo( char c )
{
/* Function body */
}
```

These two functions may look the same, but ANSI C rules require that they be treated differently. The K&R function body will have the compiler "promote" the character argument to an integer before using it in the function body, but the ANSI C function body will leave it as a character. Promoting one integral type to another lets lots of sneaky problems slip into seemingly well-written code, and the stricter compilers will issue warnings when they detect a problem of this nature.

Since K&R compilers will not accept the second form of a function body, be careful when defining character arguments to functions. Unfortunately, the solutions are once again either to not use character arguments or to resort to more of the ugly "#ifdef" preprocessor baggage.

Keeping Score

Throughout this book, there will be references to "compression ratios" and compression statistics. To keep the various forms of compression on a level playing field, compression statistics will always be in relationship to the sample compression files used in the February 1991 *Dr. Dobb's Journal* compression contest. These files consist of about 6 megabytes of data broken down into three roughly equal categories. The first category is text, consisting of manuscripts, programs, memos, and other readable files. The second category consists of binary data, including database files, executable files, and spreadsheet data. The third category consists of graphics files stored in raw screen-dump formats.

The programs created and discussed in this book will be judged by three rough measures of performance. The first will be the amount of memory consumed by the program during compression; this number will be approximated as well as it can be. The second will be the amount of time the program takes to compress the entire *Dr. Dobb's* dataset. The third will be the compression ratio of the entire set.

Different people use different formulas to calculate compression ratios. Some prefer bits/byte. Others use ratios, such as 2:1 or 3:1 (advertising people seem to like this format). In this book, we will use a simple compression-percentage formula:

```
( 1 - ( compressed_size / raw_size ) ) * 100
```

This means that a file that doesn't change at all when compressed will have a compression ratio of 0 percent. A file compressed down to one-third of its original size will have a compression ratio of 67 percent. A file that shrinks down to 0 bytes (!) will have a compression ratio of 100 percent.

This way of measuring compression may not be perfect, but it shows perfection at 100 percent and total failure at 0 percent. In fact, a file that goes through a compression program and comes out larger will show a negative compression ratio.

The Structure

This book consists of twelve chapters and a set of floppy disks. The organization roughly parallels the historical progression of data compression, starting in the "dawn age" around 1950 and working up to the present.

Chapter 2 is a reference chapter which attempts to establish the fundamental data-compression lexicon. It discusses the birth of information theory, and it introduces a series of concepts, terms, buzzwords, and theories used over and over in the rest of the book. Even if you are a data-compression novice, mastery of chapter 2 will bring you up to the "cocktail party" level of information, meaning that you will be able to carry on an intelligent-sounding conversation about data compression even if you don't fully understand its intricacies.

Chapter 3 discusses the birth of data compression, starting with variable-length bit coding. The development of Shannon-Fano coding and Huffman coding represented the birth of both data compression and information theory. These coding methods are still in wide use today. In addition, chapter 3 discusses the difference between modeling and coding—the two faces of the data-compression coin.

Standard Huffman coding suffers from a significant problem when used for high-performance data compression. The compression program has to pass a complete copy of the Huffman coding statistics to the expansion program. As the compression program collects more statistics and tries to increase its compression ratio, the statistics take up more space and work against the increased compression. Chapter 4 discusses a way to solve this dilemma: adaptive Huffman coding. This is a relatively recent innovation, due to CPU and memory requirements. Adaptive coding greatly expands the horizons of Huffman coding, leading to vastly improved compression ratios.

Huffman coding has to use an integral number of bits for each code, which is usually slightly less than optimal. A more recent innovation, arithmetic coding, uses a fractional number of bits per code, allowing it to incrementally improve compression performance. Chapter 5 explains how this recent innovation works, and it shows how to integrate an arithmetic coder with a statistical model.

Chapter 6 discusses statistical modeling. Whether using Huffman coding, adaptive Huffman coding, or arithmetic coding, it is still necessary to have a statistical model to drive the coder. This chapter shows some of the interesting techniques used to implement powerful models using limited memory resources.

Dictionary compression methods take a completely different approach to compression from the techniques discussed in the previous four chapters. Chapter 7 provides an overview of these compression methods, which represent strings of characters with single codes. Dictionary methods have become the de facto standard for general-purpose data compression on small computers due to their high-performance compression combined with reasonable memory requirements.

The fathers of dictionary-based compression, Ziv and Lempel published a paper in 1977 proposing a sliding dictionary method of data compression which has become very popular. Chapter 8 looks at recent adaptations of LZ77 compression used in popular archiving programs such as PKZIP.

Chapter 9 takes a detailed look at one of the first widely popular dictionary-based compression methods: LZW compression. LZW is the compression method used in the UNIX COMPRESS program and in earlier versions of the MS-DOS ARC program. This chapter also takes a look at the foundation of LZW compression, published in 1978 by Ziv and Lempel.

All of the compression techniques discussed through chapter 9 are "lossless." Lossy methods can be used on speech and graphics, and they are capable of achieving dramatically higher compression ratios. Chapter 10 shows how lossy compression can be used on digitized sound data with techniques like linear predictive coding and adaptive PCM.

Chapter 11 discusses lossy compression techniques applied to computer graphics. The industry is standardizing rapidly on the not-yet-complete JPEG standard. The techniques used in the JPEG standard will be presented in this chapter.

Chapter 12 describes how to put it all together into an archive program. A general-purpose archiving program should be able to compress and decompress files while keeping track of file names, dates, attributes, compression ratios, and compression methods. An archive format should ideally be portable to different types of computers. A sample archive program is developed, which applies the techniques used in previous chapters to put together a complete program.

CHAPTER 2

The Data-Compression Lexicon, with a History

Like any other scientific or engineering discipline, data compression has a vocabulary that at first can seem overwhelmingly strange to an outsider. Terms like *Lempel-Ziv compression, arithmetic coding,* and *statistical modeling* get tossed around with reckless abandon.

While the list of buzzwords is long enough to merit a glossary, mastering them is not as daunting a project as it may first seem. With a bit of study and a few notes, any programmer should hold his or her own at a cocktail-party argument over data-compression techniques.

The Two Kingdoms

Data-compression techniques can be divided into two major families: lossy and lossless. Lossy data compression concedes a certain loss of accuracy in exchange for greatly increased compression. Lossy compression proves effective when applied to graphics images and digitized voice. By their very nature, these digitized representations of analog phenomena are not perfect to begin with, so the idea of output and input not matching exactly is a little more acceptable. Most lossy compression techniques can be adjusted to different quality levels, gaining higher accuracy in exchange for less effective compression. Until recently, lossy compression has been primarily implemented using dedicated hardware. In the past few years, powerful lossy-compression programs have been moved to desktop CPUs, but even so the field is still dominated by hardware implementations.

Lossless compression consists of those techniques guaranteed to generate an exact duplicate of the input data stream after a compress/expand cycle. This is the type of compression used when storing database records, spreadsheets, or word processing files. In these applications, the loss of even a single bit could be catastrophic. Most techniques discussed in this book will be lossless.

Data Compression = Modeling + Coding

In general, data compression consists of taking a stream of symbols and transforming them into codes. If the compression is effective, the resulting stream of codes will be smaller than the original symbols. The decision to output a certain code for a certain symbol or set of symbols is based on a model. The model is simply a collection of data and rules used to process input symbols and determine which code(s) to output. A program uses the model to accurately define the probabilities for each symbol and the coder to produce an appropriate code based on those probabilities.

Modeling and coding are two distinctly different things. People frequently use the term *coding* to refer to the entire data-compression process instead of just a single component of that process. You will hear the phrases "Huffman coding" or "Run-Length Encoding," for example, to describe a data-compression technique, when in fact they are just coding methods used in conjunction with a model to compress data.

Using the example of Huffman coding, a breakdown of the compression process looks something like this:

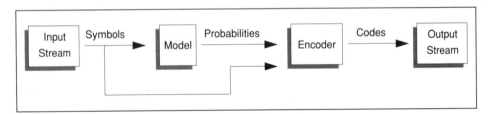

Figure 2-1. A Statistical Model with a Huffman Encoder.

In the case of Huffman coding, the actual output of the encoder is determined by a set of probabilities. When using this type of coding, a symbol that has a very high probability of occurrence generates a code with very few bits. A symbol with a low probability generates a code with a larger number of bits.

We think of the model and the program's coding process as different because of the countless ways to model data, all of which can use the same coding process to produce their output. A simple program using Huffman coding, for example, would use a model that gave the raw probability of each symbol occurring anywhere in the input stream. A more sophisticated program might calculate the probability based on the last 10 symbols in the input stream. Even though both programs use Huffman coding to produce their output, their compression ratios would probably be radically different.

So when the topic of coding methods comes up at your next cocktail party, be alert for statements like "Huffman coding in general doesn't produce very good compression ratios." This would be your perfect opportunity to respond with "That's like saying Converse sneakers don't go very fast. I always thought the leg power of the runner had a lot to do with it." If the conversation has already dropped to the point where you are discussing data compression, this might even go over as a real demonstration of wit.

The Dawn Age

Data compression is perhaps the fundamental expression of Information Theory. Information Theory is a branch of mathematics that had its genesis in the late 1940s with the work of Claude Shannon at Bell Labs. It concerns itself with various questions about information, including different ways of storing and communicating messages.

Data compression enters into the field of Information Theory because of its concern with redundancy. Redundant information in a message takes extra bits to encode, and if we can get rid of that extra information, we will have reduced the size of the message.

Information Theory uses the term *entropy* as a measure of how much information is encoded in a message. The word *entropy* was borrowed from thermodynamics, and it has a similar meaning. The higher the entropy of a message, the more information it contains. The entropy of a symbol is defined as the negative logarithm of its probability. To determine the information content of a message in bits, we express the entropy using the base 2 logarithm:

Number of bits = – Log base 2 (probability)

The entropy of an entire message is simply the sum of the entropy of all individual symbols.

Entropy fits with data compression in its determination of how many bits of information are actually present in a message. If the probability of the character 'e' appearing in this manuscript is 1/16, for example, the information content of the character is four bits. So the character string "eeeee" has a total content of 20 bits. If we are using standard 8-bit ASCII characters to encode this message, we are actually using 40 bits. The difference between the 20 bits of entropy and the 40 bits used to encode the message is where the potential for data compression arises.

One important fact to note about entropy is that, unlike the thermodynamic measure of entropy, we can use no absolute number for the information content of a given message. The problem is that when we calculate entropy, we use a number that gives us the probability of a given symbol. The probability figure we use is actually the probability for a given model, not an absolute number. If we change the model, the probability will change with it.

How probabilities change can be seen clearly when using different orders with a statistical model. A statistical model tracks the probability of a symbol based on what symbols appeared previously in the input stream. The order of the model determines how many previous symbols are taken into account. An order-0 model, for example, won't look at previous characters. An order-1 model looks at the previous character, and so on.

The different order models can yield drastically different probabilities for a character. The letter 'u' under an order-0 model, for example, may have only a 1 percent probability of occurrence. But under an order-1 model, if the previous character was 'q,' the 'u' may have a 95 percent probability.

This seemingly unstable notion of a character's probability proves troublesome for many people. They prefer that a character have a fixed "true" probability that told what the chances of its "really" occurring are. Claude Shannon attempted to determine the true information content of the English language with a "party game" experiment. He would uncover a message concealed from his audience a single character at a time. The audience guessed what the next character would be, one guess at a time, until they got it right. Shannon could then determine the entropy of the message as a whole by taking the logarithm of the guess count. Other researchers have done more experiments using similar techniques.

While these experiments are useful, they don't circumvent the notion that a symbol's probability depends on the model. The difference with these experiments is that the model is the one kept inside the human brain. This may be one of the best models available, but it is still a model, not an absolute truth.

In order to compress data well, we need to select models that predict symbols with high probabilities. A symbol that has a high probability has a low information content and will need fewer bits to encode. Once the model is producing high probabilities, the next step is to encode the symbols using an appropriate number of bits.

Coding

Once Information Theory had advanced to where the number of bits of information in a symbol could be determined, the next step was to develop new methods for encoding information. To compress data, we need to encode symbols with exactly the number of bits of information the symbol contains. If the character 'e' only gives us four bits of information, then it should be coded with exactly four bits. If 'x' contains twelve bits, it should be coded with twelve bits.

By encoding characters using EBCDIC or ASCII, we clearly aren't going to be very close to an optimum method. Since every character is encoded using the same number of bits, we introduce lots of error in both directions, with most of the codes in a message being too long and some being too short.

Solving this coding problem in a reasonable manner was one of the first problems tackled by practitioners of Information Theory. Two approaches that worked well were Shannon-Fano coding and Huffman coding—two different ways of generating variable-length codes when given a probability table for a given set of symbols.

Huffman coding, named for its inventor D. A. Huffman, achieves the minimum amount of redundancy possible in a fixed set of variable-length codes. This doesn't mean that Huffman coding is an optimal coding method. It means that it provides the best approximation for coding symbols when using fixed-width codes.

The problem with Huffman or Shannon-Fano coding is that they use an integral number of bits in each code. If the entropy of a given character is 2.5 bits, the Huffman code for that character must be either 2 or 3 bits, not 2.5. Because of this, Huffman coding can't be considered an optimal coding method, but it is the best approximation that uses fixed codes with an integral number of bits. Here is a sample of Huffman codes:

Symbol	Huffman Code
E	100
T	101
A	1100
I	11010
. . .	
X	01101111
Q	01101110001
Z	01101110000

An Improvement. Though Huffman coding is inefficient due to using an integral number of bits per code, it is relatively easy to implement and very efficient for both coding and decoding. Huffman first published his paper on coding in 1952, and it instantly became the most-cited paper in Information Theory. It probably still is. Huffman's original work spawned numerous minor variations, and it dominated the coding world till the early 1980s.

As the cost of CPU cycles went down, new possibilities for more efficient coding techniques emerged. One in particular, arithmetic coding, is a viable successor to Huffman coding.

Arithmetic coding is somewhat more complicated in both concept and implementation than standard variable-width codes. It does not produce a single code for each symbol. Instead, it produces a code for an entire message. Each symbol added to the message incrementally modifies the output code. This is an improvement because the net effect of each input symbol on the output code can be a fractional number of bits instead of an integral number. So if the entropy for character 'e' is 2.5 bits, it is possible to add exactly 2.5 bits to the output code.

An example of why this can be more effective is shown in the following table, the analysis of an imaginary message. In it, Huffman coding would yield a total message length of 89 bits, but arithmetic coding would approach the true information content of the message, or 83.69 bits. The difference in the two messages works out to approximately 6 percent. Here are some sample message probabilities:

Symbol	Information Content	Huffman Code Bit Count	Number of Occurrences
E	1.26 bit	1 bits	20
A	1.26 bit	2 bits	20
X	4.00 bit	3 bits	3
Y	4.00 bit	4 bits	3
Z	4.58 bit	4 bits	2

The problem with Huffman coding in the above message is that it can't create codes with the exact information content required. In most cases it is a little above or a little below, leading to deviations from the optimum. But arithmetic coding gets to within a fraction of a percent of the actual information content, resulting in more accurate coding.

Arithmetic coding requires more CPU power than was available until recently. Even now it will generally suffer from a significant speed disadvantage when compared to older coding methods. But the gains from switching to this method are significant enough to ensure that arithmetic coding will be the coding method of choice when the cost of storing or sending information is high enough.

Modeling

If we use a an automotive metaphor for data compression, coding would be the wheels, but modeling would be the engine. Regardless of the efficiency of the coder, if it doesn't have a model feeding it good probabilities, it won't compress data.

Lossless data compression is generally implemented using one of two different types of modeling: statistical or dictionary-based. Statistical modeling reads in and encodes a single symbol at a time using the probability of that character's appearance. Dictionary-based modeling uses a single code to replace strings of symbols. In dictionary-based modeling, the coding problem is reduced in significance, leaving the model supremely important.

Statistical Modeling. The simplest forms of statistical modeling use a static table of probabilities. In the earliest days of information theory, the CPU cost of analyzing data and building a Huffman tree was considered significant, so it wasn't frequently performed. Instead, representative blocks of data were analyzed once, giving a table of character-frequency counts. Huffman encoding/decoding trees were then built and stored. Compression programs had access to this *static model* and would compress data using it.

But using a universal static model has limitations. If an input stream doesn't match well with the previously accumulated statistics, the compression ratio will be de-graded—possibly to the point where the output stream becomes larger than the input stream. The next obvious enhancement is to build a statistics table for every unique input stream.

Building a static Huffman table for each file to be compressed has its advantages. The table is uniquely adapted to that particular file, so it should give better compres-sion than a universal table. But there is additional overhead since the table (or the statistics used to build the table) has to be passed to the decoder ahead of the compressed code stream.

For an order-0 compression table, the actual statistics used to create the table may take up as little as 256 bytes—not a very large amount of overhead. But trying to achieve better compression through use of a higher order table will make the statistics that need to be passed to the decoder grow at an alarming rate. Just moving to an order-

1 model can boost the statistics table from 256 to 65,536 bytes. Though compression ratios will undoubtedly improve when moving to order-1, the overhead of passing the statistics table will probably wipe out any gains.

For this reason, compression research in the last 10 years has concentrated on *adpative* models. When using an adaptive model, data does not have to be scanned once in order to generate statistics. Instead, the statistics are continually modified as new characters are read in and coded. The general flow of a program using an adaptive model looks something like that shown in figures 2-2 and 2-3.

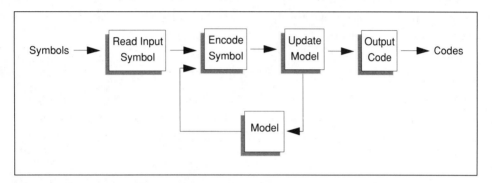

Figure 2-2. General Adaptive Compression.

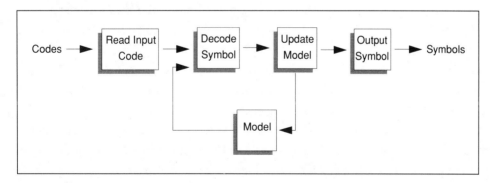

Figure 2-3. General Adaptive Decompression.

The important point in making this system work is that the box labeled "Update Model" has to work exactly the same way for both the compression and decompression programs. After each character (or group of characters) is read in, it is encoded or decoded. Only after the encoding or decoding is complete can the model be updated to take into account the most recent symbol or group of symbols.

One problem with adaptive models is that they start knowing essentially nothing about the data. So when the program first starts, it doesn't do a very good job of compression. Most adaptive algorithms tend to adjust quickly to the data stream and will begin turning in respectable compression ratios after only a few thousand bytes. Likewise, it doesn't take long for the compression-ratio curve to flatten out so that reading in more data doesn't improve the compression ratio.

One advantage that adaptive models have over static models is the ability to adapt to local conditions. When compressing executable files, for example, the character of the input data may change drastically as the program file changes from binary program code to binary data. A well-written adaptive program will weight the most recent data higher than old data, so it will modify its statistics to better suit changed data.

Dictionary Schemes. Statistical models generally encode a single symbol at a time—reading it in, calculating a probability, then outputting a single code. A dictionary-based compression scheme uses a different concept. It reads in input data and looks for groups of symbols that appear in a dictionary. If a string match is found, a pointer or index into the dictionary can be output instead of the code for the symbol. The longer the match, the better the compression ratio.

This method of encoding changes the focus of dictionary compression. Simple coding methods are generally used, and the focus of the program is on the modeling. In LZW compression, for example, simple codes of uniform width are used for all substitutions.

A static dictionary is used like the list of references in an academic paper. Through the text of a paper, the author may simply substitute a number that points to a list of references instead of writing out the full title of a referenced work. The dictionary is static because it is built up and transmitted with the text of the work—the reader does not have to build it on the fly. The first time I see a number in the text like this—[2]—I know it points to the static dictionary.

The problem with a static dictionary is identical to the problem the user of a static statistical model faces: The dictionary needs to be transmitted along with the text, resulting in a certain amount of overhead added to the compressed text. An adaptive dictionary scheme helps avoid this problem.

Mentally, we are used to a type of adaptive dictionary when performing acronym replacements in technical literature. The standard way to use this adaptive dictionary is to spell out the acronym, then put its abbreviated substitution in parentheses. So the first time I mention the Massachusetts Institute of Technology (MIT), I define both the dictionary string and its substitution. From then on, referring to MIT in the text should automatically invoke a mental substitution.

Ziv and Lempel

Until 1980, most general-compression schemes used statistical modeling. But in 1977 and 1978, Jacob Ziv and Abraham Lempel described a pair of compression methods using an adaptive dictionary. These two algorithms sparked a flood of new techniques that used dictionary-based methods to achieve impressive new compression ratios.

LZ77. The first compression algorithm described by Ziv and Lempel is commonly referred to as LZ77. It is relatively simple. The dictionary consists of all the strings in a window into the previously read input stream. A file-compression program, for example, could use a 4K-byte window as a dictionary. While new groups of symbols are being read in, the algorithm looks for matches with strings found in the previous 4K bytes of data already read in. Any matches are encoded as pointers sent to the output stream.

LZ77 and its variants make attractive compression algorithms. Maintaining the model is simple; encoding the output is simple; and programs that work very quickly can be written using LZ77. Popular programs such as PKZIP and LHarc use variants of the LZ77 algorithm, and they have proven very popular.

LZ78. The LZ78 program takes a different approach to building and maintaining the dictionary. Instead of having a limited-size window into the preceding text, LZ78 builds its dictionary out of *all* of the previously seen symbols in the input text. But instead of having carte blanche access to all the symbol strings in the preceding text, a dictionary of strings is built a single character at a time. The first time the string "Mark" is seen, for example, the string "Ma" is added to the dictionary. The next time, "Mar" is added. If "Mark" is seen again, it is added to the dictionary.

This incremental procedure works very well at isolating frequently used strings and adding them to the table. Unlike LZ77 methods, strings in LZ78 can be extremely long, which allows for high-compression ratios. LZ78 was the first of the two Ziv-Lempel algorithms to achieve popular success, due to the LZW adaptation by Terry Welch, which forms the core of the UNIX COMPRESS program.

Lossy Compression

Until recently, lossy compression has been primarily performed on special-purpose hardware. The advent of inexpensive Digital Signal Processor (DSP) chips began lossy compression's move off the circuit board and onto the desktop. CPU prices have now dropped to where it is becoming practical to perform lossy compression on general-purpose desktop PCs.

Lossy compression is fundamentally different from lossless compression in one respect: it accepts a slight loss of data to facilitate compression. Lossy compression is generally done on analog data stored digitally, with the primary applications being graphics and sound files.

This type of compression frequently makes two passes. A first pass over the data performs a high-level, signal-processing function. This frequently consists of transforming the data into the frequency domain, using FFT-like algorithms. Once the data has been transformed, it is "smoothed," rounding off high and low points. Loss of signal occurs here. Finally, the frequency points are compressed using conventional lossless techniques.

The smoothing function that operates on the frequency-domain data generally has a "quality factor" built into it that determines just how much smoothing occurs. The more the data is massaged, the greater the signal loss—and more compression will occur.

In the small systems world, a tremendous amount of work is being done on graphical image compression, both for still and moving pictures. The International Standards Organization (ISO) and the Consultive Committee for International Telegraph and Telephone (CCITT) have banded together to form two committees: The Joint Photographic Experts Group (JPEG) and the Moving Pictures Expert Group (MPEG). The JPEG committee is finalizing its compression standard, and many vendors are shipping hardware and software that work with trial versions of the standard. The MPEG committee is not as far along.

The JPEG standard uses the Discrete Cosine Transform (DCT) algorithm to convert a graphics image to the frequency domain. The DCT algorithm has been used for graphics transforms for many years, so efficient implementations are readily available. JPEG specifies a quality factor of 0 to 100, and it lets the compressor determine what factor to select.

Using the JPEG algorithm on images can result in dramatic compression ratios. With little or no degradation, compression ratios of 5-10 percent are routine. Accepting minor degradation achieves ratios as low as 1-2 percent.

Software implementations of the JPEG and MPEG algorithms are still struggling to achieve real-time performance. Most multimedia development software that uses this type of compression still depends on the use of a coprocessor board to make the compression take place in a reasonable amount of time. We are probably only a few years away from software-only compression capabilities.

Programs to Know

General-purpose data-compression programs have been available only for the past ten years or so. It wasn't until around 1980 that machines with the power to do the analysis needed for effective compression started to become commonplace.

In the Unix world, one of the first general-purpose compression programs was COMPACT. COMPACT is a relatively straightforward implementation of an order-0 compression program that uses adaptive Huffman coding. COMPACT produced good enough compression to make it useful, but it was slow. COMPACT was also a proprietary product, so it was not available to all Unix users.

COMPRESS, a somewhat improved program, became available to Unix users a few years later. It is a straightforward implementation of the LZW dictionary-based compression scheme. COMPRESS gave significantly better compression than COMPACT, and it ran faster. Even better, the source code to COMPRESS was readily available as a public-domain program, and it proved quite portable. COMPRESS is still in wide use among UNIX users, though its continued use is questionable due to the LZW patent held by Unisys.

In the early 1980s, desktop users of CP/M and MS-DOS systems were first exposed to data compression through the SQ program. SQ performed order-0 compression using a static Huffman tree passed in the file. SQ gave compression comparable to that of the COMPACT program, and it was widely used by early pioneers in desktop telecommunications.

As in the Unix world, Huffman coding soon gave way to LZW compression with the advent of ARC. ARC is a general-purpose program that performs both file compression and archiving, two features that often go hand in hand. (Unix users typically archive files first using TAR, then they compress the entire archive.) ARC could originally compress files using run-length encoding, order-0 static Huffman coding, or LZW compression. The original LZW code for ARC appears to be a derivative of the Unix COMPRESS code.

Due to the rapid distribution possible using shareware and telecommunications, ARC quickly became a de facto standard and began spawning imitators right and left. The desktop world is now littered with dozens of archive/compression utility programs, some commercial, some freeware, some shareware.

Today ARC has undergone many major revisions, and it is still a very popular commercial program. While there is not a clear-cut compression standard, in MS-DOS the title is probably held by the shareware program PKZIP. PKZIP is a relatively inexpensive program that offers both superior compression ratios and compression speed.

Two strong competitors to PKZIP's supremacy have recntly emerged. The first LHarc, comes from Japan, and has several advantages over other archiving/compression programs. First, the source to LHarc is freely available and has been ported to numerous operating systems and hardware platforms. Second, the author of LHarc, Haruyasu Yoshizaki (Yoshi), has explicitly granted the right to use his program for any purpose, personal or commercial.

The second competitor is ARJ by Robert Jung. ARJ is free for non-commercial use and has managed to achieve compression ratios slightly better than the best LHarc can offer. ARJ also has portable ANSI C source code for extracting files from ARJ archives.

Some freeware and public-domain programs are included on the source diskette with this book. See the index on the diskette for complete details.

CHAPTER 3

The Dawn Age: Minimum Redundancy Coding

In the late 1940s, the early years of information theory, the idea of developing efficient new coding techniques was just starting to be fleshed out. Researchers were exploring the ideas of entropy, information content, and redundancy. One popular notion held that if the probability of symbols in a message were known, there ought to be a way to code the symbols so that the message would take up less space.

Remarkably, this early work in data compression was being done before the advent of the modern digital computer. Today it seems natural that information theory goes hand in hand with computer programming, but just after World War II, for all practical purposes, there were no digital computers. So the idea of developing algorithms using base 2 arithmetic for coding symbols was really a great leap forward.

The first well-known method for effectively coding symbols is now known as Shannon-Fano coding. Claude Shannon at Bell Labs and R. M. Fano at M.I.T. developed this method nearly simultaneously. It depended on simply knowing the probability of each symbol's appearance in a message. Given the probabilities, a table of codes could be constructed that has several important properties:

- Different codes have different numbers of bits.
- Codes for symbols with low probabilities have more bits, and codes for symbols with high probabilities have fewer bits.
- Though the codes are of different bit lengths, they can be uniquely decoded.

The first two properties go hand in hand. Developing codes that vary in length according to the probability of the symbol they are encoding makes data compression possible. And arranging the codes as a binary tree solves the problem of decoding these variable-length codes.

An example of the type of decoding tree used in Shannon-Fano coding is shown below. Decoding an incoming code consists of starting at the root, then turning left or right at each node after reading an incoming bit from the data stream. Eventually a leaf of the tree is reached, and the appropriate symbol is decoded.

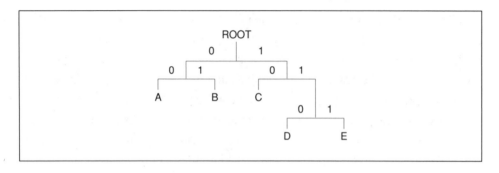

Figure 3-1. A simple Shannon-Fano tree.

Figure 3-1 is a Shannon-Fano tree designed to encode or decode a simple five-symbol alphabet consisting of the letters A through E. Walking through the tree yields the code table:

Symbol	Code
A	00
B	01
C	10
D	110
E	111

The tree structure shows how codes are uniquely defined though they have different numbers of bits. The tree structure seems designed for computer implementations, but it is also well suited for machines made of relays and switches, like the teletype machines of the 1950s.

While the table shows one of the three properties discussed earlier, that of having variable numbers of bits, more information is needed to talk about the other two properties. After all, code trees look interesting, but do they actually perform a valuable service?

The Shannon-Fano Algorithm

A Shannon-Fano tree is built according to a specific algorithm designed to define an effective code table. The actual algorithm is simple:

1. For a given list of symbols, develop a corresponding list of probabilities or frequency counts so that each symbol's relative frequency of occurence is known.

2. Sort the lists of symbols according to frequency, with the most frequently occuring symbols at the top and the least common at the bottom.

3. Divide the list into two parts, with the total frequency counts of the upper half being as close to the total of the bottom half as possible.

4. The upper half of the list is assigned the binary digit 0, and the lower half is assigned the digit 1. This means that the codes for the symbols in the first half will all start with 0, and the codes in the second half will all start with 1.

5. Recursively apply the steps 3 and 4 to each of the two halves, subdividing groups and adding bits to the codes until each symbol has become a corresponding code leaf on the tree.

The Shannon-Fano tree shown in figure 3-1 was developed from the table of symbol frequencies shown next.

Symbol	Count
A	15
B	7
C	6
D	6
E	5

Putting the dividing line between symbols B and C assigns a count of 22 to the upper group and 17 to the lower, the closest to exactly half. This means that A and B will each have a code that starts with a 0 bit, and C, D, and E are all going to start with a 1 as shown:

Symbol	Count	
A	15	0
B	7	0
		————————————First division
C	6	1
D	6	1
E	5	1

Subsequently, the upper half of the table gets a new division between A and B, which puts A on a leaf with code 00 and B on a leaf with code 01. After four division procedures, a table of codes results. In the final table, the three symbols with the highest frequencies have all been assigned 2-bit codes, and two symbols with lower counts have 3-bit codes as shown next.

Symbol	Count			
A	15	0	0	
				———Second division
B	7	0	1	
				———First division
C	6	1	0	
				———Third division
D	6	1	1	0
				———Fourth division
E	5	1	1	1

That symbols with the higher probability of occurence have fewer bits in their codes indicates we are on the right track. The formula for information content for a given symbol is the negative of the base two logarithm of the symbol's probability. For our theoretical message, the information content of each symbol, along with the total number of bits for that symbol in the message, are found in the following table.

Symbol	Count	Info Cont.	Info Bits
A:	15	1.38	20.68
B:	7	2.48	17.35
C:	6	2.70	16.20
D:	6	2.70	16.20
E:	5	2.96	14.82

The information for this message adds up to about 85.25 bits. If we code the characters using 8-bit ASCII characters, we would use 39 x 8 bits, or 312 bits. Obviously there is room for improvement.

When we encode the same data using Shannon-Fano codes, we come up with some pretty good numbers, as shown on the next page.

Symbol	Count	Info Cont.	Info Bits	SF Size	SF Bits
A:	15	1.38	20.68	2	30
B:	7	2.48	17.35	2	14
C:	6	2.70	16.20	2	12
D:	6	2.70	16.20	3	18
E:	5	2.96	14.82	3	15

With the Shannon-Fano coding system, it takes only 89 bits to encode 85.25 bits of information. Clearly we have come a long way in our quest for efficient coding methods. And while Shannon-Fano coding was a great leap forward, it had the unfortunate luck to be quickly superseded by an even more efficient coding system: Huffman coding.

The Huffman Algorithm

Huffman coding shares most characteristics of Shannon-Fano coding. It creates variable-length codes that are an integral number of bits. Symbols with higher probabilities get shorter codes. Huffman codes have the unique prefix attribute, which means they can be correctly decoded despite being variable length. Decoding a stream of Huffman codes is generally done by following a binary decoder tree.

Building the Huffman decoding tree is done using a completely different algorithm from that of the Shannon-Fano method. The Shannon-Fano tree is built from the top down, starting by assigning the most significant bits to each code and working down the tree until finished. Huffman codes are built from the bottom up, starting with the leaves of the tree and working progressively closer to the root.

The procedure for building the tree is simple and elegant. The individual symbols are laid out as a string of leaf nodes that are going to be connected by a binary tree. Each node has a weight, which is simply the frequency or probability of the symbol's appearance. The tree is then built with the following steps:

• The two free nodes with the lowest weights are located.

• A parent node for these two nodes is created. It is assigned a weight equal to the sum of the two child nodes.

• The parent node is added to the list of free nodes, and the two child nodes are removed from the list.

• One of the child nodes is designated as the path taken from the parent node when decoding a 0 bit. The other is arbitrarily set to the 1 bit.

• The previous steps are repeated until only one free node is left. This free node is designated the root of the tree.

This algorithm can be applied to the symbols used in the previous example. The five symbols in our message are laid out, along with their frequencies, as shown:

15	7	6	6	5
A	B	C	D	E

These five nodes are going to end up as the leaves of the decoding tree. When the process first starts, they make up the entire list of free nodes.

The first pass through the tree identifies the two free nodes with the lowest weights: D and E, with weights of 6 and 5. (The tie between C and D was broken arbitrarily. While the way that ties are broken effects the final value of the codes, it will not affect the compression ratio achieved.) These two nodes are joined to a parent node, which is assigned a weight of 11. Nodes D and E are then removed from the free list.

Once this step is complete, we know what the least significant bits in the codes for D and E are going to be. D is assigned to the 0 branch of the parent node, and E is assigned to the 1 branch. These two bits will be the LSBs of the resulting codes.

On the next pass through the list of free nodes, the B and C nodes are picked as the two with the lowest weight. These are then attached to a new parent node. The parent node is assigned a weight of 13, and B and C are removed from the free node list. At this point, the tree looks like that shown in figure 3-2.

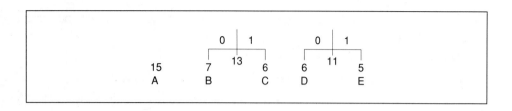

Figure 3-2. The Huffman tree after two passes.

On the next pass, the two nodes with the lowest weights are the parent nodes for the B/C and D/E pairs. These are tied together with a new parent node, which is assigned a weight of 24, and the children are removed from the free list. At this point, we have assigned two bits each to the Huffman codes for B, C, D, and E, and we have yet to assign a single bit to the code for A.

Finally, on the last pass, only two free nodes are left. The parent with a weight of 24 is tied with the A node to create a new parent with a weight of 39. After removing the two child nodes from the free list, we are left with just one parent, meaning the tree is complete. The final result looks like that shown in figure 3-3.

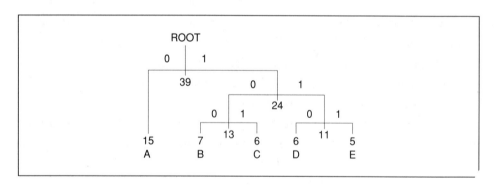

Figure 3-3 The Huffman tree.

To determine the code for a given symbol, we have to walk from the leaf node to the root of the Huffman tree, accumulating new bits as we pass through each parent node. Unfortunately, the bits are returned to us in the reverse order that we want them, which means we have to push the bits onto a stack, then pop them off to generate the code. This strategy gives our message the code structure shown in the following table.

```
A:      0
B:      100
C:      101
D:      110
E:      111
```

The Huffman Code Table

As you can see, the codes have the unique prefix property. Since no code is a prefix to another code, Huffman codes can be unambiguously decoded as they arrive in a stream. The symbol with the highest probability, A, has been assigned the fewest bits, and the symbol with the lowest probability, E, has been assigned the most bits.

Note, however, that the Huffman codes differ in length from Shannon-Fano codes. The code length for A is only a single bit, instead of two, and the B and C symbols have 3-bit codes instead of two bits. The following table shows what effect this has on the total number of bits produced by the message.

Symbol	Count	Shannon-Fano Size	Shannon-Fano Bits	Huffman Size	Huffman Bits
A:	15	2	30	1	15
B:	7	2	14	3	21
C:	6	2	12	3	18
D:	6	3	18	3	18
E:	5	3	15	3	15

This adjustment in code size adds 13 bits to the number needed to encode the B and C symbols, but it saves 15 bits when coding the A symbol, for a net savings of 2 bits. Thus, for a message with an information content of 85.25 bits, Shannon-Fano coding requires 89 bits, but Huffman coding requires only 87.

In general, Shannon-Fano and Huffman coding are close in performance. But Huffman coding will always at least equal the efficiency of Shannon-Fano coding, so it has become the predominate coding method of its type. Since both algorithms take a similar amount of processing power, it seems sensible to take the one that gives slightly better performance. And Huffman was able to prove that this coding method cannot be improved on with any other integral bit-width coding stream.

Since D. A. Huffman first published his 1952 paper, "A Method for the Construction of Minimum Redundancy Codes," his coding algorithm has been the subject of an overwhelming amount of additional research. Information theory journals to this day carry numerous papers on the implementation of various esoteric flavors of Huffman codes, searching for ever better ways to use this coding method. Huffman coding is used in commercial compression programs, FAX machines, and even the JPEG algorithm. The next logical step in this book is to outline the C code needed to implement the Huffman coding scheme.

Huffman in C

A Huffman coding tree is built as a binary tree, from the leaf nodes up. Huffman may or may not have had digital computers in mind when he developed his code, but programmers use the tree data structure all the time.

Two programs used here illustrate Huffman coding. The compressor, HUFF-C, implements a simple order-0 model and a single Huffman tree to encode it. HUFF-E expands files compressed using HUFF-C. Both programs use a few pieces of utility code that will be seen throughout this book. Before we go on to the actual Huffman code, here is a quick overview of what some of the utility modules do.

BITIO.C. Data-compression programs perform lots of input/output (I/O) that does reads or writes of unconventional numbers of bits. Huffman coding, for example, reads and writes bits one at a time. LZW programs read and write codes that can range in size from 9 to 16 bits. The standard C I/O library defined in STDIO.H only accommodates I/O on even byte boundaries. Routines like putc() and getc() read and write single bytes, while fread() and fwrite() read and write whole blocks of bytes at a time. The library offers no help for programmers needing a routine to write a single bit at a time.

To support this unconventional I/O in a conventional way, bit-oriented I/O routines are confined to a single source module, BITIO.C. Access to these routines is provided via a header file called BITIO.H, which contains a structure definition and several function prototypes.

Two routines open files for bit I/O, one for input and one for output. As defined in BITIO.H, they are

```
BIT_FILE *OpenInputBitFile( char *name );
BIT_FILE *OpenOutputBitFile( char *name );
```

These two routines return a pointer to a new structure, BIT_FILE. BIT_FILE is also defined in BITIO.H as shown:

```
typedef struct bit_file {
    FILE *file;
    unsigned char mask;
    int rack;
    int pacifier_counter;
} BIT_FILE;
```

OpenInputBitFile() or OpenOutputBitFile() perform a conventional fopen() call and store the returned FILE structure pointer in the BIT_FILE structure. The other two structure elements are initialized to their startup values, and a pointer to the resulting BIT_FILE structure is returned.

The two new structure elements, rack and mask, manage the bit-oriented aspect of a BIT_FILE. "rack" contains the current byte of data either read in from the file or waiting to be written out to the file. "mask" contains a single bit mask used either to set/clear the current output bit or to mask in the current input bit.

In BITIO.H, the most significant bit in the I/O byte gets or returns the first bit, and the least significant bit in the I/O byte gets or returns the last bit. This means that the mask element of the structure is initialized to 0x80 when the BIT_FILE is first opened. During output, the first write to the BIT_FILE will set or clear that bit, then the mask element will shift to the next. Once the mask has shifted to the point at which all the bits in the output rack have been set or cleared, the rack is written out to the file, and a new rack byte is started.

Performing input from a BIT_FILE is done in a similar fashion. The mask is first set to 0x80, and a single byte from the file is read into the rack element. Each call to read a bit from the file masks in a new bit, then shifts the mask over to the next lower significant bit. Eventually, all bits in the input rack have been returned, and the input routine can read in a new byte from the input file.

Two types of I/O routines are defined in BITIO.C. The first two routines read or write a single bit at a time. The second two read or write multiple bits, up to the size of an unsigned int. These four routines have the following ANSI prototype in BITIO.H:

```
void        OutputBit( BIT_FILE *bit_file, int bit );
void        OutputBits( BIT_FILE *bit_file,
                        unsigned long code, int count );
int         InputBit( BIT_FILE *bit_file );
unsigned  long InputBits( BIT_FILE *bit_file, int bit_count );
```

Specialized routines open a BIT_FILE, and two specialized routines close a BIT_FILE. The output routine makes sure that the last byte gets written out to the file. Both the input and output routines need to close their files, then free up the BIT_FILE structure allocated when the file was opened. The BIT_FILE routines used to close a file are defined in BITIO.H with these ANSI prototypes:

```
void        CloseInputBitFile( BIT_FILE *bit_file );
void        CloseOutputBitFile( BIT_FILE *bit_file );
```

The input and output routines in BITIO.H also have a pacifier feature that can be useful in testing compression code. Every BIT_FILE structure has a pacifier_counter that gets incremented every time a new byte is read in or written out to the corresponding file. Once every 2,048 bytes, a single character is written to stdout. This helps assure the impatient user that real work is being done. On MS-DOS systems, it also helps ensure that the user can break out of the program if it does not appear to be working correctly.

The header file and code for BITIO.H is shown next:.

```
/************************* Start of BITIO.H *************************/

#ifndef _BITIO_H
#define _BITIO_H

#include <stdio.h>

typedef struct bit_file {
    FILE *file;
    unsigned char mask;
    int rack;
    int pacifier_counter;
} BIT_FILE;

#ifdef __STDC__

BIT_FILE        *OpenInputBitFile( char *name );
BIT_FILE        *OpenOutputBitFile( char *name );
void            OutputBit( BIT_FILE *bit_file, int bit );
void            OutputBits( BIT_FILE *bit_file,
                        unsigned long code, int count );
int             InputBit( BIT_FILE *bit_file );
unsigned long   InputBits( BIT_FILE *bit_file, int bit_count );
void            CloseInputBitFile( BIT_FILE *bit_file );
void            CloseOutputBitFile( BIT_FILE *bit_file );
void            FilePrintBinary( FILE *file, unsigned int code, int
                        bits);
```

```
#else /* __STDC__ */

BIT_FILE        *OpenInputBitFile();
BIT_FILE        *OpenOutputBitFile();
void            OutputBit();
void            OutputBits();
int             InputBit();
unsigned long   InputBits();
void            CloseInputBitFile();
void            CloseOutputBitFile();
void            FilePrintBinary()

#endif /* __STDC__ */


#endif /* _BITIO_H */

/************************* End of BITIO.H *************************/

/************************* Start of BITIO.C *************************/
/*
 * This utility file contains all of the routines needed to implement
 * bit oriented routines under either ANSI or K&R C. It needs to be
 * linked with every program used in the book.
 */
#include <stdio.h>
#include <stdlib.h>
#include "bitio.h"
#include "errhand.h"

BIT_FILE *OpenOutputBitFile( name )
char *name;
{
    BIT_FILE *bit_file;

    bit_file = (BIT_FILE *) calloc( 1, sizeof( BIT_FILE ) );
    if ( bit_file == NULL )
```

```
        return( bit_file );
    bit_file->file = fopen( name, "wb" );
    bit_file->rack = 0;
    bit_file->mask = 0x80;
    bit_file->pacifier_counter = 0;
    return( bit_file );
}


BIT_FILE *OpenInputBitFile( name )
char *name;
{
    BIT_FILE *bit_file;

    bit_file = (BIT_FILE *) calloc( 1, sizeof( BIT_FILE ) );
    if ( bit_file == NULL )
        return( bit_file );
    bit_file->file = fopen( name, "rb" );
    bit_file->rack = 0;
    bit_file->mask = 0x80;
    bit_file->pacifier_counter = 0;
    return( bit_file );
}

void CloseOutputBitFile( bit_file )
BIT_FILE *bit_file;
{
    if ( bit_file->mask != 0x80 )
      if ( putc( bit_file->rack, bit_file->file ) != bit_file->rack )
          fatal_error( "Fatal error in CloseBitFile!\n" );
    fclose( bit_file->file );

    free( (char *) bit_file);
}

void CloseInputBitFile( bit_file )
BIT_FILE *bit_file;
```

```
{
    fclose( bit_file->file );
    free( (char*) bit_file );
}
void OutputBit( bit_file, bit )
BIT_FILE *bit_file;
int bit;
{
    if ( bit )
        bit_file->rack |= bit_file->mask;
    bit_file->mask >>= 1;
    if ( bit_file->mask == 0 ) {
        if ( putc( bit_file->rack, bit_file->file ) != bit_file->rack )
            fatal_error( "Fatal error in OutputBit!\n" );
        else
            if ( ( bit_file->pacifier_counter++ & 4095 ) == 0 )
                    putc( '.', stdout );
        bit_file->rack = 0;
        bit_file->mask = 0x80;
    }
}
void OutputBits( bit_file, code, count )
BIT_FILE *bit_file;
unsigned long code;
int count;
{
    unsigned long mask;

    mask = 1L << ( count - 1 );
    while ( mask != 0) {
        if ( mask & code )
            bit_file->rack |= bit_file->mask;
        bit_file->mask >>= 1;
        if ( bit_file->mask == 0 ) {
            if ( putc( bit_file->rack, bit_file->file ) != bit_file->rack )
                fatal_error( "Fatal error in OutputBit!\n" );
            else if ( ( bit_file->pacifier_counter++ & 2047 ) == 0 )
                putc( '.', stdout );
```

```
            bit_file->rack = 0;
            bit_file->mask = 0x80;
        }
        mask >>= 1;
    }
}

int InputBit( bit_file )
BIT_FILE *bit_file;
{
    int value;

    if ( bit_file->mask == 0x80 ) {
        bit_file->rack = getc( bit_file->file );
        if ( bit_file->rack == EOF )
            fatal_error( "Fatal error in InputBit!\n" );
        if ( ( bit_file->pacifier_counter++ & 2047 ) == 0 )
            putc( '.', stdout );
    }
    value = bit_file->rack & bit_file->mask;
    bit_file->mask >>= 1;
    if ( bit_file->mask == 0 )
        bit_file->mask = 0x80;
    return( value ? 1 : 0 );
}

unsigned long InputBits( bit_file, bit_count )
BIT_FILE *bit_file;
int bit_count;
{
    unsigned long mask;
    unsigned long return_value;

    mask = 1L << ( bit_count - 1 );
    return_value = 0;
    while ( mask != 0) {
```

```
            if ( bit_file->mask == 0x80 ) {
                bit_file->rack = getc( bit_file->file );
                if ( bit_file->rack == EOF )
                    fatal_error( "Fatal error in InputBit!\n" );
                if ( ( bit_file->pacifier_counter++ & 2047 ) == 0 )
                    putc( '.', stdout );
            }
            if ( bit_file->rack & bit_file->mask )
                return_value |= mask;
            mask >>= 1;
            bit_file->mask >>= 1;
            if ( bit_file->mask == 0 )
                bit_file->mask = 0x80;
    }
    return( return_value );
}


void FilePrintBinary( file, code, bits)
FILE *file;
unsigned int code;
int bits;
{
    unsigned int mask;
    mask = 1 << ( bits - 1 ):
    while ( mask != 0 ){
    if ( code & mask )
        fputc( '1', file );
    else
        fputc( '0', file);
    mask >>= 1;
    }
}


/*********************** End of BITIO.C ***********************/
```

A Reminder about Prototypes

The code in this book works on both Unix K&R and the more modern MS-DOS compilers. This affects the code in this book mainly in the area of function parameters in both prototypes and the function body itself. For the function body, all code in this book will use old-fashioned parameter specifications like this:

```
int main( argc, argv )
int argc;
char *argv[];
{

        ...
```

This is the only method of parameter declaration acceptable to K&R compilers, and as such it has the blessing of the ANSI standard. A few compilers (Microsoft C 6.0 at Warning Level 4, for example) will issue a warning when it encounters this type of function declaration, so be prepared to ignore those warnings. Declaring function parameters in this method will generally have no effect on code reliability or readability, so using the K&R style should be considered a benign anachronism.

Parameters in function declarations present a little more of a problem. The ANSI C specification will accept old style K&R function declarations (such as `int main();`), but there are good reasons to want to specify all function arguments in the declaration. When using full prototyping—as in `int main( int argc, char *argv[] );`—the compiler checks for correct parameter passing when it encounters a call to a function. This helps avoid one of the most commonplace C coding mistakes: incorrect parameter passing.

To use this prototyping, and at the same time to stay compatible with K&R compilers, all function prototypes are given in two forms: a K&R-compatible prototype and a full ANSI C prototype. The ANSI C prototypes are selected through a check for __STDC__, a predefined macro defined when a compiler conforms to the ANSI C standard. So the prototype for a set of functions in a header file will look something like this:

```
#ifdef __STDC__

int main( int argc, char *argv[] );
FOO *open_foo( char *name );

#else   /* __STDC__ */

int main();
FOO *open_foo();

#endif /* __STDC__ */
```

This compromise approach definitely hurts readability, and it is probably not the way to go during code development. But once a set of routines is working properly and not likely to be changed, this type of header file will work fine.

ANSI C compiler users will find that a problem with this header file crops up with numerous MS-DOS compilers. Compilers such as Microsoft C or Borland C++ are ANSI C compilers, but by default they include a number of language extensions, such as far pointers, alternate calling conventions, and so on. When these language extensions are enabled (as they are by default), __STDC__ is not defined, since the compiler is not operating strictly as an ANSI C compiler. This means that the correct function prototypes will not be invoked.

The solution to this problem is to compile the code in this book with the compiler in ANSI C mode. Put the compiler in this mode generally by disabling extensions. Microsoft C accomplishes this from the command line with the /Za switch. Borland C++ uses the -A switch to disable C extensions.

To adapt this code for a specific use on a specific compiler, you may want to eliminate the "#ifdef __STDC__" lines in the header file and code. As more and more compilers use ANSI C prototypes and parameter definitions, this portability machinery will become less and less useful.

MAIN-C.C and MAIN-E.C

Another piece of utility code used throughout this book is the "main()" program for the compression and expansion programs. Any piece of compression code needs to be plugged into a main program that accepts command-line arguments, opens files, calls the compression routines, then closes the files. For simplicity, I have created two versions of this code: one for the compression program (MAIN-C.C) and one for the expansion program (MAIN-E.C).

Both MAIN-C.C and MAIN-E.C expect to find a compression or expansion routine in another file, a help routine to explain command-line parameters, and an external string with the name of the compression technique being used. The declarations for the functions and name are found in MAIN.H. MAIN.H should be included in the compression module to ensure that the routines are properly typed. MAIN.H is shown next.

The idea behind these two routines is that the infrastructure of a compression test program should not have to be rewritten every time a new compression module is coded. A new routine should just have to interface with the existing compression code.

```
/************************* Start of MAIN.H *************************/

#ifndef _MAIN_H
#define _MAIN_H

#ifdef __STDC__
void CompressFile( FILE *input, BIT_FILE *output, int argc, char *argv[] );
void ExpandFile( BIT_FILE *input, FILE *output, int argc, char *argv[] );

#else  /* __STDC__ */

void CompressFile();
void ExpandFile();

#endif /* __STDC__ */

extern char *Usage;
extern char *CompressionName;

#endif /* _MAIN_H */

/************************* End of MAIN.H *************************/
```

In MAIN-C.C, a compression module supplies three things: a Usage string, which can print out a list of parameters, etc.; a CompressionName string, which lets the MAIN-C.C program print out the compression method; and a CompressFile() routine, which actually compresses the file. In this chapter, these routines are in a file called HUFF.C, which implements an order 0 model with a Huffman coder. MAIN-C.C is shown on the next page.

```
/************************ Start of MAIN-C.C ************************/
/*
 * This is the driver program used when testing compression algorithms.
 * In order to cut back on repetitive code, this version of main is
 * used with all of the compression routines. It in order to turn into
 * a real program, it needs to have another module that supplies one
 * routine and two strings, namely:
 *
 *     void CompressFile( FILE *input, BIT_FILE *output,
 *                        int argc, char *argv );
 *     char *Usage;
 *     char *CompressionName;
 *
 * The main() routine supplied here has the job of checking for valid
 * input and output files, opening them, and then calling the
 * compression routine. If the files are not present, or no arguments
 * are supplied, it prints out an error message, which includes the
 * Usage string supplied by the compression module. All of the
 * routines and strings needed by this routine are defined in the
 * main.h header file.
 *
 * After this is built into a compression program of any sort, the
 * program can be called like this:
 *
 *     main-c infile outfile [ options ]
 *
 */
#include <stdio.h>
#include <stdlib.h>
#include <string.h>
#include "bitio.h"
#include "errhand.h"
#include "main.h"
```

```
#ifdef __STDC__

void usage_exit( char *prog_name );
void print_ratios( char *input, char *output );
long file_size( char *name );

#else

void usage_exit();
void print_ratios();
long file_size();

#endif

int main( argc, argv )
int argc;
char *argv[];
{
    BIT_FILE *output;
    FILE *input;

    setbuf( stdout, NULL );
    if ( argc < 3 )
        usage_exit( argv[ 0 ] );
    input = fopen(argv[ 1 ], "rb" );
    if ( input == NULL )
        fatal_error( "Error opening %s for input\n", argv[ 1 ] );
    output = OpenOutputBitFile( argv[ 2 ] );
    if ( output == NULL )
        fatal_error( "Error opening %s for output\n", argv[ 2 ] );
    printf( "\nCompressing %s to %s\n", argv[ 1 ], argv[ 2 ] );
    printf( "Using %s\n", CompressionName );
    argc -= 3;
    argv += 3;
    CompressFile( input, output, argc, argv );
    CloseOutputBitFile( output );
```

```
    fclose( input );
    print_ratios( argv[ 1 ], argv[ 2 ] );
    return( 0 );
}


/*
 * This routine just wants to print out the usage message that is
 * called for when the program is run with no parameters. The first
 * part of the Usage statement is supposed to be just the program
 * name. argv[ 0 ] generally holds the fully qualified path name
 * of the program being run. I make a half-hearted attempt to strip
 * out that path info and file extension before printing it. It should
 * get the general idea across.
 */
void usage_exit( prog_name )
char *prog_name;
{
    char *short_name;
    char *extension;

    short_name = strrchr( prog_name, '\\' );
    if (short_name == NULL )
        short_name = strrchr( prog_name, '/' );
    if (short_name == NULL )
        short_name = strrchr( prog_name, ':' );
    if (short_name != NULL )
        short_name++;
    else
        short_name = prog_name;
    extension = strrchr( short_name, '.' );
    if ( extension != NULL )
        *extension = '\0';
    printf( "\nUsage: %s %s\n", short_name, Usage );
    exit( 0 );
}
```

```
/*
 * This routine is used by main to get the size of a file after it has
 * been closed.  It does all the work, and returns a long. The main
 * program gets the file size for the plain text, and the size of the
 * compressed file, and prints the ratio.
 */
#ifndef SEEK_END
#define SEEK_END 2
#endif


long file_size( name)
char *name;
{
    long eof ftell;
    FILE *file;

    file = fopen( name, "r");
    if ( file == NULL )
        return( OL );
    fseek( file, OL, SEEK_END );
    eof_ftell = ftell( file );
    fclose( file );
    return( eof_ftell );
}


/*
 * This routine prints out the compression ratios after the input and
 * output files have been closed.
 */
void print_ratios( input, output )
char *input;
char *output;
{
    long input_size;
    long output_size;
    int ratio;
```

```
    input_size = file_size( input );
    if ( input_size == 0 )
        input_size = 1;
    output_size = file_size * 100L / input_size );
    ratio = 100 - (int) ( output_size * 100L / input_size );
    printf( "\nInput bytes:        %ld\n", input_size );
    printf( "Output bytes:      %ld\n", output_size );
    if ( output_size == 0 )
        output_size = 1;
    printf( "Compression ratio:  %d%%\n", ratio );
}
/************************* End of MAIN-C.C *************************/
```

MAIN-C.C. There are a few expectations about how MAIN-C.C will run. MAIN-C.C is called to compress an input file supplied on the command line and send the compressed output to another file, also supplied on the command line. Thus, the basic command-line invocation of MAIN-C.C is `MAIN-C input-file output-file`. If the user invokes MAIN-C.C without any arguments, a simple usage statement prints out. The usage statement includes the usage string supplied by the compression module.

If two likely looking file names are on the command line, MAIN-C.C tries to open them both. The input file is opened as a standard file specified in STDIO.H, using fopen(). The output file is opened as a BIT_FILE, as defined in BITIO.H. If either file doesn't open, an error message is printed out and the program exits. If both files open, the next step is to call the compression routine.

MAIN-C.C expects the compression routine to be named CompressFile(). This routine is called with four arguments. The first two are pointers to the file structure for the input file and a pointer to the BIT_FILE structure for the output file. Finally, the updated values for argc and argv are passed to the compression routine. The values for argc and argv will have been adjusted to go past argv[0], which should be the program name, as well as argv[1] and argv[2], the names of the input and output files. The compression program can then scan the remaining arguments for any arguments specific to that particular compression routine. After the compression routine has finished, it returns to MAIN-C.C, which closes down the files and exits.

MAIN-E.C is the converse program to MAIN-C.C. It takes two arguments as well, but this time the input file is the compressed file and the output file is destined to be the uncompressed clear text file. Just like MAIN-C.C, it checks to be sure there are at least two arguments, then tries to open the two files. If there aren't two arguments, a usage message is printed. If either of the files fails to open, an error message is printed. MAIN-E.C is listed at the end of this chapter.

ERRHAND.C. One additional routine helps simplify the code. A production version of a program generally needs a somewhat sophisticated error-handling mechanism. In particular, it is important to let the end user know what is happening, clean up any files that may have been only partially processed, and restore any system settings that may have been changed.

In this book, our interest in compression concentrates on testing for accuracy, speed, and compression ratios. Because of this, we have created a simple universal fatal-error handler. The error handler is defined in ERRHAND.H:

```
/*********************** Start of ERRHAND.H ***********************/

    #ifndef _ERRHAND_H
    #define _ERRHAND_H

    #ifdef __STDC__

    void fatal_error( char *fmt, ... );

    #else  /* __STDC__ */

    void fatal_error();

    #endif /* __STDC__ */

    #endif /* _ERRHAND_H */

/*********************** End of ERRHAND.H ***********************/
```

The fatal-error handler is called when an unrecoverable error occurs in the program. It has the same syntax as printf, which means it can be passed a format string and arguments to format and print out.

```
/*********************** Start of ERRHAND.C***********************/

#include <stdio.h>
#include <stdlib.h>
#include <stdarg.h>
#include "errhand.h"

#ifdef __STDC__
void fatal_error( char *fmt, ... )
#else
#ifdef __UNIX__
void fatal_error( fmt )
char *fmt;
va_dcl
#else
void fatal_error( fmt )
#endif
#endif
{

    va_list argptr;

    va_start( argptr, fmt );
    printf( "Fatal error: " );
    vprintf( fmt, argptr );
    va_end(argptr );
    exit( -1 );
}

/*********************** End of ERRHAND.C ***********************/
```

Into the Huffman Code

With the infrastructure code in place, all we need to do to create a program that demonstrates Huffman coding is to write two routines, CompressFile() and ExpandFile(), and a couple of strings that describe the name of the compression method and program usage. The code for this is found in HUFF.C.

To build the Huffman decoding tree, we need to create a data structure that models the tree on the computer. In our previous examples, each node on the tree had several pieces of information: first, the weight associated with it; second, pointers to two child nodes, one associated with the 0 bit and one associated with the 1 bit. Finally, leaf nodes had the value of the symbol associated with the leaf.

The data structure used in this program to model the Huffman tree was built around the node structure:

```
typedef struct tree_node {
    unsigned int count;
    unsigned int saved_count;
    int child_0;
    int child_1;
} NODE;
```

The first thing to notice about this structure is that there is no information about the value of a leaf node. This is because the node structures are allocated as an array of 514 nodes. The lower nodes are all assigned to be leaf nodes, and the upper nodes become internal nodes. The information about the value of a leaf is encoded based on the position of the node in the array.

Instead of having 256 symbols in our alphabet for this program, we actually have 257. Values 0 through 255 are reserved for the normal range of bytes that fit into a character. The remaining symbol value of 256 is reserved for the end-of-stream indicator. This is the last code written out to the stream, and it indicates that no more data will be arriving. Because of the bit-oriented nature of compressed data, it is not ordinarily a simple matter to determine when you have reached an end-of-file state. Handling it with a special code for end-of-stream is one method for getting around this. Another would be to encode the length of the file as a prefix to the compressed data.

With 257 symbols to deal with, we know in advance the largest possible size of the Huffman tree. If all 257 symbols are in use, we will have 256 internal nodes, meaning that we have to allocate an array of 513 node structures. In the program, I actually allocate 514 and use the last one as a dummy value for comparisons when building the tree.

Counting the Symbols. To build the tree, I first calculate the relative frequencies of the symbols. In HUFF.C, I set up an array of 256 longs and count the occurences of every character in the file, from the start to the end. The position of the file input pointer is saved when the count starts and is restored when it is done. All this takes place in function count_bytes().

Though I start with 32-bit unsigned long counts, I scale the counts back signficantly in module scale_counts. Scale_counts() finds the maximum count for any symbol in the file, then develops a scaling factor to make that count and all the rest of the counts fit in a single unsigned character. These counts are then copied into the weight elements of the first 257 node elements.

There are several good reasons for scaling back the counts. First, by limiting any symbol's weight to an 8-bit unsigned character, I can confine all of the math I perform when building the tree to 16-bit unsigned integers. This helps the program run a little faster, and it cuts back on the amount of storage required for the node array. It also limits the maximum size of a Huffman code as well, ensuring that it will fit in a 16-bit unsigned integer.

Saving the Counts. For the expansion program to correctly expand the Huffman encoded bit stream it will be receiving, it needs a copy of the Huffman tree identical to the one used by the encoder. This means that the tree, or its equivalent, must be passed as a header to the file so the expander can read it in before it starts to read Huffman codes.

The easiest way for the expansion program to get this data would probably be to store the entire node array as a preamble to the compressed data. This would work well and would not be too hard for the compressor to do. An alternative method that occupies far less space in the compressed file, however, is to transmit the symbol counts to the expander. Since the Huffman tree is built up in an unambiguous manner from the symbol counts, it stands to reason that the expansion program doesn't need more to do its job. And since the scaled count array will be only 256 bytes, compared to the Huffman tree's 4K bytes, there is good reason to choose this.

I elected to try to cut down on the amount of data to be passed even further. Under many circumstances, the number of counts that stay at zero is considerable. With ASCII text files, such as program lisitings, there will generally be only around 100 symbols in use out of the possible 256. It seems a waste to transmit all those zero counts when they aren't necessary. To make this happen, I use a slightly more complicated format for the header.

The header used in HUFF.C that contains the symbol counts consists of a series of "count run" definitions, followed by a 0 terminator. A count-run definition consists of the value of the first symbol in the run, followed by the value of the last symbol in the run, followed by the counts for all of the symbols in the run from first to last. This is repeated until each run has been stored in the output file. When there is no more data to store, a first value of zero is written out to the file. Note that a value of zero for the very first run is not treated as an end of data.

For a typical ASCII file, the start of the compressed file might look something like figure 3-4.

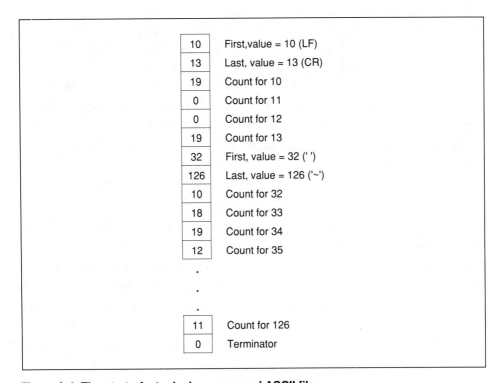

10	First,value = 10 (LF)
13	Last, value = 13 (CR)
19	Count for 10
0	Count for 11
0	Count for 12
19	Count for 13
32	First, value = 32 (' ')
126	Last, value = 126 ('~')
10	Count for 32
18	Count for 33
19	Count for 34
12	Count for 35
.	
.	
.	
11	Count for 126
0	Terminator

Figure 3-4. The start of a typical compressed ASCII file.

This symbol count format takes a fair amount of work to generate, performed in output_counts() in HUFF.C. Reading in the symbols counts is much simpler, since the work has been done in advance. Reading the counts in from the compressed file during expansion is done in the input_counts() routine.

Building the Tree. Whether compressing or expanding, once the counts have been loaded, it is time to build the Huffman tree. In HUFF.C, this is done in a function called build_tree(). Because some care was taken when creating the data structure, the actual process of creating the tree is the simple matter of sitting in a loop and combining the two free nodes with the lowest weight into a new internal node with the combined weight of the nodes. Once only one free node is left, the tree is done, and the free node is the root of the tree.

The logic of the build_tree() routine is fairly simple. When the routine is first entered, all nodes below 257 have a count value set to their frequency in the file. A nonzero value here means that this is an active node.

build_tree() also sets up a special node used as a straw man for comparison purposes. Node 513, which will never be used, is set to have a count value of 65535, which no normal node can ever exceed. When searching for the two minimum nodes, I will start by setting the minimum node to 513, knowing that any valid active node will fall below its value.

Finally, before the comparisons start, an index to the next free node is initialized. The node array is in use from 0 to 256, so the next free node will be at 257.

After things have been set up, build_tree() goes into an infinite loop. On each pass through the loop, build_tree tries to find the two active nodes with the lowest weights. If only one node is found, the tree is complete and the loop is exited. If there are two good minimum values, a new node to the tree can be created. This new node is set up using the next_free node index. Its two child pointers are set to point to the two minimum nodes found before, and its weight is their sum. The two minimum nodes are now marked as being inactive by setting their weights to 0. Nodes with a weight of 0 are considered to be unused and will never again be selected to represent a minimum.

One piece of inefficent code is deliberately left in build_tree(). There is an extra member in the node structure called saved_count. When a node is taken off the active list by having its count set to zero, the previous count is stored in saved_count. Later, if the user has selected the -d option in order to print out the model, the saved_count can be printed. This helps when debugging the program and when trying to understand how the tree works.

Using the Tree. During the expansion phase, it is easy to see how to use the Huffman tree. Starting at the root node, a single bit at a time is read in by the decoder. If the bit is a 0, the next node is the one pointed to by the child_0 index. If the bit is a 1, the next node is the one pointed to by the child_1 index. If the new node is 256 or less, we have reached a leaf of the tree and can output the corresponding symbol. If the symbol was the special end-of-stream symbol, we can exit instead of sending it out. This is what is done in the expand_node() function. It is just a few lines of code, and it decodes a compressed Huffman code file with relative ease.

Compressing the same file is a bit harder. Essentially, we want to work down the tree, outputting a 1 or a 0 bit at each node, till we get to the appropriate leaf node. Unfortunately, the tree structure makes this impossible. When we start at the root node, we have no idea whether to take the 0 or the 1 branch to arrive at a particular symbol.

One way to solve this problem when building the tree would be to add a parent member to the node structure. When combining the two minimum nodes to form a new internal node, each minimum node would have its parent structure set to point to the new node. With this new node, we could start at the leaf node and work our way up through the tree toward the root. The only problem with this procedure is that we would accumulate bits in reverse order as we went up the tree. We would have to rack them up till we reached the root node, then put them out in reverse order.

Fortunately, there is a better way to do this. Rather than trying to use the tree to code our symbols when compressing a file, we could build a code table by recursively traversing the entire tree one time only. This creates a table of codes, one for each symbol, along with the length of each code. Once the table is built, the file can be encoded by simply outputting the appropriate code for every character in the input file.

The code to convert the tree data structures into a table of codes is very simple, thanks to a recursive algorithm. We start at the root node of the tree with a zero. Then we begin working down the individual branches of the tree, adding a one or a zero to the code each time we travel down a branch. Whenever we reach a leaf, we store the code values for that leaf in the code array and back up to the previous node, where we can start searching down the other side of the tree.

The code to accomplish this is in function convert_tree_to_code(). This routine takes a fair amount of work to create the code table, but once it is done the actual file compression is very easy.

The Compression Code

The code for Huffman compression and decompression is shown in the listing below. This single file, HUFF.C, is about 500 lines long, of which probably 30 percent is comments. So we are able to implement a static dictionary Huffman compressor in only about 300 lines of code. The actual amount of code could easily be crunched down to a number much less than that. The small code and storage requirements make Huffman coding ideal for applications where both memory and CPU storage are at a premium.

```
/************************* Start of HUFF.C *************************/

#include <stdio.h>
#include <stdlib.h>
#include <string.h>
#include <ctype.h>
#include "bitio.h"
#include "errhand.h"
#include "main.h"

/*
 * The NODE structure is a node in the Huffman decoding tree. It has a
 * count, which is its weight in the tree, and the node numbers of its
 * two children. The saved_count member of the structure is only
 * there for debugging purposes, and can be safely taken out at any
 * time. It just holds the intial count for each of the symbols, since
 * the count member is continually being modified as the tree grows.
 */
typedef struct tree_node {
    unsigned int count;
    unsigned int saved_count;
    int child_0;
    int child_1;
} NODE;

/*
 * A Huffman tree is set up for decoding, not encoding. When encoding,
 * I first walk through the tree and build up a table of codes for
 * each symbol. The codes are stored in this CODE structure.
 */
```

```
typedef struct code {
    unsigned int code;
    int code_bits;
} CODE;

/*
 * The special EOS symbol is 256, the first available symbol after all
 * of the possible bytes. When decoding, reading this symbol
 * indicates that all of the data has been read in.
 */
#define END_OF_STREAM 256

/*
 * Local function prototypes, defined with or without ANSI prototypes.
 */
#ifdef __STDC__

void count_bytes( FILE *input, unsigned long *long_counts );
void scale_counts( unsigned long *long_counts, NODE *nodes );
int build_tree( NODE *nodes );
void convert_tree_to_code( NODE *nodes,
                           CODE *codes,
                           unsigned int code_so_far,
                           int bits,
                           int node );
void output_counts( BIT_FILE *output, NODE *nodes );
void input_counts( BIT_FILE *input, NODE *nodes );
void print_model( NODE *nodes, CODE *codes );
void compress_data( FILE *input, BIT_FILE *output, CODE *codes );
void expand_data( BIT_FILE *input, FILE *output, NODE *nodes,
                  int root_node );
void print_char( int c );
```

```
#else  /* __STDC__ */

void count_bytes();
void scale_counts();
int build_tree();
void convert_tree_to_code();
void output_counts();
void input_counts();
void print_model();
void compress_data();
void expand_data();
void print_char();

#endif /* __STDC__ */

/*
 * These two strings are used by MAIN-C.C and MAIN-E.C to print
 * messages of importance to the user of the program.
 */
char *CompressionName = "static order 0 model with Huffman coding";
char *Usage =
"infile outfile [-d]\n\n\ Specifying -d will dump the modeling\
  data\n";

/*
 * CompressFile is the compression routine called by MAIN-C.C. It
 * looks for a single additional argument to be passed to it from
 * the command line: "-d". If a "-d" is present, it means the
 * user wants to see the model data dumped out for debugging
 * purposes.
 *
 * This routine works in a fairly straightforward manner. First,
```

```
* it has to allocate storage for three different arrays of data.
* Next, it counts all the bytes in the input file. The counts
* are all stored in long int, so the next step is to scale them down
* to single byte counts in the NODE array. After the counts are
* scaled, the Huffman decoding tree is built on top of the NODE
* array. Another routine walks through the tree to build a table
* of codes, one per symbol. Finally, when the codes are all ready,
* compressing the file is a simple matter. After the file is
* compressed, the storage is freed up, and the routine returns.
*
*/
void CompressFile( input, output, argc, argv )
FILE *input;
BIT_FILE *output;
int argc;
char *argv[];
{
    unsigned long *counts;
    NODE *nodes;
    CODE *codes;
    int root_node;

    counts = ( unsigned long *)
                calloc( 256, sizeof( unsigned long ) );
    if ( counts == NULL )
      fatal_error( "Error allocating counts array\n" );
    if ( ( nodes = (NODE *)
                    calloc( 514, sizeof( NODE ) ) ) == NULL )
      fatal_error( "Error allocating nodes array\n" );
    if ( ( codes = (CODE *)
                    calloc( 257, sizeof( CODE ) ) ) == NULL )
      fatal_error( "Error allocating codes array\n" );
    count_bytes( input, counts );
    scale_counts( counts, nodes );
    output_counts( output, nodes );
    root_node = build_tree( nodes );
    convert_tree_to_code( nodes, codes, 0, 0, root_node );
    if ( argc > 0 && strcmp( argv[ 0 ], "-d" ) == 0 )
```

```
        print_model( nodes, codes );
    compress_data( input, output, codes );
    free( (char *) counts );
    free( (char *) nodes );
    free( (char *) codes );
}


/*
 * ExpandFile is the routine called by MAIN-E.C to expand a file that
 * has been compressed with order 0 Huffman coding. This routine has
 * a simpler job than that of the Compression routine. All it has to
 * do is read in the counts that have been stored in the compressed
 * file, then build the Huffman tree. The data can then be expanded
 * by reading in a bit at a time from the compressed file. Finally,
 * the node array is freed and the routine returns.
 *
 */
void ExpandFile( input, output, argc, argv )
BIT_FILE *input;
FILE *output;
int argc;
char *argv[];
{
    NODE *nodes;
    int root_node;

    if ( ( nodes = (NODE *)
                    calloc( 514, sizeof( NODE ) ) ) == NULL )
      fatal_error( "Error allocating nodes array\n" );
    input_counts( input, nodes );
    root_node = build_tree( nodes );
    if ( argc >0 && strcmp( argv[ 0 ], "-d" ) == 0 )
        print_model( nodes, 0 );
    expand_data( input, output, nodes, root_node );
    free( (char *) nodes );
}
```

```
/*
 * In order for the compressor to build the same model, I have to
 * store the symbol counts in the compressed file so the expander can
 * read them in. In order to save space, I don't save all 256 symbols
 * unconditionally. The format used to store counts looks like this:
 *
 * start, stop, counts, start, stop, counts, ... 0
 *
 * This means that I store runs of counts, until all the non-zero
 * counts have been stored. At this time the list is terminated by
 * storing a start value of 0. Note that at least 1 run of counts has
 * to be stored, so even if the first start value is 0, I read it in.
 * It also means that even in an empty file that has no counts, I have
 * to pass at least one count, which will have a value of 0.
 *
 * In order to efficiently use this format, I have to identify runs of
 * non-zero counts. Because of the format used, I don't want to stop a
 * run because of just one or two zeros in the count stream. So I have
 * to sit in a loop looking for strings of three or more zero values
 * in a row.
 *
 * This is simple in concept, but it ends up being one of the most
 * complicated routines in the whole program. A routine that just
 * writes out 256 values without attempting to optimize would be much
 * simpler, but would hurt compression quite a bit on small files.
 *
 */
void output_counts( output, nodes )
BIT_FILE *output;
NODE *nodes;
{
    int first;
    int last;
    int next;
    int i;
```

```
        first = 0;
        while ( first < 255 && nodes[ first ].count == 0 )
                first++;
/*
* Each time I hit the start of the loop, I assume that first is the
* number for a run of non-zero values. The rest of the loop is
* concerned with finding the value for last, which is the end of the
* run, and the value of next, which is the start of the next run.
* At the end of the loop, I assign next to first, so it starts in on
* the next run.
*/
    for ( ; first < 256 ; first = next ) {
        last = first + 1;
        for ( ; ; ) {
            for ( ; last < 256 ; last++ )
                if ( nodes[ last ].count == 0 )
                    break;
            last--;
            for ( next = last + 1; next < 256 ; next++ )
                if ( nodes[ next ].count != 0 )
                    break;
            if ( next > 255 )
                break;
            if ( ( next - last ) > 3 )
                break;
            last = next;
        };
/*
* Here is where I output first, last, and all the counts in between.
*/
        if ( putc( first, output->file ) != first )
            fatal_error( "Error writing byte counts\n" );
        if ( putc( last, output->file ) != last )
            fatal_error( "Error writing byte counts\n" );
        for ( i = first ; i <= last ; i++ ) {
            if ( putc( nodes[ i ].count, output->file ) !=
                (int) nodes[ i ].count )
```

```
            fatal_error( "Error writing byte counts\n" );
        }
    }
    if ( putc( 0, output->file ) != 0 )
            fatal_error( "Error writing byte counts\n" );
}

/*
* When expanding, I have to read in the same set of counts. This is
* quite a bit easier that the process of writing them out, since no
* decision making needs to be done. All I do is read in first, check
* to see if I am all done, and if not, read in last and a string of
* counts.
*/
void input_counts( input, nodes )
BIT_FILE *input;
NODE *nodes;
{
    int first;
    int last;
    int i;
    int c;

    for ( i = 0 ; i < 256 ; i++ )
        nodes[ i ].count = 0;
    if ( ( first = getc( input->file ) ) == EOF )
        fatal_error( "Error reading byte counts\n" );
    if ( ( last = getc( input->file ) ) == EOF )
        fatal_error( "Error reading byte counts\n" );
    for ( ; ; ) {
        for ( i = first ; i <= last ; i++ )
            if ( ( c = getc( input->file ) ) == EOF )
                fatal_error( "Error reading byte counts\n" );
            else
                nodes[ i ].count = (unsigned int) c;
        if ( ( first = getc( input->file ) ) == EOF )
            fatal_error( "Error reading byte counts\n" );
```

```
            if ( first == 0 )
                break;
            if ( ( last = getc( input->file ) ) == EOF )
                fatal_error( "Error reading byte counts\n" );
        }
    nodes[ END_OF_STREAM ].count = 1;
}


/*
 * This routine counts the frequency of occurence of every byte in
 * the input file. It marks the place in the input stream where it
 * started, counts up all the bytes, then returns to the place where
 * it started. In most C implementations, the length of a file
 * cannot exceed an unsigned long, so this routine should always
 * work.
 */
#ifndef SEEK_SET
#define SEEK_SET 0
#endif

void count_bytes( input, counts )
FILE *input;
unsigned long *counts;
{
    long input_marker;
    int c;

    input_marker = ftell( input );
    while ( ( c = getc( input )) != EOF )
        counts[ c ]++;
    fseek( input, input_marker, SEEK_SET );
}


/*
 * In order to limit the size of my Huffman codes to 16 bits, I scale
 * my counts down so they fit in an unsigned char, and then store them
 * all as initial weights in my NODE array. The only thing to be
```

```
* careful of is to make sure that a node with a non-zero count doesn't
* get scaled down to 0. Nodes with values of 0 don't get codes.
*/
void scale_counts( counts, nodes )
unsigned long *counts;
NODE   *nodes;
{
    unsigned long max_count;
    int i;

    max_count = 0;
    for ( i = 0 ; i < 256 ; i++ )
        if ( counts[ i ] > max_count )
            max_count = counts[ i ];
    if ( max_count == 0 ) {
        counts[ 0 ] = 1;
        max_count = 1;
    }
    max_count = max_count / 255;
    max_count = max_count + 1;
    for ( i = 0 ; i < 256 ; i++ ) {
        nodes[ i ].count = (unsigned int)
                              ( counts[ i ] / max_count );
        if ( nodes[ i ].count == 0 && counts[ i ] != 0 )
            nodes[ i ].count = 1;
    }
    nodes[ END_OF_STREAM ].count = 1;
}
/*
* Building the Huffman tree is fairly simple. All of the active nodes
* are scanned in order to locate the two nodes with the minimum
* weights. These two weights are added together and assigned to a new
* node. The new node makes the two minimum nodes into its 0 child
* and 1 child. The two minimum nodes are then marked as inactive.
* This process repeats until there is only one node left, which is
* the root node. The tree is done, and the root node is passed back
* to the calling routine.
*
```

```
 * Node 513 is used here to arbitratily provide a node with a guaran
 * teed maximum value. It starts off being min_1 and min_2. After all
 * active nodes have been scanned, I can tell if there is only one
 * active node left by checking to see if min_1 is still 513.
 */
int build_tree( nodes )
NODE    *nodes;
{
    int next_free;
    int i;
    int min_1;
    int min_2;


    nodes[ 513 ].count = 0xffff;
    for ( next_free = END_OF_STREAM + 1 ; ; next_free++ ) {
        min_1 = 513;
        min_2 = 513;
        for ( i = 0 ; i < next_free ; i++ )
            if ( nodes[ i ].count != 0) {
                if ( nodes[ i ].count < nodes[ min_1 ].count ) {
                  min_2 = min_1;
                  min_1 = i;
                } else if ( nodes[ i ].count
                            < nodes[ min_2 ].count )
                  min_2 = i;
            }
        if ( min_2 == 513 )
            break;
        nodes[ next_free ].count = nodes[ min_1 ].count
                                   + nodes[ min_2 ].count;
        nodes[ min_1 ].saved_count = nodes[ min_1 ].count;
        nodes[ min_1 ].count = 0;
        nodes[ min_2 ].saved_count = nodes[ min_2 ].count;
        nodes[ min_2 ].count = 0;
        nodes[ next_free ].child_0 = min_1;
        nodes[ next_free ].child_1 = min_2;
```

```
        }
    next_free--;
    nodes[ next_free ].saved_count = nodes[ next_free ].count;
    return( next_free );
}

/*
 * Since the Huffman tree is built as a decoding tree, there is
 * no simple way to get the encoding values for each symbol out of
 * it. This routine recursively walks through the tree, adding the
 * child bits to each code until it gets to a leaf. When it gets
 * to a leaf, it stores the code value in the CODE element, and
 * returns.
 */
void convert_tree_to_code( nodes, codes, code_so_far, bits, node )
NODE *nodes;
CODE *codes;
unsigned int code_so_far;
int bits;
int node;
{

    if ( node <= END_OF_STREAM ) {
        codes[ node ].code = code_so_far;
        codes[ node ].code_bits = bits;
        return;

    }
    code_so_far <<= 1;
    bits++;
    convert_tree_to_code( nodes, codes, code_so_far, bits,
                          nodes[ node ].child_0 );
    convert_tree_to_code( nodes, codes, code_so_far | 1,
                          bits, nodes[ node ].child_1 );
}
```

```
/*
 * If the -d command line option is specified, this routine is called
 * to print out some of the model information after the tree is built.
 * Note that this is the only place that the saved_count NODE element
 * is used for anything at all, and in this case it is just for
 * diagnostic information. By the time I get here, and the tree has
 * been built, every active element will have 0 in its count.
 */
void print_model( nodes, codes )
NODE *nodes;
CODE *codes;
{
    int i;

    for ( i = 0 ; i < 513 ; i++ ) {
      if ( nodes[ i ].saved_count != 0 ) {
            printf( "node=" );
            print_char( i );
            printf( " count=%3d", nodes[ i ].saved_count );
            printf( " child_0=" );
            print_char( nodes[ i ].child_0 );
            printf( " child_1=" );
            print_char( nodes[ i ].child_1 );
            if ( codes && i <= END_OF_STREAM ) {
                printf( " Huffman code=" );
                FilePrintBinary( stdout, codes[ i ].code,
                                 codes[ i ].code_bits );
            }
            printf( "\n" );
        }
    }
}
```

```
/*
 * The print_model routine uses this function to print out node num
 * bers. The catch is, if it is a printable character, it gets printed
 * out as a character. This makes the debug output a little easier to
 * read.
 */
void print_char( c )
int c;
{
    if ( c >= 0x20 && c < 127 )
        printf( "'%c'", c );
    else
        printf( "%3d", c );
}


/*
 * Once the tree gets built, and the CODE table is built, compressing
 * the data is a breeze. Each byte is read in, and its corresponding
 * Huffman code is sent out.
 */
void compress_data( input, output, codes )
FILE    *input;
BIT_FILE    *output;
CODE    *codes;
{
    int c;

    while ( ( c = getc( input ) ) != EOF )
        OutputBits( output, (unsigned long) codes[ c ].code,
                    codes[ c ].code_bits );
    OutputBits( output, (unsigned long) codes[ END_OF_STREAM ].code,
                codes[ END_OF_STREAM ].code_bits );
}


/*
 * Expanding compressed data is a little harder than the compression
 * phase. As each new symbol is decoded, the tree is traversed,
 * starting at the root node, reading a bit in, and taking either the
```

```
 * child_0 or child_1 path. Eventually, the tree winds down to a
 * leaf node, and the corresponding symbol is output. If the symbol
 * is the END_OF_STREAM symbol, it doesn't get written out, and
 * instead the whole process terminates.
 */
void expand_data( input, output, nodes, root_node )
BIT_FILE *input;
FILE *output;
NODE    *nodes;
int root_node;
{
    int node;

    for ( ; ; ) {
    node = root_node;
    do {
        if ( InputBit( input ) )
            node = nodes[ node ].child_1;
        else
            node = nodes[ node ].child_0;
    } while ( node > END_OF_STREAM );
    if ( node == END_OF_STREAM )
        break;
    if ( ( putc( node, output ) ) != node )
        fatal_error( "Error trying to write byte to output" );
    }
}
/************************** End of HUFF.C **************************/
```

Putting It All Together

The actual commands to build the compression and expansion programs will differ depending on which compiler and operating system you are using. Assuming you name the compression program HUFF-C and the expansion program HUFF-E, here are the command lines to compile the programs with various compilers:

```
Microsoft C:    cl /W3 /Za /FeHUFF-C MAIN-C.C HUFF.C BITIO.C ERRHAND.C
                cl /W3 /Za /FeHUFF-E MAIN-E.C HUFF.C BITIO.C ERRHAND.C

Borland C++:  bcc -Ax -w -eHUFF-C MAIN-C.C HUFF.C BITIO.C ERRHAND.C
```

```
       bcc -Ax -w -eHUFF-E MAIN-E.C HUFF.C BITIO.C ERRHAND.C

UNIX pcc:  cc -ohuff-c main-c.c huff.c bitio.c errhand.c
           cc -ohuff-e main-e.c huff.c bitio.c errhand.c
```

Remember that ANSI-compatible C compilers must have their extensions turned off on the command line to enable the __STDC__ macro. The __STDC__ macro is necessary to turn on the ANSI prototypes. If you don't want to continually have to add this unfamiliar command-line switch when you compile, simply strip out the "#ifdef __STDC__" line and always pull in the ANSI C prototypes. The only reason for doing this is to have code that will compile cleanly on K&R compilers. If you aren't using a K&R compiler, keeping in the K&R prototypes is of dubious value.

The module ERRHAND.C needs the __UNIX__ definition in order to use old-style variable arguments. Fully compliant ANSI C compilers may not have to turn this option on. If you are going to only be using your source code on your UNIX system, it would probably be simpler to put a "#define __UNIX__" in your ERRHAND.C file.

Performance. Order 0 Huffman coding is not going to take any prizes for compression ratios. But it does fairly well in terms of program size, memory requirements, and processing speed. To see how HUFF.C does overall, see the scorecards in appendix A.

```
/************************* Start of MAIN-E.C *************************/
* This driver program tests compression algorithms. To cut back on
* repetitive code, this version of main is used with all the expansion
* routines. The main() routine supplied here checks for valid input and
* output files, opens them, then calls the compression routine.
*
*/
#include <stdio.h>
#include <stdlib.h>
#include <string.h>
#include "bitio.h"
#include "errhand.h"
#include "main.h"

#ifdef __STDC__
void usage_exit( char *prog_name );
#else
void usage_exit();
#endif

int main( argc, argv )
int argc;
char *argv[];
{
  FILE *output;
```

```
    BIT_FILE *input;

    setbuf( stdout, NULL );
    if ( argc < 3 )
        usage_exit( argv[ 0 ] );
    input = OpenInputBitFile( argv[ 1 ] );
    if ( input == NULL )
        fatal_error( "Error opening %s for input\n", argv[ 1 ] );
    output = fopen( argv[ 2 ], "wb" );
    if ( output == NULL )
        fatal_error( "Error opening %s for output\n", argv[ 2 ] );
    printf( "\nExpanding %s to %s\n", argv[ 1 ], argv[ 2 ] );
    printf( "Using %s\n", CompressionName );
    argc -= 3;
    argv += 3;
    ExpandFile( input, output, argc, argv );
    CloseInputBitFile( input );
    fclose( output );
    putc( '\n', stdout );
    return( 0 );
}

/*
 * This routine wants to print out the usage message called for when the
 * program is run with no parameters. The first part of the Usage state-
 * ment is supposed to be just the programname. argv[ 0 ] generally holds
 * the fully qualified path name of the program being run.
 */
void usage_exit( prog_name )
char *prog_name;
{
    char *short_name;
    char *extension;

    short_name = strrchr( prog_name, '\\' );
    if ( short_name == NULL )
        short_name = strrchr( prog_name, '/' );
    if ( short_name == NULL )
        short_name = strrchr( prog_name, ':' );
    if ( short_name != NULL )
        short_name++;
    else
        short_name = prog_name;
    extension = strrchr( short_name, '.' );
    if ( extension != NULL )
        *extension = '\0';
    printf( "\nUsage: %s %s\n", short_name, Usage );
    exit( 0 );
}

/*************************** End of MAIN-E.C ***************************/
```

CHAPTER 4

A Significant Improvement: Adaptive Huffman Coding

In chapter 3 we saw how Huffman coding could perform effective data compression by reducing the amount of redundancy in the coding of symbols. Huffman coding does not in itself tell how to reduce the information content of each symbol by developing an accurate model. But any model that can predict the probability of a symbol with any accuracy should be able to use Huffman coding to compress data.

The examples in chapter 3 all used order 0 models, which are essentially context free. This means that the probability of a given character is calculated without taking into account the characters that preceded it in a message. The programs used in chapter 3 just analyzed the entire input file and created a table of probabilities for each symbol. As long as these probabilities deviated from a purely uniform distribution, we were able to compress the data.

A minor drawback to Huffman coding programs was the requirement that they transmit a copy of the probability table with the compressed data. The expansion program would have no way of correctly decoding the data without the probability table. The table requires at most the addition of an extra 250 or so bytes to the output table, and consequently it usually doesn't make much difference in the compression ratio. Even small files won't be greatly affected, since the probability table should also be small for these files.

The problem with this "minor drawback" is that as we attempt to improve the compression ability of our program, the penalty becomes more and more significant. If we move from order-0 to order-1 modeling, for example, we now have to transmit 257 probability tables instead of just one. So by using a technique that enables us to predict characters more accurately, we incur a penalty in terms of added overhead. Unless the files we are going to compress are very large, this added penalty will frequently wipe out any improvements made by increasing the order.

Adaptive Coding

This seems to lead to an impasse. To compress better, we need to accumulate more statistics. When we get more statistics, we achieve better compression but we wipe out any gains by having to send more modeling data.

Fortunately, there is a way out of this dilemma. Adaptive coding lets us use higher-order modeling without paying *any* penalty for added statistics. It does this by adjusting the Huffman tree on the fly, based on data previously seen and having no knowledge about future statistics.

Adaptive coding is not something that can just be used with Huffman coding. In principle, almost any form of coding can be converted to use an adaptive method. The high-level C program required to do adaptive compression is shown below.

```
initialize_model();
do {
    c = getc( input );
    encode( c, output );
    update_model( c );
} while ( c != EOF );
```

The decompressor works in a nearly identical fashion, as shown here:

```
initialize_model();
while ( ( c == decode( input ) ) != EOF ) {
    putc( c, output );
    update_mode( c );
}
```

Adaptive coding works since two of the routines used in these two algorithms are identical: initialize_model() and update_model(). If these routines differed even slightly between the compression and decompression programs, the whole system would fall apart.

This sort of coding is fairly simple. The compressor and decompressor start off with identical models to encode and decode. So when the compressor puts out its very first encoded symbol, the decompressor will be able to interpret it.

After the compressor emits the first symbol, it proceeds to the update_model() function. This is where the adaptive nature of the program begins. The update model takes into account the character that has just been seen and updates the frequency and encoding data used to encode that character. In a Huffman tree, it means incrementing the count for the particular symbol, then updating the Huffman coding tree.

Updating the Huffman Tree

The algorithm for constructing a Huffman coding tree is fairly simple, but it is not something we would want to do after every character is encoded. It would be relatively simple to implement adaptive Huffman coding with the following update function:

```
update_model( int c )
{
    counts[ c ]++;
    construct_tree( counts );
}
```

Unfortunately, what we would end up with would probably be the world's slowest data-compression program. Building the tree takes too much work to reasonably expect to do it after every character.

Fortunately, there is a way to take an existing Huffman coding tree and modify it to account for a new character. All it takes is a slightly different approach to building the tree in the first place. This approach introduces a concept known as the sibling property. A Huffman tree is simply a binary tree that has a weight assigned to every node, whether an internal node or a leaf node. Each node (except for the root) has a sibling, the other node that shares the same parent. The tree exhibits sibling property if the nodes can be listed in order of increasing weight and if every node appears adjacent to its sibling in the list.

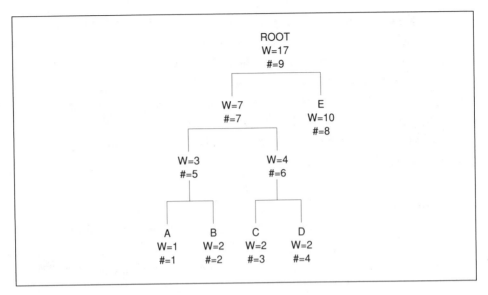

Figure 4-1. A Huffman tree.

A binary tree is a Huffman tree if and only if it obeys the sibling property. Figure 4-1 shows a Huffman tree that illustrates how this works. In this tree, the nodes have been assigned numbers, with the numbers assigned from left to right starting at the lowest row of nodes and working up. This tree was created using a conventional Huffman algorithm given the weights A=1, B=2, C=2, D=2, and E=10.

In figure 4-1, the A, B, C, and D nodes at the bottom of the tree are numbered in increasing order starting at 1. Nodes 5 and 6 are the first two internal nodes, with weights of 3 and 4. The node numbers work their way up to node 9, the root. This arrangement shows that this tree obeys the sibling property. The nodes have been numbered in order of increasing weight, and each node is adjacent to its sibling in the list.

The sibling property is important in adaptive Huffman coding since it helps show what we need to do to a Huffman tree when it is time to update the counts. Maintaining the sibling property during the update assures that we have a Huffman tree before and after the counts are adjusted.

Updating the tree consists of two basic types of operations. The first, incrementing the count, is easy to follow conceptually. To increment the count for symbol 'c', start at the leaf node for the symbol and increment the count for the leaf node. Then move up to the parent node. Since the weight of the parent node is the sum of the weight of its children, incrementing its weight by one will adjust it to its correct value. This process continues all the way up the tree till we reach the root node.

Figure 4-2 shows how the increment operation affects the tree. Starting at the leaf, the increment works its way up the tree till it reaches the parent node. Implementing this portion of the code is relatively simple. Be sure that each node has a parent pointer and that an index points to the leaf node for each symbol. This can be done using conventional data structures at a low cost. The average number of increment operations required will correspond to the average number of bits needed to encode a symbol.

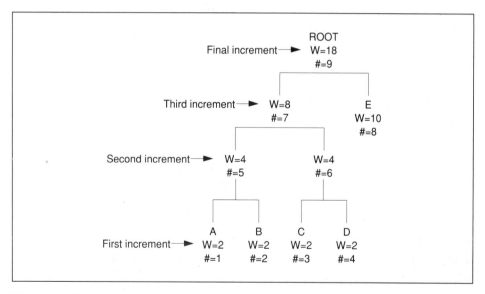

Figure 4-2. The increment process.

The second operation required in the update procedure arises when the node increment causes a violation of the sibling property. This occurs when the node being incremented has the same weight as the next highest node in the list. If the increment were to proceed as normal, we would no longer have a Huffman tree.

When we have an increment that violates the sibling property, we need to move the affected node to a higher point in the list. This means that the node is detached from its present position in the tree and swapped with a node farther up the list.

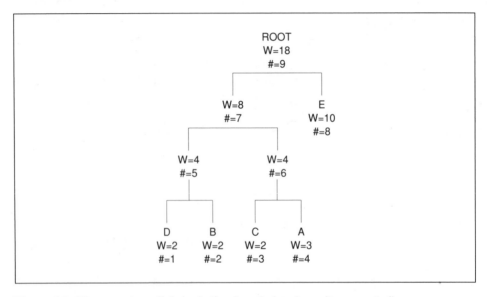

Figure 4-3. After a node switch (only the A node has been incremented).

Figure 4-3 shows the same Huffman tree from figure 4-2 after the A node has been incremented again, then switched with the D node. How was the D node selected as the one to be switched? To minimize the amount of work during the shuffle, we want to swap just two nodes. If the newly incremented node now has a weight of $W + 1$, the next higher node will have a weight of W. There may be more nodes after the next higher one that have a value of W as well. The swap procedure moves up the node list till it finds the last node with a weight of W. That node is swapped with the node with weight W + 1. The new node list will then have a string of 1 or more weight W nodes, followed by the newly incremented node with weight W + 1.

In figure 4-3, the A node was incremented from a weight of 2 to 3. Since the next node in the list, the B node, had a weight of 2, the tree no longer obeyed the sibling property. This meant it was time to swap. We worked our way up the list of nodes till we found the last node with a weight of 2, the D node. The A and D nodes were then swapped, yielding a correctly ordered tree.

After the swap is completed, the update can continue. The next node to be incremented will be the new parent of the incremented node. In figure 4-3, this would be internal node #6. As each node is incremented, a check is performed for correct ordering. A swap is performed if necessary.

What Swapping Does. The swap shown in figure 4-3 doesn't have a noticeable effect on the coding of the symbols. The A and D nodes were swapped, but the length of their codes did not change. They were both three bits long before the swap and three bits long after.

Figure 4-4 shows what happens to the tree after the A symbol has been incremented two more times. After the second increment, the A node has increased enough to swap positions with an internal node on a higher level of the tree. This reshapes the tree, impacting the length of the codes. When A had a count of two like three other symbols, it was encoded using three bits. Now, when its count has increased to five, it is encoded using only 2 bits. Symbol C is still encoded using 3 bits, but B and D have slipped down to 4 bits.

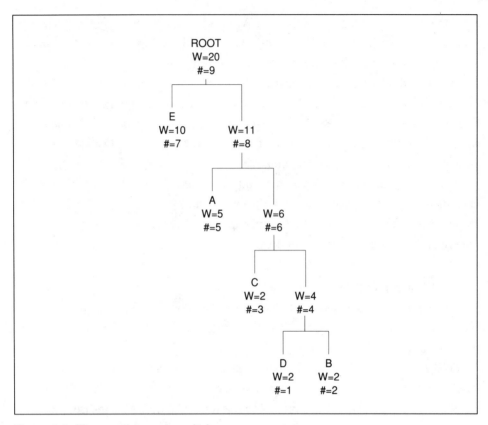

Figure 4-4. After another node switch.

The Algorithm. In summary, the algorithm for incrementing the count of a node goes something like what's shown below:

```
for ( ; ; ) {
    increment nodes[ node ].count;
    if ( node == ROOT )
        break;
    if ( nodes[ node ].count > nodes[ node + 1 ].count )
        swap_nodes();
    node = nodes[ node ].parent;
}
```

The swap_nodes() routine has to move up through the list of nodes until it finds the right node to swap with. It then performs the swap. This routine looks something like that shown below:

```
swap_node = node + 1;
while ( nodes[ swap_node + 1 ].count < nodes[ node ].count )
    swap_node++;
temp = nodes[ swap_node ].parent;
nodes[ swap_node ].parent = nodes[ node ].parent;
nodes[ node ].parent = temp;
```

An Enhancement. One way to make coding more efficient is to make sure your coder doesn't waste coding space for symbols not used in the message. With the standard Huffman coding in the previous chapter, this was easy. Since we made a pass over the data to collect statistics before building the tree, we knew in advance which symbols weren't used. So when we built the Huffman tree we didn't have to include symbols with a count of 0.

With an adaptive process, we don't know in advance which symbols will show up in the message. The simplest way to handle this problem is to initialize the Huffman tree to have all 256 possible bytes (for conventional 8-bit data messages) predefined with a count of 1. When the encoding first starts, each message will have a length of eight bits. As statistics accumulate, frequently seen characters will start to use fewer and fewer bits.

This method of encoding works, but in many cases it wastes coding capacity. Particularly in shorter messages, the extra unused codes tend to blunt the effect of compression by skewing the statistics of the message.

A better way to handle this aspect of coding is to start the encoding process with an empty table and add symbols only as they are seen in the incoming message. But this presents us with a seeming contradiction. The first time a symbol appears, it can't be encoded since it doesn't appear in the table. So how do we get around this problem?

The Escape Code. The answer to this puzzle is the escape code. The escape code is a special symbol sent out of the encoder to signify that we are going to 'escape' from the current context. The decoder knows that the next symbol will be encoded in a different context. We can use this mechanism to encode symbols that don't appear in the currently defined Huffman tree.

In the example program in this chapter, the escape code signifies that the next symbol to be encoded will be sent as a plain 8-bit character. The symbol is added to the table, and regular encoding resumes. The C code to implement the encoder for this algorithm looks something like this:

```
encode( char c )
{
    if ( in_tree( c ) )
        transmit_huffman_code( c, out_file );
    else {
        transmit_huffman_code( ESCAPE, out_file );
        putc( c, out_file );
        add_code_to_tree( c );
    }
    update_tree( c );
}
```

This example shows that the escape code is transmitted like any other symbol from the Huffman tree, so it has to appear in the Huffman tree to be properly transmitted. When the encoder first starts up, it needs to be initialized with the escape code already present.

In the implementation used in the example code for this chapter, the Huffman tree is actually initialized with two values: the escape code and the end of file code. Since both will appear in the file, we start off with them in a very small Huffman tree:

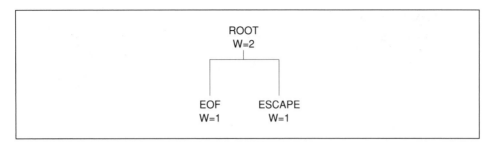

Figure 4-5. A Huffman tree initialized with two values.

As the encoding process goes on, the table fills up and the tree fleshes out. The end of file code will always have a weight of one, and in this implementation, so will the escape code. As the tree grows, these two codes will always be stuck down at the remotest branches of the tree and have the longest codes.

The Overflow Problem. As the compression program progresses, the counts in the table increase. At some point, the counts become large enough to cause trouble for the program. There are two possible areas of concern. The first occurs when the weight of the root node exceeds the capacity of the counters in the tree. For most of the programs used here, that will be 16 bits.

Another possible problem can occur even sooner. It happens when the length of the longest possible Huffman code exceeds the range of the integer used to transmit it. The decoding process doesn't care how long a code is, since it works its way down through the tree a bit at a time. The transmitter has a different problem though. It has to start at the leaf node of the tree and work up towards the root. It accumulates bits to be transmitted in reverse order, so it has to stack them up. This is conventionally done in an integer variable, so this means that when a Huffman code exceeds the size of that integer, there is a problem.

The maximum length of a Huffman code is related to the maximum count via a Fibonacci sequence. A Fibonacci function is defined as follows:

```
int fib( int n )
{
   if ( n <= 1 )
       return( 1 );
   else
      return( fib( n - 1 ) + fib( n -2 ) );
}
```

The sequence of Fibonacci numbers looks something like this: 1, 1, 2, 3, 5, 8, 13, 21, 34, etc. These numbers show up in the worst-case, lopsided Huffman tree:

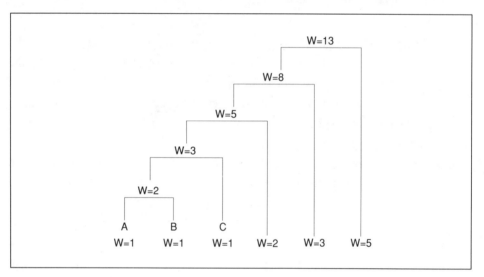

Figure 4-6. A lopsided Huffman tree produced through a sequence of Fibonacci numbers.

From this we can deduce that if the weight at the root node of a Huffman tree equals fib(i), then the longest code possible for that tree is i - 1. This means that if the integers used with our Huffman codes are only 16 bits long, a root value of 4181 could potentially introduce an overflow. (This low value is frequently overlooked in simple Huffman implementations. Setting up a file with Fibonacci counts up to fib[18] is a good way to test a Huffman program). When we update the tree, we ought to check for a maximum value. Once we reach that value, we need to rescale all the counts, typically dividing them by a fixed factor, often two.

One problem with dividing all the counts by two is that it can possibly reshape the tree. Since we are dealing with integers, dividing by two truncates the fractional part of the result, which can lead to imbalances. Consider the Huffman tree shown in figure 4-7.

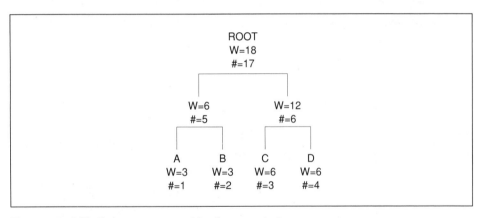

Figure 4-7. A Huffman tree created for four symbols.

This is a tree created for four symbols: A, B, C, and D, with weights of 3, 3, 6, and 6. The nodes of the tree are numbered in this diagram, and the diagram clearly shows that the tree is a Huffman tree, since it obeys the sibling property. The problem with this tree occurs if we try a rescaling operation. The simple version of the rescaling algorithm would go through the tree, dividing every leaf node weight by two, then rebuilding upwards from the leaf nodes. The resulting tree would look like what follows.

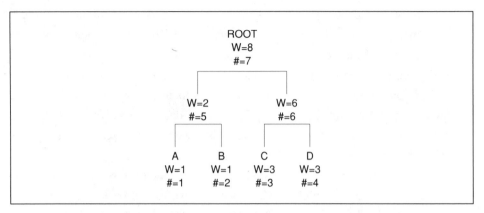

Figure 4-8. The rescaling problem after the nodes are divided by two.

The problem with the resulting tree is that it is no longer a Huffman tree. Because of the vagaries of truncation that follow integer division, we need to end up with a tree that has a slightly different shape:

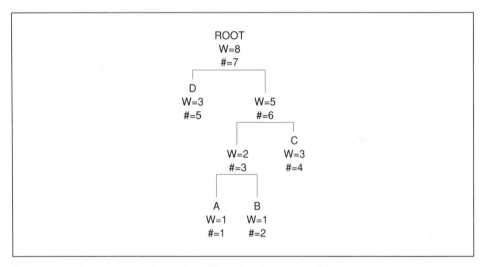

Figure 4-9. What the tree should look like after integer division.

The properly organized Huffman tree has a drastically different shape from what it had before being rescaled. This happens because rescaling loses some of the precision in our statistical base, introducing errors sometimes reflected in the rescaled tree. As time goes on, we accumulate more statistics, and the effect of the errors gradually fades away.

Unfortunately, there is no simple way to compensate for the necessary reshaping of the tree after rescaling. The sample code in this chapter merely does a brute-force rebuilding after rescaling. Rebuilding the entire tree is a relatively expensive operation, but since the rescaling operation is rare, we can live with the cost.

A Rescaling Bonus. An interesting side effect comes out of rescaling our tree at periodic intervals. Though we lose accuracy by scaling our counts, testing reveals that rescaling generally results in better compression ratios than if rescaling is postponed. This occurs because data streams frequently have a "decaying recency" effect, or the statistics for recently seen symbols are generally more valid than those accumulated farther back in the data stream. To put it simply, current symbols are more like recent symbols than older symbols.

The rescaling operation tends to discount the effect of older symbols, while increasing the importance of recent symbols. Though difficult to quantify, this seems to have a good effect on compression. Experimenting with various rescaling points will yield different results at differing values, but it doesn't seem possible to pin down an optimal strategy. There may be an optimal value for rescaling, but it moves around with different types of data streams.

The Code

The sample code for this chapter is a simple order-0 adaptive Huffman compression routine. It is linked with the standard I/O and user interface routines from the previous chapter to create a standalone compression program and a decompression program.

The key to understanding how this sample code operates lies in understanding the data structures in the program. The data structure that describes the tree is shown next.

```
struct tree {
    int leaf[ SYMBOL_COUNT ];
    int next_free_node;
    struct node {
        unsigned int weight;
        int parent;
        int child_is_leaf;
        int child;
    } nodes[ NODE_TABLE_COUNT ];
} Tree;
```

Two arrays describe the tree. The tree itself is entirely represented by the nodes[] array. This array is a set of structures with the following elements:

unsigned int weight:	This weight element is the weight of the individual node, just as it has been described previously in this chapter.
int parent:	This int is the index of the parent node. The parent node information is necessary both when encoding a symbol, and when updating the model.
int child_is_leaf:	The child of a given node can either be a leaf or a pair of nodes. This flag is used to indicate which it is.
int child:	If the child is a leaf, this int holds the value of the symbol encoded at the leaf. If the child is a pair of nodes, this value is the index to the first node. Because of the sibling property, the two nodes will always be adjacent to one another, so we know the first node will be child, and the second node will be child+1.

As described earlier in the chapter, every node in the tree is kept in a number list. When discussing the list before, we had the nodes with the lowest weight starting at 1 and working up to higher numbers until reaching the root. The implementation in this program is backwards from that, though the same principles apply. The list of nodes is the nodes[] array, with the highest number on the list appearing at nodes [0]. As we work our way down through the lower weights, we go to higher indices in the nodes list.

When the tree is first initialized, nodes[0] is the root node, nodes[1] is set to the end-of-stream symbol, and nodes[2] is set to the escape symbol. The next_free_node element in the tree is then set to 3, and the next time a character is added to the tree, it will be placed in nodes[3].

The leaf[] array in the tree data structure is used to find the leaf node for a particular symbol. To encode a symbol, start at the leaf node and work up to the root node of the tree, accumulating bits on the way (in reverse order). Without a leaf[] array to keep track of the leaf nodes, we would have to do a search through the entire tree every time we wanted to encode a character.

Initialization of the Array. Regardless of whether we perform compression or expansion, we initialize the Huffman tree using the same routine. When performing adaptive compression, it is extremely important to use an identical algorithm for both initialization and updating of the compression model. In this case, we use the same code to ensure that it happens.

The initialization routine, InitializeTree(tree), is the first thing called by both the compression and expansion code. It uses the following code to initialize nodes 0, 1, and 2:

```
tree->nodes[ ROOT_NODE ].child              = ROOT_NODE + 1;
tree->nodes[ ROOT_NODE ].child_is_leaf      = FALSE;
tree->nodes[ ROOT_NODE ].weight             = 2;
tree->nodes[ ROOT_NODE ].parent             = -1;

tree->nodes[ ROOT_NODE + 1 ].child          = END_OF_STREAM;
tree->nodes[ ROOT_NODE + 1 ].child_is_leaf  = TRUE;
```

```
tree->nodes[ ROOT_NODE + 1 ].weight          = 1;
tree->nodes[ ROOT_NODE + 1 ].parent          = ROOT_NODE;
tree->leaf[ END_OF_STREAM ]                  = ROOT_NODE + 1;

tree->nodes[ ROOT_NODE + 2 ].child           = ESCAPE;
tree->nodes[ ROOT_NODE + 2 ].child_is_leaf   = TRUE;
tree->nodes[ ROOT_NODE + 2 ].weight          = 1;
tree->nodes[ ROOT_NODE + 2 ].parent          = ROOT_NODE;
tree->leaf[ ESCAPE ]                         = ROOT_NODE + 2;

tree->next_free_node                         = ROOT_NODE + 3;

for ( i = 0 ; i < END_OF_STREAM ; i++ )
    tree->leaf[ i ] = -1;
```

The initialization of the tree->nodes[] elements is fairly direct. We assign the escape and end-of-stream nodes a weight of 1, which gives the root a weight of 2. The escape and end-of-stream elements in the tree->leaf[] array are initialized to point to the appropriate nodes, and the parent and child pointers for each of the three nodes are initialized.

The final details required during initialization are to set up the tree->next_free_node index and to initialize the remaining elements of the tree->leaf[] array. Since none of the leaf[] elements for our conventional symbols have been initialized, they are all set to values of -1. During the encoding process, we will compare the tree->leaf[] value for a given symbol to -1 to see if it has already been defined.

The Compress Main Program. The code for the compression program is short:

```
InitializeTree( &Tree );
while ( ( c = getc( input ) ) != EOF ) {
    EncodeSymbol( &Tree, c, output );
    UpdateModel( &Tree, c );
}
EncodeSymbol( &Tree, END_OF_STREAM, output );
```

Once the tree has been initialized, the program sits in a loop encoding characters and updating the model. When there are no more characters left to encode, it encodes the end-of-stream symbol, and it is done.

Complexities are hidden in these functions. The EncodeSymbol function needs to see if the symbol is already defined. If it isn't, EncodeSymbol needs to output the escape code and the unencoded symbol. EncodeSymbol then needs to add the symbol to the tree, with a count of 0.

The UpdateModel function also hides some complexity. It performs the update discussed previously in the chapter, which is fairly complex. Before doing the update, it checks to see if the root node has reached the maximum allowable weight. If it has, the tree is scaled by a factor of two and rebuilt.

The Expand Main Program. Like the compress main program, the expand program is short and to the point. After initializing the tree, it reads in symbols via the DecodeSymbol routine, then writes them to the output file. After each symbol is decoded, it is written to the output file, and the model is updated.

As in the compress program, a certain amount of complexity is concealed in the higher-level functions. The DecodeSymbol routine has to see if the symbol it decodes is an escape code. If it is, DecodeSymbol throws away the escape code and reads in an "unencoded" 8-bit symbol. The symbol is then added to the Huffman tree, with an initial count of 0.

As previously seen, the UpdateModel() routine has to see if the root node has reached the maximum allowable count. If it has, the Huffman tree is rebuilt. After that, the normal increment/test/swap routine ensues.

```
InitializeTree( &Tree );
while ( ( c = DecodeSymbol( &Tree, input ) ) != END_OF_STREAM ) {
    if ( putc( c, output ) == EOF )
        fatal_error( "Error writing character" );
    UpdateModel( &Tree, c );
}
```

Encoding the Symbol. After initializing the tree, the compress routine repeatedly calls the EncodeSymbol routine. The EncodeSymbol routine (shown below) first identifies the leaf node for the symbol to be encoded. If the leaf table returns a -1, it means that this symbol is not presently found in the Huffman tree. In that case, the symbol to be encoded is switched to the escape code, and its root node is located.

The encoding process for a Huffman tree works by starting at the leaf node and moving up through the parent nodes one at a time, until the root is reached. In a conventional Huffman tree, there will usually be two child nodes for each parent, one that encodes a 0 bit and another that encodes a 1 bit. The data structures used in this program take advantage of the sibling property by always grouping the two children of a parent node next to one another in the node list.

Grouping children together saves space by requiring only a single child pointer instead of two. It also means that a child automatically knows whether it is the child that encodes a 1 or a 0 by whether it is odd or even. In this program, the odd child is arbitrarily designated the 1, and the even is always the 0.

Given this information, the encoding process is accomplished without too many lines of C code. Starting at the leaf node, each bit is added to the cumulative Huffman code. Whether the bit is a 1 or a 0 determines whether the bit is odd or even. As each bit is encoded, the current_bit mask is shifted by one so the next bit encoded will appear in the next most significant position. A counter is also incremented that keeps track of how many bits have been accumulated in the output word so far.

```
code = 0;
current_bit = 1;
code_size = 0;
current_node = tree->leaf[ c ];
if ( current_node == -1 )
    current_node = tree->leaf[ ESCAPE ];
while ( current_node != ROOT_NODE ) {
    if ( ( current_node & 1 ) == 0 )
        code |= current_bit;
    current_bit <<= 1;
    code_size++;
```

```
    current_node = tree->nodes[ current_node ].parent;
};
OutputBits( output, code, code_size );
if ( tree->leaf[ c ] == -1 ) {
    OutputBits( output, c, 8 );
    add_new_node( tree, c );
}
```

After the bits of the Huffman code have been accumulated in the code word, the utility routine OutputBits (found in BITIO.C) is called to send out the code. There is still one piece of work left to do, however, before returning. If the code that was just output was the escape code, we have to handle the special condition created when a previously unreferenced symbol is encountered.

The first step taken after the escape code is sent is simple. The new symbol is output in an unencoded fashion, just as it was read in from the file. This lets the decoder know what symbol to add to the table. The second step is to add the new node to the Huffman tree. When the new node is added to the tree, it is inserted with a weight of 0. The 0-weight node will be incremented later when the model is updated, so it will not be 0 for long. The advantage to adding a node with a weight of zero is that it can be done without having to worry about updating any other nodes or, worse, changing the shape of the tree.

Using the sibling property definitions, we know that if the new node has a weight of 0, it will be the very first node in the list, since nodes are ranked in order of weight. We add the node to the table by finding the presently lowest-weight node and break it out into two new nodes. The old lowest-weight node will be one of the two new nodes, and the new 0-weight node will be the other one.

Figure 4-10 illustrates how this process modifies a working tree. The Huffman tree has already had the A, B, C, and D nodes defined with nonzero weights. The A node has the lowest count and consequently is at the start of the list (remember that the list in this program has the highest weights at 0). When symbol E is going to be added to the tree, we first identify A as the node at the end of the list. The position A used to occupy is converted to an internal node, and two new nodes are created. Since E is guaranteed to have the lowest weight in the tree, it is set to be the first node in the list, and A is set to be the second node.

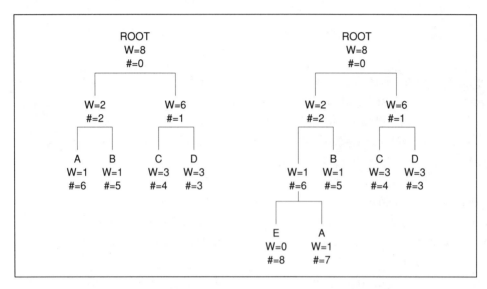

Figure 4-10. The Huffman tree before and after addition of a zero weight node.

The code needed to add the node is listed below. The first step is to find the lowest-weight node, which in the example was A. The new_node variable is the node which A will occupy, and the 0_weight_node is where E will go. Since these are two new nodes, they are set to be the next_free_node and next_free_node+1. After this is done, next_free_node is incremented by two so it will be ready for the next operation.

```
lightest_node = tree->next_free_node - 1;
new_node = tree->next_free_node;
zero_weight_node = tree->next_free_node + 1;
tree->next_free_node += 2;

tree->nodes[ new_node ] = tree->nodes[ lightest_node ];
tree->nodes[ new_node ].parent = lightest_node;
tree->leaf[ tree->nodes[ new_node ].child ] = new_node;
```

```
tree->nodes[ lightest_node ].child = new_node;
tree->nodes[ lightest_node ].child_is_leaf = FALSE;

tree->nodes[ zero_weight_node ].child         = c;
tree->nodes[ zero_weight_node ].child_is_leaf = TRUE;
tree->nodes[ zero_weight_node ].weight        = 0;
tree->nodes[ zero_weight_node ].parent        = lightest_node;
tree->leaf[ c ] = zero_weight_node;
```

After the two new nodes are created, a few more bookkeeping details are needed to link the two new children to their parent, to make sure their weights are correct, and to make sure the leaf array points to the correct nodes. After that, the routine is done, and the tree is ready to be updated.

Updating the Tree. The most complicated part of the Adaptive Huffman program is in the routines called to update the tree. Updating the model is simply a matter of incrementing a symbol weight by one and taking care of all the side effects of that action. Taking care of the side effects, however, involves some strenuous effort.

```
if ( tree->nodes[ ROOT_NODE].weight == MAX_WEIGHT )
    RebuildTree( tree );
current_node = tree->leaf[ c ];
while ( current_node != -1 ) {
    tree->nodes[ current_node ].weight++;
    for ( new_node = current_node ; new_node > ROOT_NODE ;
            new_node-- )
        if ( tree->nodes[ new_node - 1 ].weight >=
                tree->nodes[ current_node ].weight )
            break;
    if ( current_node != new_node ) {
        swap_nodes( tree, current_node, new_node );
        current_node = new_node;
    }
    current_node = tree->nodes[ current_node ].parent;
}
```

This code performs all the work needed to update the tree. The first thing it checks for is to see if the tree has reached its maximum weight. If it has, the routine invokes the RebuildTree routine to scale down all the counts.

After getting past the tree-rebuilding step, the loop that increments the node weights is entered. The first node to be incremented is the leaf node associated with the symbol. The loop increments the weight of that symbol, then moves up to the parent to increment that node. This process continues till the root is reached, at which point the update is done. The single symbol added to statistical base forming the tree has been accounted for.

There is one additional step inside the loop, however, that takes place after every node has its weight incremented. The loop immediately following the increment operation works its way back through the list of nodes to see if the increased weight of the current node means it has to move up in the list. After the loop exits, new_node has the proper new location for the current node in the node list. If new_node is the same as current_node, the incremented node is fine where it is, and we can move on to the parent node. But if new_node and current_node aren't the same, they have to be swapped.

The process of swapping nodes involves lifting two entire subtrees out of their present positions in the list and exchanging them. The use of a tree data structure makes this easier than it may first appear. The swapping process is straightforward, complicated only by the fact that each node being swapped has links to both its parent and child, and the parent and child each have links to the node. This takes no great conceptual leaps. The swapping code is illustrated:

```
struct node temp;

if ( tree->nodes[ i ].child_is_leaf )
    tree->leaf[ tree->nodes[ i ].child ] = j;
else {
    tree->nodes[ tree->nodes[ i ].child ].parent = j;
    tree->nodes[ tree->nodes[ i ].child + 1 ].parent = j;
}
if ( tree->nodes[ j ].child_is_leaf )
    tree->leaf[ tree->nodes[ j ].child ] = i;
```

```
else {
    tree->nodes[ tree->nodes[ j ].child ].parent = i;
    tree->nodes[ tree->nodes[ j ].child + 1 ].parent = i;
}
temp = tree->nodes[ i ];
tree->nodes[ i ] = tree->nodes[ j ];
tree->nodes[ i ].parent = temp.parent;
temp.parent = tree->nodes[ j ].parent;
tree->nodes[ j ] = temp;
```

An update can also force the rebuilding of the tree. Rebuilding takes a fair amount of work, unfortunately, since it amounts to building a new Huffman tree.

The rebuilding process proceeds in three discrete steps. The first step is to collect all the leaf nodes, throw away all the internal nodes, and divide the leaf-node weights by 2. The node list is compacted so that the new leaf nodes are all at the start of the list.

```
j = tree->next_free_node - 1;
for ( i = j ; i >= ROOT_NODE ; i-- ) {
    if ( tree->nodes[ i ].child_is_leaf ) {
        tree->nodes[ j ] = tree->nodes[ i ];
        tree->nodes[ j ].weight = ( tree->nodes[ j ].weight + 1 ) / 2;
        j--;
    }
}
```

The code to do this is shown above. Note that in this implementation, none of the nodes scale down to zero. This is accomplished by adding 1 to the node before dividing it by two. It may be desirable to throw away infrequently seen symbols by reducing their counts to zero and deleting them from the list, but we don't do that here.

What we end up with in the above code is a list of leaf nodes that are at the start of the list, terminating at the next_free_node index. The internal nodes which start at 0 and end at the current value of j, will now be rebuilt in the next step.

In chapter 3, we built a Huffman tree by repeatedly scanning the node list and finding the two nodes with the lowest weight. Those two nodes would be combined to form a new internal node. The tree-rebuilding phase here takes a different approach based on the sibling property.

The loop that creates internal nodes starts with j pointing to the next node that needs to be defined; i is an index that points to the next pair of nodes to be combined into an internal node. The loop progressively steps through the nodes, combining and adding new internal nodes until reaching the root node at location 0.

The process of creating the new internal node is simple. The new node, located at index j, is assigned a weight. The weight is simply the sum of the the two nodes at location i, as would be expected. The hard work comes next. After node j is created, we have to decide where it belongs in the node list. The decision on where the new node belongs is made based on the weights of the nodes in the list. Recall that the sibling property says that the nodes have to be listed based on increasing weight. We have to step through the list till we find the first node that is less than the new node j, then place the new node immediately adjacent to that node in the list. Here is the procedure for the correct location for j:

```
for ( i = tree->next_free_node - 2 ; j >= ROOT_NODE ;
     i -= 2, j-- ) {
    k = i + 1;
    tree->nodes[ j ].weight = tree->nodes[ i ].weight +
                              tree->nodes[ k ].weight;
    weight = tree->nodes[ j ].weight;
    tree->nodes[ j ].child_is_leaf = FALSE;
        for ( k = j + 1 ; weight < tree->nodes[ k ].weight ; k++)
            ;
    k--;
    memmove( &tree->nodes[ j ], &tree->nodes[ j + 1 ],
            ( k - j ) * sizeof( struct node ) );
    tree->nodes[ k ].weight = weight;
    tree->nodes[ k ].child = i;
    tree->nodes[ k ].child_is_leaf = FALSE;
}
```

The variable 'weight' is assigned the weight of the new internal node. The routine then loops back through the list until it finds the first node with a weight less than or equal to the weight of j. Node j will be placed immediately after that node in the list. Before that node can be positioned, we need to make room in the list by moving all the nodes that have higher weights up by one position. This is done with the memmove() function. After that, the new node has its child and weight assigned, and the loop continues.

This process can be seen in the short list of nodes about to be rebuilt in figure 4-11. After having been rescaled, symbols A, B, C, and D have weights 1, 3, 5, and 7 respectively. After the internal nodes have been stripped out, the list of nodes looks like figure 4-11.

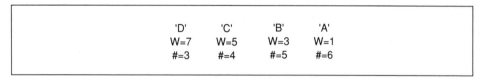

Figure 4-11: The list of nodes after the internal nodes have been stripped.

The first two nodes to be combined will be B and A, creating a new node, j, at location 2 in the table. By stepping back through the list from location 2, we see that the resulting internal node belongs between locations 4 and 5, right after B. After the memory move function is executed and the node is connected, the partial Huffman tree looks like this:

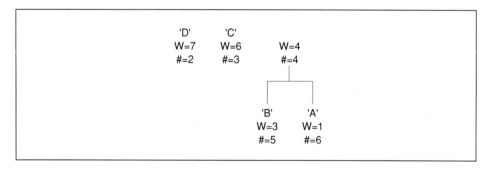

Figure 4-12. A partial Huffman tree after the memory move function is executed.

Because we are moving nodes around so freely, we do not assign parent pointers during this process. Once a node has been assigned as a child to another node, it is not going to change position in the list. But parent nodes that have yet to be combined together as children of another internal node may be moved farther up in the list as other nodes are combined. If we assigned parent nodes earlier in the process, every time we moved a node we would have to go through a backtracking procedure to locate its children and update their parent indices. We bypass this costly procedure by deferring parent node building to the third and final step in the Rebuild procedure. Assigning parent nodes is fairly simple. We start at the root node, and locate the children of each node in the tree. The children then have their parent node index set. If the child is a leaf instead of another node, the leaf[] array node index is set.

```
for ( i = tree->next_free_node - 1 ; i >= ROOT_NODE ; i-- ) {
  if ( tree->nodes[ i ].child_is_leaf ) {
    k = tree->nodes[ i ].child;
    tree->leaf[ k ] = i;
  } else {
    k = tree->nodes[ i ].child;
    tree->nodes[ k ].parent = tree->nodes[ k + 1 ].parent = i;
  }
}
```

Decoding the Symbol. The final high-level procedure to be discussed here is the routine used to decode an incoming symbol. Like the symbol encoder, this routine is short and simple. It starts at the root node of the tree and reads in a single bit at a time. As each bit is read in, one of the two children of the node is selected based on whether the input bit is a one or a zero. Eventually, this leads the routine to a leaf node.

When the leaf node is reached, we have decoded a symbol. The only possible complication at this point is if the decoded symbol is an escape code. If so, the symbol encoded by the encoder did not yet appear in the Huffman tree. This means that the next eight bits in the input stream will contain an unencoded version of the symbol. If this is the case, the input routine is called to get the plain-text version of the symbol.

```
current_node = ROOT_NODE;
while ( !tree->nodes[ current_node ].child_is_leaf ) {
  current_node = tree->nodes[ current_node ].child;
  current_node += InputBit( input );
}
c = tree->nodes[ current_node ].child;
if ( c == ESCAPE ) {
  c = (int) InputBits( input, 8 );
  add_new_node( tree, c );
}
return( c );
```

Either the decoded symbol or the escaped plain version of the symbol is passed back to the calling program where it can be placed in the output file. The hard work will come after the symbol is decoded, when the tree has to be updated to reflect the newly arrived symbol.

The Code

The code for the Adaptive Huffman compressor is listed next. This single module is contained on the source disk in the file AHUFF.C. Building the compression routine requires that you compile this file and link it with the utility routines discussed in the last chapter: BITIO.C, ERRHAND.C, and MAIN-C.C. To build the decompression routine you substitute MAIN-E.C. The two arguments for both programs are simply an input file followed by an output file.

```
/************************* Start of AHUFF.C *************************/

#include <stdio.h>
#include <stdlib.h>
#include <string.h>
#include <ctype.h>
#include "bitio.h"
#include "errhand.h"
```

```
char *CompressionName = "Adaptive Huffman coding, with escape codes";
char *Usage           = "infile outfile";

#define END_OF_STREAM     256
#define ESCAPE            257
#define SYMBOL_COUNT      258
#define NODE_TABLE_COUNT  ( ( SYMBOL_COUNT * 2 ) - 1 )
#define ROOT_NODE         0
#define MAX_WEIGHT        0x8000
#define TRUE              1
#define FALSE             0

/*
 * This data structure is all that is needed to maintain an adaptive
 * Huffman tree for both encoding and decoding. The leaf array is a
 * set of indices into the nodes that indicate which node is the
 * parent of a symbol. For example, to encode 'A', we would find the
 * leaf node by way of leaf[ 'A' ]. The next_free_node index is used
 * to tell which node is the next one in the array that can be used.
 * Since nodes are allocated when characters are read in for the first
 * time, this pointer keeps track of where we are in the node array.
 * Finally, the array of nodes is the actual Huffman tree. The child
 * index is either an index pointing to a pair of children, or an
 * actual symbol value, depending on whether 'child_is_leaf' is true
 * or false.
 */

typedef struct tree {
    int leaf[ SYMBOL_COUNT ];
    int next_free_node;
    struct node {
        unsigned int weight;
        int parent;
        int child_is_leaf;
        int child;
    } nodes[ NODE_TABLE_COUNT ];
} TREE;
```

```
/*
 * The Tree used in this program is a global structure. Under other
 * circumstances it could just as well be a dynamically allocated
 * structure built when needed, since all routines here take a TREE
 * pointer as an argument.
 */

TREE Tree;

/*
 * Function prototypes for both ANSI C compilers and their K&R breth-
 * ren.
 */

#ifdef __STDC__

void CompressFile( FILE *input, BIT_FILE *output, int argc,
                   char *argv[] );
void ExpandFile( BIT_FILE *input, FILE *output, int argc,
                 char *argv[] );
void InitializeTree( TREE *tree );
void EncodeSymbol( TREE *tree, unsigned int c, BIT_FILE *output );
int DecodeSymbol( TREE *tree, BIT_FILE *input );
void UpdateModel( TREE *tree, int c );
void RebuildTree( TREE *tree );
void swap_nodes( TREE *tree, int i, int j );
void add_new_node( TREE *tree, int c );
void PrintTree( TREE *tree );
void print_codes( TREE *tree );
void print_code( TREE *tree, int c );
void calculate_rows( TREE *tree, int node, int level );
int calculate_columns( TREE *tree, int node, int starting_guess );
int find_minimum_column( TREE *tree, int node, int max_row );
void rescale_columns( int factor );

#else
```

```
void CompressFile();
void ExpandFile();
void InitializeTree();
void EncodeSymbol();
int DecodeSymbol();
void UpdateModel();
void RebuildTree();
void swap_nodes();
void add_new_node();

#endif

/*
 * The high level view of the compression routine is very simple.
 * First, we initialize the Huffman tree, with just the ESCAPE and
 * END_OF_STREAM symbols. Then, we sit in a loop, encoding symbols,
 * and adding them to the model. When there are no more characters
 * to send, the special END_OF_STREAM symbol is encoded. The decoder
 * will later be able to use this symbol to know when to quit.
 */

void CompressFile( input, output, argc, argv )
FILE *input;
BIT_FILE *output;
int argc;
char *argv[];
{
    int c;

    InitializeTree( &Tree );
    while ( ( c = getc( input ) ) != EOF ) {
        EncodeSymbol( &Tree, c, output );
        UpdateModel( &Tree, c );
    }
    EncodeSymbol( &Tree, END_OF_STREAM, output );
    while ( argc-- > 0 ) {
        printf( "Unused argument: %s\n", *argv ); argv++;
```

```
      }
}

/*
 * The Expansion routine looks very much like the compression routine.
 * It first initializes the Huffman tree, using the same routine as
 * the compressor did. It then sits in a loop, decoding characters and
 * updating the model until it reads in an END_OF_STREAM symbol. At
 * that point, it is time to quit.
 */

void ExpandFile( input, output, argc, argv )
BIT_FILE *input;
FILE *output;
int argc;
char *argv[];
{
    int c;

    while ( argc-- > 0 )
        printf( "Unused argument: %s\n", *argv++ );
    InitializeTree( &Tree );
    while ( ( c = DecodeSymbol( &Tree, input ) ) != END_OF_STREAM ) {
        if ( putc( c, output ) == EOF )
            fatal_error( "Error writing character" );
        UpdateModel( &Tree, c );
    }
}

/*
 * When performing adaptive compression, the Huffman tree starts out
 * very nearly empty. The only two symbols present initially are the
 * ESCAPE symbol and the END_OF_STREAM symbol. The ESCAPE symbol has to
 * be included so we can tell the expansion program that we are
 * transmitting a previously unseen symbol. The END_OF_STREAM symbol
 * is here because it is greater than eight bits, and our ESCAPE
 * sequence only allows for eight bit symbols following the ESCAPE
 * code.
```

```
 *
 * In addition to setting up the root node and its two children, this
 * routine also initializes the leaf array. The ESCAPE and
 * END_OF_STREAM leaves are the only ones initially defined, the rest
 * of the leaf elements are set to -1 to show that they aren't present
 * in the Huffman tree yet.
 */

void InitializeTree( tree )
TREE *tree;
{
    int i;

    tree->nodes[ ROOT_NODE ].child              = ROOT_NODE + 1;
    tree->nodes[ ROOT_NODE ].child_is_leaf      = FALSE;
    tree->nodes[ ROOT_NODE ].weight             = 2;
    tree->nodes[ ROOT_NODE ].parent             = -1;

    tree->nodes[ ROOT_NODE + 1 ].child          = END_OF_STREAM;
    tree->nodes[ ROOT_NODE + 1 ].child_is_leaf  = TRUE;
    tree->nodes[ ROOT_NODE + 1 ].weight         = 1;
    tree->nodes[ ROOT_NODE + 1 ].parent         = ROOT_NODE;
    tree->leaf[ END_OF_STREAM ]                 = ROOT_NODE + 1;

    tree->nodes[ ROOT_NODE + 2 ].child          = ESCAPE;
    tree->nodes[ ROOT_NODE + 2 ].child_is_leaf  = TRUE;
    tree->nodes[ ROOT_NODE + 2 ].weight         = 1;
    tree->nodes[ ROOT_NODE + 2 ].parent         = ROOT_NODE;
    tree->leaf[ ESCAPE ]                        = ROOT_NODE + 2;
    tree->next_free_node                        = ROOT_NODE + 3;

    for ( i = 0 ; i < END_OF_STREAM ; i++ )
        tree->leaf[ i ] = -1; }

/*
 * This routine is responsible for taking a symbol, and converting
 * it into the sequence of bits dictated by the Huffman tree. The
```

```
 * only complication is that we are working our way up from the leaf
 * to the root, and hence are getting the bits in reverse order. This
 * means we have to rack up the bits in an integer and then send them
 * out after they are all accumulated. In this version of the program,
 * we keep our codes in a long integer, so the maximum count is set
 * to an arbitrary limit of 0x8000. It could be set as high as 65535
 * if desired.
 */

void EncodeSymbol( tree, c, output )
TREE *tree;
unsigned int c;
BIT_FILE *output;
{
    unsigned long code;
    unsigned long current_bit;
    int code_size;
    int current_node;

    code = 0;
    current_bit = 1;
    code_size = 0;
    current_node = tree->leaf[ c ];
    if ( current_node == -1 )
      current_node = tree->leaf[ ESCAPE ];
    while ( current_node != ROOT_NODE ) {
      if ( ( current_node & 1 ) == 0 )
        code |= current_bit;
      current_bit <<= 1;
      code_size++;
      current_node = tree->nodes[ current_node ].parent;
    };
    OutputBits( output, code, code_size );
    if ( tree->leaf[ c ] == -1 ) {
      OutputBits( output, (unsigned long) c, 8 );
      add_new_node( tree, c );
    }
```

```
    }

    /*
     * Decoding symbols is easy. We start at the root node, then go down
     * the tree until we reach a leaf. At each node, we decide which
     * child to take based on the next input bit. After getting to the
     * leaf, we check to see if we read in the ESCAPE code. If we did,
     * it means that the next symbol is going to come through in the next
     * eight bits, unencoded. If that is the case, we read it in here,
     * and add the new symbol to the table.
     */

    int DecodeSymbol( tree, input )
    TREE *tree;
    BIT_FILE *input;
    {
        int current_node;
        int c;

        current_node = ROOT_NODE;
        while ( !tree->nodes[ current_node ].child_is_leaf ) {
            current_node = tree->nodes[ current_node ].child;
            current_node += InputBit( input );
        }
        c = tree->nodes[ current_node ].child;
        if ( c == ESCAPE ) {
            c = (int) InputBits( input, 8 );
            add_new_node( tree, c );
        }
        return( c );
    }

    /*
     * UpdateModel is called to increment the count for a given symbol.
     * After incrementing the symbol, this code has to work its way up
     * through the parent nodes, incrementing each one of them. That is
     * the easy part. The hard part is that after incrementing each
```

```
* parent node, we have to check to see if it is now out of the proper
* order. If it is, it has to be moved up the tree into its proper
* place.
*/
void UpdateModel( tree, c )
TREE *tree;
int c;
{
    int current_node;
    int new_node;

    if ( tree->nodes[ ROOT_NODE ].weight == MAX_WEIGHT )
        RebuildTree( tree );
    current_node = tree->leaf[ c ];
    while ( current_node != -1 ) {
        tree->nodes[ current_node ].weight++;
        for ( new_node = current_node ; new_node > ROOT_NODE ;
                         new_node-- )
            if ( tree->nodes[ new_node - 1 ].weight >=
                 tree->nodes[ current_node ].weight )
                break;
        if ( current_node != new_node ) {
            swap_nodes( tree, current_node, new_node );
            current_node = new_node;
        }
        current_node = tree->nodes[ current_node ].parent;
    }
}

/*
* Rebuilding the tree takes place when the counts have gone too
* high. From a simple point of view, rebuilding the tree just means
* that we divide every count by two. Unfortunately, due to truncation
* effects, this means that the tree's shape might change. Some nodes
* might move up due to cumulative increases, while others may move
* down.
*/
```

```
void RebuildTree( tree )
TREE   *tree;
{
    int i;
    int j;
    int k;
    unsigned int weight;

/*
 * To start rebuilding the table, I collect all the leaves of the
 * Huffman tree and put them in the end of the tree. While I am doing
 * that, I scale the counts down by a factor of 2.
 */
    printf( "R" );
    j = tree->next_free_node - 1;
    for ( i = j ; i >= ROOT_NODE ; i-- ) {
      if ( tree->nodes[ i ].child_is_leaf ) {
        tree->nodes[ j ] = tree->nodes[ i ];
        tree->nodes[ j ].weight = ( tree->nodes[ j ].weight + 1 ) / 2;
        j--;
      }
    }

/*
 * At this point, j points to the first free node. I now have all the
 * leaves defined, and need to start building the higher nodes on the
 * tree. I will start adding the new internal nodes at j. Every time
 * I add a new internal node to the top of the tree, I have to check
 * to see where it really belongs in the tree. It might stay at the
 * top, but there is a good chance I might have to move it back down.
 * If it does have to go down, I use the memmove() function to scoot
 * everyone bigger up by one node.
 */
```

```
    for ( i = tree->next_free_node - 2 ; j >= ROOT_NODE ;
          i -= 2, j-- ) {
      k = i + 1;
      tree->nodes[ j ].weight =  tree->nodes[ i ].weight +
                                 tree->nodes[ k ].weight;
      weight = tree->nodes[ j ].weight;
      tree->nodes[ j ].child_is_leaf = FALSE;
      for ( k = j + 1 ; weight < tree->nodes[ k ].weight ; k++ )
        ;
      k--;
      memmove( &tree->nodes[ j ], &tree->nodes[ j + 1 ],
            ( k - j ) * sizeof( struct node ) );
      tree->nodes[ k ].weight = weight;
      tree->nodes[ k ].child = i;
      tree->nodes[ k ].child_is_leaf = FALSE;
    }
/*
 * The final step in tree reconstruction is to go through and set up
 * all of the leaf and parent members. This can be safely done now
 * that every node is in its final position in the tree.
 */
    for ( i = tree->next_free_node - 1 ; i >= ROOT_NODE ; i-- ) {
      if ( tree->nodes[ i ].child_is_leaf ) {
        k = tree->nodes[ i ].child;
        tree->leaf[ k ] = i;
      } else {
        k = tree->nodes[ i ].child;
        tree->nodes[ k ].parent = tree->nodes[ k + 1 ].parent = i;
      }
    }
}


/*
 * Swapping nodes takes place when a node has grown too big for its
 * spot in the tree. When swapping nodes i and j, we rearrange the
 * tree by exchanging the childre under i with the children under j.
```

```
void swap_nodes( tree, i, j )
TREE *tree;
int i;
int j;
{
    struct node temp;

    if ( tree->nodes[ i ].child_is_leaf )
        tree->leaf[ tree->nodes[ i ].child ] = j;
    else {
        tree->nodes[ tree->nodes[ i ].child ].parent = j;
        tree->nodes[ tree->nodes[ i ].child + 1 ].parent = j;
    }
    if ( tree->nodes[ j ].child_is_leaf )
        tree->leaf[ tree->nodes[ j ].child ] = i;
    else {
        tree->nodes[ tree->nodes[ j ].child ].parent = i;
        tree->nodes[ tree->nodes[ j ].child + 1 ].parent = i;
    }
    temp = tree->nodes[ i ];
    tree->nodes[ i ] = tree->nodes[ j ];
    tree->nodes[ i ].parent = temp.parent;
    temp.parent = tree->nodes[ j ].parent;
    tree->nodes[ j ] = temp;
}

/*
 * Adding a new node to the tree is pretty simple. It is just a matter
 * of splitting the lightest-weight node in the tree, which is the
 * highest valued node. We split it off into two new nodes, one of
 * which is the one being added to the tree. We assign the new node a
 * weight of 0, so the tree doesn't have to be adjusted. It will be
 * updated later when the normal update process occurs. Note that this
 * code assumes that the lightest node has a leaf as a child. If this
 * is not the case, the tree would be broken.
 */
```

```
 *  is not the case, the tree would be broken.
 */
void add_new_node( tree, c )
TREE    *tree;
int c;
{
    int lightest_node;
    int new_node;
    int zero_weight_node;

    lightest_node = tree->next_free_node - 1;
    new_node = tree->next_free_node;
    zero_weight_node = tree->next_free_node + 1;
    tree->next_free_node += 2;

    tree->nodes[ new_node ] = tree->nodes[ lightest_node ];
    tree->nodes[ new_node ].parent = lightest_node;
    tree->leaf[ tree->nodes[ new_node ].child ]   = new_node;

    tree->nodes[ lightest_node ].child            = new_node;
    tree->nodes[ lightest_node ].child_is_leaf    = FALSE;

    tree->nodes[ zero_weight_node ].child         = c;
    tree->nodes[ zero_weight_node ].child_is_leaf = TRUE;
    tree->nodes[ zero_weight_node ].weight        = 0;
    tree->nodes[ zero_weight_node ].parent        = lightest_node;
```

/***************************End of AHUFF.C***************************/

CHAPTER 5

Huffman One Better: Arithmetic Coding

The last two chapters show that Huffman coding uses knowledge about information content to efficiently encode symbols. If the probability of a symbol's appearance in a message is known, Huffman techniques can encode that symbol using a minimal number of bits. Huffman coding has been proven the best fixed-length coding method available.

Difficulties

Huffman codes have to be an integral number of bits long, and this can sometimes be a problem. If the probability of a character is 1/3, for example, the optimum number of bits to code that character is around 1.6. Huffman coding has to assign either one or two bits to the code, and either choice leads to a longer compressed message than is theoretically possible.

This nonoptimal coding becomes a noticeable problem when the probability of a character is very high. If a statistical method could assign a 90 percent probability to a given character, the optimal code size would be 0.15 bits. The Huffman coding system would probably assign a 1-bit code to the symbol, which is six times longer than necessary.

This would be a problem when compressing two-color images, like those coming from a fax machine. Since there are only two colors, an ordinary coding method would assign the 1 bit to one color and the 0 bit to the other. Since both codes have only a single bit, Huffman coding is not going to be able to compress this data at all. No matter how high the probability of one of the bits, we are still going to have to encode it using one bit.

The conventional solution to this problem is to group the bits into packets and apply Huffman coding. But this weakness prevents Huffman coding from being a universal compressor.

Arithmetic Coding: A Step Forward

Only in the last ten years has a respectable candidate to replace Huffman coding been successfully demonstrated: arithmetic coding. Arithmetic coding bypasses the idea of replacing an input symbol with a specific code. It replaces a stream of input symbols with a single floating-point output number. More bits are needed in the output number for longer, complex messages. This concept has been known for some time, but only recently were practical methods found to implement arithmetic coding on computers with fixed-sized registers.

The output from an arithmetic coding process is a single number less than 1 and greater than or equal to 0. This single number can be uniquely decoded to create the exact stream of symbols that went into its construction. To construct the output number, the symbols are assigned a set probabilities. The message "BILL GATES," for example, would have a probability distribution like this:

Character	Probability
SPACE	1/10
A	1/10
B	1/10
E	1/10
G	1/10
I	1/10
L	2/10
S	1/10
T	1/10

Once character probabilities are known, individual symbols need to be assigned a range along a "probability line," nominally 0 to 1. It doesn't matter which characters are assigned which segment of the range, as long as it is done in the same manner by both the encoder and the decoder. The nine-character symbol set used here would look like the following:

Character	Probability	Range
SPACE	1/10	0.00 >= r > 0.10
A	1/10	0.10 >= r > 0.20
B	1/10	0.20 >= r > 0.30
E	1/10	0.30 >= r > 0.40
G	1/10	0.40 >= r > 0.50
I	1/10	0.50 >= r > 0.60
L	2/10	0.60 >= r > 0.80
S	1/10	0.80 >= r > 0.90
T	1/10	0.90 >= r > 1.00

Each character is assigned the portion of the 0 to 1 range that corresponds to its probability of appearance. Note that the character "owns" everything up to, but not including, the higher number. So the letter T in fact has the range .90 to .9999. . .

The most significant portion of an arithmetic-coded message belongs to the first symbol—or B, in the message "BILL GATES." To decode the first character properly, the final coded message has to be a number greater than or equal to .20 and less than .30. To encode this number, track the range it could fall in. After the first character is encoded, the low end for this range is .20 and the high end is .30.

During the rest of the encoding process, each new symbol will further restrict the possible range of the output number. The next character to be encoded, the letter I, owns the range .50 to .60 in the new subrange of .2 to .3. So the new encoded number will fall somewhere in the 50th to 60th percentile of the currently established range. Applying this logic will further restrict our number to .25 to .26. The algorithm to accomplish this for a message of any length is shown here:

```
low = 0.0;
high = 1.0;
```

```
while ( ( c = getc( input ) ) != EOF ) {
    range = high - low;
    high = low + range * high_range( c );
    low = low + range * low_range( c );
}
output( low );
```

Following this process to its natural conclusion with our message results in the following table:

New Character	Low value	High Value
	0.0	1.0
B	0.2	0.3
I	0.25	0.26
L	0.256	0.258
L	0.2572	0.2576
SPACE	0.25720	0.25724
G	0.257216	0.257220
A	0.2572164	0.2572168
T	0.25721676	0.2572168
E	0.257216772	0.257216776
S	0.2572167752	0.2572167756

So the final low value, .2572167752, will uniquely encode the message "BILL GATES" using our present coding scheme.

Given this encoding scheme, it is relatively easy to see how the decoding process operates. Find the first symbol in the message by seeing which symbol owns the space our encoded message falls in. Since .2572167752 falls between .2 and .3, the first character must be B. Then remove B from the encoded number. Since we know the low and high ranges of B, remove their effects by reversing the process that put them in. First, subtract the low value of B, giving .0572167752. Then divide by the width of the range of B, or .1. This gives a value of .572167752. Then calculate where that lands, which is in the range of the next letter, I. The algorithm for decoding the incoming number is shown next:

```
number = input_code();
for ( ; ; ) {
    symbol = find_symbol_straddling_this_range( number );
    putc( symbol );
    range = high_range( symbol ) - low_range( symbol );
    number = number - low_range( symbol );
    number = number / range;
}
```

I have conveniently ignored the problem of how to decide when there are no more symbols left to decode. This can be handled either by encoding a special end-of-file symbol or by carrying the stream length with the encoded message. In the example in this chapter, as elsewhere in the book, I carry along a special end-of-stream symbol that tells the decoder when it is out of symbols. The decoding algorithm for the "BILL GATES" message will proceed as shown:

Encoded Number	Output Symbol	Low	High	Range
0.2572167752	B	0.2	0.3	0.1
0.572167752	I	0.5	0.6	0.1
0.72167752	L	0.6	0.8	0.2
0.6083876	L	0.6	0.8	0.2
0.041938	SPACE	0.0	0.1	0.1
0.41938	G	0.4	0.5	0.1
0.1938	A	0.2	0.3	0.1
0.938	T	0.9	1.0	0.1
0.38	E	0.3	0.4	0.1
0.8	S	0.8	0.9	0.1
0.0				

In summary, the encoding process is simply one of narrowing the range of possible numbers with every new symbol. The new range is proportional to the predefined probability attached to that symbol. Decoding is the inverse procedure, in which the range is expanded in proportion to the probability of each symbol as it is extracted.

Practical Matters. Encoding and decoding a stream of symbols using arithmetic coding is not too complicated. But at first glance it seems completely impractical. Most computers support floating-point numbers of around 80 bits. So do you have to start over every time you encode ten or fifteen symbols? Do you need a floating-point processor? Can machines with different floating-point formats communicate through arithmetic coding?

As it turns out, arithmetic coding is best accomplished using standard 16-bit and 32-bit integer math. Floating-point math is neither required nor helpful. What is required is an incremental transmission scheme in which fixed-size integer state variables receive new bits at the low end and shift them out at the high end, forming a single number that can be as long as the number of bits on the computer.

Earlier, we saw that the algorithm works by keeping track of a high and low number that brackets the range of the possible output number. When the algorithm first starts, the low number is set to 0 and the high number is set to 1. The first simplification made to work with integer math is to change the 1 to .999 . . . , or .111 . . . in binary. Mathematicians agree that .111 . . . binary is exactly the same as 1 binary, and we take their assurance at face value. It simplifies encoding and decoding.

To store these numbers in integer registers, first justify them so the implied decimal point is on the left side of the word. Then load as much of the initial high and low values as will fit into the word size we are working with. My implementation uses 16-bit unsigned math, so the initial value of high is 0xFFFF, and low is 0. We know that the high value continues with Fs forever, and the low continues with zeros forever—so we can shift those extra bits in with impunity when needed.

If you imagine our "BILL GATES" example in a five-decimal digit register (I use decimal digits in this example for clarity), the decimal equivalent of our setup would look like what follows on the next page.

```
HIGH: 99999 implied digits => 999999999...
LOW:  00000 implied digits => 000000000...
```

To find the new range of numbers, apply the encoding algorithm from the previous section. First, calculate the range between the low and high values. The difference between the two registers will be 100000, not 99999. This is because we assume the high register has an infinite number of 9s added to it, so we need to increment the calculated difference. We then compute the new high value using the formula from the previous section:

```
high = low + high_range(symbol)
```

In this case, the high range was .30, which gives a new value for high of 30000. Before storing the new value of high, we need to decrement it, once again because of the implied digits appended to the integer value. So the new value of high is 29999. The calculation of low follows the same procedure, with a resulting new value of 20000. So now high and low look like this:

```
high: 29999 (999...)
low:  20000 (000...)
```

At this point, the most significant digits of high and low match. Due to the nature of our algorithm, high and low can continue to grow closer together without quite ever matching. So once they match in the most significant digit, that digit will never change. We can now output that digit as the first digit of our encoded number. This is done by shifting both high and low left by one digit and shifting in a 9 in the least significant digit of high. The equivalent operations are performed in binary in the C implementation of this algorithm.

As this process continues, high and low continually grow closer together, shifting digits out into the coded word. The process for our "BILL GATES" message is shown next.

	HIGH	LOW	RANGE	CUMULATIVE OUTPUT
Initial state	99999	00000	100000	
Encode B (0.2-0.3)	29999	20000		
Shift out 2	99999	00000	10000	.2
Encode I (0.5-0.6)	59999	50000		.2
Shift out 5	99999	00000	100000	.25
Encode L (0.6-0.8)	79999	60000	20000	.25
Encode L (0.6-0.8)	75999	72000		.25
Shift out 7	59999	20000	40000	.257
Encode SPACE (0.0-0.1)	23999	20000		.257
Shift out 2	39999	00000	40000	.2572
Encode G (0.4-0.5)	19999	16000		.2572
Shift out 1	99999	60000	40000	.25721
Encode A (0.1-0.2)	67999	64000		.25721
Shift out 6	79999	40000	40000	.257216
Encode T (0.9-1.0)	79999	76000		.257216
Shift out 7	99999	60000	40000	.2572167
Encode E (0.3-0.4)	75999	72000		.2572167
Shift out 7	59999	20000	40000	.25721677
Encode S (0.8-0.9)	55999	52000		.25721677
Shift out 5	59999	20000		.257216775
Shift out 2				.2572167752
Shift out 0				.25721677520

After all the letters are accounted for, two extra digits need to be shifted out of either the high or low value to finish the output word. This is so the decoder can properly track the input data. Part of the information about the data stream is still in the high and low registers, and we need to shift that information to the file for the decoder to use later.

A Complication. This scheme works well for incrementally encoding a message. Enough accuracy is retained during the double-precision integer calculations to ensure that the message is accurately encoded. But there is potential for a loss of precision under certain circumstances.

If the encoded word has a string of 0s or 9s in it, the high and low values will slowly converge on a value, but they may not see their most significant digits match immediately. High may be 700004, and low may be 699995. At this point, the calculated range will be only a single digit long, which means the output word will not have enough precision to be accurately encoded. Worse, after a few more iterations, high could be 70000, and low could look be 69999.

At this point, the values are permanently stuck. The range between high and low has become so small that any iteration through another symbol will leave high and low at their same values. But since the most significant digits of both words are not equal, the algorithm can't output the digit and shift. It seems to have reached an impasse.

Defeat this underflow problem by preventing things from ever getting that bad. The original algorithm said something like, "If the most significant digit of high and low match, shift it out." If the two digits don't match, but are now on adjacent numbers, a second test needs to be applied. If high and low are one apart, we test to see if the second most significant digit in high is a 0 and if the second digit in low is a 9. If so, it means we are on the road to underflow and need to take action.

Head off underflow with a slightly different shift operation. Instead of shifting the most significant digit out of the word, delete the second digits from high and low and shift the rest of the digits left to fill the space. The most significant digit stays in place. Then set an underflow counter to remember that we threw away a digit and aren't quite sure whether it was going to be a 0 or a 9. This process is shown here:

	Before	After
High:	40344	43449
Low:	39810	38100
Underflow:	0	1

After every recalculation, check for underflow digits again if the most significant digits don't match. If underflow digits are present, we shift them out and increment the counter.

When the most significant digits do finally converge to a single value, output that value. Then output the underflow digits previously discarded. The underflow digits will all be 9s or 0s, depending on whether high and low converged on the higher or lower value. In the C implementation of this algorithm, the underflow counter keeps track of how many ones or zeros to output.

Decoding. In the "ideal" decoding process, we had the entire input number to work with, and the algorithm had to do things like "divide the encoded number by the symbol probability." In practice, we can't perform an operation like that on a number that could be billions of bytes long. As in the encoding process, however, the decoder can operate using 16- and 32-bit integers for calculations.

Instead of using just two numbers, high and low, the decoder has to use three numbers. The first two, high and low, correspond exactly to the high and low values maintained by the encoder. The third number, code, contains the current bits being read in from the input bit stream. The code value always falls between the high and low values. As they come closer and closer to it, new shift operations will take place, and high and low will move back away from code.

The high and low values in the decoder will be updated after every symbol, just as they were in the encoder, and they should have exactly the same values. By performing the same comparison test on the upper digit of high and low, the decoder knows when it is time to shift a new digit into the incoming code. The same underflow tests are performed as well.

In the ideal algorithm, it was possible to determine what the current encoded symbol was just by finding the symbol whose probabilities enclosed the present value of the code. In the integer math algorithm, things are somewhat more complicated. In this case, the probability scale is determined by the difference between high and low. So instead of the range being between .0 and 1.0, the range will be between two positive 16-bit integer counts. Where the present code value falls along that range determines current probability. Divide (value - low) by (high - low + 1) to get the actual probability for the present symbol.

Where's the Beef? It is not immediately obvious why this encoding process is an improvement over Huffman coding. It becomes clear when we examine a case in which the probabilities are a little different. If we have to encode the stream "AAAAAAA," and the probability of A is known to be .9, there is a 90 percent chance that any incoming character will be the letter A. We set up our probability table so that A occupies the .0 to .9 range, and the end-of-message symbol occupies the .9 to 1 range. The encoding process is shown next:

New Character	Low value	High Value
	0.0	1.0
A	0.0	0.9
A	0.0	0.81
A	0.0	0.729
A	0.0	0.6561
A	0.0	0.59049
A	0.0	0.531441
A	0.0	0.4782969
END	0.43046721	0.4782969

Now that we know the range of high and low values, all that remains is to pick a number to encode this message. The number .45 will make this message uniquely decode to "AAAAAAA." Those two decimal digits take slightly less than seven bits to specify, which means we have encoded eight symbols in less than eight bits! An optimal Huffman message would have taken a minimum of nine bits.

To take this point to an even further extreme, I set up a test that had only two symbols. In it, 0 had a 16382/16383 probability, and an end-of-file symbol had a 1/ 16383 probability. I then created a file filled with 100,000 0s. After compression using arithmetic coding, the output file was only three bytes long! The minimum size using Huffman coding would have been 12,501 bytes. This is obviously a contrived example, but it shows that arithmetic coding compresses data at rates much better than one bit per byte when the symbol probabilities are right.

The Code

The code supplied with this chapter in ARITH.C is a simple module that performs arithmetic compression and decompression using a simple order 0 model. It works exactly like the nonadaptive Huffman coding program in chapter 3. It first makes a single pass over the data, counting the symbols. The data is then scaled down to make the counts fit into single, unsigned characters. The scaled counts are saved to the output file for the decompressor to get at later, then the arithmetic coding table is built. Finally, the compressor passes through the data, compressing each symbol as it appears. When done, the end-of-stream character is sent out, the arithmetic coder is flushed, and the program exits.

The Compression Program. The compression portion of this program is shown shortly. The main module is called by the utility version of MAIN-E.C, which will have already taken care of opening files, parsing arguments, etc. Once we get to the compression phase of the program, things are ready to go.

The compressor code breaks down neatly into three sections. The first two lines initialize the model and the encoder. The while loop plus an additional line after it performs the compression, and the last three lines shut things down.

```
build_model( input, output->file );
initialize_arithmetic_encoder();

while ( ( c = getc( input ) ) != EOF ) {
   convert_int_to_symbol( c, &s );
   encode_symbol( output, &s );
}
convert_int_to_symbol( END_OF_STREAM, &s );
encode_symbol( output, &s );
flush_arithmetic_encoder( output );
OutputBits( output, 0L, 16 );
```

The build_model() routine has several responsibilities. It makes the first pass over the input data to count all the characters. It scales down the counts to fit in unsigned characters, then it takes those counts and builds the range table used by the coder. Finally, it writes the counts to the output file so the decompressor will have access to them later.

The initialize arithmetic encoder routine is fairly simple. It just sets up the high- and low-integer variables used during the encoding. The encoding loop calls two different routines to encode the symbol. The first, convert_int_to_symbol(), takes the character read in from the file and looks up the range for the given symbol. The range is then stored in the symbol object, which has the structure shown:

```
typedef struct {
    unsigned short int low_count;
    unsigned short int high_count;
    unsigned short int scale;
} SYMBOL;
```

These three values are all that are needed for the symbol to be encoded using the arithmetic encoder. The low-count and high-count values uniquely define where on the 0 to 1 range the symbol lies, and the scale value tells what the total span of the 0 to 1 scale is. If 1,000 characters had been counted in a text file, for example, the low_count and high_count for A might be 178 and 199, and the scale would be 1,000. This would indicate that on the 0 to 1 number scale, A would own the range .178 to .199.

Once the symbol object has been defined, it can be passed to the encoder. The arithmetic encoder needs only those three items to process the symbol and update the output number. It has the high- and low-range values and the underflow count stored internally as static variables, and it doesn't need anything else.

The way we detached the modeling data from the coding data gives us a convenient mechanism for experimenting with new ways of modeling. We just have to come up with the numbers that get plugged into the symbol. The encoder doesn't care how we got those numbers as long as they were derived consistently so we can decode the file later.

When we reach the end of the input file, we encode and send the end-of-stream symbol. The decompression program will use it to determine when it is done. To finish, call a routine to flush the arithmetic encoder, which takes care of any underflow bits. Finally, we have to output an extra sixteen bits. The reason for this is simple. When decoding symbols from the input bit stream, the effective bits are in the most significant bit position of the input registers. To get the bits there, we have to load other bits into the lower positions and shift them over. At least 15 insignificant bits are needed to decode the last symbol. Outputting 16 bits at the end of the program ensures that the decoder won't get a premature end of file while decoding the input file.

The Expansion Program. The main part of the expansion program follows the same pattern. First, the model is set up and the arithmetic coder is initialized. In this program, initializing the model means reading in the counts from the input file where the compressor put them. Initializing the arithmetic decoder means loading the low and high registers with 0000 and FFFF, then reading the first 16 bits from the input file into the current code.

```
input_counts( input->file );
initialize_arithmetic_decoder( input );
for ( ; ; ) {
    get_symbol_scale( &s );
    count = get_current_count( &s );
    c = convert_symbol_to_int( count, &s );
    if ( c == END_OF_STREAM )
        break;
    remove_symbol_from_stream( input, &s );
    putc( (char) c, output );
}
```

The decoding loop is a little more complicated in this routine to keep the modeling and decoding separate. First, get the scale for the current model to pass back to the arithmetic decoder. The decoder then converts its current input code into a count in the routine get_current_count. With the count, we can determine which symbol is the correct one to decode. This is done in the routine convert_symbol_to_int().

Though it seems strange, we don't remove the encoded symbol from the input bit stream till after we actually decode it. The process of removing it involves standard modifications of high and low and, if necessary, shifting in new bits from the input stream. Finally, the decoded character is written to the output file.

Initializing the Model. The model for a program using arithmetic coding needs to have three pieces of information for each symbol: the low end of its range, the high end of its range, and the scale of the entire alphabet's range (this is the same for all symbols in the alphabet). Since the top of a given symbol's range is the bottom of the next, we only need to keep track of N + 1 numbers for N symbols in the alphabet.

An example of how the range information would be created is shown for symbols A, B, C, D, and E. These symbols have the counts 5, 2, 3, 3, and 8 respectively. The numbers can be arranged in any order along the range, if done consistently.

Range	:	21
E	:	13
D	:	10
C	:	7
B	:	5
A	:	0

In this case, the alphabet has five symbols, and the number of counts to keep track of is six. The array is formed by creating the cumulative total at each symbol, starting at zero and working up to the range.

Given a structure like this, it is simple to derive the three items of information that define the symbol for the arithmetic encoder. For symbol x in the array, the low count can be found at totals[x], the high count at totals[x + 1], and the range of scale at totals[N], N being the number of symbols in the alphabet.

The routines that do compression create this array. In this program, the array is named totals[], and it has 258 elements. The number of symbols in the alphabet is 257, the normal 256 plus one for the end-of-stream symbol.

One additional constraint is placed on these counts. Two things determine the highest possible count: the number of bits available in the high and low registers and the number of bits in the code values. Since floating-point calculations are performed in fixed-length registers, we have to minimize the amount of precision needed in our calculations so errors do not occur.

As it happens, there are two restrictions on the number of bits used in arithmetic coding: (1) the bits in the frequency values must be at least two less than the number of bits in the high and low registers; and (2) the bits in the frequency values plus the bits used in either the high and low registers must not exceed the bits used in arithmetic calculations during the coding process.

During calculations on the arithmetic registers, use unsigned long values, which give 32 bits to work with. Since our high and low registers and our frequency counts are limited to 16 bits in unsigned short ints, we meet restriction 2 implicitly. Restriction 1, however, requires more modifications. Since we are only using 16-bit registers for our high and low values, we have to restrict the highest cumulative counts in the totals[] array to no more than 14 bits, or 16,384.

The code to make sure that our total count of symbols is less than 16,384 is in the build_model routine called on initialization of the model. It takes the process a step further, scaling the counts down so they all fit in a single byte. This is done so that the count data stored in the output file takes a minimal amount of space.

During the compression phase of the program, the build_model() routine is called to perform all the necessary chores associated with the order-0 modeling used in this program. The four lines of code from build_model() are shown here:

```
count_bytes( input, counts );
```

```
scale_counts( counts, scaled_counts );
output_counts( output, scaled_counts );
build_totals( scaled_counts );
```

build_model does no work on its own. It calls a series of four worker routines to handle the data for it. The first routine is count_bytes(). It does just that, counting all the occurrences of each symbol in the file and maintaining the total in an array, like so:

```
input_marker = ftell( input );
while ( ( c = getc( input )) != EOF )
   counts[ c ]++;
fseek( input, input_marker, SEEK_SET );
```

The code for count_bytes scans the entire input file, then returns the input pointer to where it was when called. We assume that the number of counts of a given symbol in the file cannot exceed the span of an unsigned long. If this is not true, other measures will need to be taken to avoid overflow of the counts[] array elements.

After the array has been counted, the counts have to be scaled down. This is done in the scale_counts() routine. The first step here is to scale down the unsigned long counts[] array to fit it in an array of unsigned characters. This stores the counts in less space in the output file. The code for this is listed here.

```
max_count = 0;
for ( i = 0 ; i < 256 ; i++ )
   if ( counts[ i ] > max_count )
      max_count = counts[ i ];
scale = max_count / 256;
scale = scale + 1;
for ( i = 0 ; i < 256 ; i++ ) {
   scaled_counts[ i ] = (unsigned char ) ( counts[ i ] /scale );
   if ( scaled_counts[ i ] == 0 && counts[ i ] != 0 )
      scaled_counts[ i ] = 1;
}
```

After this is complete, one more scaling may need to be done. As part of the limitations on performing arithmetic coding using fixed-length registers, we have to restrict the total of our counts to less than 16,384, or fourteen bits. The second part of scale_counts does this with brute force, checking the total, then dividing by either two or four to get the correct results. An additional count has to be added because of the single count used by the end-of-stream character.

```
total = 1;
for ( i = 0 ; i < 256 ; i++ )
  total += scaled_counts[ i ];
if ( total > ( 32767 - 256 ) )
  scale = 4;
else if ( total > 16383 )
  scale = 2;
else
  return;
for ( i = 0 ; i < 256 ; i++ )
  scaled_counts[ i ] /= scale;
```

There is certainly room in the scale_counts() routine for more sophistication. Every time we lose some of the accuracy in our counts by scaling, we also lose a certain amount of compression. An ideal scaling routine would scale down the counts to fit in the correct range while doing as little scaling as possible. The routines listed here don't work very hard at doing that.

Once the counts have been scaled down to fit in the unsigned character array, the output_counts() routine is called to save them to the output file. This program employs the same method to store the counts as used in chapter 3 for the Huffman coding example. Instead of storing the entire array of counts, we only store runs on nonzero values. For details on this, refer to chapter 3.

The last step in building the model is to set up the cumulative totals array in totals[]. This is the array used when actually performing the arithmetic coding. The code shown below builds that array. Remember that after the totals[] array has been built, the range for symbol x is found in totals[x] and totals[x + 1]. The range used for the entire alphabet is found in totals[END_OF_STREAM + 1].

```
totals[ 0 ] = 0;
for ( i = 0 ; i < END_OF_STREAM ; i++ )
   totals[ i + 1 ] = totals[ i ] + scaled_counts[ i ];
totals[ END_OF_STREAM + 1 ] = totals[ END_OF_STREAM ] + 1;
```

Reading the Model. For expansion, the code needs to build the same model array in totals[] that was used in the compression routine. Since the original file is not available to scan for counts, the program reads in the scaled_counts[] array stored in the compressed file. The code that accomplishes this is identical to the Huffman expansion code in chapter 3. Refer to chapter 3 for details on how this code works.

After the scaled_counts[] array has been read in, the same routine used by the compression code can be invoked to build the totals[] array. Calling build_totals() in both the compression and expansion routines helps ensure that we are working with the same array.

Initializing the Encoder. Before compression can begin, we have to initialize the variables that constitute the arithmetic encoder. Three 16-bit variables define the arithmetic encoder: low, high, and underflow_bits. When the encoder first starts to run, the range of the output floating-point number is anywhere between 0 and 1. The low variable is initialized to 0 and the high to 0xFFFF. These two variables have an implied decimal point just ahead of the most significant bit and an infinite trail of ones or zeros. The ones will be shifted into the high variable and the zeros into the low.

```
low = 0;
high = 0xffff;
underflow_bits = 0;
```

The Encoding Process. At this point, the program is ready to begin the actual encoding process. This consists of looping through the entire file, reading in a character, determining its range variables, then encoding it. After the file has been scanned, the final step is to encode the end-of-stream symbol.

```
while ( ( c = getc( input ) ) != EOF ) {
    convert_int_to_symbol( c, &s );
    encode_symbol( output, &s );
}
convert_int_to_symbol( END_OF_STREAM, &s );
encode_symbol( output, &s );
```

Two routines encode a symbol. convert_int_to_symbol() looks up the modeling information for the symbol and retrieves the numbers needed to perform the arithmetic coding. This consists of stuffing numbers into the three elements of the symbol's structure, as shown here:

```
s->scale = totals[ END_OF_STREAM + 1 ];
s->low_count = totals[ c ];
s->high_count = totals[ c + 1 ];
```

After the symbol information is present, we are ready to encode the symbol using the arithmetic encoding routine. The C code to do this, listed in encode_symbol(), has two distinct steps. The first is to adjust the high and low variables based on the symbol data passed to the encoder.

```
range = (long) ( high-low ) + 1;
high = low + (unsigned short int)
        (( range * s->high_count ) / s->scale - 1 );
low = low + (unsigned short int)
        (( range * s->low_count ) / s->scale );
```

The code shown below restricts the range of high and low by the amount indicated in the symbol information. The range of the symbol is defined by s->low_count and s->high_count. These two counts are measured relative to the s->scale variable. After the adjustments are made, low and high will both be greater than or equal to their previous values. The range, or the distance between the two, will be less than or equal to its previous value.

```
for ( ; ; ) {
   if ( ( high & 0x8000 ) == ( low & 0x8000 ) ) {
      OutputBit( stream, high & 0x8000 );
      while ( underflow_bits > 0 ) {
         OutputBit( stream, ~high & 0x8000 );
         underflow_bits--;
      }
   } else if ( ( low & 0x4000 ) && !( high & 0x4000 )) {
      underflow_bits += 1;
      low &= 0x3fff;
      high |= 0x4000;
   } else
      return ;
   low <<= 1;
   high <<= 1;
   high |= 1;
}
```

After high and low have been adjusted, the routine needs to shift out any bits available for shifting. After a given arithmetic adjustment, it is never certain how many bits will need to be shifted out. If the encoded symbol has a very high probability, the number of bits will be low. If the encoded symbol has a low probability, the number of bits may be high.

Since the number isn't known in advance, the encoding routine sits in a loop shifting bits until there are no more shifts possible. The routine tests for two conditions to see if shifting is necessary. The first occurs when the most significant bits of the low and high word are the same. Because of the math being used, once the two bits are identical, they will never change. When this occurs, the bit is sent to the output file, and the high and low values are shifted.

Before shifting out the bit found when the most MSBs match, however, we have to transmit any underflow bits previously saved up. The underflow bits will be a sequence of bits set to the opposite value of the MSB. When we have an underflow, we have a binary sequence that ends up looking like that shown above. The number of underflow bits is found in the underflow_bits variable.

```
high = .100000...
low  = .011111...
```

Which leads to the second condition under which high and low variables require shifting: underflow. This occurs when the high and low words are growing dangerously close together but have not yet had their most significant bits match, a situation similar to that shown above.

When words begin growing close together like this, the dynamic range becomes dangerously low. Test for this condition after determining that the two most significant bits don't match. If they don't, check to see if the next bit is 0 in the high word and 1 in the low word. If they are, perform an underflow shift.

The underflow shift operation consists of throwing away the underflow bit (the one next to the most significant digit), shifting the remaining bits over one by one to fill the gap, and incrementing the underflow counter. The code to do this is somewhat opaque, but it performs this operation.

The underflow code takes advantage of the fact that when in danger of underflow, we know two things. First, we know that the most significant bit in the high word is 1 and in the low word 0. Second, the bit we throw away from the high word is 0 and from the low word 1.

Since we know the value of the highest two bits, we can simplify the shift operation. The code used in this chapter toggles the second most significant bit in both the high and low registers, then performs the normal shift operation. It looks as though the lower 14 bits were shifted left and the MSB was left alone.

If we check for both possible shift conditions and don't flag either one, we are done shifting bits out and can end the encoding operation. If either of the tests passed, the actual shift operation can take place. Both the high and low words are shifted left one bit position. The high word has a 1 shifted in to the LSB, and the low word has a 0 shifted in. The loop then repeats, outputting and shifting additional bits as necessary.

Flushing the Encoder. After encoding, it is necessary to flush the arithmetic encoder. The code for this is in the flush_arithmetic_encoder() routine. It outputs two bits and any additional underflow bits added along the way.

The Decoding Process. Before arithmetic decoding can start, we need to initialize the arithmetic decoder variables. While encoding, we had just a high and low variable. Both are maintained by the decoder with a code variable, which contains the current bit stream read in from the input file.

During arithmetic decoding, the high and low variables should track exactly the same values they had during the encoding process, and the code variable should reflect the bit stream as it is read in from the input file. The only exception to this is that the code variable has underflow bits taken from it and thrown away, as with the high and low variables.

```
code = 0;
for ( i = 0 ; i < 16 ; i++ ) {
    code <<= 1;
    code += InputBit( stream );
}
low = 0;
high = 0xffff;
```

This implementation of the arithmetic decoding process requires four separate steps to decode each character. The first is to get the current scale for the symbol. This is simply a matter of looking in the current model data. In this implementation, the scale is found at totals[END_OF_STREAM + 1]. The reason for breaking this out as a separate routine rather than coding it in-line is that future expansions to the basic compression program may use different modeling techniques. If a different model is used, determining the scale of the model could end up being more complex. This happens in the program used in the next chapter.

Once the current scale for the model is known, a second call is made to get the count for the current arithmetic code. This involves translating the decoders range, expressed by the high and low variables, into the range used by the model, which is in the scale variable.

```
range = (long) ( high - low ) + 1;
count = (short int)
       (((((long) ( code - low ) + 1 ) * s->scale-1 ) / range );
return( count );
```

The count returned to the expansion program is in essence a simple translation of the code variable from one scale to another. Once the count has been determined, we can determine what symbol has been encoded. Since we know the low and high range of the count for every symbol in the alphabet, determining which symbol goes with which count is just a matter of looking through the counts listed in the totals[] array.

```
for ( c = END_OF_STREAM ; count < totals[ c ] ; c-- )
    ;
s->high_count = totals[ c + 1 ];
s->low_count = totals[ c ];
return( c );
```

The implementation of the convert_symbol_to_int() used here determines the correct symbol with brute force. It simply starts looking at the top of the totals[] array for a count that fits with the current symbol, and it works down till if finds one that does. This is not optimal, since it could take 257 comparisons to locate the correct symbol.

An improved method of decoding would keep the symbols sorted so that the most frequently used symbols would be checked first. This would reduce the average time required to locate a symbol, though with random data we would not see much improvement. For simplicity, this was not the method used here.

Once convert_symbol_to_int() locates the correct symbol in the totals[] array, it takes the high and low counts and stores them in the symbol variable. They will be used in the next step of the decoding process. The correct value of the symbol is then returned to the calling program as an int.

After the correct symbol value is set up in the symbol structure, remove_symbol_from_stream() is called. Arithmetic coding is unusual in that it determines what the symbol is *before* it removes the bits associated with it. Then it calls the routine that actually removes those bits from the code and sets up the input code for the next symbol.

```
range = (long)( high - low ) + 1;
high = low + (unsigned short int)
        (( range * s->high_count ) / s->scale - 1 );
low = low + (unsigned short int)
        (( range * s->low_count ) / s->scale );
for ( ; ; ) {
  if ( ( high & 0x8000 ) == ( low & 0x8000 ) ) {
  } else if ((low & 0x4000) == 0x4000 && (high & 0x4000) == 0 ) {
    code ^= 0x4000;
    low &= 0x3fff;
    high |= 0x4000;
  } else
    return;
  low <<= 1;
  high <<= 1;
  high |= 1;
  code <<= 1;
  code += InputBit( stream );
}
```

The code that removes the symbol from the stream is listed above. It operates almost as a mirror image of the encoding routine. It first rescales the high and low variables to their new ranges as dictated by the range of the symbol being removed. Then the shifting process begins.

As before, there are two possible reasons to shift in new bits. First, if high and low have the same most significant bit, they will be discarded and a new bit will be shifted in as a replacement. Second, if high and low don't have the same MSB, and the second most significant bits are threatening underflow, we will discard the second most significant bits and shift in new bits.

If neither of the possible shift criteria are met, we can return, since the effects of the symbol have been entirely removed from the input stream. Otherwise, we shift high, low, and code. The lowest bit of high gets a 1, the lowest bit of low gets a 0, and the lowest bit of code gets a new bit from the input stream. This process continues indefinitely until all shifting is complete, at which point we return to the calling routine.

Summary

Arithmetic coding seems more complicated than Huffman coding, but the size of the program required to implement it is not significantly different. Runtime performance *is* significantly slower than Huffman coding, however, due to the computational burden imposed on the encoder and decoder. If squeezing the last bit of performance out of the coder is important, arithmetic coding will always provide as good or better performance than Huffman coding. But careful optimization is needed to get performance up to acceptable levels.

Code

```
/************************ Start of ARITH.C ************************/
#include <stdio.h>
#include <stdlib.h>
#include "errhand.h"
#include "bitio.h"

/*
 * The SYMBOL structure is what is used to define a symbol in
 * arithmetic coding terms. A symbol is defined as a range between
 * 0 and 1. Since we are using integer math, instead of using 0 and 1
 * as our end points, we have an integer scale. The low_count and
 * high_count define where the symbol falls in the range.
```

```
*/

typedef struct {
    unsigned short int low_count;
    unsigned short int high_count;
    unsigned short int scale;
} SYMBOL;

/*
 * Internal function prototypes, with or without ANSI prototypes.
 */

#ifdef __STDC__

void build_model( FILE *input, FILE *output );
void scale_counts( unsigned long counts[],
                   unsigned char scaled_counts[] );
void build_totals( unsigned char scaled_counts[] );
void count_bytes( FILE *input, unsigned long counts[] );
void output_counts( FILE *output, unsigned char scaled_counts[] );
void input_counts( FILE *stream );
void convert_int_to_symbol( int symbol, SYMBOL *s );
void get_symbol_scale( SYMBOL *s );
int convert_symbol_to_int( int count, SYMBOL *s );
void initialize_arithmetic_encoder( void );
void encode_symbol( BIT_FILE *stream, SYMBOL *s );
void flush_arithmetic_encoder( BIT_FILE *stream );
short int get_current_count( SYMBOL *s );
void initialize_arithmetic_decoder( BIT_FILE *stream );
void remove_symbol_from_stream( BIT_FILE *stream, SYMBOL  *s);

#else

void build_model();
void scale_counts();
void build_totals();
void count_bytes();
```

```
void output_counts();
void input_counts();
void convert_int_to_symbol();
void get_symbol_scale();
int convert_symbol_to_int();
void initialize_arithmetic_encoder();
void encode_symbol();
void flush_arithmetic_encoder();
short int get_current_count();
void initialize_arithmetic_decoder();
void remove_symbol_from_stream();

#endif

#define END_OF_STREAM 256
short int totals[ 258 ];          /* The cumulative totals */

char *CompressionName  = "Adaptive order 0 model with arithmetic coding";
char *Usage            = "in-file out-file\n\n";

/*
 * This compress file routine is a fairly orthodox compress routine.
 * It first gathers statistics, and initializes the arithmetic
 * encoder. It then encodes all the characters in the file, followed
 * by the EOF character. The output stream is then flushed, and we
 * exit. Note that an extra two bytes are output. When decoding an arith-
 * metic stream, we have to read in extra bits. The decoding process
 * takes place in the msb of the low and high range ints, so when we are
 * decoding our last bit we will still have to have at least 15 junk
 * bits loaded into the registers. The extra two bytes account for
 * that.
 */
void CompressFile( input, output, argc, argv )
FILE   *input;
BIT_FILE  *output;
int argc;
char   *argv[];
```

```
{
    int c;
    SYMBOL s;

    build_model( input, output->file );
    initialize_arithmetic_encoder();

    while ( ( c = getc( input ) ) != EOF ) {
        convert_int_to_symbol( c, &s );
        encode_symbol( output, &s );
    }
    convert_int_to_symbol( END_OF_STREAM, &s );
    encode_symbol( output, &s );
    flush_arithmetic_encoder( output );
    OutputBits( output, 0L, 16 );
    while ( argc- > 0 ) {
        printf( "Unused argument: %s\n", *argv );
        argv++;
    }
}

/*
 * This expand routine is also very conventional. It reads in the
 * model, initializes the decoder, then sits in a loop reading in
 * characters. When we decode an END_OF_STREAM, it means we can close
 * up the files and exit. Note decoding a single character is a three
 * step process: first we determine what the scale is for the current
 * symbol by looking at the difference between the high an low values.
 * We then see where the current input values fall in that range.
 * Finally, we look in our totals array to find out what symbol is
 * a match. After that is done, we still have to remove that symbol
 * from the decoder. Lots of work.
 */

void ExpandFile( input, output, argc, argv )
BIT_FILE *input;
FILE *output;
```

```
int argc;
char *argv[];
{
    SYMBOL s;
    int c;
    int count;

    input_counts( input->file );
    initialize_arithmetic_decoder( input );
    for ( ; ; ) {
        get_symbol_scale( &s );
        count = get_current_count( &s );
        c = convert_symbol_to_int( count, &s );
        if ( c == END_OF_STREAM )
            break;
        remove_symbol_from_stream( input, &s );
        putc( (char) c, output );
    }
    while ( argc- > 0 ) {
        printf( "Unused argument: %s\n", *argv );
        argv++;
    }
}

/*
 * This is the routine that is called to scan the input file, scale
 * the counts, build the totals array, the output the scaled counts
 * to the output file.
 */

void build_model( input, output )
FILE *input;
FILE *output;
{
    unsigned long counts[ 256 ];
    unsigned char scaled_counts[ 256 ];
```

```
    count_bytes( input, counts );
    scale_counts( counts, scaled_counts );
    output_counts( output, scaled_counts );
    build_totals( scaled_counts );
}

/*
 * This routine runs through the file and counts the appearances of
 * each character.
 */
#ifndef SEEK_SET
#define SEEK_SET 0
#endif

void count_bytes( input, counts )
FILE *input;
unsigned long counts[];
{
    long input_marker;
    int i;
    int c;

    for ( i = 0 ; i < 256 ; i++ )
        counts[ i ] = 0;
    input_marker = ftell( input );
    while ( ( c = getc( input )) != EOF )
        counts[ c ]++;
    fseek( input, input_marker, SEEK_SET );
}

/*
 * This routine is called to scale the counts down. There are two
 * types of scaling that must be done. First, the counts need to be
 * scaled down so that the individual counts fit into a single unsigned
 * char. Then, the counts need to be rescaled so that the total of all
 * counts is less than 16384.
 */
```

```
void scale_counts( counts, scaled_counts )
unsigned long counts[];
unsigned char scaled_counts[];
{
    int i;
    unsigned long max_count;
    unsigned int total;
    unsigned long scale;

/*
 * The first section of code makes sure each count fits into a single
 * byte.
 */
    max_count = 0;
    for ( i = 0 ; i < 256 ; i++ )
        if ( counts[ i ] > max_count )
            max_count = counts[ i ];
    scale = max_count / 256;
    scale = scale + 1;
    for ( i = 0 ; i < 256 ; i++ ) {
        scaled_counts[ i ] = (unsigned char ) ( counts[ i ] / scale );
        if ( scaled_counts[ i ] == 0 && counts[ i ] != 0 )
            scaled_counts[ i ] = 1;
    }
/*
 * This next section makes sure the total is less than 16384.
 * I initialize the total to 1 instead of 0 because there will be an
 * additional 1 added in for the END_OF_STREAM symbol;
 */
    total = 1;
    for ( i = 0 ; i < 256 ; i++ )
        total += scaled_counts[ i ];
    if ( total > ( 32767 - 256 ) )
        scale = 4;
    else if ( total > 16383 )
        scale = 2;
    else
```

```
    return;
  for ( i = 0 ; i < 256 ; i++ )
    scaled_counts[ i ] /= scale;
}
```

```
/*
* This routine is used by both the encoder and decoder to build the
* table of cumulative totals. The counts for the characters in the
* file are in the counts array, and we know that there will be a
* single instance of the EOF symbol.
*/
void build_totals( scaled_counts )
unsigned char scaled_counts[];
{
  int i;

  totals[ 0 ] = 0;
  for ( i = 0 ; i < END_OF_STREAM ; i++ )
    totals[ i + 1 ] = totals[ i ] + scaled_counts[ i ];
  totals[ END_OF_STREAM + 1 ] = totals[ END_OF_STREAM ] + 1;
}
```

```
/*
* In order for the compressor to build the same model, I have to
* store the symbol counts in the compressed file so the expander can
* read them in. In order to save space, I don't save all 256 symbols
* unconditionally. The format used to store counts looks like this:
*
* start, stop, counts, start, stop, counts, ... 0
*
* This means that I store runs of counts, until all the non-zero
* counts have been stored. At this time the list is terminated by
* storing a start value of 0. Note that at least 1 run of counts has
* to be stored, so even if the first start value is 0, I read it in.
* It also means that even in an empty file that has no counts, I have
* to pass at least one count.
*
```

```
*  In order to efficiently use this format, I have to identify runs of
*  non-zero counts. Because of the format used, I don't want to stop a
*  run because of just one or two zeros in the count stream. So I have
*  to sit in a loop looking for strings of three or more zero values
*  in a row.
*
*  This is simple in concept, but it ends up being one of the most
*  complicated routines in the whole program. A routine that just
*  writes out 256 values without attempting to optimize would be much
*  simpler, but would hurt compression quite a bit on small files.
*
*/
void output_counts( output, scaled_counts )
FILE *output;
unsigned char scaled_counts[];
{
    int first;
    int last;
    int next;
    int i;

    first = 0;
    while ( first < 255 && scaled_counts[ first ] == 0 )
            first++;
/*
*  Each time I hit the start of the loop, I assume that first is the
*  number for a run of non-zero values. The rest of the loop is
*  concerned with finding the value for last, which is the end of the
*  run, and the value of next, which is the start of the next run.
*  At the end of the loop, I assign next to first, so it starts in on
*  the next run.
*/
    for ( ; first < 256 ; first = next ) {
      last = first + 1;
      for ( ; ; ) {
        for ( ; last < 256 ; last++ )
          if ( scaled_counts[ last ] == 0 )
```

```
            break;
        last--;
        for ( next = last + 1; next < 256 ; next++ )
          if ( scaled_counts[ next ] != 0 )
            break;
        if ( next > 255 )
          break;
        if ( ( next - last ) > 3 )
          break;
        last = next;
    };
/*
* Here is where I output first, last, and all the counts in between.
*/
    if ( putc( first, output ) != first )
      fatal_error( "Error writing byte counts\n" );
    if ( putc( last, output ) != last )
      fatal_error( "Error writing byte counts\n" );
    for ( i = first ; i <= last ; i++ ) {
      if ( putc( scaled_counts[ i ], output ) !=
        (int) scaled_counts[ i ] )
          fatal_error( "Error writing byte counts\n" );
    }
  }
  if ( putc( 0, output ) != 0 )
      fatal_error( "Error writing byte counts\n" );
}


/*
* When expanding, I have to read in the same set of counts. This is
* quite a bit easier that the process of writing them out, since no
* decision making needs to be done. All I do is read in first, check
* to see if I am all done, and if not, read in last and a string of
* counts.
*/

void input_counts( input )
```

```
FILE *input;
{
    int first;
    int last;
    int i;
    int c;
    unsigned char scaled_counts[ 256 ];

    for ( i = 0 ; i < 256 ; i++ )
        scaled_counts[ i ] = 0;
    if ( ( first = getc( input ) ) == EOF )
        fatal_error( "Error reading byte counts\n" );
    if ( ( last = getc( input ) ) == EOF )
        fatal_error( "Error reading byte counts\n" );
    for ( ; ; ) {
        for ( i = first ; i <= last ; i++ )
            if ( ( c = getc( input ) ) == EOF )
                fatal_error( "Error reading byte counts\n" );
            else
                scaled_counts[ i ] = (unsigned int) c;
        if ( ( first = getc( input ) ) == EOF )
            fatal_error( "Error reading byte counts\n" );
        if ( first == 0 )
            break;
        if ( ( last = getc( input ) ) == EOF )
            fatal_error( "Error reading byte counts\n" );
    }
    build_totals( scaled_counts );
}

/*
* Everything from here down define the arithmetic coder section
* of the program.
*/

/*
* These four variables define the current state of the arithmetic
```

```
* coder/decoder. They are assumed to be 16 bits long. Note that
* by declaring them as short ints, they will actually be 16 bits
* on most 80X86 and 680X0 machines, as well as VAXen.
*/
static unsigned short int code;/* The present input code value    */
static unsigned short int low; /* Start of the current code range  */
static unsigned short int high;/* End of the current code range    */
long underflow_bits;           /* Number of underflow bits pending */

/*
* This routine must be called to initialize the encoding process.
* The high register is initialized to all 1s, and it is assumed that
* it has an infinite string of 1s to be shifted into the lower bit
* positions when needed.
*/
void initialize_arithmetic_encoder() {
    low = 0;
    high = 0xffff;
    underflow_bits = 0;
}

/*
* At the end of the encoding process, there are still significant
* bits left in the high and low registers. We output two bits,
* plus as many underflow bits as are necessary.
*/
void flush_arithmetic_encoder( stream )
BIT_FILE *stream;
{
    OutputBit( stream, low & 0x4000 );
    underflow_bits++;
    while ( underflow_bits- > 0 )
        OutputBit( stream, ~low & 0x4000 );
}
```

```
/*
 * Finding the low count, high count, and scale for a symbol
 * is really easy, because of the way the totals are stored.
 * This is the one redeeming feature of the data structure used
 * in this implementation.
 */
void convert_int_to_symbol( c, s )
int c;
SYMBOL *s;
{
    s->scale = totals[ END_OF_STREAM + 1 ];
    s->low_count = totals[ c ];
    s->high_count = totals[ c + 1 ];
}


/*
 * Getting the scale for the current context is easy.
 */
void get_symbol_scale( s )
SYMBOL *s;
{
    s->scale = totals[ END_OF_STREAM + 1 ];
}


/*
 * During decompression, we have to search through the table until
 * we find the symbol that straddles the "count" parameter. When
 * it is found, it is returned. The reason for also setting the
 * high count and low count is so that symbol can be properly removed
 * from the arithmetic coded input.
 */
int convert_symbol_to_int( count, s)
int count;
SYMBOL *s;
{
    int c;
```

```
    for ( c = END_OF_STREAM ; count < totals[ c ] ; c- )
        ;
    s->high_count = totals[ c + 1 ];
    s->low_count = totals[ c ];
    return( c );
}


/*
 * This routine is called to encode a symbol. The symbol is passed
 * in the SYMBOL structure as a low count, a high count, and a range,
 * instead of the more conventional probability ranges. The encoding
 * process takes two steps. First, the values of high and low are
 * updated to take into account the range restriction created by the
 * new symbol. Then, as many bits as possible are shifted out to
 * the output stream. Finally, high and low are stable again and
 * the routine returns.
 */
void encode_symbol( stream, s )
BIT_FILE *stream;
SYMBOL *s;
{
    long range;
/*
 * These three lines rescale high and low for the new symbol.
 */
    range = (long) ( high-low ) + 1;
    high = low + (unsigned short int)
                ( ( range * s->high_count ) / s->scale - 1 );
    low = low + (unsigned short int)
                ( ( range * s->low_count ) / s->scale );
/*
 * This loop turns out new bits until high and low are far enough
 * apart to have stabilized.
 */
    for ( ; ; ) {
```

```
/*
 * If this test passes, it means that the MSDigits match, and can
 * be sent to the output stream.
 */
    if ( ( high & 0x8000 ) == ( low & 0x8000 ) ) {
      OutputBit( stream, high & 0x8000 );
      while ( underflow_bits > 0 ) {
        OutputBit( stream, ~high & 0x8000 );
        underflow_bits--;
      }
    }
/*
 * If this test passes, the numbers are in danger of underflow, because
 * the MSDigits don't match, and the 2nd digits are just one apart.
 */
    else if ( ( low & 0x4000 ) && !( high & 0x4000 )) {
      underflow_bits += 1;
      low &= 0x3fff;
      high |= 0x4000;
    } else
      return ;
    low <<= 1;
    high <<= 1;
    high |= 1;
  }
}


/*
 * When decoding, this routine is called to figure out which symbol
 * is presently waiting to be decoded. This routine expects to get
 * the current model scale in the s->scale parameter, and it returns
 * a count that corresponds to the present floating point code:
 *
 * code = count / s->scale
 */
short int get_current_count( s )
```

```
SYMBOL *s;
{
    long range;
    short int count;

    range = (long) ( high - low ) + 1;
    count = (short int)
            ((((long) ( code - low ) + 1 ) * s->scale-1 ) / range );
    return( count );
}


/*
 * This routine is called to initialize the state of the arithmetic
 * decoder. This involves initializing the high and low registers
 * to their conventional starting values, plus reading the first
 * 16 bits from the input stream into the code value.
 */
void initialize_arithmetic_decoder( stream )
BIT_FILE *stream;
{
    int i;

    code = 0;
    for ( i = 0 ; i < 16 ; i++ ) {
        code <<= 1;
        code += InputBit( stream );
    }
    low = 0;
    high = 0xffff;
}


/*
 * Just figuring out what the present symbol is doesn't remove
 * it from the input bit stream. After the character has been
 * decoded, this routine has to be called to remove it from the
 * input stream.
 */
```

```
void remove_symbol_from_stream( stream, s )
BIT_FILE *stream;
SYMBOL *s;
{
    long range;

/*
 * First, the range is expanded to account for the symbol removal.
 */
    range = (long)( high - low ) + 1;
    high = low + (unsigned short int)
            (( range * s->high_count ) / s->scale - 1 );
    low = low + (unsigned short int)
            (( range * s->low_count ) / s->scale );
/*
 * Next, any possible bits are shipped out.
 */
    for ( ; ; ) {
/*
 * If the MSDigits match, the bits will be shifted out.
 */
        if ( ( high & 0x8000 ) == ( low & 0x8000 ) ) {
        }
/*
 * Else, if underflow is threatening, shift out the 2nd MSDigit.
 */
        else if ((low & 0x4000) == 0x4000  && (high & 0x4000) == 0 ) {
            code ^= 0x4000;
            low &= 0x3fff;
            high |= 0x4000;
        } else
/*
 * Otherwise, nothing can be shifted out, so I return.
 */
```

```
        return;
    low <<= 1;
    high <<= 1;
    high |= 1;
    code <<= 1;
    code += InputBit( stream );
    }
}
```

```
/************************ End of ARITH.C ************************/
```

CHAPTER 6

Statistical Modeling

The previous three chapters have shown several coding techniques used to compress data. Huffman or arithmetic coding can be used either with fixed models or in an adaptive setting, but a statistical model needs to drive them. The chapters which discussed these coding techniques all used a simple order-0 model, which provides fairly good compression. This chapter discusses how to combine sophisticated modeling techniques with conventional coding to achieve better compression.

Higher-Order Modeling

To compress data using arithmetic or Huffman coding, we need a model of the data stream. The model needs to do two things to achieve compression: (1) it needs to accurately predict the frequency/probability of symbols in the input data stream, and (2) the symbol probabilities generated by the model need to deviate from a uniform distribution.

Accurately predicting the probability of symbols in the input data is an inherent need in arithmetic or Huffman coding. This type of coding reduces the number of bits needed to encode a character as its probability of appearance increases. If the letter E represents 25 percent of the input data, it should take only two bits to code. If the letter Z represents only .1 percent of the input data, it might take ten bits to code. If the model is not generating probabilities accurately, it might take ten bits to code E and two bits to code Z, causing data expansion instead of compression.

The model also needs to make predictions that deviate from a uniform distribution. The better the model is at making these predictions, the better the compression ratios will be. A model could be created, for example, that assigned all 256 possible symbols a uniform probability of 1/256. This model would create an output file exactly the same size as the input file, since every symbol would take exactly eight bits to encode.

Only by correctly finding probabilities that deviate from a normal distribution can the number of bits be reduced, leading to compression. The increased probabilities have to accurately reflect reality, of course, as prescribed by the first condition.

It may seem that the probability of a given symbol occurring in a data stream is fixed, but this is not quite true. The probability of a character can change quite a bit, depending on the model. When compressing a C program, for example, the probability of a new-line character in the text might be 1/40, a probability determined by scanning the entire text and dividing the number of occurrences of the character by the total number of characters. But if a modeling technique looks at a single previous character, the probabilities change. In that case, if the previous character were a '}', the probability of a new-line character goes up to 1/2. This improved modeling technique leads to better compression, though both models were generating accurate probabilities.

Finite Context Modeling

The modeling discussed in this chapter is called "finite-context" modeling. It is based on a simple idea: calculate the probabilities for each incoming symbol based on the context in which the symbol appears. In all of the examples shown here, the context consists of nothing more than symbols previously encountered. The "order" of the model refers to the number of previous symbols that make up the context.

The simplest finite-context model would be an order-0 model that calculates the probability of each symbol independently of any previous symbols. To implement this model, all that is needed is a single table containing the frequency counts for each symbol that might be encountered in the input stream. An order-1 model keeps track of 256 different tables of frequencies, since it needs a separate set of counts for each possible context. Similarly, an order-2 model needs to handle 65,536 different tables of contexts.

The models used in chapters 3, 4, and 5 were all order-0 models. They didn't take up much storage space, and they were simple to manipulate. By confining ourselves to order-0 modeling, however, we ensured that our data-compression ratios were relatively modest.

Adaptive Modeling

It seems logical that as the order of the model increases, compression ratios ought to improve as well. The probability of the letter u appearing in this text may only be 5 percent, for example, but if the previous context character is q, the probability goes up to 95 percent. Predicting characters with high probability lowers the number of bits needed, and larger contexts ought to let us make better predictions.

Unfortunately, as the order of the model increases linearly, the memory consumed by the model increases exponentially. With an order 0 model, the space consumed by the statistics could be as small as 256 bytes. Once the order of the model increases to 2 or 3, even the most cleverly designed models will consume hundreds of kilobytes.

The conventional way of compressing data is to make a pass over the symbols to gather statistics for the model. Then a second pass is made to actually encode the data. The statistics are usually carried with the compressed data so the decoder will have a copy. This approach obviously has serious problems if the statistics for the model take more space than the data to be compressed.

Adaptive compression is the solution to this problem. In adaptive data compression, both the compressor and the decompressor start with the same model. The compressor encodes a symbol using the existing model, then it updates the model to account for the new symbol. The decompressor likewise decodes a symbol using the existing model, then it updates the model. As long as the algorithm to update the model operates identically for the compressor and the decompressor, the process can operate perfectly without needing to pass a statistics table from the compressor to the decompressor.

Adaptive data compression has a slight disadvantage in that it starts compressing with less than optimal statistics. By subtracting the cost of transmitting the statistics with the compressed data, however, an adaptive algorithm will usually perform better than a fixed statistical model.

Adaptive compression also suffers in the cost of updating the model. When updating the count for a particular symbol using arithmetic coding, for example, the update code has the potential cost of updating the cumulative counts for all other symbols as well, leading to code that on the average performs 128 arithmetic operations for every symbol encoded or decoded.

Because of high cost in both memory and CPU time, higher-order adaptive models have only become practical in perhaps the last ten years. It is ironic that as the cost of disk space and memory goes down, the cost of compressing the data stored there also goes down. As these costs continue to decline, we will be able to implement even more effective programs than are practical today.

A Simple Example. The sample program in chapter 4 used Huffman coding to demonstrate adaptive compression. In this chapter, the sample program will use adaptive arithmetic coding. When performing finite-context modeling, we need a data structure to describe each context used while compressing the data. If we move up from an order-0 to an order-1 model, for example, we will use the previous symbol as a context for encoding the current symbol.

An array of 256 context arrays is probably the simplest way to create the data structures for an order-1 model. As we saw in the last chapter, a simple context model for an arithmetic encoder can be created using an array of cumulative counts for each symbol. If we have 256 symbols in our alphabet, an array of pointers to 256 different context arrays can be created like this:

```
int *totals[ 256 ];

void initialize_model()
{
    int context;
    int i;

    for ( context = 0 ; context < END_OF_STREAM ; context++ ) {
        totals[ context ] = (int *) calloc( END_OF_STREAM + 2,
                            sizeof( int ) );
    if ( totals[ context ] == NULL )
        fatal_error( "Failure allocating context %d", context );
        for ( i = 0 ; i <= ( END_OF_STREAM + 1 ) ; i++ )
            totals[ context ][ i ] = i;
    }
}
```

This code not only creates the 256 context arrays, it also initializes each symbol's count to 1. At this point, we can begin encoding symbols as they come in. The loop for encoding the symbols looks similar to the one used for other adaptive programs. Here is an order 1 arithmetic compression loop:

```
for ( ; ; ) {
   c = getc( input );
   if ( c == EOF )
     c = END_OF_STREAM;
   convert_int_to_symbol( c, context, &s );
   encode_symbol( output, &s );
   if ( c == END_OF_STREAM )
     break;
   update_model( c, context );
   context = c;
}
```

This works fairly simply. Instead of just having a single context table, like the code in chapter 5, we now have a set of 256 context tables. Every symbol is encoded using the context table from the previously seen symbol, and only the statistics for the selected context get updated after the symbol is seen. This means we can now more accurately predict the probability of a character's appearance.

The decoding process for this order-1 code is also very simple, and it looks similar to the decoding example from chapter 5. Here is the order 1 expansion loop:

```
for ( ; ; ) {
   get_symbol_scale( context, &s );
   count = get_current_count( &s );
   c = convert_symbol_to_int( count, context, &s );
   remove_symbol_from_stream( input, &s );
   if ( c == END_OF_STREAM )
     break;
```

```
    putc( (char) c, output );
    update_model( c, context );
    context = c;
}
```

The only difference between this and conventional order-0 code is the addition of the context variable, both within the loop and as a parameter to other functions. The remaining routines that differ from the code in chapter 5 are shown next. The C source for this module is included on the program disk.

```
void update_model( int symbol, int context )
{
    int i;

    for ( i = symbol + 1 ; i <= ( END_OF_STREAM + 1 ) ; i++ )
        totals[ context ][ i ]++;
    if ( totals[ context ][ END_OF_STREAM + 1 ] < MAXIMUM_SCALE )
        return;
    for ( i = 1 ; i <= ( END_OF_STREAM + 1 ) ; i++ ) {
        totals[ context ][ i ] /= 2;
        if ( totals[ context ][ i ] <= totals[ context ][ i - 1 ] )
            totals[ context ][ i ] = totals[ context ][ i - 1 ] + 1;
    }
}

void convert_int_to_symbol( int c, int context, SYMBOL *s )
{
    s->scale = totals[ context ][ END_OF_STREAM + 1 ];
    s->low_count = totals[ context ][ c ];
    s->high_count = totals[ context ][ c + 1 ];
}

void get_symbol_scale( int context, SYMBOL *s )
{
    s->scale = totals[ context][ END_OF_STREAM + 1 ];
}
```

```
int convert_symbol_to_int( int count, int context, SYMBOL *s)
{
    int c;

    for ( c = 0; count >= totals[ context ][ c + 1 ] ; c++ )
        ;
    s->high_count = totals[ context ][ c + 1 ];
    s->low_count = totals[ context ][ c ];
    return( c );
}
```

Using the Escape Code as a Fallback. The simple order-1 program does in fact do a creditable job of compression, but it has a couple of problems to address. First, the model for this program makes it a slow starter. Every context starts off with 257 symbols initialized to a single count, meaning every symbol starts off being encoded in roughly eight bits. As new symbols are added to the table, they will gradually begin to be encoded in fewer bits. This process, however, will not happen very quickly.

For the context table for the letter q, for example, we will probably see a very high number of u symbols. The very first u will have a probability of 1/257, and will accordingly be encoded in eight bits. The second u will have a probablity of 2/258, but will still require over seven bits to encode. In fact, it will take sixteen consecutive u symbols with no other appearances before the entropy of the symbol is reduced to even four bits.

The reason for this slow reduction in bit count is obvious. The probability of the u symbol is being weighed down by the other 256 symbols in the table. Though they may never appear in the message, they need a nonzero count. If their count were reduced to zero, we would not be able to encode them if and when they appeared in the message.

There is a solution to this problem, however, and it is relatively painless. Instead of having every symbol appear automatically in every table; start off with a nearly empty table and add symbols to the table only as they appear. The q table would have zero counts for all the other symbols, giving the first u that appears a low bit count.

But there is a catch here. If a symbol doesn't appear in a context table, how will it be encoded when it appears in a message? The easiest way to accomplish this is to use an escape code. The escape code is a special symbol (much like the end-of-stream symbol) that indicates we need to "escape" from the current context.

When a context issues an escape symbol, we generally fall back to a lower-order context. In our next sample program, we escape to the escape context, a context that never gets updated. It contains 258 symbols, each of which has a count of 1. This guarantees that any symbol encountered in the message can be encoded by outputting an escape code from the current context and by encoding the symbol using the escape context.

How does this affect the example used for the letter u? As it turns out, it makes an enormous difference. The first u symbol that took eight bits in the previous example will take about eight bits here as well. The escape code takes no bits to encode, and in the escape context the u has a 1/257 probability. After that, however, the u is added to the table and given a count of 1. The next appearance of u will requre only one bit to encode, since it has a probability of 1/2. By the time 16 u's have appeared, and while the previous model is still taking four bits to encode it, the escape-driven model will take only .06 bits!

The escape code frees us from burdening our models with characters that may never appear. This lets the model adjust rapidly to changing probabilities and quickly reduces the number of bits needed to encode high-probability symbols.

The encoding process for this particular implementation of a multi-order model requires only a few modfications to the previous program. The convert_int_to_symbol() routine now has to check whether a symbol is present in the given context. If not, the escape code is encoded instead, and the function returns the appropriate result to the main encoding loop, as shown:

```
context = 0;
initialize_model();
initialize_arithmetic_encoder();
for ( ; ; ) {
  c = getc( input );
  if ( c == EOF )
```

```
    c = END_OF_STREAM;
  escaped = convert_int_to_symbol( c, context, &s );
  encode_symbol( output, &s );
  if ( escaped ) {
    convert_int_to_symbol( c, ESCAPE, &s );
    encode_symbol( output, &s );
  }
  if ( c == END_OF_STREAM )
    break;
  update_model( c, context );
  context = c;
}
```

In the main compression loop shown, the compressor first tries to send the original symbol. If the convert_int_to_symbol() routine returns a true, the symbol did not appear in the current context, and the routine resends the symbol using the escape context. We update just the current context model with the symbol just sent, not the escape model.

The decompression loop for this program follows a similar pattern. The code shown next makes one or two possible passes through the loop, depending on whether an escape code is detected. The program for this order-1 context-switching program is on the program diskette that accompanies this book.

```
context = 0;
initialize_model();
initialize_arithmetic_decoder( input );
for ( ; ; ) {
  last_context = context;
  do {
    get_symbol_scale( context, &s );
    count = get_current_count( &s );
    c = convert_symbol_to_int( count, context, &s );
    remove_symbol_from_stream( input, &s );
    context = c;
  } while ( c == ESCAPE );
```

```
if ( c == END_OF_STREAM )
  break;
putc( (char) c, output );
update_model( c, last_context );
context = c;
}
```

Improvements. Some problems with the method of encoding in ARITH-1.C are the high-cost operations associated with the model. Each time we update the counts for symbol c, every count in totals[context][] from c up to 256 has to be incremented. An average of 128 increment operations have to be performed for every character encoded or decoded. For a simple demonstration program like the one shown here, this may not be a major problem, but a production program should be modified to be more efficient.

One way to reduce the number of increment operations is to move the counts for the most frequently accessed symbols to the top of the array. This makes the model keep track of each symbol's position in the totals[context] array, but it reduces the number of increment operations by an order of magnitude. This is a relatively simple enhancement to make to this program. A very good example of a program that uses this technique has been published as part of Ian H. Witten, Neal Radford, and John Cleary, "Arithmetic Coding for Data Compression," *Communications of the ACM* (June 1987). This paper is an excellent source of information regarding arithmetic coding, with some sample C source code illustrating the text.

Highest-Order Modeling

The previous sample program used order-1 statistics to compress data. It seems logical that if we move to higher orders, we should achieve better compression. The importance of the escape code becomes even more clear here. When using an order-3 model, we potentially have 16,000,000 context tables to work with. We would have to read in an incredible amount of text before those 16,000,000 tables would have enough statistics to start compressing data, and many of those 16,000,000 tables will never be used—which means they take up space in our computer's memory for no good reason. When compressing English text, for example, it does no good to allocate space for the table QQW. It will never appear.

The solution to this is, again, to set the initial probabilities of all of the symbols to 0 for a given context and to fall back to a different context when a previously unseen symbol occurs. So the obvious question is: what do we use as the fallback context after emitting an escape code? In the last example, we fell back to a default context called the escape context. The escape context was never updated, which meant that using it generally would not provide any compression.

In the higher-order models, there is a better way to compress than just automatically falling back to a default context. If an existing context can't encode a symbol, fall back to the next smaller-order context. If our existing context was REQ, for example, and U needs to be encoded for the first time, an escape code will be generated. Following that, we drop back to an order-2 model to try to encode the character U using the context EQ. This continues down through the order-0 context. If the escape code is still generated at order-0, we fall back to a special order (-1) context that is never updated and is set up at initialization to have a count of 1 for every possible symbol—so it is guaranteed to encode every symbol.

Using this escape-code technique means only a slight modification to the driver program. The program (see the code found in ARITH-N.C) now sits in a loop trying to encode its characters, as shown here:

```
do {
    escaped = convert_int_to_symbol( c, &s );
    encode_symbol( compressed_file, &s );
} while ( escaped );
```

The modeling code keeps track of what the current order is, decrementing it whenever an escape is emitted. Even more complicated is the modeling module's job of keeping track of which context table needs to be used for the current order.

Updating the Model. ARITH1E.C does a good job of compressing data. But quite a few improvements can still be made to this simple statistical method without changing the fundamental nature of its algorithm. The rest of this chapter is devoted to discussing those improvements, along with a look at a sample compression module, ARITH-N.C, that implements most of them.

Using the highest-order modeling algorithm requires that instead of keeping just one set of context tables for the highest order, we keep a full set of context tables for every order up to the highest order. If we are doing order-2 modeling, for example, there will be a single order-0 table, 256 order-1 tables, and 65,536 order-2 tables. When a new character is encoded or decoded, the modeling code updates one of these tables for each order. In the example of U following REQ, the modeling code would update the U counters in the order-3 REQ table, the order-2 EQ table, the order-1 Q table, and the order-0 table. The code to update all of these tables is shown next:

```
for ( order = 0 ; order <= max_order ; order++ )
    update_model( order, symbol );
```

A slight modification to this algorithm results in both faster updates and better compression. Instead of updating all the different order models for the current context, we can instead update only those models actually used to encode the symbol. This is called "update exclusion," since it excludes unused lower-order models from being updated. It will generally give a small but noticeable improvement in the compression ratio. Update exclusion works since symbols showing up frequently in the higher-order models won't be seen as often in the lower-order models, which means we shouldn't increment the counters in the lower-order models. The modified code for update exclusion will look like this:

```
for ( order=encoding_order ; order <= max_order ; order++ )
    update_model( order, symbol );
```

Escape Probabilities. When the program first starts encoding a text stream, it will emit quite a few escape codes. The number of bits used to encode escape characters will probably have a large effect on the compression ratio, particularly in small files. In our first attempts to use escape codes, we set the escape count to 1 and left it there, regardless of the state of the rest of the context table. Bell, Cleary, and Witten call this "Method A." Method B sets the count for the escape character at the number of symbols presently defined for the context table. If eleven different characters have been seen so far, for example, the escape symbol count will be set at eleven, regardless of what the counts are.

Both methods seem to work fairly well. The code in our previous program can easily be modified to support either one. Probably the best thing about methods A and B is that they are not computationally intensive. Adding the escape symbol to the Method A table can be done so that it takes almost no more work to update the table with the symbol than without it.

The next sample program, ARITH-N.C, implements a slightly more complicated escape-count calculation algorithm. It tries to take into account three different factors when calculating the escape probability. First, as the number of symbols defined in the context table increases, the escape probability naturally decreases. This reaches its maximum when the table has all 256 symbols defined, making the escape probability 0.

Second, it takes into account a measure of randomness in the table. It calculates this by dividing the maximum count in the table by the average count. The higher the ratio, the less random the table. The REQ table, for example, may have only three symbols defined: U, with a count of 50; u, with a count of 10; and e, with a count of 3. The ratio of U's count, 50, to the average, 21, is fairly high. The U is thus predicted with a relatively high amount of accuracy, and the escape probability ought to be lower. In a table where the high count was 10 and the average was 8, things would seem a little more random, and the escape probability should be higher.

The third factor taken into account is simply the raw count of how many symbols have been seen for the particular table. As the number of symbols increases, the predictability of the table should go up, making the escape probability go down.

The formula I use for calculating the number of counts for the escape symbol is on the next page.

```
count = (256 - number of symbols seen)*number of symbols seen
count = count /(256 * the highest symbol count)
if count is less than 1
   count = 1
```

The missing variable in this equation is the raw symbol count. This is implicit in the calculation, because the escape probability is the escape count divided by the raw count. The raw count will automatically scale the escape count to a probability.

Scoreboarding. When using highest-order modeling techniques, an additional enhancement, scoreboarding, can improve compression efficiency. When we first try to compress a symbol, we can generate either the code for the symbol or an escape code. If we generate an escape code, the symbol had not previously occurred in that context, so we had a count of 0. But we do gain some information about the symbol just by generating an escape. We can now generate a list of symbols that did not match the symbol to be encoded. These symbols can temporarily have their counts set to 0 when we calculate the probabilities for lower-order models. The counts will be reset back to their permanent values after the encoding for the particular character is complete. This process is called scoreboarding.

An example of this is shown below. If the present context is HAC and the next symbol is K, we will use the tables shown next to encode the K. Without scoreboarding, the HAC context generates an escape with a probability of 1/6. The AC context generates an escape with a probability of 1/8. The C context generates an escape with a probability of 1/40, and the "" context finally generates a K with a probability of 1/73.

""	"C"	"AC"	"HAC"
ESC 1	ESC 1	ESC 1	ESC 1
'K' 1	'H' 20	'C' 5	'E' 3
'E' 40	'T' 11	'H' 2	'L' 1
'I' 22	'L' 5		'C' 1
'A' 9	'A' 3		

If we use scoreboarding to exclude counts of previously seen characters, we can make a significant improvement in these probabilities. The first encoding of an escape from HAC isn't affected, since no characters were seen before. But the AC escape code eliminates the C from its calculations, resulting in a probability of 1/3. The C escape code excludes the H and the A counts, increasing the probability from 1/40 to 1/17. And finally, the "" context excludes the E and A counts, reducing that probability from 1/73 to 1/24. This reduces the number of bits required to encode the symbol from 14.9 to 12.9, a significant savings.

Keeping a symbol scoreboard will almost always result in some improvement in compression, and it will never make things worse. The major problem with scoreboarding is that the probability tables for all of the lower-order contexts have to be recalculated every time the table is accessed. This results in a big increase in the CPU time required to encode text. Scoreboarding is left in ARITH-N.C to demonstrate the gains possible when compressing text using it.

Data Structures. All improvements to the basic statistical modeling assume that higher-order modeling can actually be accomplished on the target computer. The problem with increasing the order is one of memory. The cumulative totals table in the order-0 model in chapter 5 occupied 516 bytes of memory. If we used the same data structures for an order-1 model, the memory used would shoot up to 133K, which is still probably acceptable. But going to order-2 will increase the RAM requirements for the statistics unit to thirty-four megabytes! Since we would like to try orders even higher than 2, we need to redesign the data structures that hold the counts.

To save memory space, we have to redesign the context statistics tables. In chapter 5, the table is about as simple as it can be, with each symbol being used as an index directly into a pair of counts. In the order-1 model, the appropriate context tables would be found by indexing once into an array of context tables, then indexing again to the symbol in question, a procedure like that shown here:

```
low_count = totals[ last_char ][ current_char ];
high_count = totals[ last_char ][ current_char + 1 ];
range = totals[ last_char ][ 256 ];
```

This is convenient, but enormously wasteful. Full context space is allocated even for unused tables, and within the tables space is allocated for all symbols, seen or not. Both factors waste enormous amounts of memory in higher-order models.

The solution to the first problem, reserving space for unused contexts, is to organize the context tables as a tree. Place the order-0 context table at a known location and use it to contain pointers to order-1 context tables. The order-1 context tables will hold their own statistics and pointers to order-2 context tables. This continues until reaching the "leaves" of the context tree, which contain order-n tables but no pointers to higher orders. Using a tree structure can keep the unused pointer nodes set to null pointers until a context is seen. Once the context is seen, a table is created and added to the parent node of the tree.

The second problem is creating a table of 256 counts every time a new context is created. In reality, the highest-order contexts will frequently have only a few symbols, so we can save a lot of space by only allocating space for symbols seen for a particular context.

After implementing these changes, we have a set of data structures that look like this:

```
typedef struct {
    unsigned char symbol;
    unsigned char counts;
} STATS;

typedef struct {
    struct context *next;
} LINKS;

typedef struct context {
    int max_index;
    STATS *stats;
    LINKS *links;
    struct context *lesser_context;
} CONTEXT;
```

The new context structure has four major elements. The first is the counter, max_index, which tells how many symbols are presently defined for this particular context table. When a table is first created, it has no defined symbols, and max_index is -1. A completely defined table will have a max_index of 255. max_index tells how many elements are allocated for the arrays pointed to by stats and links. Stats is an array of structures, each containing a symbol and a count for that symbol. If the context table is not one of the highest-order tables, it will also have a links array. Each symbol defined in the stats array will have a pointer to the next higher-order context table in the links table.

A sample of the context table tree is shown in Figure 6-1. The table shown is one that will have just been created after the input text "ABCABDABE" when keeping maximum order-3 statistics. Just nine input symbols have already generated a fairly complicated data structure, but it is orders of magnitude smaller than one consisting of arrays of arrays.

Order 0	Order 1	Order 2	Order 3
Context: "" Lesser: NULL Symbol Count Link A 3 "A" B 3 "B" C 1 "C" D 1 "D" E 1 "E"	Context: "A" Lesser: "" Symbol Count Link B 3 "AB" Context: "B" Lesser: "" Symbol Count Link C 1 "BC" D 1 "BD" E 1 "BE" Context "C" Lesser "" Symbol Count Link A 1 "CA" Context "D" Lesser "" Symbol Count Link A 1 "DA" Context "E" Lesser "" Symbol Count Link	Context: "AB" Lesser: "B" Symbol Count Link C 1 "ABC" D 1 "ABD" E 1 "ABE" Context: "BC" Lesser: "C" Symbol Count Link A 1 "BCA" Context: "CA" Lesser: "A" Symbol Count Link B 1 "CAB" Context: "BD" Lesser: "D" Symbol Count Link A 1 "BDA" Context: "BE" Lesser: "E" Symbol Count Link	Context: "ABC" Lesser: "BC" Symbol Count Link A 1 NULL Context: "BCA" Lesser: "CA" Symbol Count Link B 1 NULL Context: "CAB" Lesser: "AB" Symbol Count Link D 1 NULL Context: "ABD" Lesser: "BD" Symbol Count Link A 1 NULL Context: "BDA" Lesser: "DA" Symbol Count Link B 1 NULL Context: "DAB" Lesser: "AB" Symbol Count Link E 1 NULL Context: "ABE" Lesser: "BE" Symbol Count Link

Figure 6-1. A context table tree: "ABCABDABE."

One element in this structure that hasn't been explained is the lesser_context pointer. This pointer is needed when using higher-order models. If the modeling code is trying to locate an order-3 context table, it first has to scan through the order-0 symbol list looking for the first symbol, the match, the order-1 symbol list, and so on.

If the symbol lists in the lower orders are relatively full, this can be a lengthy process. Even worse, every time an escape is generated, the process has to be repeated when looking up the lower-order context. These searches can consume an inordinate amount of CPU time.

The solution to this is to maintain a pointer for each table that points to the table for the context one order less. The context table ABC should have its back pointer point to BC, for example, which should have a back pointer to C, which should have a pointer to "", the null table. Then the modeling code only needs to keep a pointer to the current highest order context. Given that, finding the order-1 context table is simply a matter of performing (n-1) pointer operations.

With the table shown in figure 6-1, for example, suppose the next incoming text symbol is X and the current context is ABE. Without the benefit of the lesser context pointers, I have to check the order-3, 2, 1, and 0 tables for X. This takes 15 symbol comparisons and three table lookups. Using reverse pointers eliminates all the symbol comparisons and performs just three table lookups.

To update the figure 6-1 context tree to contain an X after ABE, the modeling code has to perform a single set of lookups for each order/context. This code is shown in ARITH-N.C in the add_character_to_model() routine. Every time a new table is created, it needs to have its back pointer created properly at the same time, which requires a certain amount of care in the design of update procedures.

The Finishing Touches: Tables 1 and 2. The final touch to the context tree in ARITH-N.C is the addition of two special tables. The order-1 table has been discussed previously. This is a table with a fixed probability for every symbol. If a symbol is not found in any of the higher-order models, it will show up in the order-1 model. This is the table of last resort. Since it guarantees that it will always provide a code for every symbol in the alphabet, we don't update this table, which means it uses a fixed probability for every symbol.

ARITH-N.C also has a special order(-2) table used for passing control information from the encoder to the decoder. The encoder can pass a -1 to the decoder to indicate end-of-file. Since normal symbols are always defined as unsigned values ranging from 0 to 255, the modeling code recognizes a negative number as a special symbol that will generate escapes all the way back to the order(-2) table. The modeling code can also determine that since -1 is a negative number, the symbol should just be ignored when the update_model() code is called.

Model Flushing. The creation of the order(-2) model allows us to pass a second control code from the encoder to the expander—the flush code, which tells the decoder to flush statistics out of the model. The compressor does this when the performance of the model starts to slip. The ratio is adjustable and is set in this implementation to 10 percent. When compression falls belows this ratio, the model is "flushed" by dividing all counts by two. This gives more weight to newer statistics, which should improve the compression.

In reality the model should probably be flushed whenever the input symbol stream drastically changes character. If the program is compressing an executable file, for example, the statistics accumulated during the compression of the executable code are probably of no value when compressing the program's data. Unfortunately, it isn't easy to define an algorithm that detects a "change in the nature" of the input.

Implementation. Even with the Byzantine data structures used here, the compression and expansion programs built around ARITH-N.C have prodigious memory requirements. When running on DOS machines limited to 640K, these programs have to be limited to order-1, or perhaps order-2 for text that has a higher redundancy ratio.

To examine compression ratios for higher orders on binary files, there are a couple of choices for these programs. First, they can be built using a DOS Extender, such as Rational Systems /16M. Or they can be built on a machine that has either a larger address space or support for virtual memory, such as VMS or UNIX. The code distributed here was written in an attempt to be portable across all these options.

Testing shows that with an extra megabyte of extended memory and a DOS Extender, virtually any ASCII file can be compressed on a PC using order-3 compression. Some binary files require more memory. A UNIX system had no problem with order-3 compression and turned in the best performance overall in terms of speed.

Conclusions

Compression-ratio tests show that statistical modeling can perform at least as well as dictionary-based methods. But these programs are at present somewhat impractical because of their high resource requirements. ARITH-N is fairly slow, compressing data with speeds in the range of 1K per second and needing huge amounts of memory to use higher-order modeling. As memory becomes cheaper and processors become more powerful, however, schemes such as the ones shown here may become practical. They could be applied today to circumstances in which either storage or transmission costs are extremely high.

Order-0 adaptive modeling using arithmetic coding could be useful today in situations requiring extremely low consumption of memory. The compression ratios might not be as good as those gained with sophisticated models, but memory consumption is minimized.

Enhancement. The performance of these algorithms could be improved significantly beyond the implementations discussed here. The first area for improvement would be in memory management. Right now, when the programs run out of memory, they abort. A more sensible approach would be to have the programs start with fixed amounts of memory available for statistics. When the statistics fill the space, the program should then stop updating the tables and just use what it had. This would mean implementing internal memory-management routines instead of using the C run-time library routines.

Another potential improvement could come in the tree structure for the context tables. Locating tables through the use of hashing could be quite a bit faster and might require less memory. The context tables themselves could also be improved. When a table has over 50 percent of the potential symbols defined for it, an alternate data structure could be used with the counts stored in a linear array. This would allow for faster indexing and would reduce memory requirements.

Finally, it might be worth trying ways to adaptively modify the order of the model being used. When compressing using order-3 statistics, early portions of the input text generate a lot of escapes while the statistics tables fill up. It ought to be possible to start encoding using order-0 statistics while keeping order-3 statistics. As the table fills up, the order used for encoding could be incremented until it reaches the maximum.

ARITH-N Listing

```
/*********************** Start of ARITH-N.C ***********************
* * This is the order-n arithmetic coding module used in the final
* part of chapter 6.
*
* Compile with BITIO.C, ERRHAND.C, and either MAIN-C.C or MAIN-E.C. This
* program should be compiled in large model. An even better alternative
* is a DOS extender.
*
*/
#include <stdio.h>
#include <stdlib.h>
#include <string.h>
#include "errhand.h"
#include "bitio.h"

/*
* The SYMBOL structure is what is used to define a symbol in
* arithmetic coding terms. A symbol is defined as a range between
* 0 and 1. Since we are using integer math, instead of using 0 and 1
* as our end points, we have an integer scale. The low_count and
* high_count define where the symbol falls in the range.
*/

typedef struct {
    unsigned short int low_count;
    unsigned short int high_count;
    unsigned short int scale;
} SYMBOL;
```

```
#define MAXIMUM_SCALE 16383    /* Maximum allowed frequency count  */
#define ESCAPE     256         /* The escape symbol                */
#define DONE     (-1)          /* The output stream empty  symbol  */
#define FLUSH    (-2)          /* The symbol to flush the model    */


/*
 * Function prototypes.
 */

#ifdef __STDC__

void initialize_options( int argc, char **argv );
int check_compression( FILE *input, BIT_FILE *output );
void initialize_model( void );
void update_model( int symbol );
int convert_int_to_symbol( int symbol, SYMBOL *s );
void get_symbol_scale( SYMBOL *s );
int convert_symbol_to_int( int count, SYMBOL *s );
void add_character_to_model( int c );
void flush_model( void );
void initialize_arithmetic_decoder( BIT_FILE *stream );
void remove_symbol_from_stream( BIT_FILE *stream, SYMBOL *s );
void initialize_arithmetic_encoder( void );
void encode_symbol( BIT_FILE *stream, SYMBOL *s );
void flush_arithmetic_encoder( BIT_FILE *stream );
short int get_current_count( SYMBOL *s );

#else

void initialize_options();
int check_compression();
void initialize_model();
void update_model();
int convert_int_to_symbol();
void get_symbol_scale();
int convert_symbol_to_int();
void add_character_to_model();
```

```
void flush_model();
void initialize_arithmetic_decoder();
void remove_symbol_from_stream();
void initialize_arithmetic_encoder();
void encode_symbol();
void flush_arithmetic_encoder();
short int get_current_count();

#endif


char *CompressionName = "Adaptive order n model with arithmetic coding";
char *Usage          = "in-file out-file [ -o order ]\n\n";
int max_order        = 3;

/*
 *
 * The main procedure is similar to the main found in ARITH1E.C. It has
 * to initialize the coder and the model. It then sits in a loop reading
 * input symbols and encoding them. One difference is that every 256
 * symbols a compression check is performed. If the compression ratio
 * falls below 10%, a flush character is encoded. This flushes the encod
 * ing model, and will cause the decoder to flush its model when the
 * file is being expanded. The second difference is that each symbol is
 * repeatedly encoded until a successful encoding occurs. When trying to
 * encode a character in a particular order, the model may have to
 * transmit an ESCAPE character. If this is the case, the character has
 * to be retransmitted using a lower order. This process repeats until a
 * successful match is found of the symbol in a particular context.
 * Usually this means going down no further than the order -1 model.
 * However, the FLUSH and DONE symbols drop back to the order -2 model.
 *
 */

void CompressFile( input, output, argc, argv )
FILE *input;
BIT_FILE *output;
```

```
int argc;
char *argv[];
{
   SYMBOL s;
   int c;
   int escaped;
   int flush = 0;
   long int text_count = 0;

   initialize_options( argc, argv );
   initialize_model();
   initialize_arithmetic_encoder();
   for ( ; ; ) {
      if ( ( ++text_count & 0x0ff ) == 0 )
         flush = check_compression( input, output );
      if ( !flush )
         c = getc( input );
      else
         c = FLUSH;
      if ( c == EOF )
         c = DONE;
      do {
         escaped = convert_int_to_symbol( c, &s );
         encode_symbol( output, &s );
      } while ( escaped );
      if ( c == DONE )
         break;
      if ( c == FLUSH ) {
         flush_model();
         flush = 0;
      }
      update_model( c );
      add_character_to_model( c );
   }
   flush_arithmetic_encoder( output );
}
```

THE DATA COMPRESSION BOOK

```
/*
 * The main loop for expansion is very similar to the expansion
 * routine used in the simpler compression program, ARITH1E.C. The
 * routine first has to initialize the the arithmetic coder and the
 * model. The decompression loop differs in a couple of respects.
 * First of all, it handles the special ESCAPE character, by
 * removing them from the input bit stream but just throwing them
 * away otherwise. Secondly, it handles the special FLUSH character.
 * Once the main decoding loop is done, the cleanup code is called,
 * and the program exits.
 *
 */

void ExpandFile( input, output, argc, argv )
BIT_FILE *input;
FILE *output;
int argc;
char *argv[];
{
    SYMBOL s;
    int c;
    int count;

    initialize_options( argc, argv );
    initialize_model();
    initialize_arithmetic_decoder( input );
    for ( ; ; ) {
        do {
            get_symbol_scale( &s );
            count = get_current_count( &s );
            c = convert_symbol_to_int( count, &s );
            remove_symbol_from_stream( input, &s );
        } while ( c == ESCAPE );
        if ( c == DONE )
            break;
        if ( c != FLUSH )
            putc( (char) c, output );
```

```
      else
        flush_model();
      update_model( c );
      add_character_to_model( c );
    }
}


/*
 * This routine checks for command line options. At present, the only
 * option being passed on the command line is the order.
 */

void initialize_options( argc, argv )
int argc;
char *argv[];
{
    while ( argc-- > 0 ) {
      if ( strcmp( *argv, "-o" ) == 0 ) {
        argc--;
        max_order = atoi( *++argv );
      } else
        printf( "Uknown argument on command line: %s\n", *argv );
      argc--;
      argv++;
    }
}


/*
 * This routine is called once every 256 input symbols. Its job is to
 * check to see if the compression ratio falls below 10%. If the
 * output size is 90% of the input size, it means not much compression
 * is taking place, so we probably ought to flush the statistics in the
 * model to allow for more current statistics to have greater impact.
 * This heuristic approach does seem to have some effect.
 */
```

```
int check_compression( input, output )
FILE *input;
BIT_FILE *output;
{
    static long local_input_marker = 0L;
    static long local_output_marker = 0L;
    long total_input_bytes;
    long total_output_bytes;
    int local_ratio;

    total_input_bytes = ftell( input ) - local_input_marker;
    total_output_bytes = ftell( output->file );
    total_output_bytes -= local_output_marker;
    if ( total_output_bytes == 0 )
        total_output_bytes = 1;
    local_ratio = (int)( ( total_output_bytes * 100 ) /
                                    total_input_bytes );

    local_input_marker = ftell( input );
    local_output_marker = ftell( output->file );

    return( local_ratio > 90 );
}

/*
 *
 * The next few routines contain all of the code and data used to
 * perform modeling for this program. This modeling unit keeps track
 * of all contexts from 0 up to max_order, which defaults to 3. In
 * addition, there is a special context -1 which is a fixed model used
 * to encode previously unseen characters, and a context -2 which is
 * used to encode EOF and FLUSH messages.
 *
 * Each context is stored in a special CONTEXT structure, which is
 * documented below. Context tables are not created until the context
 * is seen, and they are never destroyed.
 *
 */
```

```
/*
 * A context table contains a list of the counts for all symbols
 * that have been seen in the defined context. For example, a
 * context of "Zor" might have only had 2 different characters
 * appear. 't' might have appeared 10 times, and 'l' might have
 * appeared once. These two counts are stored in the context
 * table. The counts are stored in the STATS structure. All of
 * the counts for a given context are stored in and array of STATS.
 * As new characters are added to a particular contexts, the STATS
 * array will grow. Sometimes the STATS array will shrink
 * after flushing the model.
 */
typedef struct {
    unsigned char symbol;
    unsigned char counts;
}STATS;


/*
 * Each context has to have links to higher order contexts. These
 * links are used to navigate through the context tables. For example,
 * to find the context table for "ABC", I start at the order 0 table,
 * then find the pointer to the "A" context table by looking through
 * the LINKS array. At that table, we find the "B" link and go to
 * that table. The process continues until the destination table is
 * found. The table pointed to by the LINKS array corresponds to the
 * symbol found at the same offset in the STATS table. The reason that
 * LINKS is in a separate structure instead of being combined with
 * STATS is to save space. All of the leaf context nodes don't need
 * next pointers, since they are in the highest order context. In the
 * leaf nodes, the LINKS array is a NULL pointer.
 */
typedef struct {
    struct context *next;
} LINKS;
```

```
/*
 * The CONTEXT structure holds all of the known information about
 * a particular context. The links and stats pointers are discussed
 * immediately above here. The max_index element gives the maximum
 * index that can be applied to the stats or link array. When the
 * table is first created, and stats is set to NULL, max_index is set
 * to -1. As soon as single element is added to stats, max_index is
 * incremented to 0.
 *
 * The lesser context pointer is a navigational aid. It points to
 * the context that is one less than the current order. For example,
 * if the current context is "ABC", the lesser_context pointer will
 * point to "BC". The reason for maintaining this pointer is that
 * this particular bit of table searching is done frequently, but
 * the pointer only needs to be built once, when the context is
 * created.
 */
typedef struct context {
    int max_index;
    LINKS *links;
    STATS *stats;
    struct context *lesser_context;
} CONTEXT;

/*
 * *contexts[] is an array of current contexts. If I want to find
 * the order 0 context for the current state of the model, I just
 * look at contexts[0]. This array of context pointers is set up
 * every time the model is updated.
 */
CONTEXT **contexts;

/*
 * current_order contains the current order of the model. It starts
 * at max_order, and is decremented every time an ESCAPE is sent. It
 * will only go down to -1 for normal symbols, but can go to -2 for
 * EOF and FLUSH.
 */
```

```
int current_order;

/*
* This table contains the cumulative totals for the current context.
* Because this program is using exclusion, totals has to be calculated
* every time a context is used. The scoreboard array keeps track of
* symbols that have appeared in higher order models, so that they
* can be excluded from lower order context total calculations.
*/

short int totals[ 258 ];
char scoreboard[ 256 ];

/*
* Local procedure declarations for modeling routines.
*/
#ifdef __STDC__
void update_table( CONTEXT *table, int symbol );
void rescale_table( CONTEXT *table );
void totalize_table( CONTEXT *table );
CONTEXT *shift_to_next_context( CONTEXT *table, int c, int order);
CONTEXT *allocate_next_order_table( CONTEXT *table,
                                    int symbol,
                                    CONTEXT *lesser_context );
void recursive_flush( CONTEXT *table );
#else
void update_table();
void rescale_table();
void totalize_table();
CONTEXT *shift_to_next_context();
CONTEXT *allocate_next_order_table();
void recursive_flush();
#endif

/*
* This routine has to get everything set up properly so that
* the model can be maintained properly. The first step is to create
```

```
 * the *contexts[] array used later to find current context tables.
 * The *contexts[] array indices go from -2 up to max_order, so
 * the table needs to be fiddled with a little. This routine then
 * has to create the special order -2 and order -1 tables by hand,
 * since they aren't quite like other tables. Then the current
 * context is set to \0, \0, \0, ... and the appropriate tables
 * are built to support that context. The current order is set
 * to max_order, the scoreboard is cleared, and the system is
 * ready to go.
 */

void initialize_model()
{
    int i;
    CONTEXT *null_table;
    CONTEXT *control_table;

    current_order = max_order;
    contexts = (CONTEXT **) calloc( sizeof( CONTEXT * ), 10 );
    if ( contexts == NULL )
      fatal_error( "Failure #1: allocating context table!" );
    contexts += 2;
    null_table = (CONTEXT *) calloc( sizeof( CONTEXT ), 1 );
    if ( null_table == NULL )
      fatal_error( "Failure #2: allocating null table!" );
    null_table->max_index = -1;
    contexts[ -1 ] = null_table;
    for ( i = 0 ; i <= max_order ; i++ )
      contexts[ i ] = allocate_next_order_table( contexts[ i-1 ],
                                                 0,
                                                 contexts[ i-1 ] );
    free( (char *) null_table->stats );
    null_table->stats =
      (STATS *) calloc( sizeof( STATS ), 256 );
    if ( null_table->stats == NULL )
      fatal_error( "Failure #3: allocating null table!" );
    null_table->max_index = 255;
```

```
    for ( i=0 ; i < 256 ; i++ ) {
      null_table->stats[ i ].symbol = (unsigned char) i;
      null_table->stats[ i ].counts = 1;
    }

    control_table = (CONTEXT *) calloc( sizeof(CONTEXT), 1 );
    if ( control_table == NULL )
      fatal_error( "Failure #4: allocating null table!" );
    control_table->stats =
      (STATS *) calloc( sizeof( STATS ), 2 );
    if ( control_table->stats == NULL )
      fatal_error( "Failure #5: allocating null table!" );
    contexts[ -2 ] = control_table;
    control_table->max_index = 1;
    control_table->stats[ 0 ].symbol = -FLUSH;
    control_table->stats[ 0 ].counts = 1;
    control_table->stats[ 1 ].symbol =- DONE;
    control_table->stats[ 1 ].counts = 1;

    for ( i = 0 ; i < 256 ; i++ )
      scoreboard[ i ] = 0;
}


/*
* This is a utility routine used to create new tables when a new
* context is created. It gets a pointer to the current context,
* and gets the symbol that needs to be added to it. It also needs
* a pointer to the lesser context for the table that is to be
* created. For example, if the current context was "ABC", and the
* symbol 'D' was read in, add_character_to_model would need to
* create the new context "BCD". This routine would get called
* with a pointer to "BC", the symbol 'D', and a pointer to context
* "CD". This routine then creates a new table for "BCD", adds it
* to the link table for "BC", and gives "BCD" a back pointer to
* "CD". Note that finding the lesser context is a difficult
* task, and isn't done here. This routine mainly worries about
* modifying the stats and links fields in the current context.
*/
```

```
CONTEXT *allocate_next_order_table( table, symbol, lesser_context )
CONTEXT *table;
int symbol;
CONTEXT *lesser_context;
{
    CONTEXT *new_table;
    int i;
    unsigned int new_size;

    for ( i = 0 ; i <= table->max_index ; i++ )
        if ( table->stats[ i ].symbol == (unsigned char) symbol )
            break;
    if ( i > table->max_index ) {
        table->max_index++;
        new_size = sizeof( LINKS );
        new_size *= table->max_index + 1;
        if ( table->links == NULL )
            table->links = (LINKS *) calloc( new_size, 1 );
        else
            table->links = (LINKS *)
                realloc( (char *) table->links, new_size );
        new_size = sizeof( STATS );
        new_size *= table->max_index + 1;
        if ( table->stats == NULL )
            table->stats = (STATS *) calloc( new_size, 1 );
        else
            table->stats = (STATS *)
                realloc( (char *) table->stats, new_size );
        if ( table->links == NULL )
            fatal_error( "Failure #6: allocating new table" );
        if ( table->stats == NULL )
            fatal_error( "Failure #7: allocating new table" );
        table->stats[ i ].symbol = (unsigned char) symbol;
        table->stats[ i ].counts = 0;
```

```
   }
   new_table = (CONTEXT *) calloc( sizeof( CONTEXT ), 1 );
   if ( new_table == NULL )
      fatal_error( "Failure #8: allocating new table" );
   new_table->max_index = -1;
   table->links[ i ].next = new_table;
   new_table->lesser_context = lesser_context;
   return( new_table );
}


/*
 * This routine is called to increment the counts for the current
 * contexts. It is called after a character has been encoded or
 * decoded. All it does is call update_table for each of the
 * current contexts, which does the work of incrementing the count.
 * This particular version of update_model() practices update exclusion,
 * which means that if lower order models weren't used to encode
 * or decode the character, they don't get their counts updated.
 * This seems to improve compression performance quite a bit.
 * To disable update exclusion, the loop would be changed to run
 * from 0 to max_order, instead of current_order to max_order.
 */
void update_model( symbol )
int symbol;
{

   int i;
   int local_order;

   if ( current_order < 0 )
      local_order = 0;
   else
      local_order = current_order;
   if ( symbol >= 0 ) {
      while ( local_order <= max_order ) {
         if ( symbol >= 0 )
            update_table( contexts[ local_order ], symbol );
```

```
      local_order++;
    }
  }
  current_order = max_order;
  for ( i = 0 ; i < 256 ; i++ )
    scoreboard[ i ] = 0;
}

/*
* This routine is called to update the count for a particular symbol
* in a particular table. The table is one of the current contexts,
* and the symbol is the last symbol encoded or decoded. In principle
* this is a fairly simple routine, but a couple of complications make
* things a little messier. First of all, the given table may not
* already have the symbol defined in its statistics table. If it
* doesn't, the stats table has to grow and have the new guy added
* to it. Secondly, the symbols are kept in sorted order by count
* in the table so that the table can be trimmed during the flush
* operation. When this symbol is incremented, it might have to be moved
* up to reflect its new rank. Finally, since the counters are only
* bytes, if the count reaches 255, the table absolutely must be rescaled
* to get the counts back down to a reasonable level.
*/

void update_table( table, symbol )
CONTEXT *table;
int symbol;
{
   int i;
   int index;
   unsigned char temp;
   CONTEXT *temp_ptr;
   unsigned int new_size;
/*
* First, find the symbol in the appropriate context table. The first
* symbol in the table is the most active, so start there.
*/
```

```
    index = 0;
    while ( index <= table->max_index &&
          table->stats[index].symbol != (unsigned char) symbol )
        index++;
    if ( index > table->max_index ) {
      table->max_index++;
      new_size = sizeof( LINKS );
      new_size *= table->max_index + 1;
      if ( current_order < max_order ) {
        if ( table->max_index == 0 )
          table->links = (LINKS *) calloc( new_size, 1 );
        else
          table->links = (LINKS *)
              realloc( (char *) table->links, new_size );
        if ( table->links == NULL )
          fatal_error( "Error #9: reallocating table space!" );
        table->links[ index ].next = NULL;
      }
      new_size = sizeof( STATS );
      new_size *= table->max_index + 1;
      if (table->max_index==0)
        table->stats = (STATS *) calloc( new_size, 1 );
      else
        table->stats = (STATS *)
            realloc( (char *) table->stats, new_size );
      if ( table->stats == NULL )
        fatal_error( "Error #10: reallocating table space!" );
      table->stats[ index ].symbol = (unsigned char) symbol;
      table->stats[ index ].counts = 0;
    }
/*
* Now I move the symbol to the front of its list.
*/
    i = index;
    while ( i > 0 &&
      table->stats[ index ].counts == table->stats[ i-1 ].counts )
      i--;
```

```
  if ( i != index ) {
    temp = table->stats[ index ].symbol;
    table->stats[ index ].symbol = table->stats[ i ].symbol;
    table->stats[ i ].symbol = temp;
    if ( table->links != NULL ) {
      temp_ptr = table->links[ index ].next;
      table->links[ index ].next = table->links[ i ].next;
      table->links[ i ].next = temp_ptr;
    }
    index = i;
  }
/*
 * The switch has been performed, now I can update the counts
 */
  table->stats[ index ].counts++;
  if ( table->stats[ index ].counts == 255 )
    rescale_table( table ); }


/*
 * This routine is called when a given symbol needs to be encoded.
 * It is the job of this routine to find the symbol in the context
 * table associated with the current table, and return the low and
 * high counts associated with that symbol, as well as the scale.
 * Finding the table is simple. Unfortunately, once I find the table,
 * I have to build the table of cumulative counts, which is
 * expensive, and is done elsewhere. If the symbol is found in the
 * table, the appropriate counts are returned. If the symbols is
 * not found, the ESCAPE symbol probabilities are returned, and
 * the current order is reduced. Note also the kludge to support
 * the order -2 character set, which consists of negative numbers
 * instead of unsigned chars. This insures that no match will ever
 * be found for the EOF or FLUSH symbols in any "normal" table.
 */
int convert_int_to_symbol( c, s )
int c;
SYMBOL *s;
{
```

```
    int i;
    CONTEXT *table;

    table = contexts[ current_order ];
    totalize_table( table );
    s->scale = totals[ 0 ];
    if ( current_order == -2 )
      c = -c;
    for ( i = 0 ; i <= table->max_index ; i++ ) {
      if ( c == (int) table->stats[ i ].symbol ) {
        if ( table->stats[ i ].counts == 0 )
          break;
        s->low_count = totals[ i+2 ];
        s->high_count = totals[ i+1 ];
        return( 0 );
      }
    }
    s->low_count = totals[ 1 ];
    s->high_count = totals[ 0 ];
    current_order--;
    return( 1 );
}


/*
 * This routine is called when decoding an arithmetic number. In
 * order to decode the present symbol, the current scale in the
 * model must be determined. This requires looking up the current
 * table, then building the totals table. Once that is done, the
 * cumulative total table has the symbol scale at element 0.
 */

void get_symbol_scale( s )
SYMBOL *s;
{
    CONTEXT *table;

    table = contexts[ current_order ];
```

```
  totalize_table( table );
  s->scale = totals[ 0 ];
}


/*
 * This routine is called during decoding. It is given a count that
 * came out of the arithmetic decoder, and has to find the symbol that
 * matches the count. The cumulative totals are already stored in the
 * totals[] table, from the call to get_symbol_scale, so this routine
 * just has to look through that table. Once the match is found,
 * the appropriate character is returned to the caller. Two possible
 * complications. First, the character might be the ESCAPE character,
 * in which case the current_order has to be decremented. The other
 * complication is that the order might be -2, in which case we return
 * the negative of the symbol so it isn't confused with a normal
 * symbol.
 */
int convert_symbol_to_int( count, s )
int count;
SYMBOL *s;
{
    int c;
    CONTEXT *table;

    table = contexts[ current_order ];
    for ( c = 0; count < totals[ c ] ; c++ )
      ;
    s->high_count = totals[ c - 1 ];
    s->low_count = totals[ c ];
    if ( c == 1 ) {
      current_order--;
      return( ESCAPE );
    }
    if ( current_order < -1 )
      return( (int) -table->stats[ c-2 ].symbol );
    else
      return( table->stats[ c-2 ].symbol );
}
```

```
/*
 * After the model has been updated for a new character, this routine
 * is called to "shift" into the new context. For example, if the
 * last context was "ABC", and the symbol 'D' had just been processed,
 * this routine would want to update the context pointers to that
 * contexts[1]=="D", contexts[2]=="CD" and contexts[3]=="BCD". The
 * potential problem is that some of these tables may not exist.
 * The way this is handled is by the shift_to_next_context routine.
 * It is passed a pointer to the "ABC" context, along with the symbol
 * 'D', and its job is to return a pointer to "BCD". Once we have
 * "BCD", we can follow the lesser context pointers in order to get
 * the pointers to "CD" and "C". The hard work was done in
 * shift_to_context().
 */

void add_character_to_model( c )
int c;
{
    int i;
    if ( max_order < 0 || c < 0 )
      return;
    contexts[ max_order ] =
      shift_to_next_context( contexts[ max_order ], c, max_order );
    for ( i = max_order-1 ; i > 0 ; i-- )
      contexts[ i ] = contexts[ i+1 ]->lesser_context;
}

/*
 * This routine is called when adding a new character to the model. From
 * the previous example, if the current context was "ABC", and the new
 * symbol was 'D', this routine would get called with a pointer to
 * context table "ABC", and symbol 'D', with order max_order. What this
 * routine needs to do then is to find the context table "BCD". This
 * should be an easy job, and it is if the table already exists. All
 * we have to in that case is follow the back pointer from "ABC" to "BC".
 * We then search the link table of "BC" until we find the link to "D".
 * That link points to "BCD", and that value is then returned to the
```

```
 * caller. The problem crops up when "BC" doesn't have a pointer to
 * "BCD". This generally means that the "BCD" context has not appeared
 * yet. When this happens, it means a new table has to be created and
 * added to the "BC" table. That can be done with a single call to
 * the allocate_new_table routine. The only problem is that the
 * allocate_new_table routine wants to know what the lesser context for
 * the new table is going to be. In other words, when I create "BCD",
 * I need to know where "CD" is located. In order to find "CD", I
 * have to recursively call shift_to_next_context, passing it a pointer
 * to context "C" and the symbol 'D'. It then returns a pointer to
 * "CD", which I use to create the "BCD" table. The recursion is
 * guaranteed to end if it ever gets to order -1, because the null table
 * is guaranteed to have a link for every symbol to the order 0 table.
 * This is the most complicated part of the modeling program, but it is
 * necessary for performance reasons.
 */
CONTEXT *shift_to_next_context( table, c, order )
CONTEXT *table;
int c;
int order;
{
    int i;
    CONTEXT *new_lesser;
/*
 * First, try to find the new context by backing up to the lesser
 * context and searching its link table. If I find the link, we take
 * a quick and easy exit, returning the link. Note that there is a
 * special kludge for context order 0. We know for a fact that
 * the lesser context pointer at order 0 points to the null table,
 * order -1, and we know that the -1 table only has a single link
 * pointer, which points back to the order 0 table.
 */
    table = table->lesser_context;
    if ( order == 0 )
        return( table->links[ 0 ].next );
    for ( i = 0 ; i <= table->max_index ; i++ )
        if ( table->stats[ i ].symbol == (unsigned char) c )
```

```
        if ( table->links[ i ].next != NULL )
          return( table->links[ i ].next );
        else
          break;
/*
 * If I get here, it means the new context did not exist. I have to
 * create the new context, add a link to it here, and add the backwards
 * link to *his* previous context. Creating the table and adding it to
 * this table is pretty easy, but adding the back pointer isn't. Since
 * creating the new back pointer isn't easy, I duck my responsibility
 * and recurse to myself in order to pick it up.
 */
    new_lesser = shift_to_next_context( table, c, order-1 );
/*
 * Now that I have the back pointer for this table, I can make a call
 * to a utility to allocate the new table.
 */
    table = allocate_next_order_table( table, c, new_lesser );
    return( table );
}


/*
 * Rescaling the table needs to be done for one of three reasons.
 * First, if the maximum count for the table has exceeded 16383, it
 * means that arithmetic coding using 16 and 32 bit registers might
 * no longer work. Secondly, if an individual symbol count has
 * reached 255, it will no longer fit in a byte. Third, if the
 * current model isn't compressing well, the compressor program may
 * want to rescale all tables in order to give more weight to newer
 * statistics. All this routine does is divide each count by 2.
 * If any counts drop to 0, the counters can be removed from the
 * stats table, but only if this is a leaf context. Otherwise, we
 * might cut a link to a higher order table.
 */
```

```
void rescale_table( table )
CONTEXT *table;
{
    int i;

    if ( table->max_index == -1 )
        return;
    for ( i = 0 ; i <= table->max_index ; i++ )
        table->stats[ i ].counts /= 2;
    if ( table->stats[ table->max_index ].counts == 0 &&
        table->links == NULL ) {
        while ( table->stats[ table->max_index ].counts == 0 &&
            table->max_index >= 0 )
            table->max_index--;
        if ( table->max_index == -1 ) {
            free( (char *) table->stats );
            table->stats = NULL;
        } else {
            table->stats = (STATS *)
                realloc( (char *) table->stats,
                        sizeof( STATS ) * ( table->max_index + 1 ) );
            if ( table->stats == NULL )
                fatal_error( "Error #11: reallocating stats space!" );
        }
    }
}

/*
 * This routine has the job of creating a cumulative totals table for
 * a given context. The cumulative low and high for symbol c are going to
 * be stored in totals[c+2] and totals[c+1]. Locations 0 and 1 are
 * reserved for the special ESCAPE symbol. The ESCAPE symbol
 * count is calculated dynamically, and changes based on what the
 * current context looks like. Note also that this routine ignores
 * any counts for symbols that have already shown up in the scoreboard,
 * and it adds all new symbols found here to the scoreboard. This
 * allows us to exclude counts of symbols that have already appeared in
```

```
* higher order contexts, improving compression quite a bit.
*/
void totalize_table( table )
CONTEXT *table;
{
   int i;
   unsigned char max;

   for ( ; ; ) {
     max = 0;
     i = table->max_index + 2;
     totals[ i ] = 0;
     for ( ; i > 1 ; i- ) {
       totals[ i-1 ] = totals[ i ];
       if ( table->stats[ i-2 ].counts )
         if ( ( current_order == -2 ) ||
            scoreboard[ table->stats[ i-2 ].symbol ] == 0 )
            totals[ i-1 ] += table->stats[ i-2 ].counts;
       if ( table->stats[ i-2 ].counts > max )
         max = table->stats[ i-2 ].counts; }
/*
* Here is where the escape calculation needs to take place.
*/
     if ( max == 0 )
       totals[ 0 ] = 1;
     else {
       totals[ 0 ] = (short int) ( 256 - table->max_index );
       totals[ 0 ] *= table->max_index;
       totals[ 0 ] /= 256;
       totals[ 0 ] /= max;
       totals[ 0 ]++;
       totals[ 0 ] += totals[ 1 ];
     }
     if ( totals[ 0 ] < MAXIMUM_SCALE )
       break;
     rescale_table( table );
```

```
  }
  for ( i = 0 ; i < table->max_index ; i++ )
    if (table->stats[i].counts != 0)
      scoreboard[ table->stats[ i ].symbol ] = 1;
}

/*
 * This routine is called when the entire model is to be flushed.
 * This is done in an attempt to improve the compression ratio by
 * giving greater weight to upcoming statistics. This routine
 * starts at the given table, and recursively calls itself to
 * rescale every table in its list of links. The table itself
 * is then rescaled.
 */
void recursive_flush( table )
CONTEXT *table;
{
  int i;

  if ( table->links != NULL )
    for ( i = 0 ; i <= table->max_index ; i++ )
      if ( table->links[ i ].next != NULL )
        recursive_flush( table->links[ i ].next );
  rescale_table( table );
}

/*
 * This routine is called to flush the whole table, which it does
 * by calling the recursive flush routine starting at the order 0
 * table.
 */
void flush_model()
{
  putc( 'F', stdout );
  recursive_flush( contexts[ 0 ] );
}
```

```
/*
 * Everything from here down define the arithmetic coder section
 * of the program.
 */

/*
 * These four variables define the current state of the arithmetic
 * coder/decoder. They are assumed to be 16 bits long. Note that
 * by declaring them as short ints, they will actually be 16 bits
 * on most 80X86 and 680X0 machines, as well as VAXen.
 */
static unsigned short int code; /* The present input code value   */
static unsigned short int low;  /* Start of the current code range */
static unsigned short int high; /* End of the current code range   */
long underflow_bits;            /* Number of underflow bits pending */

/*
 * This routine must be called to initialize the encoding process.
 * The high register is initialized to all 1s, and it is assumed that
 * it has an infinite string of 1s to be shifted into the lower bit
 * positions when needed.
 */
void initialize_arithmetic_encoder()
{
    low = 0;
    high = 0xffff;
    underflow_bits = 0;
}

/*
 * At the end of the encoding process, there are still significant
 * bits left in the high and low registers. We output two bits,
 * plus as many underflow bits as are necessary.
 */
void flush_arithmetic_encoder( stream )
BIT_FILE *stream;
{
```

```
    OutputBit( stream, low & 0x4000 );
    underflow_bits++;
    while ( underflow_bits-- > 0 )
        OutputBit( stream, ~low & 0x4000 );
    OutputBits( stream, OL, 16 );
}


/*
 * This routine is called to encode a symbol. The symbol is passed
 * in the SYMBOL structure as a low count, a high count, and a range,
 * instead of the more conventional probability ranges. The encoding
 * process takes two steps. First, the values of high and low are
 * updated to take into account the range restriction created by the
 * new symbol. Then, as many bits as possible are shifted out to
 * the output stream. Finally, high and low are stable again and
 * the routine returns.
 */
void encode_symbol( stream, s )
BIT_FILE *stream;
SYMBOL *s;
{
    long range;
/*
 * These three lines rescale high and low for the new symbol.
 */
    range = (long) ( high-low ) + 1;
    high = low + (unsigned short int)
                ( ( range * s->high_count ) / s->scale - 1 );
    low = low + (unsigned short int)
                ( ( range * s->low_count ) / s->scale );
/*
 * This loop turns out new bits until high and low are far enough
 * apart to have stabilized.
 */
    for ( ; ; ) {
```

```
/*
 * If this test passes, it means that the MSDigits match, and can
 * be sent to the output stream.
 */
    if ( ( high & 0x8000 ) == ( low & 0x8000 ) ) {
      OutputBit( stream, high & 0x8000 );
      while ( underflow_bits > 0 ) {
        OutputBit( stream, ~high & 0x8000 );
        underflow_bits--;
      }
    }
/*
 * If this test passes, the numbers are in danger of underflow, because
 * the MSDigits don't match, and the 2nd digits are just one apart.
 */
    else if ( ( low & 0x4000 ) && !( high & 0x4000 )) {
      underflow_bits += 1;
      low &= 0x3fff;
      high |= 0x4000;
    } else
      return ;
    low <<= 1;
    high <<= 1;
    high |= 1;
  }
}


/*
 * When decoding, this routine is called to figure out which symbol
 * is presently waiting to be decoded. This routine expects to get
 * the current model scale in the s->scale parameter, and it returns
 * a count that corresponds to the present floating point code:
 *
 * code = count / s->scale
 */
short int get_current_count( s )
SYMBOL *s;
```

```
{
  long range;
  short int count;

  range = (long) ( high - low ) + 1;
  count = (short int)
        (((((long) ( code - low ) + 1 ) * s->scale-1 ) / range );
  return( count );
}


/*
 * This routine is called to initialize the state of the arithmetic
 * decoder. This involves initializing the high and low registers
 * to their conventional starting values, plus reading the first
 * 16 bits from the input stream into the code value.
 */
void initialize_arithmetic_decoder( stream )
BIT_FILE *stream;
{
  int i;

  code = 0;
  for ( i = 0 ; i < 16 ; i++ ) {
    code <<= 1;
    code += InputBit( stream );
  }
  low = 0;
  high = 0xffff;
}


/*
 * Just figuring out what the present symbol is doesn't remove
 * it from the input bit stream. After the character has been
 * decoded, this routine has to be called to remove it from the
 * input stream.
 */
```

```
void remove_symbol_from_stream( stream, s )
BIT_FILE *stream;
SYMBOL *s;
{
   long range;

/*
* First, the range is expanded to account for the symbol removal.
*/
    range = (long)( high - low ) + 1;
    high = low + (unsigned short int)
                ((  range * s->high_count ) / s->scale - 1 );
    low = low + (unsigned short int)
                (( range * s->low_count ) / s->scale );
/*
* Next, any possible bits are shipped out.
*/
   for ( ; ; ) {
/*
* If the MSDigits match, the bits will be shifted out.
*/
     if ( ( high & 0x8000 ) == ( low & 0x8000 ) ) {
     }
/*
* Else, if underflow is threatening, shift out the 2nd MSDigit.
*/
     else if ((low & 0x4000) == 0x4000  && (high & 0x4000) == 0 ) {
       code ^= 0x4000;
       low &= 0x3fff;
       high |= 0x4000;
     } else
```

```
/*
 * Otherwise, nothing can be shifted out, so I return.
 */
        return;
    low <<= 1;
    high <<= 1;
    high |= 1;
    code <<= 1;
    code += InputBit( stream );
  }
}
/*************************** End of ARITH-N.C ***************************/
```

CHAPTER 7

Dictionary-Based Compression

So far, the compression methods we have looked at used a statistical model to encode single symbols. They achieve compression by encoding symbols into bit strings that use fewer bits than the original symbols. The quality of the compression goes up or down depending on how good the program is at developing a model. The model not only has to accurately predict the probabilities of symbols, it also has to predict probabilities that deviate from the mean. More deviation achieves better compression.

But dictionary-based compression algorithms use a completely different method to compress data. This family of algorithms does not encode single symbols as variable-length bit strings; it encodes variable-length strings of symbols as single tokens. The tokens form an index to a phrase dictionary. If the tokens are smaller than the phrases they replace, compression occurs.

In many respects, dictionary-based compression is easier for people to understand. It represents a strategy that programmers are familiar with—using indexes into databases to retrieve large amounts of storage. In everyday life, we use phone numbers, Dewey Decimal numbers, and postal codes to encode larger strings of text. This is essentially what a dictionary-based encoder does.

An Example

A good example of how dictionary based compression works can be created by using a standard dictionary. For this example, I will use the *Random House Dictionary of the English Language, Second Edition, Unabridged.* Using this dictionary's system as a key for encoding messages, I can achieve a reasonable amount of compression. Using my proprietary scheme, the first eight words of the first sentence in this paragraph would read:

1/1 822/3 674/4 1343/60 928/75 550/32 173/46 421/2

This dictionary-based encoding scheme consists of a simple lookup table. The first number gives the page of the dictionary, and the second number tells the number of the word on that page. The dictionary has 2,200 pages with less than 256 entries on each page. Thus, 1/1 encodes the first word on the first page, which is "A." 822/3 encodes the third word on the 822nd page, which is "good."

To see how much space this scheme would save, look at the number of bits actually used to encode a word. Since a word can land on any of 2,200 pages, we need 12 bits to encode the page number. Each page has fewer than 256 entries, so the number of the entry will take just 8 bits to encode. This gives a total of 20 bits to encode any word in the dictionary, or 2.5 bytes per word.

The ASCII representation of the eight words in our encoded message takes 43 bytes. The encoded message takes 2.5 x 8 bytes, or 20 bytes. Thus, we compressed our text to 50 percent of its original size using dictionary encoding.

In theory, a different encoding method can probably improve on this. The dictionary has about 315,000 words. Shannon's formula for information content tells us that any one of the words in the dictionary can be encoded using just a little over eighteen bits. We used the page number/entry number scheme to make it easier to look up the encoded word, a general theme in dictionary-based compression.

Static vs. Adaptive

In general, dictionary-based compression replaces phrases with tokens. If the number of bits in the token is less than the number of bits in the phrase, compression will occur. But this definition of dictionary-based compression still leaves enormous room for variation. Consider, for example, the methods for building and maintaining a dictionary.

In some cases, it is advantageous to use a predefined dictionary to encode text. If the text to be encoded is a database containing all motor-vehicle registrations for Texas, we could develop a dictionary with only a few thousand entries that concentrated on words like "General Motors," "Smith," "Main," and "1977." Once this dictionary were compiled, it could be kept on-line and used by both the encoder and decoder as needed.

A dictionary like this is called a static dictionary. It is built up before compression occurs, and it does not change while the data is being compressed. It has advantages and disadvantages. One of the biggest advantages is that a static dictionary can be "tuned" to fit the data it is compressing. With the motor-vehicle registration database, for example, Huffman encoding could allocate fewer bits to strings such as "Ford" and more bits to "Yugo." Of course, we could use different bit strings depending on which field is being compressed.

Adaptive compression schemes can't tune their dictionaries in advance, which in principle would seem a major disadvantage. But static dictionary schemes have to deal with the problem of how to pass the dictionary from the encoder to the decoder. Chapters 3 and 5 showed that passing statistics along with compressed data can significantly harm compression, particularly on small files.

But this doesn't have to be a disadvantage in every case. In many situations, a static dictionary could remain the same over long periods of time and be kept on line, available to both the compressor and the decompressor. The motor-vehicle database dictionary could be calculated once, for example, then kept on hand. In the case of an exceptionally large amount of data, the compression ratio may not be significantly degraded if the dictionary is passed with the compressed text.

Adaptive Methods. At present, dictionary-based compression schemes using static dictionaries are mostly ad hoc, implementation dependent, and not general purpose. Most well-known dictionary algorithms are adaptive. Instead of having a completely defined dictionary when compression begins, adaptive schemes start out either with no dictionary or with a default baseline dictionary. As compression proceeds, the algorithms add new phrases to be used later as encoded tokens.

The basic principle behind adaptive dictionary programs is relatively easy to follow. Imagine a section of code that compressed text using an algorithm that looked something like this:

```
for ( ; ; ) {
   word = read_word( input_file );
   dictionary_index = look_up( word, dictionary );
   if ( dictionary_index < 0 ) {
      output( word, output_file );
      add_to_dictionary( word, dictionary );
   } else
      output( dictionary_index, output_file );
}
```

If the dictionary index used here could be encoded as an integer index into a table, we would achieve respectable compression with what is actually a very simple algorithm. This code is a specialized one set up to apply to written documents, but the principle behind it is similar to that behind many more sophisticated algorithms. It illustrates the basic components of an adaptive dictionary compression algorithm:

1. To parse the input text stream into fragments tested against the dictionary.
2. To test the input fragments against the dictionary; it may or may not be desirable to report on partial matches.
3. To add new phrases to the dictionary.
4. To encode dictionary indices and plain text so that they are distinguishable.

The corresponding decompression program has a slightly different set of requirements. It no longer has to parse the input text stream into fragments, and it doesn't have to test fragments against the dictionary. Instead, it has the following requirements: (1) to decode the input stream into either dictionary indices or plain text; (2) to add new phrases to the dictionary; (3) to convert dictionary indices into phrases; and (4) to output phrases as plain text. The ability to accomplish these tasks with relatively low costs in system resources made dictionary-based programs popular over the last ten years.

A Representative Example. Compressing data when sending it to magnetic tape has several nice side effects. First, it reduces the use of magnetic tape. Though magnetic tape is not particulary expensive, some applications make prodigous use of it. Second, the effective transfer rate to and from the tape is increased. Improvements in transfer speed through hardware are generally expensive, but compression through software is in a sense "free." Finally, in some cases, the overall CPU time involved may actually be reduced. If the CPU cost of writing a byte to magnetic tape is sufficiently high, writing half as many compressed bytes may save enough cycles to pay for the compression.

While the benefits of compressing data before sending it to magnetic tape have been clear, only sporadic methods were used until the late 1980s. In 1989, however, Stac Electronics successfully implemented a dictionary-based compression algorithm on a chip. This algorithm was quickly embraced as an industry standard and is now widely used by tape-drive manufacturers worldwide.

This compression method is generally referred to by the standard which defines it: QIC-122. (QIC refers to the Quarter Inch Cartridge industry group, a trade association of tape-drive manufacturers.) Stac Electronics is now attempting to expand the scope of this algorithm beyond tape drives to the hard disk market.

QIC-122 provides a good example of how a sliding-window, dictionary-based compression algorithm actually works. It is based on the LZ77 sliding-window concept. As symbols are read in by the encoder, they are added to the end of a 2K window that forms the phrase dictionary. To encode a symbol, the encoder checks to see if it is part of a phrase already in the dictionary. If it is, it creates a token that defines the location of the phrase and its length. If it is not, the symbol is passed through unencoded.

The output of a QIC-122 encoder consists of a stream of data, which, in turn, consists of tokens and symbols freely intermixed. Each token or symbol is prefixed by a single bit flag that indicates whether the following data is a dictionary reference or a plain symbol. The definitions for these two sequences are: (1) plaintext: <1> <eight-bit-symbol>; (2) dictionary reference: <0> <window-offset> <phrase-length>.

The QIC-122 encoder complicates things by further encoding the window-offset and phrase-length codes. Window offsets of less than 128 bytes are encoded in seven bits. Offsets between 128 bytes and 2,047 bytes are encoded in eleven bits. The phrase length uses a variable-bit coding scheme which favors short phrases over long. This explanation will gloss over these as "implementation details." The glossed-over version of the C code for this algorithm is shown here:

```
while ( !out_of_symbols ) {
    length = find_longest_match( &offset );
    if ( length > 1 ) {
        output_bit( 0 );
        output_bits( offset );
        output_bits( length );
        shift_input_buffer( length );
    } else {
        output_bit( 1 );
        output_byte( buffer[ 0 ] );
        shift_input_buffer( 1 );
    }
}
```

Following is an example of what this sliding window looks like when used to encode some C code, in this case the phrase "output_byte." The previously encoded text, which ends with the phrase "output_bit(1);\r," is at the end of the window. The find_longest_match routine will return a value of 8, since the first eight characters of "output_byte" match the first eight characters of "output_bit." The encoder will then output a 0 bit to indicate that a dictionary reference is following. Next it will output a 15 to indicate that the start of the phrase is fifteen characters back into the window ('\r' is a single symbol). Finally, it will output an 8 to indicate that there are eight matching symbols from the phrase.

```
output_bit(1);\r  output_byte(buffer[0]);
```

Figure 7-1. A sliding window used to encode some C code.

Using QIC-122 encoding, this will take exactly sixteen bits to encode, which means it encodes 8 bytes of data with only 2 bytes. This is clearly a respectable compression ratio, typical of how QIC-122 works under the best circumstances as shown here:

```
output_bit(1);\routput_b  yte(buffer[0]);
```

Figure 7-2. Encoding 8 bytes of data using only 2 bytes.

After the dictionary reference is output, the input stream shifts over eight characters, with the last symbol encoded becoming the last symbol in the window. The next three symbols will not match anything in the window, so they will have to be individually encoded.

This example of QIC-122 gives a brief look at how a dictionary-based compression scheme might work. Chapter 8 will take a more extensive look at LZ77 and its derivatives.

Israeli Roots

Dig beneath the surface of virtually any dictionary-based compression program, and you will find the work of Jacob Ziv and Abraham Lempel. For all practical purposes, these two Israeli researchers gave birth to this branch of information theory in the late 1970s.

Research in data compression up to 1977 included work on entropy, character and word frequencies, and various other facets of statistical modeling. There were minor forays into other esoteric areas of interest, such as finite state machines and linguistic models, but research went mainly into new and improved methodologies for driving Huffman coders.

All this changed in 1977 with the publication of Jacob Ziv's and Abraham Lempel's "A Universal Algorithm for Sequential Data Compression" in *IEEE Transactions on Information Theory*. This paper, with its 1978 sequel "Compression of Individual Sequences via Variable-Rate Coding," triggered a flood of dictionary-based compression research, algorithms, and programs.

The two compression techniques developed in these papers are called LZ77 and LZ78 (the transposition of the author's initials is apparently an innocent historical accident, but one that is here to stay). LZ77 is a "sliding window" technique in which the dictionary consists of a set of fixed-length phrases found in a "window" into the previously processed text. The size of the window is generally somewhere between 2K and 16K bytes, with the maximum phrase length ranging from perhaps 16 to 64 bytes. LZ78 takes a completely different approach to building a dictionary. Instead of using fixed-length phrases from a window into the text, LZ78 builds phrases up one symbol at a time, adding a new symbol to an existing phrase when a match occurs.

It is easy to think that these two compression methods are closely related, particularly since people will casually speak of "Lempel Ziv Compression" as if it were just one thing. These are, however, two very different techniques. They have different implementation problems and solutions, different strengths and weaknesses. Since they have had such a large impact on the world of data compression, the next two chapters of this book will take a detailed look at an LZ77 and an LZ78 implementation.

History. While the publication of the two papers in 1977 and 1978 may have had an immediate impact in the world of information theory, it was some time before programmers noticed the effects. In fact, it took the publication of another paper in 1984 to really get things moving.

The June 1984 issue of *IEEE Computer* had an article entitled "A Technique for High-Performance Data Compression" by Terry Welch. Welch described work performed at Sperry Research Center (now part of Unisys). His paper was a practical description of his implementation of the LZ78 algorithm, which he called LZW. It discussed the LZW compression algorithm in reference to its possible use in disk and tape-drive controllers, but it was clear that the same algorithm could easily be built into a general-purpose compression program.

Almost immediately after the article appeared, work began on the Unix Compress program. Compress is a C program developed initially on the DEC's VAX. Ports to other machines, including the IBM PC, followed shortly. The public release of Compress became available almost exactly a year after the publication of the IEEE article.

Compress was a very influential program for a number of reasons. The program was well written. It performed well, and it had a reasonable level of documentation. Many UNIX installations began actively using Compress soon after its release. Manual pages distributed with UNIX systems are now routinely shipped in compressed form, and they are not decompressed until accessed for the first time by the man program. The code was in the public domain from its initial release, which made for wide distribution and study. Perhaps most importantly, the authors went out of their way to ensure that the code was portable so that it could be used on a wide variety of systems with no modifications.

While Compress was becoming a standard in the UNIX community, desktop software was still struggling along with a rather inefficient order-0 Huffman coding program known as SQ. But in 1985, desktop power was increasing; more and more people were using modems to communicate; and hard-disk space was still relatively expensive. Conditions were ripe for an improvement in compression, and dictionary-based coding stepped in.

ARC: The Father of MS-DOS Dictionary Compression

In 1985, System Enhancement Associates released a general-purpose compression and cataloging program called ARC. ARC quickly took the MS-DOS desktop world by storm, becoming a de facto standard for PC users in a matter of months. Several factors helped ARC gain this position. First, it ordinarily used a close derivative of Compress to compress files. At the time, this provided state-of-the-art compression and was essentially without peer. Second, ARC provided a cataloging or archiving function as an integral part of the program. UNIX users were accustomed to using the "tar" program to combine groups of files into a single archive, but PC users did not have a similar function as part of their operating system. ARC added that capability, vital for transferring groups of files by modem or even floppy diskette. Finally, ARC was distributed as shareware, which helped saturate the user base in a short time.

With Compress reigning supreme in the UNIX world and ARC ruling the MS-DOS world, it seemed LZ78 would be the dominant compression method for years. Imitators such as PKWare's PKARC only strengthened LZ78's hold by providing performance improvements in both speed and compression ratios. But oddly enough, in recent years the field has taken a step back.

ARC lost its dominance of the desktop world to new contenders, most notably PKZIP, by PKWare; but also LHarc, by Haruyasu Yoshizaki; and ARJ, by Robert Jung. These programs are built on an LZ77 algorithm which uses a dictionary based on a sliding window that moves through the text. LZ77 was not a practical algorithm to implement until refinements were made in the mid 1980s. Now LZ77 has a legitimate position alongside LZ78 as co-ruler of the general-purpose compression world.

Dictionary Compression: Where It Shows Up. Dictionary-based compression has found more and more homes in the last ten years as both hardware and software improvements make it practical. We can subdivide applications for dictionary-based compression into two areas: general-purpose programs and hardware-specific code.

As shown, dictionary-based coding took over desktop general-purpose compression. In the MS-DOS world, programs such as PKZIP, ARC, ARJ, and LHarc all use dictionary-based algorithms to compress and archive files in a general-purpose manner. Most of these programs have ports to at least one or two other platforms, UNIX being the most popular.

Dictionary-based compression is also used in some special-purpose desktop programs. Most backup programs, for example, use some form of compression to make their operation faster and more efficient. PC Backup, by Central Point Software, uses a dictionary-based algorithm from Stac Electronics, the company that produced the QIC-122 compression standard.

Compuserve Information Service developed a dictionary-based compression scheme used to encode bit-mapped graphical images. The GIF format uses an LZW variant to compress repeated sequences in screen images. Compression is clearly needed when using these type of images. Computer images take up lots of storage space. As video resolutions improve, the size of the saved images grows dramatically. Compuserve users also typically use modems to upload or download these images. When confined to a maximum of 2,400 baud, compressing images becomes even more crucial.

Compressing files before transmitting them saves telecommunications bandwidth. But this requires compatible compression software on both ends. An even more effective method of utililizing bandwidth would be to build data compression directly into the modem. Microcom Corp. originally developed this idea, which used Huffman coding to compress data before it was transmitted by its modems. Microcom's compression algorithm, MNP-5, uses a dynamic Huffman coding scheme that performs well as a general-purpose compressor on most data streams.

But the international telecommunications industry has recently ratified and is rapidly adopting a new compression algorithm used by modem manufacturers: V.42*bis*, a dictionary-based compression scheme which offers better compression ratios than MNP-5. With the adoption of an international standard, modem builders can now implement data compression in their modems and have confidence that they will pass this data on to modems from other manufacturers.

As mentioned previously, tape drive manufacturers are also rapidly adopting an industry-standard compression algorithm: QIC-122. QIC-122 is generally implemented on the tape drive itself or on the tape controller using a dedicated microcontroller or the Stac Electronics compression engine chip. Hewlett-Packard has proposed an alternative compression standard known as DCLZ. DCLZ uses an LZ78-type algorithm, which supposedly offers better compression performance than programs based on QIC-122.

The hard disk is a new frontier being tackled using dictionary-based compression. At present, general-purpose programs are frequently used to compress data stored on a hard disk. But no popular disk drives or controllers compress data transparently to the host computer. Several MS-DOS software companies are working at the device driver level to make compression transparent to the application program. Some operating-system implications, however, still make it difficult to implement compression on random-access devices.

One of the primary difficulties with compressing data on the hard disk is that most of today's dictionary schemes are adaptive. A general-purpose algorithm would be needed to operate on a disk drive or controller, making a static dictionary difficult to implement. Most adaptive algorithms do not perform very well until they have built up some statistical information, which may take several K of input data.

Unfortunately, disk drives are used in a random-access mode, which means a program can begin reading data at any point in the file. If the file were compressed using a conventional adaptive method, we might have to go back to the start and begin reading there in order to properly decompress the file. This may not be much of a problem in a 16 Kbyte text file, but imagine the performance problems in a 16-Mbyte database!

At present, manufactures of software- and hardware-based disk compression drivers avoid these problems by compressing at the sector level. Since the device driver typically reads in a sector or more at a time, the adaptive algorithm will restart at the begining of each sector boundary. Even better, if the device driver controls the size of the sector, it can be set to a somewhat larger value than might normally be used, giving the adaptive algorithm a chance to improve its compression.

With algorithms such as QIC-122, increasing the sector size past a certain point will not likely improve matters, since the dictionary is only composed of the previous 2K bytes of data. But more powerful compression algorithms that take advantage of older information will frequently want to increase the sector size.

Danger Ahead—Patents

The fact that most work on dictionary-based compression has been done over the last ten or fifteen years has a potentially dangerous side effect. Till the early 1980s, it was generally not possible to patent software. But during the past ten years, increasingly large numbers of patents were awarded for what are clearly algorithms.

One of the first data-compression patents was granted to Sperry Corp. (now Unisys) for the improvements to LZ78 developed by Terry Welch at the Sperry Research Center. In fact, this patent became a point of contention during the standardization process for the V.42*bis* data-communications standard. Since V.42*bis* is based on the LZW algorithm, Unisys claimed the right to collect royalties on implementations which use V.42*bis*. There was some concern in the CCITT about the effect of basing a standard on a patented technique. Unisys dampened concern while protecting its patent rights by publicly offering to license the algorithm to any modem manufacturer for a onetime $25,000 fee.

As research in dictionary-based compression continues, patents are being filed at a relatively rapid pace. Since patent filings are not a matter of public record, it is not possible to know if and when certain techniques will be freely available. At present, the most prudent course for potential data-compression users would be to conduct a patent search and to contact the inventors of any techniques they intend to use.

Fortunately, manufacturers can generally come to terms on patent royalties for relatively modest terms. The danger comes when the owner of the patent is competing for the same market as a potential licensee. Unisys was only too happy to license the LZW algorithm to modem manufacturers, for example, but it may have adopted an entirely different strategy if the market being discussed was that of mid-sized minicomputers.

Conclusion

Dictionary-based compression techniques are presently the most popular forms of compression in the lossless arena. Almost without exception, these techniques can trace their origins back to the original work published by Ziv and Lempel in 1977 and 1978. Refinements on these algorithms yield better performance at lower cost, but both types of improvements are evolutionary, not revolutionary.

CHAPTER 8

Sliding Window Compression

The genesis of modern dictionary-based compression can be traced to the 1977 Ziv and Lempel paper, "A Universal Algorithm for Sequential Data Compression," published in *IEEE Transactions on Information Theory*. In retrospect, this algorithm (referred to hereafter as LZ77) does not seem particularly remarkable. It is simple enough that it could have easily been described thirty or forty years earlier, and there is no doubt that it could have been implemented at least as a "proof of principle" program well before 1977.

However, as was discussed in the previous chapter, till the late 1970s most data compression work concentrated on improved ways to drive Huffman coders and perhaps on more exotic studies of digrams or other statistical topics. So the LZ77 paper truly broke new ground.

The Algorithm

LZ77 compression uses previously seen text as a dictionary. It replaces phrases in the input text with pointers into the dictionary to achieve compression. The amount of compression depends on how long the dictionary phrases are, how large the window into previously seen text is, and the entropy of the source text with respect to the LZ77 model.

The main data structure in LZ77 is a text window, divided into two parts. The first consists of a large block of recently decoded text. The second, normally much smaller, is a look-ahead buffer. The look-ahead buffer has characters read in from the input stream but not yet encoded.

The normal size of the text window is several thousand characters. The look-ahead buffer is generally much smaller, maybe ten to one hundred characters. The algorithm tries to match the contents of the look-ahead buffer to a string in the dictionary. A simplistic example of a text window is shown in figure 8-1.

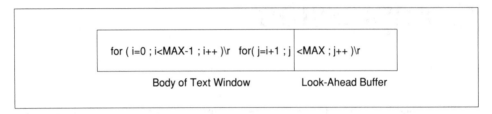

Body of Text Window   Look-Ahead Buffer

Figure 8-1. A text window in use.

Figure 8-1 shows a snippet of C code being compressed. The text window has a total width of 64 characters, with 16 of those characters used by the look-ahead buffer. The LZ77 algorithm, as originally conceived, issued sequences of tokens. Each token consisted of three different data items which defined a phrase of variable length in the current look-ahead buffer. The three items in the token are: (1) an offset to a phrase in the text window; (2) the length of the phrase; and (3) the first symbol in the look-ahead buffer that follows the phrase.

In the above example, the look-ahead buffer contains the phrase "<MAX ; j++)\r. " By searching through the buffer, we find that "<MAX" is located at position 14 in the text window. It matches the look-ahead buffer for the first four symbols. The first symbol not present in the look-ahead buffer is the space character. So this token is encoded as: 14, 4, ''.

The compression program that implements the LZ77 algorithm first emits the token, then shifts the text window over by five characters, which is the width of the phrase just encoded. Five new symbols are then read into the look-ahead buffer, and the process repeats.

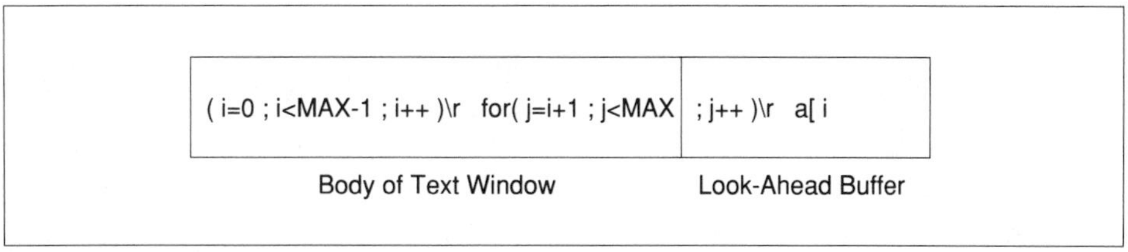

(i=0 ; i<MAX-1 ; i++)\r for(j=i+1 ; j<MAX	; j++)\r a[i
Body of Text Window	Look-Ahead Buffer

Figure 8-2. The window after encoding 14, 4, ' '

The next token issued by the compression algorithm would encode the phrase "; j+" as "40, 2, '+' ." The syntax of this token allows for phrases that have no match of any length in the window. If the look-ahead buffer shown above had no match, for example, it could be encoded a single character at a time using a phrase length of zero: "0, 0, ';' ." This method is not efficient, but it ensures that the algorithm can encode any message.

The code to implement this compression algorithm should be fairly simple. It merely has to look through the entire text window for the longest match, encode it, then shift. A brute force application of this algorithm might look something like this:

```
int window_cmp( char *w, int i, int j, int length )
{
    int count = 0;

    while ( length-- ) {
        if ( w[ i++ ] == w[ j++ ] )
            count++;
        else
            return( count );
    }
    return( count );
}




    .

    .

    .

    match_position = 0;
```

```
match_length = 0;
for ( i = 0 ; i < ( WINDOW_SIZE - LOOK_AHEAD_SIZE ); i++ ) {
   length = window_cmp( window, i, LOOK_AHEAD, LOOK_AHEAD_SIZE );
   if ( length > match_length ) {
     match_position = i;
     match_length = length;
   }
}
encode( match_position, match_length,
                       window[ LOOK_AHEAD+match_length ] );
memmove( window, window+match_length+1, WINDOW_SIZE - match_length );
for ( i = 0 ; i < match_length+1 ; i++ )
   window[ WINDOW_SIZE - match_length + i ] = getc( input );

     .
     .
     .
```

The decompression algorithm for LZ77 is even simpler, since it doesn't have to do comparisons. It reads in a token, outputs the indicated phrase, outputs the following character, shifts, and repeats. It maintains the window, but it does not work with string comparisons. A decompression program that used the output of the previous program might have a loop like this:

```
decode( &match_position, &match_length, &character );
fwrite( window+match_position, 1, match_length, output );
putc( character, output );
for ( i = 0 ; i < match_length ; i++ )
   window[ LOOK_AHEAD+i ] = window[ match_position+i ];
window[ LOOK_AHEAD+i ] = character;
memmove( window, window+match_length+1, WINDOW_SIZE - match_length );
```

One interesting side effect of this decompression method is that it can use phrases that have not yet been encoded to encode existing phrases. In a file that had one hundred consecutive 'A' characters, for example, we would encode the first A as (0, 0, 'A'). Our window would then look like that shown in figure 8-3.

Figure 8-3. Coding for one hundred consecutive A characters.

We could then encode the next nine A characters as (38, 9, 'A'). It may seem odd to use a nine-character phrase here. Though we can see the eight characters in the phrase presently in the look-ahead buffer, the decoder won't be able to. When the decoder receives the (38, 9, 'A') token, its buffer will look like figure 8-4.

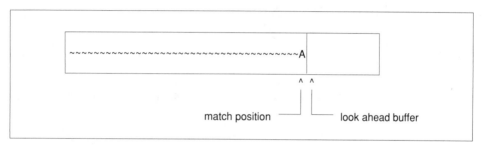

Figure 8-4 The buffer for the decoder when it receives the (38, 9, 'A') token.

But by examining the decompression algorithm, you can see how the decompression routine manages this trick. It sits in a loop, copying from the match position to the look-ahead buffer. After the first character has been copied, the buffer looks like figure 8-5.

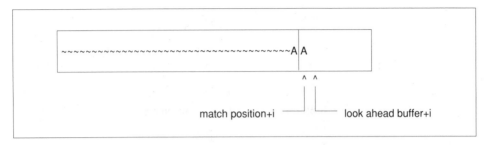

8-5. What the buffer looks like after it copies the first character.

The next time through the loop the second A character will be available to be copied though it was not in the window when the decoding started. After the entire copy is complete, along with the single character store, the buffer is ready to shift, as shown in figure 8-6.

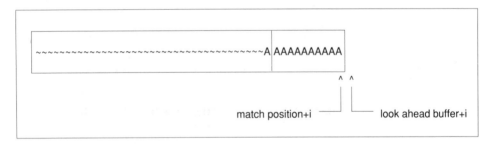

8-6. The buffer, when ready to shift.

This illustrates a powerful feature of LZ77 compression: rapid adaptation to the character of the input stream. In this example, it encoded a sequence of ten characters when its "dictionary" had only been loaded with a single character.

Problems with LZ77. The implementation of LZ77 shown here is deliberately crude. It also has to be considered a somewhat liberal interpretation of the algorithm. The authors presented little discussion of implementation details when they presented their method.

There is clearly a major performance bottleneck in the LZ77 approach. When encoding, it has to perform string comparisons against the look-ahead buffer for every position in the text window. As it tries to improve compression performance by increasing the size of the window, and thus the dictionary, this performance bottleneck only gets worse. On the bright side, however, the decompression portion of this algorithm does not have to suffer through this bottleneck. Since it only copies the phrases, it can operate at a much higher rate. Even better, the LZ77 decompressor will not be severely affected by increases in either the size of the text window or the look-ahead buffer.

A second performance problem occurs with the way the sliding window is managed. For conceptual convenience, the discussion here treated the sliding window as though it were truly sliding "across" the text, progressing from the end of the buffer to the front as the encoding process was executed.

This may be conceptually superior, but it is certainly not the best way to code an LZ77 program. In fact, it is much better to have a sliding index or pointer into a fixed buffer. Instead of moving the phrases toward the front of the window, a sliding pointer would keep the text in the same place in the window and move the start and end pointers along the buffer as text is encoded.

Using sliding pointers does create a few problems. For one, we can't use a straightforward string-compare function like strncmp() to look for longest phrases because a phrase may land across the end of the physical window, with the first character at window[WINDOW_SIZE - 1] and the second at window[0]. This means that as we do string comparisons we need to use a modulo index into the window instead of a normal index. A recoded version of strncmp() that would work properly under these revised circumstances might look like this:

```
int window_cmp( char *w, int i, int j, int length )
{
  int count = 0;

  while ( length- ) {
    if ( w[ i ] == w[ j ] )
      count++;
```

```
    else
      return( count );
    i = ++i % WINDOW_SIZE;
    j = ++j % WINDOW_SIZE;
  }
  return( count );
}
```

This routine is slightly more complicated, but it will pay for itself in savings on calls to memmove(). Keeping the buffer in one place is a big savings in CPU cycles. In addition, the routine can be made even more efficient if WINDOW_SIZE is an integral power of 2. The modulus operator can then be replaced by a logical, saving even more time.

An Encoding Problem. Besides the CPU cost problems, the LZ77 algorithm has a major efficiency problem. When encoding phrases, LZ77 achieves good compression rapidly. Even if the phrases being substituted for input text are short, they will still generally cause very effective compression to take place.

The problem occurs when matching phrases are not found in the dictionary. When this is the case, the compression program still has to use the same three component tokens to encode a single character. To realize the cost of this, imagine encoding a single character when using a 4,096-byte window and a sixteen-byte look-ahead buffer. This would take twelve bits to encode a window position and another four bits to encode a phrase length. Using this system, encoding the (0, 0, c) token would take twenty-four bits, all to encode a single eight-bit symbol. This is a very high price to pay, and there ought to be a way to improve it.

LZSS Compression

LZSS compression seeks to avoid some of the bottlenecks and performance problems in the original LZ77 algorithm. It makes two major changes to the way the algorithm works. The first is in the way the text window is maintained. Under LZ77, the phrases in the text window were stored as a single contiguous block of text, with no other organization on top of it. LZSS still stores text in contiguous windows, but it creates an additional data structure that improves on the organization of the phrases.

As each phrase passes out of the look-ahead buffer and into the encoded portion of the text windows, LZSS adds the phrase to a tree structure. In the implementation that will be used in this chapter, the tree is a binary search tree. By sorting the phrases into a tree such as this, the time required to find the longest matching phrase in the tree will no longer be proportional to the product of the window size and the phrase length. Instead, it will be proportional to the base 2 logarithm of the window size multiplied by the phrase length.

The savings created by using the tree not only makes the compression side of the algorithm much more efficient, it also encourages experimentation with longer window sizes. Doubling the size of the text window now might only cause a small increase in the compression time, whereas before it would have doubled it.

The second change lies in the actual tokens output by the compression algorithm. Recall that LZ77 output tokens consisted of a phrase offset, a match length, and the character that followed the phrase. This meant that LZ77 was compelled to alternate pointers with plain characters, regardless of the nature of the input text.

LZSS instead allows pointers and characters to be freely intermixed. When first starting up, for example, the compression algorithm may not find any phrase matches to output for the first dozen or so input symbols. Under the LZ77 system, the encoder would still have to output a dummy match position with a length of zero for every symbol it output.

LZSS instead uses a single bit as a prefix to every output token to indicate whether it is an offset/length pair or a single symbol for output. When outputting several consecutive single characters, this method reduces the overhead from possibly several bytes per character down to a single byte per character.

Once the data is well characterized, the compressor may efficiently match up pointers every time it loads new data into the look-ahead buffer. LZ77 had some inefficiency here as well, since every offset/length pair had to be accompanied by a single character. This is not as bad as the previous type of inefficiency, but it still reduces the compression ratio.

Data Structures. Two important data structures are used in the implementation of LZSS shown in this chapter. They are the text window, which contains the previously encoded text buffer and the look-ahead buffer. The text buffer is a simple character buffer declared and used as might normally be expected in a C program:

```
unsigned char window[ WINDOW_SIZE ];
```

As discussed previously, while the idea of a sliding window might imply that the text should "slide" through the window, this would actually be an inefficient way to implement it. Instead, the look-ahead buffer moves through the array and tracks its index as it goes along. This means that once a phrase is stored in the array, it stays there until it is overwritten after WINDOW_SIZE characters have been encoded.

This method of working with the text window also means that all string operations, copies, etc. performed on the window have to be done using modulo WINDOW_SIZE arithmetic. Computing (i + 1) mod WINDOW_SIZE is usually done most efficiently if WINDOW_SIZE is an integral power of 2, and this implementation of LZSS expects that to be the case. Having WINDOW_SIZE an integral power of 2 also leads to the most efficient way of encoding the window indices, so this is almost always the method used in sliding-window data compression.

The second data structure in this program is the binary tree used to store the phrases currently in the text window. The tree is defined by the tree structure shown here:

```
struct {
   int parent;
   int smaller_child;
   int larger_child;
} tree[ WINDOW_SIZE + 1 ];
```

For every phrase in the window, a corresponding structure element defines the position that phrase occupies in the tree. Each phrase has a parent and up to two children. Since this is a binary tree, the two child nodes are defined as "smaller" and "larger" children. Every phrase that resides under the smaller_child node must be smaller than the phrase defined by the current node, and every phrase under the larger_child node must be larger. The terms "larger" and "smaller" refer to where the phrases fall in the collating sequence used by the compression program. In this particular program, one phrase is "larger" or "smaller" in the same sense as that used by the standard library strcmp() function.

The tree used in this program has a couple of unusual features that need to be explained. First, though only WINDOW_SIZE phrases are in the window, we have defined the tree to have WINDOW_SIZE + 1 elements. In the implementation used here, tree[WINDOW_SIZE] is the special node used to locate the tree's root. This element doesn't have a phrase of its own, as do all other nodes in the tree. It also doesn't have smaller and greater children like the other nodes. Instead, it has the index of a larger_child only, and this index points to the root node of the tree.

Pointing to the root node in this fashion saves processing time and simplifies the code. When working our way up through the tree during an insertion or deletion, therefore, we don't have to check to see if a parent node points to the root or to another node. Instead, we can assume that a node's parent node is always a valid tree element. When deleting node i from the tree, for example, you will typically have a section of code that looks something like this: tree[tree[i].parent].child = tree[i].child. Because the pointer to the root node is stored in the same tree, we don't have to perform any special checks to see if i is the root node. Even if i is the root node, tree[i].parent still points to a valid node in the tree.

The second unusual feature is the use of another node for special purposes. Like the other programs in this book, LZSS uses a special code to indicate when the end of the compressed data is reached. In this case, a window index of zero indicates an end-of-stream condition.

Since index 0 has a special purpose, it can never be used as a valid phrase. So the code to insert a new phrase into the tree automatically returns without even trying to insert the phrase at index 0. Since phrase 0 is not used, we can achieve even more code savings by using node 0 as the special UNUSED index. This becomes useful when writing code to maintain the tree. A typical operation performed when deleting node i from the tree, for example, is to reassign a new parent node to i's children. Code to perform this might look like what follows.

```
if ( tree[ i ].smaller_child != UNUSED )
  tree[ tree[ i ].smaller_child ].parent = tree[ i ].parent;
if ( tree[ i ].larger_child != UNUSED )
  tree[ tree[ i ].larger_child ].parent = tree[ i ].parent;
```

But if the UNUSED index actually points to a legitimate storage area, the test for validity can be bypassed, with the resulting code looking like the following:

```
tree[ tree[ i ].smaller_child ].parent = tree[ i ].parent;
tree[ tree[ i ].larger_child ].parent = tree[ i ].parent;
```

If either of the children in this example are UNUSED, no harm is done—the parent node for tree[0] will merely be modified. Since tree[0] is never used for any tree navigation, no harm is done, and significant CPU time is saved during tree updates.

A Balancing Act. Saving phrases in a binary tree can simplify the search for the best match. But a binary tree can deteriorate when given data that is ordered in some fashion. In the worst case, a binary tree can turn into nothing more than a linked list. Imagine a file that had the string "ABCDEFGHIJKLMNOP" in it. Since the phrases in that string would have to be added to the tree in order, the structure in figure 9-7 would evolve.

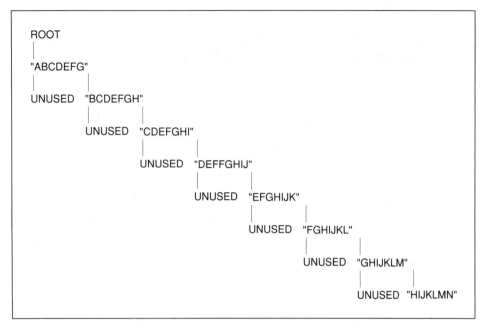

Figure 8-7. The structure that would evolve from the sequence "ABCDEFGHIJKLMNOP."

This structure may have a pleasing pattern, but it is not well built for locating strings. Given that data compressed from computer files will frequently have patterns of increasing or decreasing phrases, what can we do to avoid this problem?

Of course we can do a lot to help maintain a balanced tree. Many well-known algorithms are built expressly to keep nicely built trees from turning into cycle-stealing unbalanced lists.

In the case of sliding-window data compression, however, it is relatively safe to ignore the problem. Severely unbalanced trees may develop as data is compressed, but the nature of the sliding window almost mandates that unbalanced situations quickly converge to more balanced states. Since old phrases are pulled out of the tree as rapidly as new ones are put in, the effects of an ordered sequence quickly disappear.

As a result, tree balancing is usually not built into sliding-window programs. Probably the only time it would be considered would be in a production version of a compression program that was under severe constraints in terms of CPU cost allowed per byte compressed.

Greedy vs. Best Possible. Both LZ77 and LZSS are called "greedy" algorithms: They don't look ahead into the input stream to analyze it for the best combination of indices and characters. Consider a dictionary-based encoding scheme that used nine bits to encode a single character and twenty-five bits to encode a combined index/offset pair. This scheme would have a break-even point somewhere between two and three characters, which means it would encode a match of two characters as two individual symbols and a match of three symbols as an index/offset token.

Consider now how we would go about encoding the phrase "Go To Statement Considered Harmful" if the contents of the phrase dictionary contained the following fragments: "Go T" "o S" "tat" " Stat." A greedy encoder would naturally encode the "Go T" phrase of four characters length first, followed by the "o S" phrase of three characters length, then the "tat" phrase of three characters length. The output of the encoder up to this point would look like this:

Offset/Length of "Go T"	:	25 bits
Offset/Length of "o S"	:	25 bits
Offset/Length of "tat"	:	25 bits
		———————
		75 bits

The encoder looks like it was doing what makes sense, trying to build phrases up instead of characters. But an optimal encoder would encode the fragment as shown:

Offset/Length of "Go "	:	25 bits
Character	'T' :	9 bits
Character	'o' :	9 bits
Offset/Length of " Stat"	:	25 bits
		———————
		68 bits

These figures clearly show that the greedy encoder did not do as well as the optimal encoder. But it should also be noted that even in this contrived example, the difference between the two is only about 10 percent. When using dictionary coding, it is difficult to find examples of optimal encoders outperforming greedy encoders by more than a few percent. The largest differences occur when only short phrases are in the dictionary, and there is a real possibility that encoding single symbols will take less space than a phrase.

The problem with optimal coding is simply one of payback. Implementing an optimal encoder generally means that encoding speed will be drastically reduced. While optimizing algorithms are available, they tend to be CPU intensive, and the profit derived is generally small. In the world of data compression, a few good heuristics are often more respected than a provably superior algorithm. The greedy heuristic in this case is definitely the choice of most compression programmers.

The Code

The C implementation of LZSS shown here is relatively simple. A production program would probably want to take advantage of numerous potential improvements, which will be discussed at the end of the chapter.

By the very nature of LZSS compression, the compression program will be considerably more complicated than the decoder. The decoder does not have to worry about maintaining the tree or searching for matches. Those two activities are what the encoder spends most of its time doing.

Constants and Macros. All of the constants and global data used in this program are shown following. The parameters of the text window are initially defined by deciding how many bits to allocate to the two fields used to define a pointer or index into the text window. In this example, INDEX_BIT_COUNT is set to twelve: It will use twelve bits to define an index into the text window. The LENGTH_BIT_COUNT macro is set to four bits, which means it will use a four-bit field to encode the length of a matching phrase.

After determining the size of the two bit fields, other macros can be given values derived from them. First, the WINDOW_SIZE is directly determined by the size of the INDEX_BIT_COUNT. In this case, our text window will consist of 4,096 bytes, or 1 << 12. Since we have allocated four bits for the length parameter used to encode a phrase, we will be able to encode a length of up to sixteen bits, or 1 << 4. This is defined as the RAW_LOOK_AHEAD_SIZE.

The next macro defined, BREAK_EVEN, determines whether it is better to encode a phrase as an index/length pair or as single characters. In this program, the BREAK_EVEN point is determined by adding up the INDEX_BIT_COUNT and the LENGTH_BIT_COUNT plus 1. These add up to seventeen: it takes seventeen bits to encode an index/length pair. Because of this, we set our BREAK_EVEN point to one character. This means that in the program, any matching phrase that is one character or fewer will be encoded as single characters instead of as a phrase.

```
#define INDEX_BIT_COUNT      12
#define LENGTH_BIT_COUNT     4
#define WINDOW_SIZE          ( 1 << INDEX_BIT_COUNT )
#define RAW_LOOK_AHEAD_SIZE( 1 << LENGTH_BIT_COUNT )
#define BREAK_EVEN     ( ( 1 + INDEX_BIT_COUNT + LENGTH_BIT_COUNT ) / 9 )
#define LOOK_AHEAD_SIZE      ( RAW_LOOK_AHEAD_SIZE + BREAK_EVEN )
#define TREE_ROOT            WINDOW_SIZE
#define END_OF_STREAM        0
#define UNUSED               0
#define MOD_WINDOW( a )      ( ( a ) & ( WINDOW_SIZE - 1 ) )
```

The BREAK_EVEN point adjusts our LOOK_AHEAD_SIZE. Since we aren't going to code any phrases with lengths 0 or 1, we can adjust our LOOK_AHEAD_SIZE upward by two. So when we want to encode a phrase length, instead of outputting the length, we output the length - BREAK_EVEN - 1. This means that the length numbers 0 through 15 will actually correspond to phrases of length 2 through 17.

The TREE_ROOT macro defines the node that points to the binary tree root. Since TREE_ROOT is defined as index WINDOW_SIZE, it is a special node that actually lies outside the binary tree. Whenever the program searches the binary tree, it looks at the child of the node at TREE_ROOT to find the root of the tree.

The END_OF_STREAM constant defines the special index used to place an end-of-file indicator in the output stream. In this implementation, END_OF_STREAM is set to zero, specifically because the UNUSED node index is also set to zero. Having the UNUSED node index set to zero leads to a slight improvement in the program's performance. By using static initialization or by creating the tree with calloc(), we will automatically have a tree with every node pointer set to UNUSED—which means we don't have to have a specific initialization step.

The final macro used in the program is MOD_WINDOW. Since input strings can wrap around the end of the tree and head back to the front, we need to perform all of our arithmetic on window indices modulo the tree size. The MOD_WINDOW macro provides a convenient way to do that.

Global Variables. The data structures that hold both the text window and the binary tree are defined as global variables in this program. They could just as easily be dynamically allocated and passed to the encoder and decoder as arguments, but this implementation cuts a few corners by using globals.

The window[WINDOW_SIZE] variable holds the last 4,096 characters read in from the input file. The last seventeen of those characters will have been read in from the file but not yet encoded. These constitute the look-ahead buffer.

For comparison purposes, we also consider those 4,096 characters to be 4,096 strings, with each character being the first character in an 17-byte string. The code in this program also universally refers to a string by the index of its first character in the text window. So when a piece of code does a comparison on string 'r,' it is looking at the seventeen-byte string starting at position 'r' in the text window.

```
unsigned char window[ WINDOW_SIZE ];

struct {
   int parent;
   int smaller_child;
   int larger_child;
} tree[ WINDOW_SIZE + 1 ];
```

The binary tree in this program is defined as the unnamed structure tree. Each tree node has only three elements: a parent index, a smaller_child index, and a larger_child index. Each of these indices are single numbers referring to the string at that position in the text window. An example of how this tree might look after reading in twenty-five characters follows. Remember that position 0 in the text window is used for other purposes, so strings starting there don't get added to the tree.

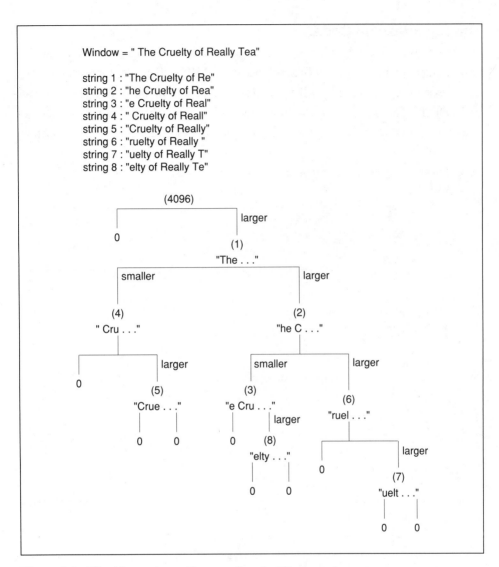

Window = " The Cruelty of Really Tea"

string 1 : "The Cruelty of Re"
string 2 : "he Cruelty of Rea"
string 3 : "e Cruelty of Real"
string 4 : " Cruelty of Reall"
string 5 : "Cruelty of Really"
string 6 : "ruelty of Really "
string 7 : "uelty of Really T"
string 8 : "elty of Really Te"

Figure 8-8. The binary tree after reading in 25 characters.

One nice feature of this binary tree is that we know in advance how many total nodes will be in it, so we can allocate the space in advance instead of while building the tree. This saves the code needed for allocating and freeing nodes, and we know that the node for the string at position 'i' will be in the tree structure at position 'i.'

The Compression Code

The compression code follows. Like all previous programs in this book, it is called with pointers to an open input file and to a special BIT_FILE structure that takes the compressed output. The BIT_FILE structure lets us use the bit-oriented I/O routines in BITIO.H. The compression routine breaks down into three different sections of code: an initialization section, the main compression loop, and a termination section.

```
void CompressFile( FILE *input, BIT_FILE *output, int argc,
                                                char *argv[] )
{
    int i;
    int c;
    int look_ahead_bytes;
    int current_position;
    int replace_count;
    int match_length;
    int match_position;

    current_position = 1;
    for ( i = 0 ; i < LOOK_AHEAD_SIZE ; i++ ) {
        if ( ( c = getc( input ) ) == EOF )
            break;
        window[ current_position + i ] = c;
    }
    look_ahead_bytes = i;
    InitTree( current_position );
    match_length = 0;
    while ( look_ahead_bytes > 0 ) {
        if ( match_length > look_ahead_bytes )
            match_length = look_ahead_bytes;
        if ( match_length <= BREAK_EVEN ) {
            replace_count = 1;
            OutputBit( output, 1 );
            OutputBits( output, window[ current_position ], 8 );
        } else {
            OutputBit( output, 0 );
```

```
        OutputBits( output, match_position, INDEX_BIT_COUNT );
        OutputBits( output, match_length - ( BREAK_EVEN + 1 ),
                    LENGTH_BIT_COUNT );
        replace_count = match_length;
    }
    for ( i = 0 ; i < replace_count ; i++ ) {
      DeleteString( MOD_WINDOW( current_position + LOOK_AHEAD_SIZE ) );
      if ( ( c = getc( input ) ) == EOF )
        look_ahead_bytes--;
      else
        window[ MOD_WINDOW( current_position + LOOK_AHEAD_SIZE ) ] = c;
      current_position = MOD_WINDOW( current_position + 1 );
      if ( look_ahead_bytes )
        match_length = AddString( current_position, &match_position );
    }

  }
  OutputBit( output, 0 );
  OutputBits( output, END_OF_STREAM, INDEX_BIT_COUNT );
}
```

Initialization. The compression main loop needs a steady state before it can start. Two things need to be done: first, the look-ahead buffer needs to be loaded; and second, the tree needs to be initialized.

The code to load the look-ahead buffer is shown next. It tries to load up to seventeen bytes into the buffer. After the loading is complete, two local variables are set up so that the main loop can begin executing. First, current_position is set to one. This means that the look-ahead buffer now starts at position 1. Second, look_ahead_bytes is set to the number of bytes left to be encoded in the look-ahead buffer.

```
    current_position = 1;
    for ( i = 0 ; i < LOOK_AHEAD_SIZE ; i++ ) {
      if ( ( c = getc( input ) ) == EOF )
        break;
      window[ current_position + i ] = c;
```

```
        }
    look_ahead_bytes = i;
```

The look_ahead_bytes variable will be set to seventeen most of the time the main loop executes. Usually seventeen characters are left in the look-ahead buffer to encode. Once the program approaches the end of the file, that number will start to drop.

The next step in the initialization program calls InitTree(). InitTree() establishes a root node for the tree. The first node put into the tree will be at the current position, position 1. The code in InitTree() executes a standard insertion algorithm, establishing the child of the root pointer node and setting up the parents and children of position 1.

```
void InitTree( int r )
{
    tree[ TREE_ROOT ].larger_child = r;
    tree[ r ].parent = TREE_ROOT;
    tree[ r ].larger_child = UNUSED;
    tree[ r ].smaller_child = UNUSED;
}
```

The final step in the initialization of CompressFile sets up a match_length of one. This forces the encoding loop to output the first character of the look-ahead buffer as a single character instead of as a phrase. It would not be possible at this point even to search for a match to the string at position 1, since it is the only string in the tree.

The Main Loop. The main loop runs as long as characters are left in the look-ahead buffer to encode. It does three things in the loop: (1) It encodes the current phrase in the look-ahead buffer; (2) it reads new characters into the look-ahead buffer while deleting the oldest from the tree; and (3) it inserts the new strings defined by the new characters into the binary tree while the new characters being loaded into the look-ahead buffer.

```
while ( look_ahead_bytes > 0 ) {
    if ( match_length > look_ahead_bytes )
```

```
        match_length = look_ahead_bytes;
    if ( match_length <= BREAK_EVEN ) {
      replace_count = 1;
      OutputBit( output, 1 );
      OutputBits( output, window[ current_position ], 8 );
    } else {
      OutputBit( output, 0 );
      OutputBits( output, match_position, INDEX_BIT_COUNT );
      OutputBits( output, match_length - ( BREAK_EVEN + 1 ),
                  LENGTH_BIT_COUNT );
      replace_count = match_length;
    }
    for ( i = 0 ; i < replace_count ; i++ ) {
      DeleteString( MOD_WINDOW( current_position + LOOK_AHEAD_SIZE ) );
      if ( ( c = getc( input ) ) == EOF )
        look_ahead_bytes—;
      else
        window[ MOD_WINDOW( current_position + LOOK_AHEAD_SIZE ) ] = c;
      current_position = MOD_WINDOW( current_position + 1 );
      if ( look_ahead_bytes )
        match_length = AddString( current_position, &match_position );
    }
  }
}
```

The main loop assumes that at the top of the loop, the best match length and position are stored in variables match_length and match_position. The AddString() operation normally does this at the bottom of the loop, but the first time through the loop the initialization code set match_length to zero.

Since the match_length is known, the code just has to decide whether to encode the current phrase in the look-ahead buffer as an index/length pair or whether to output a single character. All that is necessary here is a simple comparison against BREAK_EVEN. If the current phrase match length is more than BREAK_EVEN, it makes sense to encode it as a phrase. Otherwise it is encoded as a single character.

The encoding process is straightforward. Solo characters are output as a single bit, followed by the eight bits in the character. Index/position tokens are output as a zero bit, followed by the twelve-bit position and the four-bit length. The length is encoded as a number from zero to fifteen that corresponds to a length of two to seventeen.

After encoding, the look-ahead buffer has to be loaded with new characters to replace the ones that have been output. If a phrase was encoded, the variable replace_count is set to the length of the phrase, otherwise, replace_count is set to one to indicate that a single character needs to be replaced.

The replacement loop code is shown in figure below. New characters read into the look-ahead buffer land on top of the oldest phrases in the text window. Accordingly, before each character is read in, the DeleteString() routine deletes the older phrase.

```
for ( i = 0 ; i < replace_count ; i++ ) {
  DeleteString( MOD_WINDOW( current_position + LOOK_AHEAD_SIZE ) );
  if ( ( c = getc( input ) ) == EOF )
    look_ahead_bytes--;
  else
    window[ MOD_WINDOW( current_position + LOOK_AHEAD_SIZE ) ] = c;
  current_position = MOD_WINDOW( current_position + 1 );
  if ( look_ahead_bytes )
    match_length = AddString( current_position, &match_position );
}
```

After the new character is read in, the current_position is updated, and the AddString() routine adds a new phrase to the tree. AddString() also returns the position and length of the best match for the inserted string. These variables will then be used at the top of the loop to encode the current phrase in the look-ahead buffer.

The Exit Code. The exit code for the compression routine is very simple to implement in this program. All that needs to be done is to encode the special END_OF_STREAM position code so that the decoder will know that there is no more data to pull out of the compressed stream. Its job is completed, and it can then return.

AddString(). The bulk of the work done by the compression routine takes place in AddString(). This routine does two jobs. First, it adds a new string to the binary tree. Second, it tracks the string currently in the tree that best matches the one being inserted.

The process of locating the node for insertion of the new string uses standard techniques for traversing a binary tree. AddString first checks to see if the new string is the END_OF_STREAM node. If it is, it shouldn't be inserted into the tree, so it takes an immediate return with a match_length of zero. This forces the encoder to output a single character instead of trying to encode a phrase at index 0.

After checking for a bad node, the test_node and initial match_length are set up. Throughout the main loop, test_node will point to the current node that will be compared to the new_node. The match_length variable will contain the current longest match found during traversal of the tree.

```
int AddString( int new_node, int *match_position )
{
    int i;
    int test_node;
    int delta;
    int match_length;
    int *child;

    if ( new_node == END_OF_STREAM )
        return( 0 );
    test_node = tree[ TREE_ROOT ].larger_child;
    match_length = 0;
    for ( ; ; ) {
        for ( i = 0 ; i < LOOK_AHEAD_SIZE ; i++ ) {
            delta = window[ MOD_WINDOW( new_node + i ) ] -
                window[ MOD_WINDOW( test_node + i ) ];
            if ( delta != 0 )
                break;
        }
        if ( i >= match_length ) {
            match_length = i;
            *match_position = test_node;
```

```
        if ( match_length >= LOOK_AHEAD_SIZE ) {
          ReplaceNode( test_node, new_node );
          return( match_length );
        }
      }
      if ( delta >= 0 )
        child = &tree[ test_node ].larger_child;
      else
        child = &tree[ test_node ].smaller_child;
      if ( *child == UNUSED ) {
        *child = new_node;
        tree[ new_node ].parent = test_node;
        tree[ new_node ].larger_child = UNUSED;
        tree[ new_node ].smaller_child = UNUSED;
        return( match_length );
      }
      test_node = *child;
  }
}
```

At this point, the main comparison loop is entered. The first section executes a comparison of the test_node and the new_node. Two pieces of information are available after falling out of the loop. The first is the value of delta. The delta variable will be less than one if the string at new_node is less than the test_node, zero if they are the same, and one if the new_node is greater. The second, found in the loop variable i, tells how many characters in the two strings were identical, or the match_length for a particular string.

```
    for ( i = 0 ; i < LOOK_AHEAD_SIZE ; i++ ) {
      delta = window[ MOD_WINDOW( new_node + i ) ] -
        window[ MOD_WINDOW( test_node + i ) ];
      if ( delta != 0 )
        break;
    }
```

After the comparison code completes, the main loop tests whether the match for this phrase is the longest one recorded so far. If it is, the match_length variable is updated, and the test_node position is saved.

```
if ( i >= match_length ) {
  match_length = i;
  *match_position = test_node;
  if ( match_length >= LOOK_AHEAD_SIZE ) {
    ReplaceNode( test_node, new_node );
    return( match_length );
  }
}
```

Frequently, the phrase in the look-ahead buffer is an exact match for the test_node. When this is the case, two things happen. First, since the longest match is found, the code will exit the AddString() routine. But before exiting, it performs a node replacement by deleting the test_node and replacing it with the new_node. It could just add new_node to the binary tree, but there is really no point to it. test_node will be redundant data taking up time in the search path if it just uses the normal insertion code. Instead, a special routine replaces test_node with new_node and returns. This leaves a sparser tree that can be searched more quickly. And, since test_node would have been deleted before new_node, it doesn't sacrifice any compression by doing this.

The final section of the main test loop is the tree navigation step. The delta variable tells whether to follow the larger_child or smaller_child branches from the test_node. If the child we are supposed to follow is UNUSED, we have gone as far as we can in the tree. At this point, the code inserts new_node into the binary tree at the correct child and returns. Otherwise, it moves to the new test_node and goes back to the start of the test loop.

```
if ( delta >= 0 )
  child = &tree[ test_node ].larger_child;
else
  child = &tree[ test_node ].smaller_child;
if ( *child == UNUSED ) {
```

```
        *child = new_node;
        tree[ new_node ].parent = test_node;
        tree[ new_node ].larger_child = UNUSED;
        tree[ new_node ].smaller_child = UNUSED;
        return( match_length );
    }
    test_node = *child;
```

DeleteString(). DeleteString() is called from the main compression loop every time a new character is read into the look-ahead buffer. It uses a standard binary tree deletion algorithm to delete a phrase from the text window.

DeleteString() first determines whether the node is really in the tree. It is possible for the AddString() routine to have already deleted a string because it was a duplicate. If this is the case, the work has been done, and the routine can return.

```
void DeleteString( int p )
{
    int   replacement;

    if ( tree[ p ].parent == UNUSED )
        return;
    if ( tree[ p ].larger_child == UNUSED )
        ContractNode( p, tree[ p ].smaller_child );
    else if ( tree[ p ].smaller_child == UNUSED )
        ContractNode( p, tree[ p ].larger_child );
    else {
        replacement = FindNextNode( p );
        DeleteString( replacement );
        ReplaceNode( p, replacement );
    }
}
```

If the string is presently in the tree, there are two possibilities for a deletion strategy. If either of the node's children are unused, deleting the node is just a matter of closing the link between the current node's parent and the child in use, effectively pulling the node out of the tree. This is done by a routine called ContractNode().

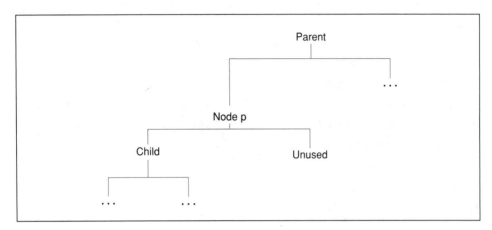

Figure 8-9. Tree before contraction of node p.

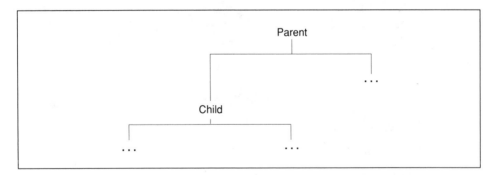

Figure 8-10. Tree after contraction of node p.

The situation is a little more complicated if the node to be deleted has children on both the larger_child and smaller_child nodes. When this is the case, the alternate deletion algorithm has to be used. The way to delete node p when both children are used is to find the node in the tree either directly before or directly after node p in the ordered list of nodes. In this program, we find the next smaller node. This is done in the FindNextNode() routine and is accomplished by taking the first smaller_child branch, then following the larger_child branches until an UNUSED smaller_child is found. This next smaller node in the list is the replacement node.

The replacement node is then deleted from the tree, with a recursive call to DeleteString(). Out of control recursion is not a worry at this point, since the replacement node by definition has at least one UNUSED child. This means we will never go more than one level deep in our recursion.

After the replacement node has been deleted, it is used to replace the original deleted node. This is done by a routine called ReplaceNode() which simply inserts it in the tree in the same position as the original node.

Binary Tree Support Routines. The support routines used by AddString() and DeleteString() are ContractNode(), ReplaceNode(), and FindNextNode(). ContractNode() deletes a node when one of the children is UNUSED. To do this, the used child is linked with the parent, effectively pulling the node out of the tree. The deleted node has its parent node set to UNUSED, which is what is used internally to determine if a node is in use.

```
void ContractNode( int old_node, int new_node )
{
    tree[ new_node ].parent = tree[ old_node ].parent;
    if ( tree[ tree[ old_node ].parent ].larger_child == old_node )
      tree[ tree[ old_node ].parent ].larger_child = new_node;
    else
      tree[ tree[ old_node ].parent ].smaller_child = new_node;
    tree[ old_node ].parent = UNUSED;
}
```

ReplaceNode() is used during the deletion process when a new_node is going to be dropped into the tree on top of the old_node. It is assumed that the new_node is not currently linked to the tree. When the operation completes, the old_node will have been removed, and this is indicated by setting the parent to UNUSED.

```
void ReplaceNode( int old_node, int new_node )
{
    int parent;

    parent = tree[ old_node ].parent;
    if ( tree[ parent ].smaller_child == old_node )
        tree[ parent ].smaller_child = new_node;
    else
        tree[ parent ].larger_child = new_node;
    tree[ new_node ] = tree[ old_node ];
    tree[ tree[ new_node ].smaller_child ].parent = new_node;
    tree[ tree[ new_node ].larger_child ].parent = new_node;
    tree[ old_node ].parent = UNUSED;
}
```

FindNextNode() is called when the DeleteString() routine needs to find the next smaller node in the sorted list. It first takes the smaller branch from the starting node, then follows the larger branches until an UNUSED child is located. The node with the UNUSED larger_child is the next highest in the list. This routine assumes that the node has a next smallest node, meaning it has to have a smaller_child branch.

```
int FindNextNode( int node )
{
    int next;

    next = tree[ node ].smaller_child;
    while ( tree[ next ].larger_child != UNUSED )
        next = tree[ next ].larger_child;
    return( next );
}
```

The Expansion Routine

The LZSS compression algorithm is highly asymmetrical. The compression routine is fairly complicated, and it does quite a bit of work for every character or phrase that is compressed. In comparison, the expansion code is extremely simple. It has very little work to do, and in fact it can operate nearly as fast as an ordinary copy routine. This makes LZSS an excellent choice for data that needs to be compressed once and expanded many times.

```
void ExpandFile( BIT_FILE *input, FILE *output, int argc, char *argv[] )

{
    int i;
    int current_position;
    int c;
    int match_length;
    int match_position;

    current_position = 1;
    for ( ; ; ) {
        if ( InputBit( input ) ) {
            c = InputBits( input, 8 );
            putc( c, output );
            window[ current_position ] = c;
            current_position = MOD_WINDOW( current_position + 1 );
        } else {
            match_position = InputBits( input, INDEX_BIT_COUNT );
            if ( match_position == END_OF_STREAM )
                break;
            match_length = InputBits( input, LENGTH_BIT_COUNT );
            match_length += BREAK_EVEN;
            for ( i = 0 ; i <= match_length ; i++ ) {
                c = window[ MOD_WINDOW( match_position + i ) ];
                putc( c, output );
                window[ current_position ] = c;
                current_position = MOD_WINDOW( current_position + 1 );
            }
        }
    }
}
```

Virtually all the time in the expansion routine is spent in the main loop. The first step reads in a single bit. If this is a zero, the next byte will contain an unencoded character. The character is read in, output to the file, and put in the text window at the current position.

If the input bit was a one instead of a zero, the expansion routine reads in a match_position and length instead of a character. It checks to see if the match_position is actually the encoded END_OF_STREAM message. If so, the program is done, and it can exit. Otherwise, the match_length is read in and adjusted to range 2 through 17.

Once the match_position and length are known, a short loop executes. In this loop, the character from the match string is pulled out of the text window, stored in the file, and put in the window at the current position, which is then updated.

That is the entire expansion routine. It is easy to see why expansion takes place so quickly.

Improvements. While LZSS makes for a fairly good compression algorithm, improvements can be made to it. For instance, LZSS compresses poorly when it starts since it does not have any data in the text window for matches. It is fairly simple to preload the window with WINDOW_SIZE - LOOK_AHEAD_SIZE characters, then add all the appropriate strings to the binary tree.

The trouble with preloading the window is deciding what to preload it with, since we have no idea what type of data will come up in the input stream. Probably the easiest thing to do is to insert 256 strings that contain 16 consecutive occurrences of all of the possible symbols in the alphabet. Unfortunately, runs of repeated characters are the types of initial data that will be helped the least by preloading, but there will be some improvement.

Much experimentation can be done with the number of bits used in the index and the length codes. It is possible to achieve better compression by increasing the number of bits used for each of these, but there are at least two negative effects. First, the compression speed will suffer as the window grows, due to the extra work required to navigate and maintain a larger binary tree. Second, compression of smaller files will suffer due to the increased time needed to build a full dictionary. Some of this startup overhead can be reduced by starting the compression code with a smaller code size and working up to the larger sizes as the dictionary fills up.

One way the programs used here can be sped up dramatically is by using blocked I/O. The tokens output by the compression program here are all exactly either one or two bytes. It is possible to buffer these bytes up while accumulating the flag bits. When eight flag bits have been output, the flag byte can be sent, followed by between 8 and 16 bytes of byte-oriented data. Since the eight to sixteen bytes can be written using conventional byte-oriented code, the compression routines will run considerably faster.

Another technique which speeds up both compression and expansion is to create a "ghost buffer" at the end of the text window. In the case of this program the ghost buffer would hold seventeen characters, which would be identical to the characters in the first seventeen locations of the window. By maintaining a copy of the first seventeen bytes in the ghost buffer, the comparison routines can run without using modulo arithmetic on the indices. Since the compression program spends so much time on string comparison, this results in big time savings.

One final bit of inefficiency found in LZSS relates to the handling of duplicate strings. We remove duplicate strings from the binary tree, but we leave them in the text window, where they take up valuable space. It is possible to free up the space used by these duplicate strings in the text window, allowing for expansion of the dictionary. However, the side effect of this is that the decompression program has to keep track of duplicate strings, which will result in a significant cutback in expansion speed.

The Code

```
/************************* Start of LZSS.C *************************
 *
 * This is the LZSS module, which implements an LZ77 style compression
 * algorithm. As implemented here it uses a 12 bit index into the sliding
 * window, and a 4 bit length, which is adjusted to reflect phrase
 * lengths of between 2 and 17 bytes.
 */
```

```
#include <stdio.h>
#include <stdlib.h>
#include <string.h>
#include <ctype.h>
#include "bitio.h"

/*
 * Various constants used to define the compression parameters. The
 * INDEX_BIT_COUNT tells how many bits we allocate to indices into the
 * text window. This directly determines the WINDOW_SIZE. The
 * LENGTH_BIT_COUNT tells how many bits we allocate for the length of
 * an encode phrase. This determines the size of the look-ahead buffer.
 * The TREE_ROOT is a special node in the tree that always points to
 * the root node of the binary phrase tree. END_OF_STREAM is a special
 * index used to flag the fact that the file has been completely
 * encoded, and there is no more data. UNUSED is the null index for
 * the tree. MOD_WINDOW() is a macro used to perform arithmetic on tree
 * indices.
 *
 */

#define INDEX_BIT_COUNT       12
#define LENGTH_BIT_COUNT      4
#define WINDOW_SIZE           ( 1 << INDEX_BIT_COUNT )
#define RAW_LOOK_AHEAD_SIZE   ( 1 << LENGTH_BIT_COUNT )
#define BREAK_EVEN            ( ( 1 + INDEX_BIT_COUNT +
                                  LENGTH_BIT_COUNT ) / 9 )

#define LOOK_AHEAD_SIZE       ( RAW_LOOK_AHEAD_SIZE + BREAK_EVEN )
#define TREE_ROOT             WINDOW_SIZE
#define END_OF_STREAM         0
#define UNUSED                0
#define MOD_WINDOW( a )       ( ( a ) & ( WINDOW_SIZE - 1 ) )

char *CompressionName = "LZSS Encoder";
char *Usage           = "in-file out-file\n\n";
```

```
/*
 * These are the two global data structures used in this program.
 * The window[] array is exactly that, the window of previously seen
 * text, as well as the current look-ahead text. The tree[] structure
 * contains the binary tree of all of the strings in the window sorted
 * in order.
 */

unsigned char window[ WINDOW_SIZE ];

struct {
    int parent;
    int smaller_child;
    int larger_child;
} tree[ WINDOW_SIZE + 1 ];

/*
 * Function prototypes for both ANSI C compilers and their K&R brethren.
 */

#ifdef __STDC__

void InitTree( int r );
void ContractNode( int old_node, int new_node );
void ReplaceNode( int old_node, int new_node );
int FindNextNode( int node );
void DeleteString( int p );
int AddString( int new_node, int *match_position );
void CompressFile( FILE *input, BIT_FILE *output,
                   int argc, char *argv[] );
void ExpandFile( BIT_FILE *input, FILE *output, int argc, char *argv[] );

#else

void InitTree();
void ContractNode();
void ReplaceNode();
```

```
int  FindNextNode();
void DeleteString();
int  AddString();
void CompressFile();
void ExpandFile();

#endif

/*
 * Since the tree is static data, it comes up with every node
 * initialized to 0, which is good, since 0 is the UNUSED code.
 * However, to make the tree really usable, a single phrase has to be
 * added to the tree so it has a root node. That is done right here.
 */
void InitTree( r )
int r;
{
    tree[ TREE_ROOT ].larger_child = r;
    tree[ r ].parent = TREE_ROOT;
    tree[ r ].larger_child = UNUSED;
    tree[ r ].smaller_child = UNUSED;
}


/*
 * This routine is used when a node is being deleted. The link to
 * its descendant is broken by pulling the descendant in to overlay
 * the existing link.
 */
void ContractNode( old_node, new_node )
int old_node;
int new_node;
{
    tree[ new_node ].parent = tree[ old_node ].parent;
    if ( tree[ tree[ old_node ].parent ].larger_child == old_node )
        tree[ tree[ old_node ].parent ].larger_child = new_node;
    else
        tree[ tree[ old_node ].parent ].smaller_child = new_node;
```

```
    tree[ old_node ].parent = UNUSED;
}


/*
 * This routine is also used when a node is being deleted. However,
 * in this case, it is being replaced by a node that was not previously
 * in the tree.
 */
void ReplaceNode( old_node, new_node )
int old_node;
int new_node;
{
    int parent;

    parent = tree[ old_node ].parent;
    if ( tree[ parent ].smaller_child == old_node )
        tree[ parent ].smaller_child = new_node;
    else
        tree[ parent ].larger_child = new_node;
    tree[ new_node ] = tree[ old_node ];
    tree[ tree[ new_node ].smaller_child ].parent = new_node;
    tree[ tree[ new_node ].larger_child ].parent = new_node;
    tree[ old_node ].parent = UNUSED;
}


/*
 * This routine is used to find the next smallest node after the node
 * argument. It assumes that the node has a smaller child. We find
 * the next smallest child by going to the smaller_child node, then
 * going to the end of the larger_child descendant chain.
 */
int FindNextNode( node )
int node;
{
    int next;

    next = tree[ node ].smaller_child;
```

```
   while ( tree[ next ].larger_child != UNUSED )
     next = tree[ next ].larger_child;
   return( next );
}


/*
* This routine performs the classic binary tree deletion algorithm.
* If the node to be deleted has a null link in either direction, we
* just pull the non-null link up one to replace the existing link.
* If both links exist, we instead delete the next link in order, which
* is guaranteed to have a null link, then replace the node to be deleted
* with the next link.
*/
void DeleteString( p )
int p;
{
   int  replacement;

   if ( tree[ p ].parent == UNUSED )
     return;
   if ( tree[ p ].larger_child == UNUSED )
     ContractNode( p, tree[ p ].smaller_child );
   else if ( tree[ p ].smaller_child == UNUSED )
     ContractNode( p, tree[ p ].larger_child );
   else {
     replacement = FindNextNode( p );
     DeleteString( replacement );
     ReplaceNode( p, replacement );
   }
}


/*
* This where most of the work done by the encoder takes place. This
* routine is responsible for adding the new node to the binary tree.
* It also has to find the best match among all the existing nodes in
* the tree, and return that to the calling routine. To make matters
* even more complicated, if the new_node has a duplicate in the tree,
```

```
 * the old_node is deleted, for reasons of efficiency.
 */

int AddString( new_node, match_position )
int new_node;
int *match_position;
{
   int i;
   int test_node;
   int delta;
   int match_length;
   int *child;

   if ( new_node == END_OF_STREAM )
     return( 0 );
   test_node = tree[ TREE_ROOT ].larger_child;
   match_length = 0;
   for ( ; ; ) {
     for ( i = 0 ; i < LOOK_AHEAD_SIZE ; i++ ) {
           delta = window[ MOD_WINDOW( new_node + i ) ] -
                   window[ MOD_WINDOW( test_node + i ) ];
           if ( delta != 0 )
         break;
     }
     if ( i >= match_length ) {
       match_length = i;
       *match_position = test_node;
       if ( match_length >= LOOK_AHEAD_SIZE ) {
         ReplaceNode( test_node, new_node );
         return( match_length );
       }
     }
     if ( delta >= 0 )
       child = &tree[ test_node ].larger_child;
     else
       child = &tree[ test_node ].smaller_child;
     if ( *child == UNUSED ) {
```

```
        *child = new_node;
        tree[ new_node ].parent = test_node;
        tree[ new_node ].larger_child = UNUSED;
        tree[ new_node ].smaller_child = UNUSED;
        return( match_length );
    }
    test_node = *child;
  }
}


/*
 * This is the compression routine. It has to first load up the look
 * ahead buffer, then go into the main compression loop. The main loop
 * decides whether to output a single character or an index/length
 * token that defines a phrase. Once the character or phrase has been
 * sent out, another loop has to run. The second loop reads in new
 * characters, deletes the strings that are overwritten by the new
 * character, then adds the strings that are created by the new
 * character.
 */

void CompressFile( input, output, argc, argv )
FILE *input;
BIT_FILE *output;
int argc;
char *argv[];
{
    int i;
    int c;
    int look_ahead_bytes;
    int current_position;
    int replace_count;
    int match_length;
    int match_position;

    current_position = 1;
    for ( i = 0 ; i < LOOK_AHEAD_SIZE ; i++ ) {
```

```
   if ( ( c = getc( input ) ) == EOF )
      break;
   window[ current_position + i ] = (unsigned char) c;
}
look_ahead_bytes = i;
InitTree( current_position );
match_length = 0;
match_position = 0;
while ( look_ahead_bytes > 0 ) {
   if ( match_length > look_ahead_bytes )
      match_length = look_ahead_bytes;
   if ( match_length <= BREAK_EVEN ) {
      replace_count = 1;
      OutputBit( output, 1 );
      OutputBits( output,
                  (unsigned long)window[ current_position ], 8 );
   } else {
      OutputBit( output, 0 );
      OutputBits( output,
                  (unsigned long) match_position, INDEX_BIT_COUNT );
      OutputBits( output,
                  (unsigned long) ( match_length - ( BREAK_EVEN + 1 ) ),
                  LENGTH_BIT_COUNT );
      replace_count = match_length;
   }
   for ( i = 0 ; i < replace_count ; i++ ) {
      DeleteString( MOD_WINDOW( current_position + LOOK_AHEAD_SIZE ) );
      if ( ( c = getc( input ) ) == EOF )
         look_ahead_bytes--;
      else
         window[ MOD_WINDOW( current_position + LOOK_AHEAD_SIZE ) ]
                           = (unsigned char) c;
      current_position = MOD_WINDOW( current_position + 1 );
      if ( look_ahead_bytes )
         match_length = AddString( current_position, &match_position );
   }
}
OutputBit( output, 0 );
```

```
  OutputBits( output,
                 (unsigned long) END_OF_STREAM, INDEX_BIT_COUNT );
  while ( argc-- > 0 )
    printf( "Unknown argument: %s\n", *argv++ );
}

/*
 * This is the expansion routine for the LZSS algorithm. All it has
 * to do is read in flag bits, decide whether to read in a character or
 * a index/length pair, and take the appropriate action.
 */

void ExpandFile( input, output, argc, argv )
BIT_FILE *input;
FILE *output;
int argc;
char *argv[];
{
  int i;
  int current_position;
  int c;
  int match_length;
  int match_position;

  current_position = 1;
  for ( ; ; ) {
    if ( InputBit( input ) ) {
      c = (int) InputBits( input, 8 );
      putc( c, output );
      window[ current_position ] = (unsigned char) c;
      current_position = MOD_WINDOW( current_position + 1 );
    } else {
      match_position = (int) InputBits( input, INDEX_BIT_COUNT );
      if ( match_position == END_OF_STREAM )
        break;
      match_length = (int) InputBits( input, LENGTH_BIT_COUNT );
      match_length += BREAK_EVEN;
```

```
        for ( i = 0 ; i <= match_length ; i++ ) {
          c = window[ MOD_WINDOW( match_position + i ) ];
          putc( c, output );
          window[ current_position ] = (unsigned char) c;
          current_position = MOD_WINDOW( current_position + 1 );
        }
      }
  }
  while ( argc-- > 0 )
    printf( "Unknown argument: %s\n", *argv++ );
}


/************************ End of LZSS.C ************************/
```

CHAPTER 9

LZ78 Compression

The LZ77 algorithms have a deficiency that must have troubled their creators, Jacob Ziv and Abraham Lempel. These algorithms use only a small window into previously seen text, which means they continuously throw away valuable dictionary entries because they slide out of the dictionary. The phrase "Jacob Ziv," for example, may have appeared in the text in chapter 7. If this book were being compressed using an LZ77 algorithm, it almost certainly would not appear in the sliding window by the time we arrived at this chapter. But the book would compress better if "Jacob Ziv" did appear in the dictionary, since it shows up four or five times in scattered locations throughout the text.

The sliding window makes LZ77 algorithms biased toward exploiting recency in the text. Many, but not all, streams of data tend to "look" more like what has been seen recently than what was seen long ago. Encoding a telephone book is a good example of this. After encoding the first "Jones" entry, it would seem that the word "Jones" was showing up everywhere. But the word "Adams," seen long ago, would probably not show up at all. As we moved through the phone book, recency effects would be patently obvious, and LZ77 would take advantage of them.

While compressing the phone book, if we looked carefully, we would also notice that some data was more or less immune to recency effects. The street address associated with each listing, for example, would only show the effect faintly, when two listings with the same last name lived at the same address. This would result in fewer matches to text in the window, leading to less effective compression.

A second deficiency in LZ77 compression is the limited size of a phrase that can be matched. The longest match is approximately the size of the look-ahead buffer, which in the previous chapter was just 17 bytes. Many of the seventeen-byte matches found when compressing using that algorithm may actually be much longer.

Can LZ77 Improve?

One obvious way to tackle these problems is simply to start tinkering with the size of the window and the size of the look-ahead buffer. Instead of using a 4K window and a seventeen-byte buffer, for example, why not use a 64K text window and a 1K look-ahead buffer? Wouldn't that address both problems effectively?

While raising the size of both parameters does seem to address these problems, the scheme has two major drawbacks. First, when we increase the buffer size from 4K to 64K, we now need sixteen bits to encode an index location instead of twelve. And instead of needing four bits to encode a phrase length, we now need ten. So the cost of encoding a phrase rises from seventeen bits to twenty-seven.

This 50 percent increase in the bit size of an index/length token can have a severely negative impact on the compression algorithm. For one thing, it will change the BREAK_EVEN point in the program from just under two characters to three characters. This means that matches of three or fewer characters will no longer be effectively coded as index/length tokens and will instead have to be encoded as single characters. Encoding data as single characters is actually less efficient than plain text, since it needs an additional bit to indicate that a normal character is coming.

An even more distressing effect is that changing these parameters will drastically increase the amount of CPU time needed to perform compression. Under LZ77, just changing the text window size from 4K to 64K will result in the average search taking sixteen times longer, since every string in the window is compared to the look-ahead buffer. The situation is somewhat better under LZSS, since the strings are kept in a binary tree. In this case, the runtime cost of the window size is proportional to the logarithm of the window size. But this still means over a 30 percent increase in runtime.

The real penalty comes when the size of the look-ahead buffer is increased. Since our string comparisons between the text window phrases and the look-ahead buffer proceed sequentially, the runtime here will increase in direct proportion to the length of the look-ahead buffer. Going from sixteen to 1,024 characters means this portion of the program is going to run sixty-four times more slowly—a costly penalty indeed.

These effects combine to effectively cancel out any gains from increasing either of these parameters in an LZ77 algorithm. And even with a 64K text window, we are still effectively tied to an algorithm that depends on recency to perform adequate compression.

Enter LZ78

To effectively sidestep these problems, Ziv and Lempel developed a different form of dictionary-based compression. This algorithm, popularly referred to as LZ78, was published in "Compression of Individual Sequences via Variable-Rate Coding" in *IEEE Transactions on Information Theory* (September 1978).

LZ78 abandons the concept of a text window. Under LZ77 the dictionary of phrases was defined by a fixed window of previously seen text. Under LZ78, the dictionary is a potentially unlimited list of previously seen *phrases*.

LZ78 is similar to LZ77 in some ways. LZ77 outputs a series of tokens. Each token has three components: a phrase location, the phrase length, and a character that follows the phrase. LZ78 also outputs a series of tokens with essentially the same meanings. Each LZ78 token consists of a code that selects a given phrase and a single character that follows the phrase. Unlike LZ77, the phrase length is not passed since the decoder knows it.

Unlike LZ77, LZ78 does not have a ready-made window full of text to use as a dictionary. It creates a new phrase each time a token is output, and it adds that phrase to the dictionary. After the phrase is added, it will be available to the encoder at any time in the future, not just for the next few thousand characters.

LZ78 Details. When using the LZ78 algorithm, both the encoder and the decoder start off with a nearly empty dictionary. By definition, the dictionary has a single encoded string—the null string. As each character is read in, it is added to the current string. As long as the current string matches some phrase in the dictionary, this process continues.

But eventually the string will no longer have a corresponding phrase in the dictionary. This is when LZ78 outputs a token and a character. Remember that the string did have a match in the dictionary until the last character was read in. The current string, therefore, is defined as that last match with one new character added on. This is what LZ77 outputs: the index for the previous match and the character that broke that match.

But at this point, LZ78 takes an additional step. The new phrase, consisting of the dictionary match and the new character, is added to the dictionary. The next time that phrase appears, it can be used to build an even longer phrase.

A code fragment to implement this algorithm is shown next. Some of the detail has been glossed over, but this is a fairly faithful representation of the algorithm.

```
for ( ; ; ) {
    current_match = 1;
    current_length = 0;
    memset( test_string, '\0', MAX_STRING );
    for ( ; ; ) {
        test_string[ current_length++ ] = getc( input );
        new_match = find_match( test_string );
        if ( new_match == -1 )
            break;
        current_match = new_match;
    }
    output_code( current_match );
    output_char( test_string[ current_length - 1 ] );
    add_string_to_dictionary( test_string );
}
```

By definition, the empty string will always match string 0, the null node in the dictionary. Thus, when we encounter a character for the first time, it is encoded as phrase 0 plus the new character. The next time that character appears, it will be encoded as part of a phrase.

An example of the encoder output follows. The input text is a sequence of words from the dictionary of a spelling checker. The LZ78 encoder starts encoding with no phrases in the dictionary; therefore, the first character it reads in from the input text, "D," creates a string that has no match in the dictionary. The encoder will then output a phrase/character pair, in this case 0 and D. Remember that the dictionary starts up with zero defined as the empty phrase.

Input text: "DAD DADA DADDY DADO..."

Output Phrase	Output Character	Encoded String
0	'D'	"D"
0	'A'	"A"
1	' '	"D "
1	'A'	"DA"
4	' '	"DA "
4	'D'	"DAD"
1	'Y'	"DY"
0	' '	" "
6	'O'	"DADO"

The first two characters to come through the encoder, D and A, have not been seen before. Each will have to be encoded as a phrase, 0 + character pair. D is added to the dictionary as phrase 1, and A is added as phrase 2.

When the third character, "D," is read in, it matches an existing dictionary phrase. The " " character, the next character read in, creates a new phrase with no match in the dictionary. LZ78 will output code 1 for the previous match (the D string), then the " " character.

As the encoding continues, the dictionary quickly builds up fairly long phrases. Of course, since these entries are from a dictionary sorted in alphabetical order, we probably build up phrases much faster than would normally be the case. After just nineteen characters have been read in and encoded, the dictionary looks like the one following.

0	" "
1	"D"
2	"A"
3	"D "
4	"DA"
5	"DA "
6	"DAD"
7	"DY"
8	" "
9	"DADO"

LZ78 Implementation. Like LZ77, LZ78 can arbitrarily set the size of the phrase dictionary. And like LZ77, in LZ78 we have to worry about the effects of this in two ways. First, we have to consider the number of bits allocated in the output token for the phrase code. Second, and more importantly, we have to consider how much CPU time managing the dictionary will take.

In theory, LZ78 should compress better and better as the size of the dictionary increases. But this only holds true as the length of the input text tends towards infinity. In practice, smaller files will quickly begin to suffer as the code size grows larger.

The real difficulty with LZ78 actually comes in managing the dictionary. If we use a sixteen-bit code for the phrase index, for example, we can accommodate 65,536 phrases, including the null code. The phrases can vary tremendously in length, including the improbable possibility of 65,536 different versions of a phrase composed of runs of a single, repeated character.

These phrases are conventionally stored in a multiway tree. The tree starts at a root node, 0, the null string. Each possible character that can be added to the null string is a new branch of the tree, with each phrase created that way getting a new node number.

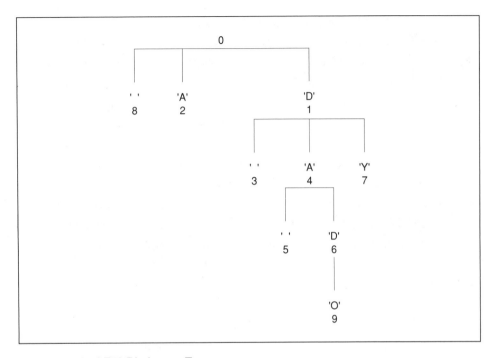

Figure 9-1. An LZ78 Dictionary Tree.

The dictionary tree shown here would be created after the previous nineteen-character phrase was encoded. The major difficulty with managing a tree such as this is the potentially large number of branches off of each node. When compressing binary files with an eight-bit alphabet, 256 branches off of each node are possible. We could simply allocate an array of indices or pointers at each node that was large enough to accommodate all 256 possible descendants. But since most nodes will not have that many descendants, it would be incredibly wasteful to allocate so much storage. Instead, descendant nodes are usually managed as a list of indices no longer than the number of descendant nodes that actually exits. This technique makes better use of available memory, but it is also significantly slower. It is essentially the same technique used in chapter 6 to perform higher-order modeling of data streams.

With a tree like this, comparing an existing string to the dictionary is simple. It is just a matter of walking through the tree, traversing a single node of the tree for every character in the phrase. If the phrase terminates at a particular node, we have a match. If there are more phrases but we have reached a leaf node, there is not a match. After the symbol has been encoded, adding it to the leaf node is also simple—just a matter of adding space to the descendant list, then inserting a new descendant node at the node last matched.

One negative side effect of LZ78 not found in LZ77 is that the decoder has to maintain this tree as well. With LZ77, a dictionary index was just a pointer or index to a previous position in the data stream. But with LZ78, the index is the number of a node in the dictionary tree. The decoder, therefore, has to keep up the tree in exactly the same fashion as the encoder, or a disastrous mismatch will occur.

One issue ignored so far is that of the dictionary filling up. Regardless of how big the dictionary space is, it is going to fill up sooner or later. If we are using a sixteen-bit code, the dictionary will fill up after it has 65,535 phrases defined in it.

There are several alternative choices regarding a full dictionary. Probably the safest default choice is to stop adding new phrases to the dictionary after it is full. This only requires an extra line or two of code in the add_phrase_to_dictionary() routine.

But just leaving the dictionary alone may not be the best choice. When compressing large streams of data, we may see significant changes in the character of the incoming data. When compressing a program's binary image (such as an EXE file), for example, we would expect to see a major shift in the statistical model of the data as we move out of the code section of the file and into the data section.

If we keep using our existing phrase dictionary, we may be stuck with an out-of-date dictionary that isn't compressing very well. At the same time, we have to be careful not to throw away a dictionary that is compressing well.

The UNIX COMPRESS program, which uses an LZ78 variant, manages the full dictionary problem by monitoring the compression ratio of the file. If the compression ratio ever starts to deteriorate, the dictionary is deleted and the program starts over from scratch. Otherwise, the existing dictionary continues to be used, though no new phrases are added to it.

An Effective Variant

As with LZ77, LZ78 was first published in a research journal and discussed in a very technical and abstract fashion. It wasn't until 1984 that a variant of LZ78 made headway in the programming world. This was when Terry Welch published "A Technique for High-Performance Data Compression" in *IEEE Computer*.

Work on the UNIX COMPRESS program began almost immediately after Terry Welch's article appeared. The technique Welch described, and the implementation in COMPRESS, are referred to as LZW compression.

LZSS improved on LZ77 compression by eliminating the requirement that each token output a phrase and a character. LZW makes the same improvement on LZ78. In fact, under LZW, the compressor never outputs single characters, only phrases.

To do this, the major change in LZW is to preload the phrase dictionary with single-symbol phrases equal to the number of symbols in the alphabet. Thus, there is no symbol that cannot be immediately encoded even if it has not already appeared in the input stream.

The LZW compression algorithm in its simplest form follows. A quick examination of the algorithm shows that LZW always tries to output codes for strings that are already known. And each time a new code is output, a new string is added to the string table.

```
old_string[ 0 ] = getc(input);
old_string[ 1 ] = '\0';
while ( !feof( input ) ) {
   character = getc( input );
   strcpy( new_string, old_string );
   strncat( new_string, &character, 1 );
   if ( in_dictionary( new_string ) )
      strcpy( old_string, new_string );
   else {
      code = look_up_dictionary( old_string );
      output_code( code );
      add_to_dictionary( new_string );
      old_string[ 0 ] = character;
      old_string[ 1 ] = '\0';
   }
```

```
        }
        code = look_up_dictionary( old_string );
        output_code( code );
```

A sample string used to demonstrate the algorithm is shown next. The input string is a set of English words from a spelling dictionary, separated by the " " character. On the first pass through the loop, a check is performed to see if the string " W" is in the table. Since it isn't, the code for " " is output, and the string " W" is added to the table. Since the dictionary has codes 0-255 already defined as the 256 possible character values, the first string definition is assigned to code 256. After the third letter, "E", has been read in, the second string code, "WE", is added to the table, and the code for letter "W" is output. In the second word, the characters " " and "W" are read in, matching string number 256. Code 256 is then output, and a three-character string is added to the string table. The process continues until the string is exhausted and all codes have been output.

Input String: " WED WE WEE WEB WET"

Characters Input	Code Output	New code value and associated string
" W"	' '	256 = " W"
"E"	'W'	257 = "WE"
"D"	'E'	258 = "ED"
" "	"D"	259 = "D "
"WE"	256	260 = " WE"
" "	'E'	261 = "E "
"WEE"	260	262 = " WEE"
" W"	261	263 = "E W"
"EB"	257	264 = "WEB"
" "	B	265 = "B "
"WET"	260	266 = " WET"
<EOF>	T	

The sample output for the string is shown with the resulting string table. The string table fills up rapidly, since a new string is added each time a code is output. In this highly redundant input, five code substitutions were output, along with seven characters.

If we were using nine-bit codes for output, the nineteen-character input string would be reduced to a 13.5-byte output string. Of course, this example was carefully chosen to demonstrate code substitution. In real world examples, compression usually doesn't begin until a sizable table has been built, usually after at least one hundred or so bytes have been read in.

Decompression

The companion algorithm for compression is the decompression algorithm. It takes the stream of codes output from the compression algorithm and uses them to recreate the exact input stream. One reason for the efficiency of the LZW algorithm is that it does not need to pass the dictionary to the decompressor. The table can be built exactly as it was during compression, using the input stream as data. This is possible because the compression algorithm always outputs the phrase and character components of a code before it uses it in the output stream, so the compressed data is not burdened with carrying a large dictionary.

```
old_string[ 0 ] = input_bits();
old_string[ 1 ] = '\0';
putc( old_string[ 0 ], output )
while ( ( new_code = input_bits() ) != EOF )
   new_string = dictionary_lookup( new_code );
   fputs( new_string, output );
   append_char_to_string( old_string, new_string[ 0 ] );
   add_to_dictionary( old_string );
   strcpy( old_string, new_string );
}
```

Preceding is a rough C implementation. Like the compression algorithm, it adds a new string to the string table each time it reads in a new code. In addition, it translates each incoming code into a string and sends it to the output.

Following is the output of the algorithm given the input created by the earlier compression. Note that the string table ends up looking exactly like the table built during compression. The output string is identical to the input string from the compression algorithm. Note also that the first 256 codes are already defined to translate to single-character strings, as in the compression code.

Input Codes: " WED<256>E<260><261><257>B<260>T"

Input/ NEW_CODE	OLD_CODE	STRING/ Output	CHARACTER	New table entry
' '	' '	" "		
'W'	' '	"W"	'W'	256 = " W"
'E'	'W'	"E"	'E'	257 = "WE"
'D'	'E'	"D"	'D'	258 = "ED"
256	'D'	" W"	' '	259 = "D "
'E'	256	"E"	'E'	260 = " WE"
260	'E'	" WE"	' '	261 = "E "
261	260	"E "	'E'	262 = " WEE"
257	261	"WE"	'W'	263 = "E W"
'B'	257	"B"	'B'	264 = "WEB"
260	'B'	" WE"	' '	265 = "B "
'T'	260	"T"	'T'	266 = " WET"

The Catch. Unfortunately, the decompression algorithm shown is just a little too simple. A single exception in the LZW compression algorithm causes some trouble in decompression. Each time the compressor adds a new string to the phrase table, it does so before the entire phrase has actually been output to the file. If for some reason the compressor used that phrase as its next code, the expansion code would have a problem. It would be expected to decode a string that was not yet in its table.

Unfortunately, there is a way this can occur. If there is a phrase already in the table composed of a CHARACTER, STRING pair, and the input stream then sees a sequence of CHARACTER, STRING, CHARACTER, STRING, CHARACTER, the compression algorithm will output a code before the decompressor defines it.

A simple example will illustrate the point. Imagine the string IWOMBAT is defined in the table as code 300. Later, the sequence IWOMBATIWOMBATI occurs in the table. The compression output will look like the following:

Input String: IWOMBAT.......IWOMBATIWOMBATIXXX
< Problem section >

Character Input	New code value and associated string	Code Output
...I		
WOMBATA	300 = IWOMBAT	288 (IWOMBA)
.	.	.
.	.	.
...I	.	.
WOMBATI	400 = IWOMBATI	300 (IWOMBAT)
WOMBATIX	401 = IWOMBATIX	400 (IWOMBATI)

When the decompression algorithm sees this input stream, it first decodes code 300 and outputs the IWOMBATI string. It will then add the definition for code 399 to the table, whatever that may be. It then reads the next input code, 400, and finds that it is not in the table.

Fortunately, this is the only time when the decompression algorithm will encounter an undefined code. Since it is the only time, we can add an exception handler to the algorithm. The modified algorithm just looks for the special case of an undefined code and handles it. In the sample, the decompression routine sees a code of 400. Since 400 is undefined, the program goes back to the previous code/string, which was "IWOMBAT", or code 300. It then appends the first character of the string to the end of the string, yielding "IWOMBATI," the correct value for code 400. Processing then proceeds as normal.

The exception handler takes advantage of the knowledge that this problem can happen only in the special circumstances of CHARACTER+STRING+CHARACTER+STRING+CHARACTER. Given that, any time an unknown code occurs, it can determine what the unknown code is given knowledge of the previous string from the input.

```
old_string[ 0 ] = input_bits();
old_string[ 1 ] = '\0';
putc( old_string[ 0 ], output )
while ( ( new_code = input_bits() ) != EOF )
  new_string = dictionary_lookup( new_code );
  if ( new_string == NULL ) {
    strcpy( new_string, old_string );
    append_character_to_string( new_string, new_string[ 0 ] );
  }
  fputs( new_string, output );
  append_character_to_string( old_string, new_string[ 0 ] );
  add_to_dictionary( old_string );
  strcpy( old_string, new_string );
}
```

LZW Implementation. The concepts in the compression algorithm are so simple that the whole algorithm can be expressed in a dozen lines. Implementation of this algorithm is somewhat more complicated, mainly due to management of the dictionary. A short example program that uses twelve-bit codes is in LZW12.C, and it will illustrate some of the techniques used here.

Tree Maintenance and Navigation. As in the LZ78 algorithm, the LZW dictionary is maintained as a multiway tree. But in the case of LZW, the way the data is stored doesn't look much like a tree. A little analysis, however will reveal a multiway tree hidden behind the dictionary data structures.

```
struct dictionary {
  int code_value;
  int parent_code;
  char character;
} dict[ TABLE_SIZE ];
```

The structure shown in the preceding figure holds the entire dictionary tree. Each element in the data structure represents a single node. The node is defined by three items: (1) Code_value. This number is the actual code for the string that terminates at this node and is what the compression program emits when it wants to encode the string; (2) Parent_code. Under LZ78-style compression, every string in the dictionary has a parent string one character shorter than it. This integer is the code for that parent string; (3) Character. This is the character for this particular node. If the string encoded by the parent of a node were "GREENLEA," and the character value was "F," this node would encode "GREENLEAF."

Something that immediately becomes noticeable as a problem here is that each dictionary node does not have a pointer or pointers to its child nodes. As we navigate the tree, how are we supposed to find the children of each node if there are no pointers to children?

The answer is that this tree maintains the dictionary pointers through a hashed array of nodes. To find the child of a particular node, we apply a hashing function to see where that puts us in the list. The hashing function used in LZW12.C is shown next.

```
unsigned int find_child_node( parent_code, child_character )
int parent_code;
int child_character;
{
    int index;
    int offset;

    index = ( child_character << ( BITS - 8 ) ) ^ parent_code;
    if ( index == 0 )
        offset = 1;
    else
        offset = TABLE_SIZE - index;
    for ( ; ; ) {
        if ( dict[ index ].code_value == UNUSED )
            return( index );
        if ( dict[ index ].parent_code == parent_code &&
            dict[ index ].character == (char) child_character )
```

```
        return( index );
    index -= offset;
    if ( index < 0 )
        index += TABLE_SIZE;
    }
}
```

This hashing function is essentially the same one used in the UNIX COMPRESS program. It combines the numeric values of the parent_code and the child_character to form a sixteen-bit offset into the list of nodes. After finding the target node, it checks for collisions, since that node may be in use by some other element in the tree. Eventually, one of two things happens. Either this function finds a node already defined as belonging to the parent and child, or it finds an empty node that can be used that way.

This hashing function performs fairly well. The collision avoidance mechanism depends on having TABLE_SIZE be a prime number, and performance depends on it being at least 20 percent larger than two raised to the BITS power. In LZW12.C, TABLE_SIZE needs to be larger than 4,096. The number actually used was 5,021.

With the hashing function in place, we can now effectively navigate down through the tree. The data structures used to maintain the dictionary during compression don't help us move up the tree, but during compression we don't need to move up the tree, only down.

During decompression, the hashing function is no longer used. Instead, each node in the tree has its parent code and character value stored at the array offset defined by its own code. This allows for quick lookup of dictionary values, which lets us move up the tree quickly. We need to move up the tree during decompression to determine the entire contents of a string, and this different storage method makes this possible. We never need to move down the tree during decompression, so the hashing function is no longer needed.

One additional feature of the dictionary tree used in LZW12.C needs explanation. The first 256 nodes are considered "special" nodes by the program. Each of them represents the one character string that corresponds with its node value. In other words, code 65 will always represent the character "A," and it will automatically be assumed not to have a parent. These nodes are all predefined when the program is first initialized.

Compression

Armed just with the hashing function and the data structure, the compression program can be written fairly easily. The program goes through a short initialization phase, then sits in an encoding loop reading characters in and sending codes out. Finally, it does a small amount of cleanup work, then exits.

```
next_code = FIRST_CODE;
for ( i = 0 ; i < TABLE_SIZE ; i++ )
  dict[ i ].code_value = UNUSED;
if ( ( string_code = getc( input ) ) == EOF )
  string_code = END_OF_STREAM;
while ( ( character = getc( input ) ) != EOF ) {
  index = find_child_node( string_code, character );
  if ( dict[ index ].code_value != - 1)
    string_code = dict[ index ].code_value;
  else {
    if ( next_code <= MAX_CODE ) {
      dict[ index ].code_value = next_code++;
      dict[ index ].parent_code = string_code;
      dict[ index ].character = (char) character;
    }
    OutputBits( output, string_code, BITS );
    string_code = character;
  }
}
OutputBits( output, string_code, BITS );
OutputBits( output, END_OF_STREAM, BITS );
```

This routine first initializes the dictionary array. It does this by marking all nodes in the tree as unused. Remember that the first 256 nodes are special and will be considered used automatically.

The next_code variable is then set to the first available code. This program uses code 256 as an end-of-file marker, so the first code defined will have a value of 257. As new strings are read in and defined, this number grows until it reaches the maximum code value of 4,095.

Finally, the first character is read in and assigned to the loop variable string_code. We can arbitrarily assign the first character to a code value, since it is a special single-character string.

After initialization, the main encoding loop begins. The working variable, string_code, keeps track of which code matches the characters read in so far. When the program first starts, that is just a single-character string, but as the dictionary grows, string_code can represent very long strings.

A single character is read in from the input file, then find_child_node() is called to see if the current string_code has a child node that corresponds to that character. If it does, the child's code is assigned to string_code, and we move back to the top of the loop.

If there is no child node, we have reached the end of our string match. When this occurs, we output the current code, then start over with a new string_code. Finally, we add the new string created by the combination of string_code and character to the dictionary so the next time it occurs we will get a match.

The main loop repeats until an end-of-file is read in. When this occurs, we output the string_code built up so far. Finally, the END_OF_STREAM code is output, which tells the decoder when we are at the end of the data stream.

Decompression

As mentioned previously, maintaining the dictionary is simpler during decompression. We don't ever have to navigate down through the tree. Instead, we read in codes straight from the encoded stream, then work our way up through the tree. As long as the parent nodes are properly defined in the data structure, everything works fine.

The only problem with working up through the tree is that the decoded characters are gathered in reverse order, so they have to be pushed into a stack, popped off in reverse order, and written to the output file. This is done with the decode_string routine, shown next.

Decode_string() follows the parent pointers up through the dictionary until it finds a code less than 256, which we have defined as the first character in the string. A count of characters in the decode stack is then returned to the calling program.

```
unsigned int decode_string( count, code )
unsigned int count;
unsigned int code;
{
    while ( code > 255 ) {
        decode_stack[ count++ ] = dict[ code ].character;
        code = dict[ code ].parent_code;
    }
    decode_stack[ count++ ] = (char) code;
    return( count );
}
```

Once the decode routine is in place, the decompression routine falls into order fairly easily. The routine has a few lines of initialization code, followed by a main decoding loop.

The initialization section of the decompression routine in LZW12.C sets up the next_code variable. This lets it track the code value of each string as it is added to the table. Next, it reads in the first code and copies it to the output file. Once that is done, it can enter the main decoding loop.

```
next_code = FIRST_CODE;
old_code = InputBits( input, BITS );
if ( old_code == END_OF_STREAM )
    return;
character = old_code;
putc( old_code, output );
while ( ( new_code = InputBits( input, BITS ) ) != END_OF_STREAM ) {
    if ( new_code >= next_code ) {
        decode_stack[ 0 ] = (char) character;
        count = decode_string( 1, old_code );
    }
    else
        count = decode_string( 0, new_code );
    character = decode_stack[ count - 1 ];
    while ( count > 0 )
        putc( decode_stack[ --count ], output );
    if ( next_code <= MAX_CODE ) {
```

```
      dict[ next_code ].parent_code = old_code;
      dict[ next_code ].character = (char) character;
      next_code++;
    }
    old_code = new_code;
  }
```

Normally, decoding is a simple matter. The loop reads in a code value, looks up the string, and outputs it. Then it creates a new string by adding the old_code and the first character of the current string to the string table. It then goes back to the top of the loop and starts over.

But an additional complication is created when the CHARACTER+STRING+ CHARACTER+STRING+CHARACTER sequence shows up. This creates a code larger than the largest currently defined code. Fortunately, we know what to do in this case. Our new string will be the same as our last string, defined by old_code, with a copy of its first character appended to its end. This is handled by preinitializing the decoding_stack with a single character, then decoding the old_code string into the stack with an offset of one instead of zero.

The Code

The source code for a complete twelve-bit version of LZW compression and decompression follows.

```
/*************************** Start of LZW12.C ***************************
*
* This is 12 bit LZW program, which is discussed in the first part
* of the chapter. It uses a fixed size code, and does not attempt
* to flush the dictionary after it fills up.
*/
#include <stdio.h>
#include <stdlib.h>
#include <string.h>
#include "errhand.h"
#include "bitio.h"
```

```
/*
 * Constants used throughout the program. BITS defines how many bits
 * will be in a code. TABLE_SIZE defines the size of the dictionary
 * table.
 */
#define BITS            12
#define MAX_CODE        ( ( 1 << BITS ) - 1 )
#define TABLE_SIZE      5021
#define END_OF_STREAM   256
#define FIRST_CODE      257
#define UNUSED          -1
/*
 * Local prototypes.
 */
#ifdef _STDC_
unsigned int find_child_node( int parent_code, int child_character );
unsigned int decode_string( unsigned int offset, unsigned int code );
#else
unsigned int find_child_node ();
unsigned int decode_string ();
#endif

char *CompressionName = "LZW 12 Bit Encoder";
char *Usage           = "in-file out-file\n\n";

/*
 * This data structure defines the dictionary. Each entry in the
 * dictionary has a code value. This is the code emitted by the
 * compressor. Each code is actually made up of two pieces: a
 * parent_code, and a character. Code values of less than 256 are
 * actually plain text codes.
 */

struct dictionary {
    int code_value;
    int parent_code;
    char character;
```

```
} dict[ TABLE_SIZE ];

char decode_stack[ TABLE_SIZE ];

/*
 * The compressor is short and simple. It reads in new symbols one
 * at a time from the input file. It then checks to see if the
 * combination of the current symbol and the current code are already
 * defined in the dictionary. If they are not, they are added to the
 * dictionary, and we start over with a new one symbol code. If they
 * are, the code for the combination of the code and character becomes
 * our new code.
 */

void CompressFile( input, output, argc, argv )
FILE *input;
BIT_FILE *output;
int argc;
char *argv[];
{
    int next_code;
    int character;
    int string_code;
    unsigned int index;
    unsigned int i;

    next_code = FIRST_CODE;
    for ( i = 0 ; i < TABLE_SIZE ; i++ )
        dict[ i ].code_value = UNUSED;
    if ( ( string_code = getc( input ) ) == EOF )
        string_code = END_OF_STREAM;
    while ( ( character = getc( input ) ) != EOF ) {
        index = find_child_node( string_code, character );
        if ( dict[ index ].code_value != - 1)
            string_code = dict[ index ].code_value;
        else {
            if ( next_code <= MAX_CODE ) {
```

```
        dict[ index ].code_value = next_code++;
        dict[ index ].parent_code = string_code;
        dict[ index ].character = (char) character;
      }
      OutputBits( output, (unsigned long) string_code, BITS );
      string_code = character;
    }
  }
  OutputBits( output, (unsigned long) string_code, BITS );
  OutputBits( output, (unsigned long) END_OF_STREAM, BITS );
  while ( argc-- > 0 )
    printf( "Unknown argument: %s\n", *argv++ ); }

/*
 * The file expander operates much like the encoder. It has to
 * read in codes, the convert the codes to a string of characters.
 * The only catch in the whole operation occurs when the encoder
 * encounters a CHAR+STRING+CHAR+STRING+CHAR sequence. When this
 * occurs, the encoder outputs a code that is not presently defined
 * in the table. This is handled as an exception.
 */
void ExpandFile( input, output, argc, argv )
BIT_FILE *input;
FILE *output;
int argc;
char *argv[];
{
  unsigned int next_code;
  unsigned int new_code;
  unsigned int old_code;
  int character;
  unsigned int count;

  next_code = FIRST_CODE;
  old_code = (unsigned int) InputBits( input, BITS );
  if ( old_code == END_OF_STREAM )
    return;
```

```
  character = old_code;
  putc( old_code, output );

while ( ( new_code = (unsigned int) InputBits( input, BITS ) )
        != END_OF_STREAM ) {
/*
** This code checks for the CHARACTER+STRING+CHARACTER+STRING+CHARACTER
** case which generates an undefined code. It handles it by decoding
** the last code, and adding a single character to the end of the
** decode string.
*/
    if ( new_code >= next_code ) {
      decode_stack[ 0 ] = (char) character;
      count = decode_string( 1, old_code );
    }
    else
      count  = decode_string( 0, new_code );
    character = decode_stack[ count - 1 ];
    while ( count > 0 )
      putc( decode_stack[ --count ], output );
    if ( next_code <= MAX_CODE ) {
      dict[ next_code ].parent_code = old_code;
      dict[ next_code ].character = (char) character;
      next_code++;
    }
    old_code = new_code;
  }
  while ( argc-- > 0 )
    printf( "Unknown argument: %s\n", *argv++ );
}

/*
* This hashing routine is responsible for finding the table location
* for a string/character combination. The table index is created
* by using an exclusive OR combination of the prefix and character.
* This code also has to check for collisions, and handles them by
* jumping around in the table.
```

```
*/
unsigned int find_child_node( parent_code, child_character )
int parent_code;
int child_character;
{
   int index;
   int offset;

   index = ( child_character << ( BITS - 8 ) ) ^ parent_code;
   if ( index == 0 )
     offset = 1;
   else
     offset = TABLE_SIZE - index;
   for ( ; ; ) {
     if ( dict[ index ].code_value == UNUSED )
       return( index );
     if ( dict[ index ].parent_code == parent_code &&
       dict[ index ].character == (char) child_character )
       return( index );
     index -= offset;
     if ( index < 0 )
       index += TABLE_SIZE;
   }
}
/*
* This routine decodes a string from the dictionary, and stores it
* in the decode_stack data structure. It returns a count to the
* calling program of how many characters were placed in the stack.
*/

unsigned int decode_string( count, code )
unsigned int count;
unsigned int code;
{
   while ( code > 255 ) {
     decode_stack[ count++ ] = dict[ code ].character;
     code = dict[ code ].parent_code;
```

```
    }
    decode_stack[ count++ ] = (char) code;
    return( count );
}
```

/*********************** End of LZW12.C ***********************/

Improvements

A second version of the LZW program, LZW15V.C, follows. It contains several enhancements, most of which are also found in the UNIX COMPRESS program.

LZW can be improved by increasing the size of the dictionary. As it becomes possible to store more and longer phrases, the program compresses to higher ratios. In this case, LZW15V.C uses a maximum code size of fifteen bits, which allows for a 32K phrase dictionary. While there is enough memory available on most MS-DOS machines to accommodate sixteen-bit code sizes, the program has to convert most of the indices used during compression from unsigned int values to long ints. This usually exacts a fairly heavy performance penalty on a sixteen-bit machine, so this program stayed with fifteen-bit values.

Unfortunately, moving to a larger code size actually retards compression when the file to be compressed is small. Since phrases are initially found and added to the dictionary at the same pace, whether the code is nine bits or fifteen bits long, the nine-bit code will actually produce a smaller file.

There is a simple solution to this problem, however. Instead of always outputting codes using fifteen bits, LZW15V.C starts out using a nine-bit code, and it doesn't advance to ten bits until the dictionary has added 256 new entries. It progresses through ten, eleven, twelve, etc, until it starts using fifteen-bit codes. This puts it on an equal footing with compressors using a smaller code size.

To let the decompression program know when the bit size of the output code is going to change, a special BUMP_CODE is used. This code tells the decompression program to increase the bit size immediately. While it is possible to synchronize the compressor and decompressor so that they don't need to explicitly use a code, the BUMP_CODE was employed for purposes of clarity.

One final enhancement in LZW15V.C is the FLUSH_CODE. This tells the decompressor to throw away all phrases currently in the dictionary and to start over with a blank slate. When compressing files several hundred K bytes long, the dictionary will ordinarily fill up with phrases. At this point, the UNIX COMPRESS program starts to monitor the compression ratio, looking for signs of decay. This type of algorithm could be employed in LZW15V.C, but a simpler heuristic was chosen: when the dictionary fills up, it is discarded. In practice this method generally gives results comparable to those of the COMPRESS algorithm.

```
/************************* Start of LZW15V.C *************************
*
* This is the LZW module which implements a more powerful version
* of the algorithm. This version of the program has three major
* improvements over LZW12.C. First, it expands the maximum code size
* to 15 bits. Second, it starts encoding with 9 bit codes, working
* its way up in bit size only as necessary. Finally, it flushes the
* dictionary when done.
*
* Note that under MS-DOS this program needs to be built using the
* Compact or Large memory model.
*
*/
#include <stdio.h>
#include <stdlib.h>
#include <string.h>
#include "errhand.h"
#include "bitio.h"

/*
* Constants used throughout the program. BITS defines the maximum
* number of bits that can be used in the output code. TABLE_SIZE defines
* the size of the dictionary table. TABLE_BANKS are the number of
* 256 element dictionary pages needed. The code defines should be
* self-explanatory.
*/
```

```
#define BITS            15
#define MAX_CODE        ( ( 1 << BITS ) - 1 )
#define TABLE_SIZE      35023L
#define TABLE_BANKS     ( ( TABLE_SIZE >> 8 ) + 1 )
#define END_OF_STREAM   256
#define BUMP_CODE       257
#define FLUSH_CODE      258
#define FIRST_CODE      259
#define UNUSED          -1

/*
 * Local prototypes.
 */
#ifdef_STDC_
unsigned int find_child_node( int parent_code, int child_character );
unsigned int decode_string( unsigned int offset, unsigned int code );
#else
unsigned int find_child_node();
unsigned int decode_string();
#endif

char *CompressionName = "LZW 15 Bit Variable Rate Encoder";
char *Usage           = "in-file out-file\n\n";

/*
 * This data structure defines the dictionary. Each entry in the
 * dictionary has a code value. This is the code emitted by the
 * compressor. Each code is actually made up of two pieces: a
 * parent_code, and a character. Code values of less than 256 are
 * actually plain text codes.
 *
 * Note that in order to handle 16 bit segmented compilers, such as most
 * of the MS-DOS compilers, it was necessary to break up the dictionary
 * into a table of smaller dictionary pointers. Every reference to the
 * dictionary was replaced by a macro that did a pointer dereference
 * first. By breaking up the index along byte boundaries we should be as
 * efficient as possible.
 */
```

```
struct dictionary
{
    int code_value;
    int parent_code;
    char character;
} *dict[ TABLE_BANKS ];

#define DICT( i ) dict[ i >> 8 ][ i & 0xff ]

/*
 * Other global data structures. The decode_stack is used to reverse
 * strings that come out of the tree during decoding. next_code is the
 * next code to be added to the dictionary, both during compression and
 * decompression. current_code_bits defines how many bits are currently
 * being used for output, and next_bump_code defines the code that will
 * trigger the next jump in word size.
 */

char decode_stack[ TABLE_SIZE ];
unsigned int next_code;
int current_code_bits;
unsigned int next_bump_code;

/*
 * This routine is used to initialize the dictionary, both when the
 * compressor or decompressor first starts up, and also when a flush
 * code comes in. Note that even though the decompressor sets all
 * the code_value elements to UNUSED, it doesn't really need to.
 */

void InitializeDictionary( void )
{
    unsigned int i;

    for ( i = 0 ; i < TABLE_SIZE ; i++ )
        DICT( i ).code_value = UNUSED;
    next_code = FIRST_CODE;
```

```
    putc( 'F', stdout );
    current_code_bits = 9;
    next_bump_code = 511;
}


/*
 * This routine allocates the dictionary. Since the total size of the
 * dictionary is much larger than 64K, it can't be allocated as a single
 * object. Instead, it is allocated as a set of pointers to smaller
 * dictionary objects. The special DICT() macro is used to translate
 * indices into pairs of references.
 */

void InitializeStorage( void )
{
    int i;

    for ( i = 0 ; i < TABLE_BANKS ; i++ ) {
        dict[ i ] = (struct dictionary *)
                    calloc( 256, sizeof ( struct dictionary ) );
        if ( dict[ i ] == NULL )
            fatal_error( "Error allocating dictionary space" );
    }
}


/*
 * The compressor is short and simple. It reads in new symbols one
 * at a time from the input file. It then checks to see if the
 * combination of the current symbol and the current code are already
 * defined in the dictionary. If they are not, they are added to the
 * dictionary, and we start over with a new one symbol code. If they
 * are, the code for the combination of the code and character becomes
 * our new code. Note that in this enhanced version of LZW, the
 * encoder needs to check the codes for boundary conditions.
 */

void CompressFile( input, output, argc, argv )
```

```
FILE *input;
BIT_FILE *output;
int argc;
char *argv[];
{
  int character;
  int string_code;
  unsigned int index;

  InitializeStorage();
  InitializeDictionary();
  if ( ( string_code = getc( input ) ) == EOF )
    string_code = END_OF_STREAM;
  while ( ( character = getc( input ) ) != EOF ) {
    index = find_child_node( string_code, character );
    if ( DICT( index ).code_value != - 1)
      string_code = DICT( index ).code_value;
    else {
      DICT( index ).code_value = next_code++;
      DICT( index ).parent_code = string_code;
      DICT( index ).character = (char) character;
      OutputBits( output,
                  (unsigned long) string_code, current_code_bits );
      string_code = character;
      if ( next_code > MAX_CODE ) {
        OutputBits( output,
                    (unsigned long) FLUSH_CODE, current_code_bits );
        InitializeDictionary();
      } else if ( next_code > next_bump_code ) {
        OutputBits( output,
                    (unsigned long) BUMP_CODE, current_code_bits );
        current_code_bits++;
        next_bump_code <<= 1;
        next_bump_code |= 1;
        putc( 'B', stdout );
      }
    }
```

```
    }
    OutputBits( output, (unsigned long) string_code, current_code_bits );
    OutputBits( output, (unsigned long) END_OF_STREAM, current_code_bits);
    while ( argc-- > 0 )
        printf( "Unknown argument: %s\n", *argv++ );
}


/*
 * The file expander operates much like the encoder. It has to
 * read in codes, then convert the codes to a string of characters.
 * The only catch in then whole operation occurs when the encoder
 * encounters a CHAR+STRING+CHAR+STRING+CHAR sequence. When this
 * occurs, the encoder outputs a code that is not presently defined
 * in the table. This is handled as an exception. All of the special
 * input codes are handled in various ways.
 */

void ExpandFile( input, output, argc, argv )
BIT_FILE *input;
FILE *output;
int argc;
char *argv[];
{
    unsigned int new_code;
    unsigned int old_code;
    int character;
    unsigned int count;

    InitializeStorage();
    while ( argc-- > 0 )
        printf( "Unknown argument: %s\n", *argv++ );
    for ( ; ; ) {
        InitializeDictionary();
        old_code = (unsigned int) InputBits( input, current_code_bits );
        if ( old_code == END_OF_STREAM )
            return;
        character = old_code;
```

```
    putc( old_code, output );
    for ( ; ; ) {
      new_code = (unsigned int) InputBits( input, current_code_bits );
      if ( new_code == END_OF_STREAM )
        return;
      if ( new_code == FLUSH_CODE )
        break;
      if ( new_code == BUMP_CODE ) {
        current_code_bits++;
        putc( 'B', stdout );
        continue;
      }
      if ( new_code >= next_code ) {
        decode_stack[ 0 ] = (char) character;
        count = decode_string( 1, old_code );
      }
      else
        count = decode_string( 0, new_code );
      character = decode_stack[ count - 1 ];
      while ( count > 0 )
        putc( decode_stack[ -count ], output );
      DICT( next_code ).parent_code = old_code;
      DICT( next_code ).character = (char) character;
      next_code++;
      old_code = new_code;
    }
  }
}


/*
 * This hashing routine is responsible for finding the table location
 * for a string/character combination. The table index is created
 * by using an exclusive OR combination of the prefix and character.
 * This code also has to check for collisions, and handles them by
 * jumping around in the table.
 */
```

```
unsigned int find_child_node( parent_code, child_character )
int parent_code;
int child_character;
{
  unsigned int index;
  int offset;

  index = ( child_character << ( BITS - 8 ) ) ^ parent_code;
  if ( index == 0 )
    offset = 1;
  else
    offset = TABLE_SIZE - index;
  for ( ; ; ) {
    if ( DICT( index ).code_value == UNUSED )
      return( (unsigned int) index );
    if ( DICT( index ).parent_code == parent_code &&
      DICT( index ).character == (char) child_character )
      return( index );
    if ( index >= offset )
      index -= offset;
    else
      index += TABLE_SIZE - offset;
  }
}

/*
* This routine decodes a string from the dictionary, and stores it
* in the decode_stack data structure. It returns a count to the
* calling program of how many characters were placed in the stack.
*/

unsigned int decode_string( count, code )
unsigned int count;
unsigned int code;
{
  while ( code > 255 ) {
    decode_stack[ count++ ] = DICT( code ).character;
```

```
      code = DICT( code ).parent_code;
   }
   decode_stack[ count++ ] = (char) code;
   return( count );
}


/************************* End of LZW15V.C *************************/
```

Patents

One note of caution regarding the use of the LZW algorithm. Terry Welch filed for, and was awarded, a U.S. patent covering at least some portions of his algorithm. This patent is presently assigned to Unisys, which has made public its intention to protect its intellectual property rights. LZW compression is defined as part of the CCITT V.42*bis* specification, and Unisys has defined specific terms under which it will license the algorithm to modem manufacturers. It has not stated that it will apply the same terms to any and all parties manufacturing other types of products.

Clearly LZW is a derivative work of the LZ78 algorithm, but defining the boundaries of what is covered by the patent and what is not probably requires the assistance of a skilled patent attorney. Over the past ten years, quite a few software copyright battles have been fought in the courts, enough so that software developers can sensibly use some general rules. The same cannot be said for software patents. The U.S. patent office has only begun issuing these patents in a major way since the mid 1980s, and very little significant litigation has made its way through the courts. Programmers and manufacturers would be wise to seek competent counsel before stepping into these waters.

CHAPTER 10

Speech Compression

Manipulation of sound by computers is a relatively new development. It has been possible since the birth of digital computers, but only in the last five years or so has inexpensive hardware brought this to the average user's desktop. Now the ability to play digitized sound is expected to be an integral part of the up-and-coming "multimedia revolution."

The use of multimedia focuses the issue of data compression for must users. Computer graphics in particular quickly take up all available disk space. Digitized audio is far less voracious in its storage requirements, but even so it can quickly swallow up all free space on the average user's hard disk.

Fortunately for computer users, the world of telephony has used digitized audio since the 1960s, and extensive research has been done on effective methods of encoding and compressing audio data. The world's telecommunications companies were intensely aware of the cost of transmission bandwidth and made efforts to reduce expenses in this area. Computer users today benefit from much of this research.

This chapter looks first at some of the basic concepts involved in using digital audio, including the software and hardware in today's generation of computers. Next, it looks at how well conventional lossless compression techniques work on digitized voice. Finally, it explores some lossy techniques.

Digital Audio Concepts

For modern computers to manipulate sound, they first have to convert it to a digital format. The sound samples can then be processed, transmitted, and converted back to analog format, where they can finally be received by the human ear.

Digitization of sound began in earnest in the early 1960s. Like much of our early computer technology, credit for development lies with AT&T, which at that time had a regulated monopoly on long-distance service in the United States. In 1962, AT&T established the first commercial digital telephone link, a T1 interoffice trunk in Chicago.

In the short space of thirty years, we have seen the long-distance network in the United States convert almost entirely from analog to digital transmission. Virtually all new switching equipment installed by telephone companies today is digital. But analog switching is still found in older installations and in the smaller PBX and key systems installed in businesses. Of course, the final subscriber loop between the telephone company and the end user is still persistently analog.

Digital audio is now coming of age in the highly visible consumer electronics arena as well. The digital compact disk has nearly completed its displacement of analog LP records. It remains to be seen whether digital audio tape will do the same thing to analog cassette tape, but it seems likely that some day most recorded music will be distributed in digital format.

Fundamentals. While this book cannot give a complete course in digital signal processing, it certainly has room to cover a few basic concepts involved in digital sound. Figure 10-1 shows a typical audio waveform as it might be displayed on an oscilloscope. The X axis in this diagram represents time. The Y axis represents a voltage measured at an input device, typically a microphone. The microphone attempts to faithfully reproduce changes in air pressure caused by sound waves traveling through it.

Some human ears can hear sounds at frequencies as high as 20,000Hz and nearly as low as DC. The dynamic range of our hearing is so wide that we have to employ a logarithmic scale of measurement, the decibel, to reasonably accommodate it. This presents a unique set of requirements for digitization.

A waveform like that shown in figure 10-1 is typical of audio sample. It isn't a nice, clean sine wave that has a regular period and can be described as a simple mathematical function. Instead, it is a combination of various frequencies at different amplitudes and phases. When combined, we see something that looks fairly irregular and not easy to characterize.

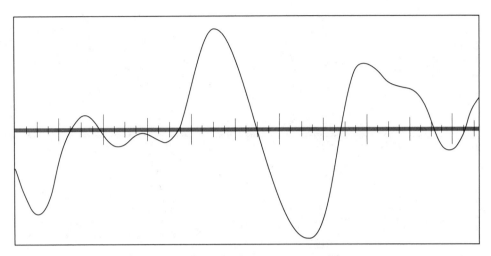

Figure 10-1. A typical audio waveform.

This particular "snapshot" shows about 5 milliseconds (ms) of output. Notice that the largest recognizable components of the waveform appear to have a period of roughly two milliseconds. This corresponds to a frequency of about 500Hz, a fairly characteristic frequency found in speech or music.

The first step in working with digital audio is "sampling." Sampling consists of taking measurements of the input signal at regular times, converting them to an appropriate scale, and storing them. Figure 10-2 shows the same waveform sampled at an 8KHz rate. This means that 8,000 times per second a measurement is taken of the voltage level of the input signal. The measurement points are marked with an "x" on the waveform.

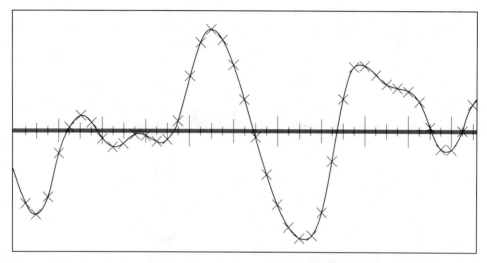

Figure 10-2. A typical audio waveform being sampled at 8KHz.

In most computer systems, this first step of digitization is done with an analog-to-digital converter (ADC). The ADC takes a given voltage and scales it to an appropriate digital measurement. An eight-bit ADC, for example, might have a "full scale" input voltage of 500 millivolts (mv)—it would output an eight-bit value of 255 if the input voltage were 500mv and zero if the input voltage were zero. A voltage between these values would be scaled to fit in the linear range of zero to 255.

Since audio signals are AC in nature, the ranges are usually adjusted so that a zero voltage signal falls in the middle of the range. For the previous example, the range would be adjusted to between -250mv and +250mv. Outputs from the eight-bit ADC would range from -128 to +127.

The stored sample points then represent a series of voltages that were measured at the input of the ADC. Figure 10-3 shows the representation of those voltages overlaid with the input AC signal. Note that since the sample points in this case are occurring many times more frequently than the period of the waveform, the digital samples themselves trace the analog signal very accurately.

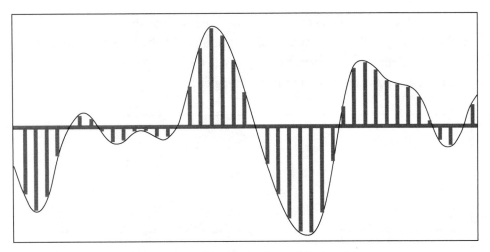

Figure 10-3. Sample voltages overlaid with the input AC signal

Now that the sound has been digitized, it can be stored via computer using any number of technologies, ranging from fast storage, such as main processor RAM, to off-line slow storage on magnetic tape. The actual speed of the storage medium is relatively unimportant with digital sound, since the bandwidth needed to accurately store the sound is relatively slow compared to most digital media.

Eventually, the sound needs to be played back. This is done via another electronic component that is the converse of the ADC: the digital-to-analog converter (DAC). The DAC is responsible for taking a digital value and converting it to a corresponding analog signal. To be effective, the conversion process needs to be the mirror image of that performed when converting the analog signal to digital. While the exact voltages produced at the output of the DAC do not need to be identical to those seen at the input, they do need to be proportional to one another so that one waveform corresponds to the other. In addition, the samples need to be output at exactly the same rate that they were read in. Any deviation here will cause the output frequencies to be shifted up or down from the input, generally not a good thing.

Figure 10-4 shows the output of the DAC when given the same set of samples produced in figure 10-2. At first glance, it seems that this is a radically different waveform. All the nice, smooth shapes shown in the earlier figures are gone, replaced by this stair-step, rectangular, artificial-looking creation.

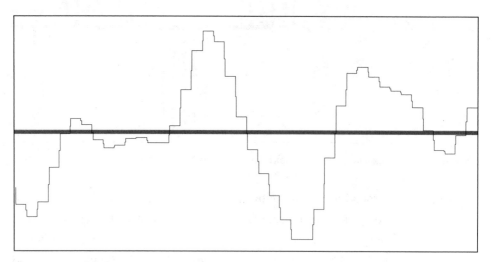

Figure 10-4. DAC output.

Fortunately, figure 10-4 is not that far removed from figure 10-1. Mathematically, the sharp jumps that occur when we move from sample to sample represent high-frequency components in the output signal. These can (and must) be eliminated from the signal by means of a low-pass filter that lies between the output of the DAC and the final amplification stage of the audio output.

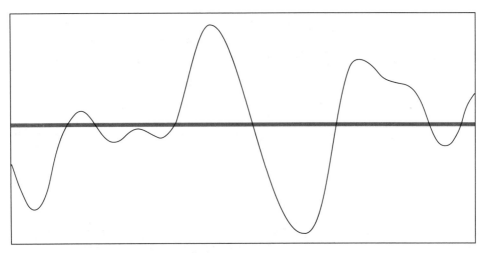

Figure 10-5. Sampling at a much higher rate.

A low-pass filter is a network of electrical components designed to let frequencies below a certain value pass through it unhindered, while attenuating frequencies above that point. An ideal low-pass filter used with the samples shown here would completely stop any frequency above 4KHz and let frequencies below 4KHz pass through with no attenuation.

In practice, low-pass filters don't work perfectly, but even a low-budget filter can take figure 10-4 and create a nearly indistinguishable copy of figure 10-1. Without the filter, the sound sample will still be intelligible, but it will be filled with distracting high-frequency "noise" that is part of the reproduction process.

Figure 10-5 shows the same figure when the sampling rate has been stepped up to a much higher rate. This increase in sampling rate clearly does a more accurate job of reproducing the signal. The next section discusses how variations in these parameters affect the output signal.

Sampling Variables. When an audio waveform is sampled, two important variables affect the quality of the reproduction: the sample rate and the sample resolution. Both are important factors, but they play different roles in determining the level of distortion produced when a sample is played back.

The sample resolution is simply a measure of how accurately the digital sample can measure the voltage it is recording. When the input range is -500mv to +500mv, for example, an eight-bit ADC can resolve the input signal down to about 4mv. So an input signal of 2mv will either get rounded up to 4mv or down to 0mv. This is called a quantization error.

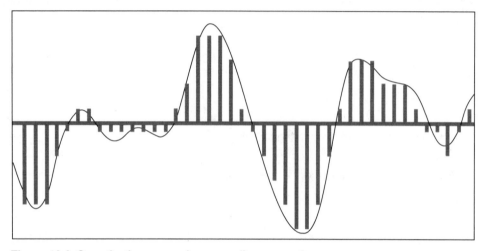

Figure 10-6. Quantization error when sampling a waveform

Figure 10-6 shows the results of quantization error when sampling a waveform. In some cases the sample point has a larger magnitude than the audio signal, but in other places it has less. When the digitized signal is played back through a DAC, the output waveform will closely track the sample points, resulting in a certain amount of distortion.

It might seem that eight bits should be enough to accurately record audio data, but this may not be the case because of the large dynamic range of audio the human ear can detect. If our 500mv range example were used, we might find that our input signal magnitudes range from 1mv to 500mv in a single recording session. The crash of drums in an orchestra could push the ADC to its limits, while a delicate violin solo may never go outside 5mv. If the minimum digital resolution is only 5mv, a very noticeable level of distortion will be introduced during this part of a recording session.

The sampling rate plays a different role in determining the quality of digital sound reproduction. One classic law in digital signal processing was published by Harry Nyquist in 1933. He determined that to accurately reproduce a signal of frequency f, the sampling rate has to be greater than 2*f. This is commonly called the Nyquist Rate.

The audio signal in figure 10-7 is being measured at a considerably slower rate than that shown in the previous examples, with noticeably negative consequences. At several places in the waveform it is not even sampled a single time during an excursion above or below the center line.

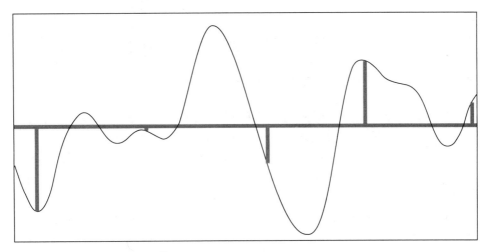

Figure 10-7. A slower sampling rate.

Figure 10-8 shows the waveform we could expect after playing back the digitized samples stored from figure 10-7. Clearly, after the digitized output is filtered, the resulting waveform differs quite a bit from that shown in the previous figure. What has happened is that the high-frequency components of the waveform have been lost by the slower sampling rate, letting only the low-frequency parts of the sample through.

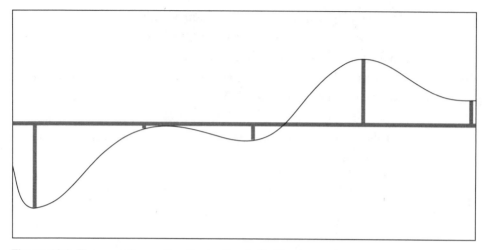

Figure 10-8. The waveform after playing back digitized samples.

The human ear hears sounds up to 20KHz, which implies that we need to sample audio at 40KHz or better to achieve good reproduction. In fact, the sampling rate used for digital reproduction of music via compact disk or digital audio tape is 44KHz, using sixteen-bit samples. The quality of sound achieved at this sampling rate is generally acknowledged to be superior.

This does not mean that all digital recordings have to be done at 44KHz rates. Virtually every digital phone system in the world uses an 8KHz sampling rate to record human speech, with generally good results. This means that the phone system is unable to pass any signal with a frequency of 4KHz or higher. This clearly does not render the system useless—millions of long-distance calls over digital lines are made every day. The average speech signal is composed of many different frequencies, and even if everything above 4KHz is discarded, most of the speech energy still makes it through the system. Our ears detect this loss as a lower-fidelity signal, but they still understand it quite well.

The ultimate test of all this is how the audio output sounds to our ears. It is difficult to quantify a "quality of sound" measurement in strictly mathematical terms, so when discussing audio output, it is always best to temper judgments with true listener trials.

PC-Based Sound. Some exotic work in digital signal processing has been going on for years, but it usually involved expensive special-purpose peripherals far out of reach of the average computer installation.

Early desktop computers did not really push the state of the art in sound reproduction. Original IBM and Apple computers both had built-in speakers as standard equipment, but they gave the programmer only a single bit with which to control the speaker. This meant the speaker could generally be used only to emit beeps and buzzes, not true digitized sound.

In the early 1980s, however, many computer manufacturers saw that a true digitized sound capability could be added to their computers at a relatively low cost. Apple was the most prominent manufacturer, adding an eight-bit DAC to the Macintosh, which opened the door to the use of true digitized audio.

Most desktop computers today are IBM compatible ISA computers based on Intel's 80x86 CPU chips. Unfortunately for sound enthusiasts, IBM has not yet elected to add sound capability to the PC, but third-party solutions are relatively inexpensive. The sound samples used in this book have been created and manipulated using the Sound Blaster card, manufactured by Creative Labs. But several other cards are on the market that can play digitized sound samples, and any of these can be used, provided file-format conversion utilities exist.

The next generation of digitized sound on the desktop is just coming. Newer machines are being built which not only digitize and play back 44KHz sixteen-bit CD-quality sound data, but also have built in digital signal-processing chips to manipulate stored voice data. These capabilities let users produce the high-fidelity sounds that enable the so-called multimedia revolution. But these high-sampling rates and wide samples only highlight the need for data compression, since they fill up a hard disk faster than ever before.

The files in this book will be "raw" sound files. These will be pure binary recordings of eight-bit input data. Virtually all sound software on desktop machines today expects more than that for a sound file, but many software packages have utilities to convert raw sound files to a particular format. The Sound Blaster, for example, includes an executable program called VOC-HDR.EXE that prepends a header file to a raw sound file. The sound samples here were all sampled at 11KHz, a commonly used rate for medium-fidelity digital recording.

By supplying sound data only, the code here can concentrate on compression, without worries about additional superfluous data in the file. A full-fledged sound-file compression package by necessity needs to support the dozens of different file formats in existence, but that mostly consists of implementation details.

Some sound capability resources are available for a relatively small investment. Many on-line services, such as Compuserve, GEnie, and BIX, have active forums for audio manipulation. Freeware and shareware utility programs available in these forums do a passable job of playing sound out of the PC speaker. Other programs convert sound files between various formats. It wouldn't be feasible to try to list specific examples here, but it should be relatively simple to find this type of software. In addition, third-party sound cards are available for a relatively low investment.

Lossless Compression of Sound

The original applications for sound compression could not take advantage of lossless data-compression techniques. One characteristic of all the compression techniques discussed so far in this book is that the amount of compression they achieve on a given data set is not known in advance. In some cases, the compression program can actually cause the data to expand, taking up more space than it occupied before.

In the 1960s, telecommunications researchers were trying to find ways to put more conversations on digital trunk lines, particularly on "expensive" lines, such as undersea cables or satellite links. Unlike disk space, which is somewhat flexible, these links have a fixed total bandwidth. A single telephone conversation might be allocated a 64Kbps slot on one of these channels. If it suddenly needed 100Kbps because the compression code hit a rough spot, there would be a major problem.

These early researchers were attempting to divide a 64Kbps channel into two 32Kbps channels to get two for the price of one. This required compression techniques that would consistently compress data by 50 percent, even if it meant losing some resolution.

Today, when trying to compress sound on disk for multimedia applications, we are in a slightly better position. We store and retrieve data from fixed disks, a more flexible medium for our work. If our files are compressed by 95 percent in some cases, and -10 percent in others, it will not really cause any trouble.

Problems and Results. How much can we compress voice files using conventional lossless techniques? To answer this question, a set of six short sound files were created, ranging in length from about one second to about seven seconds. To determine how compressible these files were, they were packed into an archive using ARJ 2.10, a shareware compression program that generally compresses as well or better than any other general-purpose program.

ARJ results showed that voice files did in fact compress relatively well. The six sample raw sound files gave the following results:

Filename	Original	Compressed	Ratio
SAMPLE-1.RAW	50777	33036	35%
SAMPLE-2.RAW	12033	8796	27%
SAMPLE-3 RAW	73091	59527	19%
SAMPLE-4.RAW	23702	9418	60%
SAMPLE-5.RAW	27411	19037	30%
SAMPLE-6.RAW	15913	12771	20%

These compression results look relatively promising. All the files were compressible to some extent, and some were reduced to less than half their original size. This level of compression is undoubtedly useful and may well be enough for some applications.

ARJ.EXE performs two sorts of compression on an input data stream. First, it does an LZSS type of windowed string matching on the string. The output from LZSS is, of course, a stream of tokens referring to either individual characters or matched strings. ARJ, like LHArc, takes LZSS a step further by performing Huffman compression on the output stream. Compressing these sound files using just LZSS compression and simple order-0 Huffman coding might tell us a little bit about what kind of redundancy is in these voice files.

To check the results, the files were compressed again with the LZSS program from chapter 8 and the HUFF program from chapter 3. The results of these experiments are shown in the following table.

Filename	ARJ Ratio	LZSS Ratio	HUFF Ratio
SAMPLE-1.RAW	35%	23%	26%
SAMPLE-2.RAW	27%	5%	30%
SAMPLE-3.RAW	19%	-3%	17%
SAMPLE-4.RAW	60%	25%	27%
SAMPLE-5.RAW	30%	15%	32%
SAMPLE-6.RAW	20%	2%	18%

The table shows that in every case, we perform more compression with simple order-0 Huffman coding than we do with LZSS dictionary compression. Since LZSS is normally a much more powerful compression technique, this is a telling result.

What LZSS takes advantage of when compressing is repeated strings of characters in the file. Order-0 Huffman coding just takes advantage of overall frequency differences for individual sequences. What we see in these sound files is some overall frequency difference between the various codes that make up the files, but not as many repeated strings as we might normally expect.

A look at snapshots of these sound files reveals some of the character of the data we are trying to compress. Figure 10-9 shows a section of about 600 sample points from SAMPLE-3.RAW. In this case, the sound samples are only taking up about 30 percent of the possible range allocated for them by the hardware. While individual samples can range from +127 to -128, in this snapshot they run only from about +30 to -30.

By only using a portion of the available bandwidth, a sound file automatically makes itself a good candidate for Huffman compression. The sample shown in figure 10-9 can probably be compressed by about 30 percent by just squeezing the samples down from eight bits to six or so bits. This is, in effect, what the Huffman coder does.

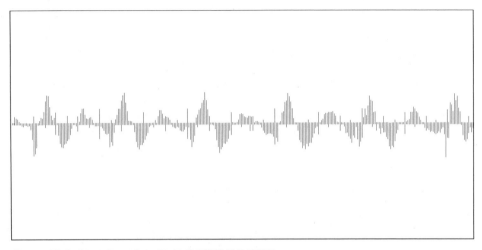

Figure 10-9. Sample points from SAMPLE-3.RAW.

Looking for repeated sequences in a sample such as this is less fruitful. We can certainly see a pattern in the waveform, but it is somewhat irregular, and it is not likely to produce many repeated patterns of even length 2. If we keep sampling long enough, random chance dictates that repeated strings will recur, but the compression will be much less than in a data or program file.

Figure 10-10 shows a sound sample that is a much more difficult candidate for compression. Unlike figure 10-9, this sound sample utilizes nearly the entire dynamic range of the ADC, so an order-0 Huffman encoder will be much less effective. Likewise, the chances of finding repeated patterns with an LZSS algorithm diminish considerably here. This is the type of file that gives us only a few percentage points of compression.

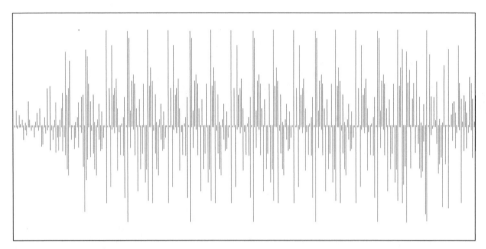

Figure 10-10. A sound sample that is difficult to compress.

Of course, even when looking at a "busy" sample like this, the human eye picks out patterns. The peaks and valleys of the waveform occur at somewhat regular intervals, telling us that sinusoidal waveforms are present in the signal. Unfortunately, our existing compression algorithms aren't equipped to find this type of redundancy in an input waveform. To do better, we need to move to a new frontier: lossy compression.

Lossy Compression. The very word "lossy" implies that when using this type of compression we are going to give up a certain amount of precision. This would certainly not be acceptable when compressing the data or text files we use on our computers. We could probably compress the M&T Books annual financial statement if we rounded all figures off to the nearest million dollars, for example, but the accounting department would definitely have a problem working with the books after that.

By digitizing sound samples, however, we have in effect given up quite a bit of precision. For example, our sound samples used in this chapter were all recorded at 11KHz. This means that we have thrown away the entire portion of every sample greater than 5.5KHz in frequency. We are also using only eight-bit samples, so we are introducing a significant amount of distortion in the form of quantization error.

All these factors are taken into account when designing the hardware and software for digitization. Instead of trying to perfectly reproduce analog phenomena, we instead make compromises that give us reproduction that is satisfactory for our purposes.

Likewise, when we look at lossy compression, we once again accept a certain loss in fidelity. The signal we get after going through a compression/expansion cycle will not be identical to the original, but we can adjust the parameters to get better or worse fidelity, and likewise better or worse compression.

Lossy compression is not necessarily an end to itself. We frequently use lossy compression in a two-phase process: a lossy stage followed by a lossless stage. One nice thing about lossy compression is that it frequently smooths out the data, which makes it even more suitable for lossless compression. So we get an extra unexpected benefit from lossy compression, above and beyond the compression itself.

Silence Compression. Silence compression on sound files is the equivalent of run-length encoding on normal data files. In this case, however, the runs we encode are sequences of relative silence in a sound file. This is a lossy technique because we replace the sequences of relative silence with absolute silence.

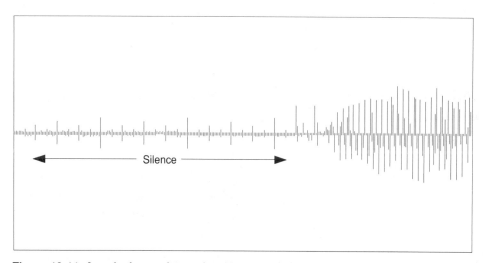

Figure 10-11. A typical sound sample with a long sequence of silence.

Figure 10-11 shows a typical sound sample that has a long sequence of silence. The first two thirds of it is composed of silence. Note that though we call it "silence," there are actually very small "blips" in the waveform. These are normal background noise and can be considered inconsequential.

A compression program for a sample like this needs to work with a few parameters. First, it needs a threshold value for what can be considered silence. With our eight-bit samples, for example, 80H is considered "pure" silence. We might want to consider any sample value within a range of plus or minus three from 80H to be silence.

Second, it needs a way to encode a run of silence. The sample program that follows creates a special SILENCE_CODE with a value of FF used to encode silence. The SILENCE_CODE is followed by a single byte that indicates how many consecutive silence codes there are.

Third, it needs a parameter that gives a threshold for recognizing the start of a run of silence. We wouldn't want to start encoding silence after seeing just a single byte of silence. It doesn't even become economical until three bytes of silence are seen. We may want to experiment with even higher values than three to see how it affects the fidelity of the recording.

Finally, we need another parameter that indicates how many consecutive non-silence codes need to be seen in the input stream before we declare the silence run to be over. Setting this parameter to a value greater than one filters out anomalous spikes in the input data. This can also cut back on noise in the recording.

The code to implement this silence compression follows. It incorporates a starting threshold of four and a stop threshold of two, so we have to see four consecutive silence codes before we consider a run started.

SILENCE.C by definition spends a lot of time looking ahead at upcoming input data. For example, to see if a silence run has really started the program must look at the next upcoming four input values. To simplify this, the program keeps a look-ahead buffer full of input data. It never directly examines the upcoming data read in via getc(). Instead, it looks at the bytes read into the buffer. This makes it easy to write functions to determine if a silence run has been started or if one is now over.

```
/*************************** Start of SILENCE.C **************************
* * This is the silence compression coding module used in chapter 10.
* Compile with BITIO.C, ERRHAND.C, and either MAIN-C.C or MAIN-E.C
*/

#include <stdio.h>
#include <stdlib.h>
#include <string.h>
#include <ctype.h>
#include "bitio.h"
#include "errhand.h"
#include "main.h"

/*
* These two strings are used by MAIN-C.C and MAIN-E.C to print
* messages of importance to the user of the program.
*/
char *CompressionName = "Silence compression";
char *Usage = "infile outfile\n";

/*
* These macros define the parameters used to compress the silent
* sequences. SILENCE_LIMIT is the maximum size of a signal that can
* be considered silent, in terms of offset from the center point.
* START_THRESHOLD gives the number of consecutive silent codes that
* have to be seen before a run is started. STOP_THRESHOLD tells how
* many non-silent codes need to be seen before a run is considered to
* be over. SILENCE_CODE is the special code output to the compressed
* file to indicate that a run has been detected. SILENCE_CODE is always
* followed by a single byte indicating how many consecutive silence
* bytes are to follow.
*/

#define SILENCE_LIMIT     4
#define START_THRESHOLD   5
#define STOP_THRESHOLD    2
#define SILENCE_CODE      0xff
```

```
#define IS_SILENCE( c ) ( (c) >( 0x7f - SILENCE_LIMIT ) && \
                          (c) < ( 0x80 + SILENCE_LIMIT ) )

/*
 * BUFFER_SIZE is the size of the look-ahead buffer. BUFFER_MASK is
 * the mask applied to a buffer index when performing index math.
 */
#define BUFFER_SIZE 8
#define BUFFER_MASK 7

/*
 * Local function prototypes.
 */

#ifdef __STDC__

int silence_run( int buffer[], int index )
int end_of_silence( int buffer[], int index )

#else

int silence_run();
int end_of_silence();

#endif

/*
 * The compression routine has the hard job here. It has to detect when
 * a silence run has started and when it is over. It does this by keeping
 * up-and-coming bytes in a look-ahead buffer. The buffer and the
 * current index are passed ahead to routines that check to see if a run
 * has started or if it has ended.
 */

void CompressFile( input, output, argc, argv )
FILE *input;
BIT_FILE *output;
```

```
int argc;
char *argv[];
{
   int look_ahead[ BUFFER_SIZE ];
   int index;
   int i;
   int run_length;

   for ( i = 0 ; i < BUFFER_SIZE ; i++ )
     look_ahead[ i ] = getc( input );
   index = 0;
   for ( ; ; ) {
     if ( look_ahead[ index ] == EOF )
       break;
/*
* If a run has started, I handle it here. I sit in the do loop until
* the run is complete, loading new characters all the while.
*/
     if ( silence_run( look_ahead, index ) ) {
       run_length = 0;
       do {
         look_ahead[ index++ ] = getc( input );
         index &= BUFFER_MASK;
         if ( ++run_length == 255 ) {
           putc( SILENCE_CODE, output->file );
           putc( 255, output->file );
           run_length = 0;
         }
       } while ( !end_of_silence( look_ahead, index ) );
       if ( run_length > 0 ) {
         putc( SILENCE_CODE, output->file );
         putc( run_length, output->file );
       }
     }
   }
/*
* Eventually, any run of silence is over, and I output some plain codes.
* Any code that accidentally matches the silence code gets silently
```

```
 * changed.
 */
    if ( look_ahead[ index ] == SILENCE_CODE )
      look_ahead[ index ]--;
    putc( look_ahead[ index ], output->file );
    look_ahead[ index++ ] = getc( input );
    index &= BUFFER_MASK;
  }
  while ( argc- > 0 )
    printf( "Unused argument: %s\n", *argv++ );
}


/*
 * The expansion routine used here has a very easy time of it. It just
 * has to check for the run code, and when it finds it, pad out the
 * output file with some silence bytes.
 */
void ExpandFile( input, output, argc, argv )
BIT_FILE *input;
FILE *output;
int argc;
char *argv[];
{
  int c;
  int run_count;

  while ( ( c = getc( input->file ) ) != EOF ) {
    if ( c == SILENCE_CODE ) {
      run_count = getc( input->file );
      while ( run_count-- > 0 )
        putc( 0x80, output );
    } else
      putc( c, output );
  }
  while ( argc- > 0 )
    printf( "Unused argument: %s\n", *argv++ );
}
```

```
/*
 * This support routine checks to see if the look-ahead buffer contains
 * the start of a run, which by definition is START_THRESHOLD consecutive
 * silence characters.
 */

int silence_run( buffer, index )
int buffer[];
int index;
{
    int i;

    for ( i = 0 ; i < START_THRESHOLD ; i++ )
      if ( !IS_SILENCE( buffer[ ( index + i ) & BUFFER_MASK ] ) )
        return( 0 );
    return( 1 );
}

/*
 * This support routine is called while we are in the middle of a run of
 * silence. It checks to see if we have reached the end of the run.
 * By definition this occurs when we see STOP_THRESHOLD consecutive
 * non-silence characters.
 */

int end_of_silence( buffer, index )
int buffer[];
int index;
{
    int i;

    for ( i = 0 ; i < STOP_THRESHOLD ; i++ )
      if ( IS_SILENCE( buffer[ ( index + i ) & BUFFER_MASK ] ) )
        return( 0 );
    return( 1 );
}
/*************************** End of SILENCE.C ***************************/
```

Just how effective silence compression can be at compressing files is shown in the following table. As expected, files without much silence in them were not greatly affected. But files that contained significant gaps were compressed quite a bit.

File Name	Raw Size	Compressed Size	Compression
SAMPLE-1.RAW	50777	37769	26%
SAMPLE-2.RAW	12033	11657	3%
SAMPLE-3.RAW	73091	73072	0%
SAMPLE-4.RAW	13852	10962	21%
SAMPLE-5.RAW	27411	22865	17%

The final question to ask about silence detection is how it affects the fidelity of input files. The best way to answer that is to take the sample files, compress them, then expand them into new files. The expanded files should differ only from the originals in that strings of characters near the silence value of 80H should all have been arbitrarily made exactly 80H, changing slightly noisy silence to pure silence.

In most cases, it is not possible to tell the sound samples that have been through a compression/expansion cycle from the originals. By tinkering with the parameters, it is possible to start erasing significant sections of speech, but that obviously means the parameters are not set correctly. All in all, when applied correctly, silence compression provides an excellent way to squeeze redundancy out of sound files.

Companding

Silence compression can be a good way to remove redundant information from sound files, but in some cases it may be ineffective. In the preceding examples, SAMPLE-3.RAW had so few silent samples it was only reduced by a few bytes out of 73K. This situation is somewhat analogous to using run-length encoding on standard text or data files: it will sometimes produce great gains, but it is not particularly reliable.

In the early 1960s, telecommunications researchers were looking for a method of data compression that could always reduce the number of bits in a sound sample. Customer satisfaction tests showed that it took about thirteen bits of resolution in the DAC sampled at 8,000Hz to provide an acceptable voice connection, but it seemed likely that much of that resolution was going to waste.

We need thirteen bits of resolution in a phone conversation because of the large dynamic range of the human voice. To accommodate a loud speaker, the voltage input range of the ADC has to be set at a fairly high level. The problem is that the input voltage from a very soft voice is several orders of magnitude lower than this. If the ADC had eight bits of resolution, it would only detect input signals close to 1 percent of the magnitude of the highest input. This proved unacceptable.

It turns out, however, that the thirteen bits of resolution needed to pick up the voice of the quietest speaker is overkill for resolution of the loudest speaker. If our microphone input for a loud speaker is in the neighborhood of 100mv, we might only need one millivolt of resolution to provide good sound reproduction. The thirteen-bit ADC might be giving 200 microvolt resolution, which turns out to be more than is necessary.

The telecommunications industry solved this using a non-linear matched set of ADCs and DACs. The normal ADC equipment used in desktop computers (and most electronic equipment) uses a linear conversion scheme in which each increase in a code value corresponds to a uniform increase in input/output voltage. This arrangement is shown in figure 10-12.

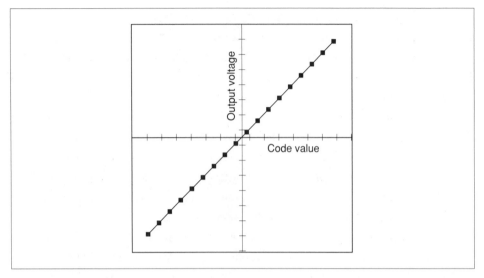

Figure 10-12. A linear conversion scheme in which each increase in a code value corresponds to a uniform increase in input/output voltage

Using a linear conversion scheme such as this, when we go from code 0 to code 1, the output voltage from the DAC might change from 0mv to 1mv. Likewise, going from code 100 to code 101 will change the DAC output voltage from 100mv to 101mv.

The system in our telecommunications equipment today uses a "companding codec"—jargon for "compressing/expanding coder/decoder." The codec is essentially a chip that combines several functions, including those of the DAC, ADC, and input and output filters. We are concerned with the DAC and ADC.

The codec used in virtually all modern digital telephone equipment does not use a standard linear function when converting codes to voltages and voltages to codes. Instead, it uses an exponential function that changes the size of the voltage step between codes as the codes grow larger. Figure 10-13 shows an example of what this curve looks like. The resolution for smaller code values is much finer than at the extremes of the range. For example, the difference between a code of zero and a code of one might be 1mv, while the difference between code 100 and code 101 could be 10mv.

The exponential curve defined for telecommunications codecs gives an effective range of thirteen bits out of a codec that only uses eight-bit samples. We can do the same thing with our eight-bit sound files by squeezing eight-bit samples into a smaller number of codes.

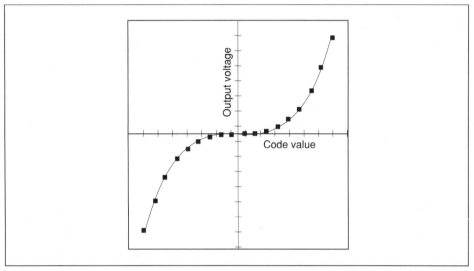

Figure 10-13. An exponential function that changes the size of voltage steps.

Our eight-bit sound files can be considered approximately seven-bit samples with a single sign bit, indicating whether the output voltage is positive or negative. This gives us a range running from zero to 128 to encode for the output of our non-linear compression function.

If we assume that we will have N codes to express the range of zero to 127, we can develop a transfer function for each code using the following equation:

```
output = 127.0 * ( pow( 2.0, code / N ) - 1.0 )
```

In other words, we calculate the output by raising 2 to the code/N power. The value of code/N will range from zero for code 0 up to one for code N, resulting in an output range that runs from zero to 127, with a decidedly non-linear look.

An example of how this might work would be found if we used eight samples to encode the range zero to 128. This, in effect, compresses seven bits to three. The output value produced by an input code is shown in the table that follows.

Input Code	Output Value
0	0
1	13
2	28
3	44
4	62
5	81
6	103
7	127

Transforming three bits to seven

The output step taken here between codes 0 and 1 is 13, but between 6 and 7 it goes up to 24. This means that we have more resolution in the smaller input ranges, where we need it, and less resolution for the loud sounds, where we don't need it.

This compression algorithm does an excellent job of compressing sound without damaging quality. It also has several nice features. First, both decompression and compression can take place via table lookup, resulting in extremely fast processing. Second, the amount of compression is known in advance, since the amount of compression does not vary based on the input data stream. Finally, the algorithm can be tuned to any desired compression ratio simply by varying the number of codes used in the compressed file.

The code to implement a simple version of this compression scheme follows. File COMPAND.C can be called with an additional parameter that tells how many bits to use per code during the compression process. Experimental results show that compressing eight-bit samples to four bits results in very little degradation. Three bits or fewer starts to generate high-frequency components in the output, which are heard as static, or noise. But it is a tribute to the human ear to note that even samples compressed down to one bit per sample are still frequently intelligible.

```
/*********************** Start of COMPAND.C ***********************
*
* This is the companding module used in chapter 10.
* Compile with BITIO.C, ERRHAND.C, and either MAIN-C.C or MAIN-E.C
*/


#include <stdio.h>
#include <stdlib.h>
#include <string.h>
#include <ctype.h>
#include <math.h>
#include "bitio.h"
#include "errhand.h"
#include "main.h"

/*
* These two strings are used by MAIN-C.C and MAIN-E.C to print
* messages of importance to the user of the program.
*/
char *CompressionName = "Sound sample companding";
char *Usage =
"infile outfile [n]\n\n n optionally sets the bits per sample\n\n";

#ifdef __STDC__

long get_file_length( FILE *file );

#else

long get_file_length();

#endif

#ifndef SEEK_END
#define SEEK_END 2
#endif
```

```
#ifndef SEEK_SET
#define SEEK_SET 0
#endif

/*
 * The compression routine runs very quickly, since all it does is
 * perform a table lookup on each input byte. The first part of the
 * routine builds that table. After that it is just a matter of
 * reading bytes in and writing out the compressed value.
 *
 * Unlike all of the other compression routines in the book, this
 * routine does not have a special END_OF_STREAM code. With as few
 * as four or eight codes, they seem too precious to give one up.
 * Instead, the file length is written out at the very start of the
 * compressed file, along with the number of bits used to encode the
 * data.
 */

void CompressFile( input, output, argc, argv )
FILE *input;
BIT_FILE *output;
int argc;
char *argv[];
{
    int compress[ 256 ];
    int steps;
    int bits;
    int value;
    int i;
    int j;
    int c;

/*
 * The first section of code determines the number of bits to use for
 * output codes, then writes it to the compressed file. The
 * length of the input file is also written out.
```

```
*/
  if ( argc-- > 0 )
    bits = atoi( *argv );
  else
    bits = 4;
  printf( "Compressing using %d bits per sample...\n", bits );
  steps = ( 1 << ( bits - 1 ) );
  OutputBits( output, (unsigned long) bits, 8 );
  OutputBits( output, (unsigned long) get_file_length( input), 32 );
/*
* The compression table is built here. Each input code maps to
* a single output code. There are "steps" codes to be used in
* the output space. This builds an exponential output function.
*/
  for ( i = steps ; i > 0; i-- ) {
    value = 128.0 * ( pow( 2.0, (double) i / steps ) - 1.0 ) + 0.5;
    for ( j = value ; j > 0 ; j-- ) {
      compress[ j + 127 ] = i + steps - 1;
      compress[ 128 - j ] = steps - i;
    }
  }
/*
* The actual compression takes place here.
*/
  while ( ( c = getc( input ) ) != EOF )
    OutputBits( output, (unsigned long) compress[ c ], bits ); }


/*
* The expansion routine gets the number of bits per code from the
* compressed file, then builds an expansion table. Each of the
* "steps" codes expands to a unique eight-bit code that lies on
* the exponential encoding curve.
*/

void ExpandFile( input, output, argc, argv )
BIT_FILE *input;
FILE *output;
int argc;
```

```
char *argv[];
{
    int steps;
    int bits;
    int value;
    int last_value;
    int i;
    int c;
    long count;
    int expand[ 256 ];

/*
 * First this routine reads in the number of bits, then it builds the
 * expansion table. Once the table is built, expanding the file
 * is simply a matter of performing a table lookup on each code.
 */
    bits = (int) InputBits( input, 8 );
    printf( "Expanding using %d bits per sample...\n", bits );
    steps = ( 1 << ( bits - 1 ) );
    last_value = 0;
    for ( i = 1; i <= steps; i++ ) {
        value = 128.0 * ( pow( 2.0, (double) i / steps ) - 1.0 ) + 0.5;
        expand[ steps + i - 1 ] = 128 + ( value + last_value ) / 2;
        expand[ steps - i ] = 127 - ( value + last_value ) / 2;
        last_value = value;
    }
/*
 * The actual file size is stored at the start of the compressed file.
 * It is read in to determine how many codes need to be expanded. Once
 * that is done, expansion takes place rapidly.
 */
    for ( count = InputBits( input, 32 ) ; count > 0 ; count-- ) {
        c = (int) InputBits( input, bits );
        putc( expand[ c ], output );
    }
    while ( argc-- > 0 )
        printf( "Unused argument: %s\n", *argv++ );
}
```

```
/*
 * This utility routine determines the size of the input file.
 */

long get_file_length( file )
FILE *file;
{
    long marker;
    long eof_ftell;

    marker = ftell( file );
    fseek( file, 0L, SEEK_END );
    eof_ftell = ftell( file );
    fseek( file, marker, SEEK_SET );
    return( eof_ftell - marker );
}

/************************* End of COMPAND.C *************************/
```

As was mentioned before, lossy compression is frequently used as a front end to a lossless compressor. In the case of COMPAND.C, this is a very effective strategy. After the files have been processed, far fewer codes are present in the output file, which makes string matching more likely, such as that used by LZSS compressors. By compressing a file by 50 percent using the companding strategy, then by applying LZSS compression, we can frequently achieve upwards of 90 percent compression on sound samples.

Other Techniques

This chapter covered some of the simpler techniques used to compress sound samples. As the level of processing power available for processing goes up, far more complicated algorithms are being applied.

One of the most common compression algorithms in use today has been sanctioned by the CCITT in their recommendation G.721. The G.721 algorithm uses Adaptive Differential Pulse Code Modulation (ADPCM) to encode digital signals at 16Kbps or 32Kbps. This algorithm is commonly performed by digital signal processors, and it is generally applied to data that has already been digitized using standard codes.

The ADPCM algorithm combines two techniques. The first, delta pulse code modulation, encodes sound signals by measuring the difference between two consecutive samples, not their absolute values. The quantization level adapts itself to the changing input signal, so the size of the encoded voltage changes as the input signal changes. When the signal moves from a high voltage to a low voltage at a steep rate, the encoded step value will be high. If a quiet input signal is being encoded, the step value will be low.

This becomes complicated because the ADPCM algorithm requires that the transmitter predict in advance where the input signal is headed. If this prediction is not made accurately, it is not possible to make good judgments about the size of the step defined by each code. The process of predicting where a waveform is headed occupies most of the processor's time.

To compress sound samples to even lower bit rates, even more sophisticated techniques, such as Linear Predictive Coding (LPC), are used. Human speech can be compressed and replayed in a recognizable state with rates as low as 2,400 bits per second using LPC.

LPC attempts to compress human speech by modeling the vocal tract that produces the speech. Instead of storing thousands of samples per second, LPC instead attempts to determine just a few parameters that model the process used to create the sound. The success or failure of LPC hinges on the ability of the compressor to execute millions of instructions per second during the compression process.

Processes such as LPC and ADPCM represent the type of algorithms that will be used more and more frequently on the desktop. Unfortunately, the complexity of these algorithms are far beyond the scope of a sample program in this chapter.

Lossy Graphics Compression

Desktop computers communicate information primarily via their screens, so graphics are a major concern for computer programmers and designers. Programmers spend enormous amounts of time and effort trying to accommodate the proliferation of the Graphical User Interface (GUI). Millions of man hours and billions of dollars worth of equipment are being allocated just to make improvements in the way programs display data.

The money being spent on computers equipped to perform properly under GUIs such as Microsoft Windows or Motif has created a vast array of computers capable of displaying complex graphical images, with resolution approaching that of conventional media, such as television or magazines. In turn, this capability has spawned new software designed to exploit these capabilities.

Programs using complex graphics are showing up in virtually every area of computing applications: games, education, desktop publishing, and graphical design, just to mention a few. These programs have one factor in common: The images they use consume prodigious amounts of disk storage.

In the IBM world, for example, the VGA display is probably the current lowest common denominator for high-quality color graphics. VGA displays 256 simultaneous colors selected from a palette of 262,144 colors. This lets the VGA display continuous tone images, such as color photographs, with a reasonable amount of fidelity.

The problem with using images of photographic quality is the amount of storage required to use them in a program. For the previously mentioned VGA, a 256-color screen image has 200 rows of 320 pixels, each consuming a single byte of storage.

This means that a single screen image consumes a minimum of 64K! It isn't hard to imagine applications that would require literally hundreds of these images to be accessed. An on-line catalog for a retail sales outlet, for example, could easily have 1,000 images stored for immediate access. The problem is that 1,000 images of this quality would consume 64MB of storage. And this is not an unreasonable number: We are just beginning to see game programs being distributed on CD-ROM, due to the enormous amounts of storage required by screen images.

This chapter discusses the use of lossy compression techniques to achieve very high levels of data compression on continuous tone graphical images, such as digitized images of photographs.

Enter Compression

There has been an explosion of research into graphics storage during the last decade, and many interesting results have been published. In the late 1970s and early 1980s, most graphics compression concentrated on using conventional lossless techniques. Popular PC file formats now use techniques discussed earlier in the book to achieve savings ranging from 10 to 90 percent on graphics images. Well-known formats using compression include the PCX, GIF, and BMP standards.

As the use of stored graphical images increased, file formats such as PCX began to appear inadequate. Cutting file sizes in half certainly is a worthwhile thing to do, but developers and users were filling their storage space up so fast that system requirements for multimedia systems appeared prohibitively expensive. Worse yet, the promise of full motion video on the desktop was simply not possible until some method was developed for radically reducing storage needs. Clearly, compression capabilities needed to improve, perhaps by as much as an order of magnitude.

Statistical and Dictionary Compression Methods. Conventional programs and data on computers respond well to compression based on exploiting statistical variations in the frequency of both individual symbols and strings of symbols or phrases. Dictionary-based systems are in fact just statistical programs in disguise. Unfortunately, these types of compression don't tend to do very well on continuous tone images.

The primary problem these programs have stems from the fact that pixels in photographic images tend to be well spread out over their entire range. If the colors in an image are plotted as a histogram based on frequency, the histogram is not as "spiky" as we would like for statistical compression to succeed. In fact, over the long run, histograms for live images from sources such as television tend to be flat. This means that each pixel code has approximately the same chance of appearing as any other, negating any opportunity for exploiting entropy differences.

Dictionary-based compression programs run into similar problems. Images based on scanned photographs just don't have the right kind of data characteristics to create multiple occurrences of the same phrase. In a rasterized image, for example, a vertical structure such as the side of a house may give similar strings in many consecutive rows of a picture. Unfortunately, because of the vagaries of the real world, the same feature in each row will tend to be slightly different from the one before. Out of a string of twenty pixels, one or two will vary by a single step from the scans before and after. And while these differences are small enough that they are either undetectable or meaningless to the human eye, they throw a monkey wrench into the works of dictionary-based compression. Strings have to match exactly for this compression method to work. Because of minute variations, the length of matching strings tends to be small, which limits the effectiveness of compression.

Lossy Compression. Just like audio data, graphical images have an advantage over conventional computer data files: They can be slightly modified during the compression/expansion cycle without affecting the perceived quality on the part of the user. Minor changes in the exact shade of a pixel here and there can easily go completely unnoticed if the modifications are done carefully. Since the graphical images on a computer are generally scanned from real-world sources, they usually represent an already imperfect representation of a photograph or some other printed media. A lossy compression program that doesn't change the basic nature of the image ought to be feasible.

Given that lossy compression for graphical images is possible, how is it implemented? Researchers initially tried some of the same techniques that worked on speech, such as differential coding and adaptive coding. While these techniques helped compress graphics, they did not do as well as hoped. One reason for this lies in the fundamental difference between audio and video data.

Audio data sampled using conventional formats tends to be very repetitive. Sounds, including speech, are made of sine waves that repeat for seconds at a time. Though the input stream at the DAC on a computer may consist of dozens of different frequencies added together, sine waves generally combine to produce repetitive waveforms.

The repetitive nature of audio data naturally lends itself to compression. Techniques such as linear predictive coding and adaptive differential pulse code modulation take advantage of this fact to compress audio streams anywhere from 50 to 95 percent.

When research began on compression of graphics, attempts were made to apply similar techniques to digitized images, with some success. Initially, researchers worked on the compression of streams of rasterized data, such as would be displayed on a television set.

When graphics data is rasterized, it is displayed as a sequential stream of pixels. One row at time is displayed on a screen, working from left to right, then top to bottom. Thus, a thin slice of the picture is painted as each row is completed, until the complete screen is filled. When digitized, pixels can range in size from a single bit to as many as twenty-four bits. Desktop graphics today frequently uses eight bits to define a single pixel.

Differential Modulation. Differential modulation depends on the notion that analog data tends to vary in "smooth" patterns, with radical jumps in the magnitude of a signal being the exception, not the rule. In audio data, this is true as long as the sampling rate of the signal is somewhat higher than its maximum frequency component.

Differential modulation of an audio signal takes advantage of this fact by encoding each sample as the difference from its predecessor. If audio samples are eight bits each, for example, a differential encoding system might encode the difference between samples in four bits, compressing the input data by 50 percent. The lossy part of the compression scheme arises from the fact that an exact difference can't always be encoded using the standard differential method. The signal may be rising faster than the encoding permits, or the encoding may be too coarse to accommodate a small difference. The lossy aspect of differential encoding can be managed well enough to produce a good signal.

Differential modulation has more of a problem when compressing graphical data. For one thing, pixels in a graphical image can't be reliably depended on to vary upward or downward in smooth increments. Sharp dividing lines between different components of an image are the rule. This means that a system that relies on differential encoding needs to accommodate both small and large differences between samples, limiting its effectiveness. Many images will feature long stretches of data where pixels have little or no difference between one another, and these will compress well; however, others will feature many abrupt changes, and these may not compress at all.

In general, differential encoding of graphical images doesn't seem to produce compression that is significantly greater than that of the best lossless algorithms. It certainly doesn't yield the order of magnitude of improvement in compression that is needed.

Adaptive Coding. Adaptive coding (which is often used with differential coding) relies on predicting some information about upcoming pixels based on previously seen pixels. If the last ten pixels in a grey-scale photograph all had values between forty-five and fifty, for example, an adaptive compression system might predict with high probability that the next pixel would be in the same range. An entropy-based encoding scheme, such as Huffman or arithmetic coding, could then assign probabilities to various incoming codes. An alternative would be to use a companding scale, with the finest granularity assigned to the range nearest the predicted guess. Assuming that the prediction method enabled you to make an educated guess about the probabilities of the pixels, you should achieve some data compression.

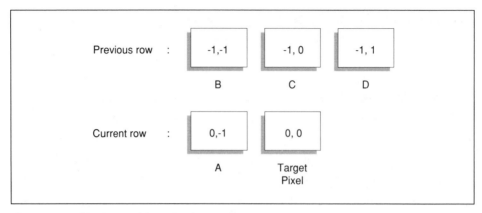

Figure 11-1. Pixels used for adaptive coding.

Most adaptive schemes rely on using just a few of the surrounding pixels as part of the calculation for probabilities of the upcoming pixel. In figure 11-1, the pixel to be encoded is shown at position 0,0. Pixels that are most commonly used when calculating probabilities are shown at positions A, B, C, and D. Predictions about the upcoming value of the target pixel can be made based on any of several predicting equations:

```
A
B
C
( A + C ) / 2
( A + D ) / 2
( A + ( C + D ) / 2 ) / 2
( A + ( C - B ) )
( A + ( ( D - B ) / 2 ) )
```

Figure 11-2. Pixel predictors.

These techniques use previous data to calculate the most likely value of the target pixel, and they adjust the coding scheme accordingly. While these calculations produce good results, once again they are certainly not the order of magnitude needed to perform effective compression.

A Standard That Works: JPEG

In the late 1970s and early 1980s, research began on new types of image compression that promised to greatly outperform the more conventional compression techniques discussed earlier. By the late 1980s, this work was beginning to find commercial applications for image processing on desktop systems, mostly in the form of add-on coprocessor cards for UNIX and Macintosh workstations. These cards were able to perform lossy compression on images at ratios of as much as 95 percent without visible degradation of the image quality.

Other forces at this time combined to start development of an international standard that would encompass these new varieties of compression. There are clear advantages to all parties if standards allowed for easy interchange of graphical formats. The main concern regarding early standardization is the possibility that it would constrain further innovation. The two standardization groups involved, the CCITT and the ISO, worked actively to get input from both industry and academic groups concerned with image compression, and they seem to have avoided the potentially negative consequences of their actions.

The standards group created by these two organizations is the Joint Photographic Experts Group (JPEG). It is in the final stages of the standardization process, having produced a draft proposal which is being voted on in several stages during 1991.

The JPEG specification consists of several parts, including a specification for both lossless and lossy encoding. The lossless compression uses the predictive/adaptive model described earlier in this chapter, with a Huffman code output stage, which produces good compression of images without the loss of any resolution.

The most interesting part of the JPEG specification is its work on a lossy compression technique. The rest of this chapter discusses the basics of this technique, with sample code to illustrate its components.

JPEG Compression. The JPEG lossy compression algorithm operates in three successive stages, shown in figure 11-3.

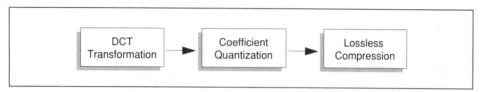

Figure 11-3. JPEG lossy compression.

These three steps combine to form a powerful compressor, capable of compressing continuous tone images to less than 10 percent of their original size, while losing little, if any, of their original fidelity.

The Discrete Cosine Transform. The key to the compression process discussed here is a mathematical transformation known as the Discrete Cosine Transform (DCT). The DCT is in a class of mathematical operations that includes the well-known Fast Fourier Transform (FFT), as well as many others. The basic operation performed by these transforms is to take a signal and transform it from one type of representation to another.

This transformation is done frequently when analyzing digital audio samples using the FFT. When we collect a set of sample points from an incoming audio signal, we end up with the representation of a signal in the time domain. That is, we have a collection of points that show what the voltage level was for the input signal at each point in time. The FFT transforms the set of sample points into a set of frequency values that describes exactly the same signal.

Figure 11-4 shows the classic time domain representation of an analog signal. This particular signal is composed of three different sine waves added together to form a single, slightly more complicated waveform. Each of the sample points represents the relative voltage or amplitude of the signal at a specific point in time.

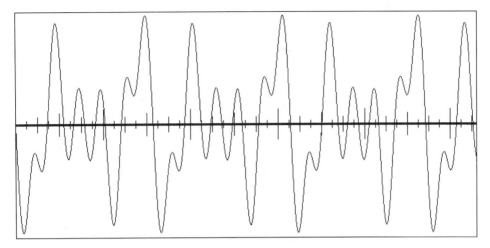

Figure 11-4.The classic time domain representation of an analog signal.

Figure 11-5 shows what happens to the same set of data points after FFT processing. In the time-domain representation of the signal, each of the points on the X axis
represents a different point in time, and each of the points on the Y axis represents a
specific magnitude of the signal. After processing the data points with an FFT, the X
axis no longer has the same meaning. Now, each point on the X axis represents a
specific frequency, and the Y axis represents the magnitude of that frequency.

Given that interpretation of the output of the FFT, figure 11-5 makes immediate
sense. It says that the signal displayed in the earlier figure can also be represented as
the sum of three different frequencies of what appears to be identical magnitude.
Given this information, it should be just as easy to construct the signal as it would be
with figure 11-4.

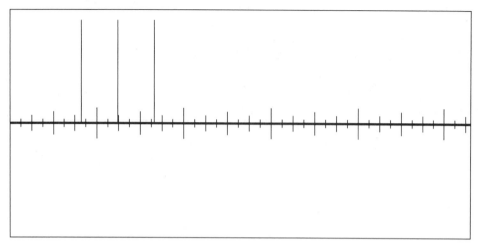

Figure 11-5. Data points after FFT processing.

Another important point to make about the this type of transformation function is that the function is reversible. In principle, the same set of points shown in figure 11-5 can be processed through an inverse FFT function, and the points shown in figure 11-4 should result. The two transformation cycles are essentially lossless, except for loss of precision resulting from rounding and truncation errors.

The DCT is closely related to the Fourier Transform, and produces a similar result. It takes a set of points from the spatial domain and transforms them into an identical representation in the frequency domain; however, we are going to introduce an additional complication in this particular instance. Instead of a two-dimensional signal plotted on an X and Y axis, the DCT will operate on a three-dimensional signal, plotted on an X, Y, and Z axis.

In this case, the "signal" is a graphical image. The X and Y axes are the two dimensions of the screen. The amplitude of the "signal" in this case is simply the value of a pixel at a particular point on the screen. For the examples used in this chapter, that is simply an eight-bit value used to represent a grey-scale value. So a graphical image displayed on the screen can be thought of as a complex three-dimensional signal, with the value on the Z axis denoted by the color on the screen at a given point. This is the spatial representation of the signal.

The DCT can be used to convert spatial information into "frequency" or "spectral" information, with the X and Y axes representing frequencies of the signal in two different dimensions. And like the FFT, there is an Inverse DCT (IDCT) function that can convert the spectral representation of the signal back to a spatial one.

DCT Specifics. The actual formula for the two-dimensional DCT is shown in figure 11-6, with its partner, the IDCT, shown immediately below in figure 11-7. The DCT is performed on an N x N square matrix of pixel values, and it yields an N x N square matrix of frequency coefficients. The formula looks somewhat intimidating at first glance, but it can be done with a relatively straightforward piece of code.

$$DCT(i,j) = \frac{1}{\sqrt{2N}} C(i) \, C(j) \sum_{x=0}^{N-1} \sum_{y=0}^{N-1} pixel(x,y) \cos\left[\frac{(2x+1)i\pi}{2N}\right] \cos\left[\frac{(2y+1)j\pi}{2N}\right]$$

$$C(x) = \frac{1}{\sqrt{2}} \text{ if x is } 0 \text{, else } 1 \text{ if x} > 0$$

Figure 11-6. The Discrete Cosine Transform

$$Pixel(x,y) = \frac{1}{\sqrt{2N}} \sum_{i=0}^{N-1} \sum_{j=0}^{N-1} C(i) \, C(j) DCT(i,j) \cos\left[\frac{(2x+1)i\pi}{2N}\right] \cos\left[\frac{(2y+1)j\pi}{2N}\right]$$

$$C(x) = \frac{1}{\sqrt{2}} \text{ if x is } 0 \text{, else } 1 \text{ if x} > 0$$

Figure 11-7. The Inverse DCT

To write code to implement this function, it first becomes clear that simple table lookups can replace many terms of the equation. The two cosine terms that have to be multiplied together only need to be calculated once at the beginning for the program, and they can be stored for later use. Likewise, the C(x) terms that fall outside the summation loops can also be replaced with table lookups. Once that is done, code to compute the N-by-N portion of a display looks somewhat like that shown below:

```
for ( i = 0 ; i < N ; i++ )
  for ( j = 0 ; j < N ; j++ ) {
    temp = 0.0;
    for ( x = 0 ; x < N ; x++ )
      for ( y = 0 ; y < N ; y++ ) {
        temp += Cosines[ x ][ i ] *
                Cosines[ y ][ j ] *
                pixel[ x ][ y ];
      }
    temp *= sqrt( 2 * N ) * Coefficients[ i ][ j ];
    DCT[ i ][ j ] = INT_ROUND( temp );
  }
```

Why Bother?

While this code fragment looks as though it may be somewhat interesting to a mathematician, why anyone would want to use it on a graphical image is not immediately obvious. After we transform the pixels to frequency coefficients, we still have just as many points as before. It doesn't seem as if that is a particularly good way to go about compressing data. It would be much more impressive if the DCT took an N-by-N matrix of data and transformed it to an N/2 by N/2 matrix.

However, figure 11-5 provides a clue as to what the JPEG committee sees in this algorithm. Figure 11-5 shows that the spectral representation of the audio waveform takes all the information needed to describe the waveform and packs it into the three non-zero points on the graph. So in principle we could describe the 512 points that make up the input waveform with just three points of frequency data.

The DCT accomplishes something similar when it transforms data. In the N-by-N matrix, all the elements in row 0 have a frequency component of zero in one direction of the signal. All the elements in column 0 have a frequency component of zero in the other direction. As the rows and columns move away from origin, the coefficients in the transformed DCT matrix begin to represent higher frequencies, with the highest frequencies found at position N-1 of the matrix.

This is significant because most graphical images on our computer screens are composed of low-frequency information. As it turns out, the components found in row and column 0 (the DC components) carry more useful information about the image than the higher-frequency components. As we move farther away from the DC components in the picture, we find that the coefficients not only tend to have lower values, but they become far less important for describing the picture.

So the DCT transformation identifies pieces of information in the signal that can be effectively "thrown away" without seriously compromising the quality of the image. It is hard to imagine how we would do this with a picture that hadn't been transformed. With the image still described in spatial terms, using pixels, a program would have a difficult time figuring out which pixels are important to the overall look of the picture and which aren't.

After defining the DCT as the transformation to be used, the JPEG committee then tackled the truly difficult work: how to "throw away" the insignificant portions of the picture. Details on that come later in this chapter.

Implementing the DCT

One of the first things that shows up when examining the DCT algorithm is that the calculation time required for each element in the DCT is heavily dependent on the size of the matrix. Since a doubly nested loop is used, the number of calculations is O(N squared): as N goes up, the amount of time required to process each element in the DCT output array will go up dramatically.

One of the consequences of this is that it is virtually impossible to perform a DCT on an entire image. The amount of calculation needed to perform a DCT transformation on even a 256-by-256 grey-scale block is prohibitively large. To get around this, DCT implementations typically break the image down into smaller, more manageable blocks. The JPEG group selected an 8-by-8 block for the size of their DCT calculation.

While increasing the size of the DCT block would probably give better compression, it doesn't take long to reach a point of diminishing returns. Research shows that the connections between pixels tend to diminish quickly, such that pixels even fifteen or twenty positions away are of very little use as predictors. This means that a DCT block of 64-by-64 might not compress much better than if we broke it down into four 16-by-16 blocks. And to make matters worse, the computation time would be much longer.

While there is probably a good argument for using 16-by-16 blocks as the basis for DCT computations, the JPEG committee elected to stick with 8-by-8. Much of this was motivated by a desire to allow for practical implementations that could be built using today's technology. This type of compression is referred to as "block coding."

Matrix Multiplication. The definition of the DCT shown above is a relatively straightforward, doubly nested loop. The inner element of the loop gets executed N*N times for every DCT element that is calculated. The inner line of the loop has two multiplication operations and a single addition operation.

A considerably more efficient form of the DCT can be calculated using matrix operations. To perform this operation, we first create an N-by-N matrix known as the Cosine Transform matrix, C. This matrix is defined by the equation shown in figure 11-8.

$$C_{i,j} = \begin{cases} \dfrac{1}{\sqrt{N}} & \text{if } i = 0 \\[4mm] \sqrt{\dfrac{2}{N}} \cos\left[\dfrac{(2j+1)i\pi}{2N}\right] & \text{if } i > 0 \end{cases}$$

Figure 11-8. The Cosine Tranform Matrix.

Once the Cosine Transform matrix has been built, we transpose it by rotating it around the main diagonal. This matrix is referred to in code as Ct, the Transposed Cosine Transform matrix. Building this matrix is done only once during program initialization. Both matrices can be built at the same time with a relatively short loop, shown below:

```
for ( j = 0 ; j < N ; j++ ) {
    C[ 0 ][ j ] = 1.0 / sqrt( N );
    Ct[ j ][ 0 ] = C[ 0 ][ j ];
}
for ( i = 1 ; i < N ; i++ ) {
    for ( j = 0 ; j < N ; j++ ) {
        C[ i ][ j ] = sqrt( 2.0 / N ) *
                      cos( ( 2 * j + 1 ) * i * pi
                      / ( 2.0 * N ) );
        Ct[ j ][ i ] = C[ i ][ j ];
    }
}
```

Once these two matrices have been built, we can take advantage of the alternate definition of the DCT function:

```
DCT = C * Pixels * Ct
```

In this particular equation, the '*' operator refers to matrix multiplication, not normal arithmetic multiplication. Each factor in the equation is an N-by-N matrix. In the case of the JPEG algorithm and the program used to illustrate this chapter, the matrices are 8 by 8.

When multiplying two square matrices together, the arithmetic cost of each element of the output matrix will be N multiplication operations and N addition operations. Since we perform two matrix multiplications to create the DCT matrix, each element in the transformed DCT matrix was created at the cost of 2N multiplications and additions, a considerable improvement over the nested loop definition of the DCT used earlier.

```
/* MatrixMultiply( temp, input, Ct ); */
  for ( i = 0 ; i < N ; i++ ) {
    for ( j = 0 ; j < N ; j++ ) {
      temp[ i ][ j ] = 0.0;
      for ( k = 0 ; k < N ; k++ )
        temp[ i ][ j ] += ( pixel[ i ][ k ] ) * Ct[ k ][ j ];
    }
  }


/* MatrixMultiply( output, C, temp ); */

  for ( i = 0 ; i < N ; i++ ) {
    for ( j = 0 ; j < N ; j++ ) {
      temp1 = 0.0;
      for ( k = 0 ; k < N ; k++ )
        temp1 += C[ i ][ k ] * temp[ k ][ j ];
      DCT[ i ][ j ] = temp1;
    }
  }
```

A sample piece of code that implements the DCT via matrix arithmetic is shown above. Note that the code is essentially nothing more than a set of two triply nested loops. The first set of loops multiplies the transposed Cosine Transform Matrix by the input set of pixels, creating a temporary matrix. The temporary matrix is then multiplied by the Cosine Transform matrix, which results in the output, the DCT matrix.

Continued Improvements

The versions of the DCT presented here perform the same operations as those used in commercial implementations, but without several more optimization steps needed to produce JPEG compressors that operate in something approaching real time.

One improvement that can be made to the algorithm is to develop versions of the algorithm that only use integer arithmetic. To achieve the accuracy needed for faithful reproduction, the versions of the program tested in this chapter all stick with reliable floating point math. It is possible, however, to develop versions of the DCT that use scaled integer math, which is considerably faster on most platforms.

Since the DCT is related to the Discrete Fourier Transform, it shouldn't be surprising that many of the techniques used to speed up the family of Fourier Transforms can also be applied to the DCT. In fact, people all over the world are working full time on applying Digital Signal Processing techniques to the DCT. Every cycle shaved off the time taken to perform the transform can be worth a small fortune, so there is good incentive for these research efforts.

Output of the DCT. Figure 11-9 shows a representative input block from a grey-scale image. As can be seen, the input consists of an 8-by-8 matrix of pixel values which are somewhat randomly spread around the 140 to 175 range. These integer values are fed to the DCT algorithm, creating the output matrix shown below it.

Input Pixel matrix:

140	144	147	140	140	155	179	175
144	152	140	147	140	148	167	179
152	155	136	167	163	162	152	172
168	145	156	160	152	155	136	160
162	148	156	148	140	136	147	162
147	167	140	155	155	140	136	162
136	156	123	167	162	144	140	147
148	155	136	155	152	147	147	136

Output DCT matrix:

186	-18	15	-9	23	-9	-14	19
21	-34	26	-9	-11	11	14	7
-10	-24	-2	6	-18	3	-20	-1
-8	-5	14	-15	-8	-3	-3	8
-3	10	8	1	-11	18	18	15
4	-2	-18	8	8	-4	1	-7
9	1	-3	4	-1	-7	-1	-2
0	-8	-2	2	1	4	-6	0

Figure 11-9. The DCT on a Block of Pixels from CHEETAH.GS

The output matrix shows the spectral compression characteristic the DCT is supposed to create. The "DC coefficient" is at position 0,0 in the upper left-hand corner of the matrix. This value represents an average of the overall magnitude of the input matrix, since it represents the DC component in both the X and the Y axis. Note that the DC coefficient is almost an order of magnitude greater than any of the other values in the DCT matrix. In addition, there is a general trend in the DCT matrix. As the elements move farther and farther from the DC coefficient, they tend to become lower and lower in magnitude.

This means that by performing the DCT on the input data, we have concentrated the representation of the image in the upper left coefficients of the output matrix, with the lower right coefficients of the DCT matrix containing less useful information. The next section discusses how this can help compress data.

Quantization. Figure 11-3 shows the JPEG compression process as a three-step procedure, the first step being a DCT transformation. DCT is a lossless transformation that doesn't actually perform compression. It prepares for the "lossy," or quantization, stage of the process.

The DCT output matrix takes more space to store than the original matrix of pixels. The input to the DCT function consists of eight-bit pixel values, but the values that come out can range from a low of -1,024 to a high of 1,023, occupying eleven bits. Something drastic needs to happen before the DCT matrix can take up less space.

The "drastic" action used to reduce the number of bits required for storage of the DCT matrix is referred to as "Quantization." Quantization is simply the process of reducing the number of bits needed to store an integer value by reducing the precision of the integer. Once a DCT image has been compressed, we can generally reduce the precision of the coefficients more and more as we move away from the DC coefficient at the origin. The farther away we are from 0,0, the less the element contributes to the graphical image, so the less we care about maintaining rigorous precision in its value.

The JPEG algorithm implements Quantization using a Quantization matrix. For every element position in the DCT matrix, a corresponding value in the quantization matrix gives a quantum value. The quantum value indicates what the step size is going to be for that element in the compressed rendition of the picture, with values ranging from one to 255.

The elements that matter most to the picture will be encoded with a small step size, size 1 offering the most precision. Values can become higher as we move away from the origin. The actual formula for quantization is quite simple:

$$\text{Quantized Value}(i, j) = \frac{\text{DCT}(i, j)}{\text{Quantum}(i, j)} \text{ Rounded to nearest integer}$$

From the formula, it becomes clear that quantization values above twenty-five or perhaps fifty assure that virtually all higher-frequency components will be rounded down to zero. Only if the high-frequency coefficients get up to unusually large values will they be encoded as non-zero values.

During decoding, the dequantization formula operates in reverse:

$$\text{DCT}(i, j) = \text{Quantized Value}(i, j) * \text{Quantum}(i, j)$$

Once again, from this we can see that when you use large quantum values, you run the risk of generating large errors in the DCT output during dequantization. Fortunately, errors generated in the high-frequency components during dequantization normally don't have a serious effect on picture quality.

Selecting a Quantization Matrix. Clearly an enormous number of schemes could be used to define values in the quantization matrix. At least two experimental approaches can test different quantization schemes. One measures the mathematical error found between an input and output image after it has been decompressed, trying to determine an acceptable level of error. A second approach tries to judge the effect of decompression on the human eye, which may not always correspond exactly with mathematical differences in error levels.

Since the quantization matrix can obviously be defined at runtime when compression takes place, JPEG allows for the use of any quantization matrix; however, the ISO has developed a standard set of quantization values supplied for use by implementers of JPEG code. These tables are based on extensive testing by members of the JPEG committee, and they provide a good baseline for established levels of compression.

One nice feature about selecting quantization matrices at runtime is that it is quite simple to "dial in" a picture quality value when compressing graphics using the JPEG algorithm. By choosing extraordinarily high step sizes for most DCT coefficients, we get excellent compression ratios and poor picture quality. By choosing cautiously low step sizes, compression ratios will begin to slip to not so impressive levels, but picture quality should be excellent. This allows for a great deal of flexibility for the user of JPEG code, choosing picture quality based on both imaging requirements and storage capacity.

The quantization tables used in the test code supplied with this program are created using a very simple algorithm. To determine the value of the quantum step sizes, the user inputs a single "quality factor" which should range from one to about twenty-five. Values larger than twenty-five would work, but picture quality has degraded far enough at quality level 25 to make going any farther an exercise in futility.

```
for ( i = 0 ; i < N ; i++ )
    for ( j = 0 ; j < N ; j++ )
        Quantum[ i ][ j ] = 1 + ( ( 1 + i + j )  * quality );
```

The quality level sets the difference between adjoining bands of the same quantization level. These bands are oriented on diagonal lines across the matrix, so quantization levels of the same value are all roughly the same distance from the origin. An example of what the quantization matrix looks like with a quality factor of two follows.

3	5	7	9	11	13	15	17
5	7	9	11	13	15	17	19
7	9	11	13	15	17	19	21
9	11	13	15	17	19	21	23
11	13	15	17	19	21	23	25
13	15	17	19	21	23	25	27
15	17	19	21	23	25	27	29
17	19	21	23	25	27	29	31

Figure 11-10. The matrix at quality factor 2.

As a result of this configuration, the DCT coefficient at 7,7 would have to reach a value of sixteen to be encoded as a value other than zero. This sets the threshold for the value of an element before it is going to contribute any meaningful information to the picture. Any contribution under the value of this threshold is simply thrown out. This is the exact point in the algorithm where the "lossy" effect takes place. The first DCT step is lossless except for minor mathematical precision loss. And the step following quantization is a lossless encoding step. So this is the only place where we get a chance to actually discard data.

DCT Matrix before	92	3	-9	-7	3	-1	0	2
Quantization:	-39	-58	12	17	-2	2	4	2
	-84	62	1	-18	3	4	-5	5
	-52	-36	-10	14	-10	4	-2	0
	-86	-40	49	-7	17	-6	-2	5
	-62	65	-12	-2	3	-8	-2	0
	-17	14	-36	17	-11	3	3	-1
	-54	32	-9	-9	22	0	1	3
DCT Matrix after	90	0	-7	0	0	0	0	0
Dequantization:	-35	-56	9	11	0	0	0	0
	-84	54	0	-13	0	0	0	0
	-45	-33	0	0	0	0	0	0
	-77	-39	45	0	0	0	0	0
	-52	60	0	0	0	0	0	0
	-15	0	-19	0	0	0	0	0
	-51	19	0	0	0	0	0	0

Figure 11-11. The effects of quantization.

Figure 11-11 shows the effects of quantization on a DCT matrix. The quantization matrix shown in the previous figure was applied to this block of DCT, which comes from the first block of test file CHEETAH.GS. The quantization/dequantization cycle has readily apparent effects. The high-frequency portions of the matrix have for the most part been truncated down to zero, eliminating their effect on the decompressed image. The coefficients in the matrix that are close to the DC coefficient may have been modified, but only by small amounts.

The interesting thing is that while we appear to be making wholesale changes to the saved image, quality factor 2 makes only minor changes that are barely noticeable. Yet the clearing of so many of the coefficients allows the image to be compressed by 60 percent, even in the very simple compression program used in this chapter.

Coding

The final step in the JPEG process is coding the quantized images. The JPEG coding phase combines three different steps to compress the image. The first changes the DC coefficient at 0, 0 from an absolute value to a relative value. Since adjacent blocks in an image exhibit a high degree of correlation, coding the DC element as the difference from the previous DC element typically produces a very small number. Next, the coefficients of the image are arranged in the "zig-zag sequence." Then they are encoded using two different mechanisms. The first is run-length encoding of zero values. The second is what JPEG calls "Entropy Coding." This involves sending out the coefficient codes, using either Huffman codes or arithmetic coding depending on the choice of the implementer.

The Zig-Zag Sequence. One reason the JPEG algorithm compresses so effectively is that a large number of coefficients in the DCT image are truncated to zero values during the coefficient quantization stage. So many values are set to zero that the JPEG committee elected to handle zero values differently from other coefficient values.

Instead of relying on Huffman or arithmetic coding to compress the zero values, they are coded using a Run-Length Encoding (RLE) algorithm. A simple code is developed that gives a count of consecutive zero values in the image. Since over half of the coefficients are quantized to zero in many images, this gives an opportunity for outstanding compression.

One way to increase the length of runs is to reorder the coefficients in the zig-zag sequence. Instead of compressing the coefficient in row-major order, as a programmer would probably do, the JPEG algorithm moves through the block along diagonal paths, selecting what should be the highest value elements first, and working its way toward the values likely to be lowest.

The actual path of the zig-zag sequence is shown in figure 11-12. In the code used in this chapter, the diagonal sequences of quantization steps follow exactly the same lines, so the zig-zag sequence should be optimal for our purposes.

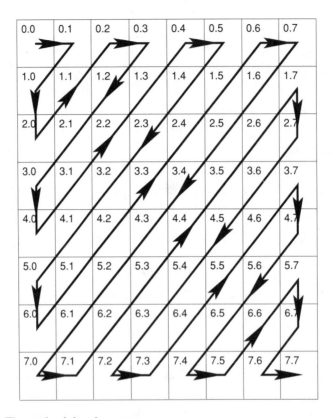

Figure 11-12. The path of the zig-zag sequence.

Implementing the zig-zag sequence in C is probably done best using a simple lookup table. In our sample code for this chapter, the sequence is coded as part of a structure that can be accessed sequentially to determine which row and column to encode:

```
struct zigzag {
    int row;
    int col;
} ZigZag[ N * N ] =
```

```
{
    {0, 0},
    {0, 1}, {1, 0},
    {2, 0}, {1, 1}, {0, 2},
    {0, 3}, {1, 2}, {2, 1}, {3, 0},
    {4, 0}, {3, 1}, {2, 2}, {1, 3}, {0, 4},
    {0, 5}, {1, 4}, {2, 3}, {3, 2}, {4, 1}, {5, 0},
    {6, 0}, {5, 1}, {4, 2}, {3, 3}, {2, 4}, {1, 5}, {0, 6},
    {0, 7}, {1, 6}, {2, 5}, {3, 4}, {4, 3}, {5, 2}, {6, 1}, {7, 0},
    {7, 1}, {6, 2}, {5, 3}, {4, 4}, {3, 5}, {2, 6}, {1, 7},
    {2, 7}, {3, 6}, {4, 5}, {5, 4}, {6, 3}, {7, 2},
    {7, 3}, {6, 4}, {5, 5}, {4, 6}, {3, 7},
    {4, 7}, {5, 6}, {6, 5}, {7, 4},
    {7, 5}, {6, 6}, {5, 7},
    {6, 7}, {7, 6},
    {7, 7}
};
```

The C code that sends each of the DCT results to the compressor follows. Note that instead of directly looking up each result, we instead determine which row and column to use next by looking it up in the zig-zag structure. We then encode the element determined by the row and column from the zig-zag structure.

```
for ( i = 0 ; i < ( N * N ) ; i++ ) {
    row = ZigZag[ i ].row;
    col = ZigZag[ i ].col;
    result = DCT[ row ][ col ] / Quantum[ row ][ col ];
    OutputCode( output_file, ROUND( result ) );
}
```

Entropy Encoding. After converting the DC element to a difference from the last block, then reordering the DCT block in the zig-zag sequence, the JPEG algorithm outputs the elements using an "entropy encoding" mechanism. The output has RLE built into it as an integral part of the coding mechanism. Basically, the output of the entropy encoder consists of a sequence of three tokens, repeated until the block is complete. The three tokens look like this:

- **Run Length:** The number of consecutive zeros that preceded the current element in the DCT output matrix.

- **Bit Count:** The number of bits to follow in the amplitude number.

- **Amplitude:** The amplitude of the DCT coefficient.

The coding sequence used in this chapter's test program is a combination of Run Length Encoding and variable-length integer coding. The run-length and bit-count values are combined to form a code that is output. The bit count refers to the number of bits used to encode the amplitude as a variable-length integer.

The variable-length integer coding scheme takes advantage of the fact that the DCT output should consist of mostly smaller numbers, which we want to encode with smaller numbers of bits. The bit counts and the amplitudes which they encode follow.

Bit Count	Amplitudes
1	-1, 1
2	-3 to -2, 2 to 3
3	7 to -4, 4 to 7
4	-15 to -8, 8 to 15
5	-31 to -16, 16 to 31
6	-63 to -32, 32 to 64
7	-127 to -64, 64 to 127
8	-255 to -128, 128 to 255
9	-511 to -256, 256 to 511
10	-1023 to -512, 512 to 1023

Note that each bit count encodes a symmetrical set of high and low values. The values skipped over in the middle will be encoded with a lower bit count from one in the table.

While this form of variable-bit coding is not quite as efficient as Huffman coding, it works fairly well, particularly if the data performs as expected, which means smaller values dominate and larger values are rare.

What About Color? The sample programs in this chapter and most of the text have talked about how to compress images that have only one color component, usually a grey scale. This leaves the question of what to do with color images.

Color images are generally composed of three components, such as the red, green, and blue of RGB, or the luminance and chrominance of YUV. In these cases, JPEG treats the image as if it were actually three separate images. An RGB image would first have its red component compressed, then its green, then its blue. This is essentially just more of the same.

The Sample Program

The sample program used to demonstrate DCT compression in this chapter is in the C source file DCT.C. It can be compiled and linked with the standard support source files, BITIO.C, ERRHAND.C, and either MAIN-C.C for compression or MAIN-E.C for expansion.

The DCT compression program takes an additional parameter on the command line, the quality factor. A factor of zero through twenty-five can be selected, zero being the best quality and twenty-five being the lowest. As was discussed earlier in this chapter, the quality factor is used to initialize the quantum table with the step sizes for each DCT element.

The command syntax for the compression program is:

```
DCT-C  input-file  output-file  [quality]
```

If no quality value is selected, it defaults to a value of three, which is an arbitrarily chosen constant. The quality factor is encoded in the compressed file, so the expansion program doesn't need that parameter on the command line. The syntax for expansion is:

```
DCT-E    input-file   output-file
```

The DCT sample program in this chapter is not an implentation of JPEG compression. It does closely duplicate the first and second stages of the algorithm, however, which are the DCT transformation of the input, followed by the quantization and zig-zag coding steps. The only significant difference from the JPEG algorithm at this point is that the DC coefficient at 0,0 is not encoded as a difference from the last coefficient.

The test program used here departs from being a JPEG implementation in the encoding phase after quantization is complete. DCT.C does not implement Huffman coding on the output, but it does implement a slightly different form of RLE and uses variable-length integer codes for output.

Input Format. Graphics files come in a plethora of formats. Decoding and understanding every format can become a bewildering problem, and the purpose of this book is not to be a treatise on file formats. Thus, the graphics examples used in this chapter are stored in the closest thing possible to a "non-format."

All of the graphics files used in this section are stored in a row-major order, so that all the pixels in each row are stored adjacent to one another. The top of the screen is stored first, with subsequent rows working their way down the screen. Each file is a 320 column by 200 row grey-scale image, with pixels having eight bits, ranging from zero to 255. The grey-scale files have a file suffix of "GS," which identifies them as "non-formatted" grey-scale files.

This format is particularly easy to display on IBM VGA displays, but should be easy to adapt to any system that can display 256 colors. A short program, GS.C, is included to display the files on IBM VGA displays. Since VGA displays can only handle sixty-four grey-scale colors, some of the resolution of the image is lost on display, but the effect is relatively insignificant to the human eye.

In addition to GS.C, which displays GS files on an IBM compatible VGA adaptor, there is a second display program called GSDIFF.C. This tests the differences between an original file and its reproduction after a compression/decompression cycle. First it gives a visual display of the differences between the two files. Then the root mean squared (rms) error is written to the screen. While the rms value is not the best way to assign a quality factor to a compression cycle, it does provide a good way to see how well compression is working.

The Code. A summarized version of the main compression module follows (a complete listing is at the end of the chapter). The main program first calls the initialization module, which sets up the quantization table and the cosine transform matrices. The quality parameter must be passed to this module to have it set up the quantization matrix properly.

The next step is to write out the quality factor to the output file. By outputting this information, we eliminate the possibility of inadvertently trying to decompress using the wrong quantization matrix. This would cause the output to be catastrophically in error if it happened.

```
void CompressFile( FILE *input, BIT_FILE *output,
                   int argc, char *argv[] )
{
    int row;
    int col;
    int i;
    unsigned char *input_array[ N ];
    int output_array[ N ][ N ];
    int quality;

    quality = atoi( argv[ 0 ] );
    printf( "Using quality factor of %d\n", quality );
    Initialize( quality );
    OutputBits( output, quality, 8 );
    for ( row = 0 ; row < ROWS ; row += N ) {
        ReadPixelStrip( input, PixelStrip );
```

```
    for ( col = 0 ; col < COLS ; col += N ) {
      for ( i = 0 ; i < N ; i++ )
        input_array[ i ] = PixelStrip[ i ] + col;
      ForwardDCT( input_array, output_array );
      WriteDCTData( output, output_array );
    }
  }
  OutputCode( output, 1 );
}
```

Finally, the main compression loop is entered. Since the data is stored a single row at a time, we need to read in a block of eight rows together before we can begin building 8-by-8 blocks to compress. This is accomplished in the routine called ReadPixelStrip. It reads an entire strip of pixels 8 rows deep and 320 columns wide.

The next part of the loop sets up the input_array. This actually gets passed to the DCT routine. It consists of a block of eight pointers into the pixel strip. When it is passed to the DCT routine, the input_array can be treated in the code as an 8-by-8 input matrix.

The DCT routine is then called. It is passed an 8-by-8 unsigned character matrix and returns an 8-by-8 integer matrix. The integer matrix is then passed to the WriteDCTData() routine for compression and to be written to the file.

The final step in the program is to call the OutputCode() routine one last time with a dummy non-zero value. The OutputCode() routine tracks consecutive zeros for the run-length encoding portion of the program. If the file ends with several consecutive zeros, they may need to be flushed before the program exits.

Initialization. DCT.C has single initialization routine that is called for both compression and expansion. It first sets up the quantization matrix, using the quality parameter passed to it. This uses the simple formula for defining step sizes discussed earlier.

Once the quantization matrix is set up, the next step is to set up the cosine transform matrix and the transposed cosine transform matrix. These matrices are used by the forward DCT and the inverse DCT, so they can be set up in a common routine. Setting them up involves nothing more than a simple translation of the formula shown in figure 11-8.

The final step in initialization is to initialize the run-length encoding counters used on input and output. These values are used when either outputting or inputting codes, and they track the number of consecutive zero codes that have output or will be input.

```
void Initialize( int quality )
{
    int i;
    int j;

    for ( i = 0 ; i < N ; i++ )
      for ( j = 0 ; j < N ; j++ )
        Quantum[ i ][ j ] = 1 + ( ( 1 + i + j ) * quality );
    for ( j = 0 ; j < N ; j++ ) {
      C[ 0 ][ j ] = 1.0 / sqrt( N );
      Ct[ j ][ 0 ] = C[ 0 ][ j ];
    }
    for ( i = 1 ; i < N ; i++ ) {
      for ( j = 0 ; j < N ; j++ ) {
        C[ i ][ j ] = sqrt( 2.0 / N ) *
                      cos( ( 2 * j + 1 ) * i * pi / ( 2.0 * N ) );
        Ct[ j ][ i ] = C[ i ][ j ];
      }
    }
    OutputRunLength = 0;
    InputRunLength = 0;
}
```

The Forward DCT Routine. Despite the seeming complexity of the DCT, it is accomplished in a very short routine. All it does is first perform a matrix multiplication of the input pixel data matrix by the transposed cosine transform matrix and store the result in a temporary N-by-N matrix. Then the temporary matrix is multiplied by the cosine transform matrix, and the result is stored in the output matrix, which is passed back to the caller.

Note here that all input pixel values are scaled before being multiplied by the transposed cosine transform matrix. After being scaled, they have a range of -128 to 127 instead of the zero to 255 range they had before. This is consistent with the way the JPEG algorithm handles input data.

```
void ForwardDCT( input, output )
unsigned char *input[ N ];
int output[ N ][ N ];
{
    double temp[ N ][ N ];
    double temp1;
    int i;
    int j;
    int k;

/* MatrixMultiply( temp, input, Ct ); */

    for ( i = 0 ; i < N ; i++ ) {
      for ( j = 0 ; j < N ; j++ ) {
        temp[ i ][ j ] = 0.0;
        for ( k = 0 ; k < N ; k++ )
          temp[ i ][ j ] += ( input[ i ][ k ] - 128 ) *
                            Ct[ k ] [ j ];
      }
    }

/* MatrixMultiply( output, C, temp ); */

    for ( i = 0 ; i < N ; i++ ) {
      for ( j = 0 ; j < N ; j++ ) {
```

```
        temp1 = 0.0;
        for ( k = 0 ; k < N ; k++ )
          temp1 += C[ i ][ k ] * temp[ k ][ j ];
        output[ i ][ j ] = ROUND( temp1 );
      }
    }
  }
```

Another point to observe is that we are dealing with several different data types here, and a certain amount of care needs to be exercised so as not to cause problems during conversions. The input data coming from the pixel strip is unsigned character converted during the matrix multiplication to integer, then multiplied by a double. The result is stored in a double temporary matrix. Finally, the last matrix multiplication produces double values, which are then rounded to integers for storage in the output matrix. If everything goes as planned, the integers should be in the range of -1,024 to 1,023, and they are ready for quantization.

WriteDCTData(). This routine is responsible for ordering the DCT result matrix into the zigzag pattern, then quantizing the data. Both of these just involve table lookups of values that have been stored either during initialization or at compile time. Then, the quantized value is rounded to the nearest integer and sent to the routine that outputs codes.

```
void WriteDCTData( BIT_FILE *output_file, output_data[ N ][ N ] )
{
   int i;
   int row;
   int col;
   double result;

   for ( i = 0 ; i < ( N * N ) ; i++ ) {
     row = ZigZag[ i ].row;
     col = ZigZag[ i ].col;
     result = output_data[ row ][ col ] / Quantum[ row ][ col ];
     OutputCode( output_file, ROUND( result ) );
   }
}
```

OutputCode(). This routine is complicated by the fact that it has to handle quite a few different situations in the output data. In general, this routine puts out two numbers every time it is called. The first number is the number of bits used in the output word to follow. The second number is the actual amplitude of the output, encoded using a variable-length word, as in the JPEG algorithm.

The number of bits parameter that is output first can range anywhere from zero to ten. To encode this number using standard binary arithmetic would take four bits for every number. To achieve a minor amount of savings, this routine uses a simple prefix code to output the number of bits, which will result in a small net savings.

```
void OutputCode( BIT_FILE *output_file, int code )
{
    int top_of_range;
    int abs_code;
    int bit_count;

    if ( code == 0 ) {
        OutputRunLength++;
        return;
    }
    if ( OutputRunLength != 0 ) {
        while ( OutputRunLength > 0 ) {
            OutputBits( output_file, 0, 2 );
            if ( OutputRunLength <= 16 ) {
                OutputBits( output_file, OutputRunLength - 1, 4 );
                OutputRunLength = 0;
            } else {
                OutputBits( output_file, 15, 4 );
                OutputRunLength -= 16;
            }
        }
    }

    if ( code < 0 )
        abs_code = -code;
```

```
else
   abs_code = code;
top_of_range = 1;
bit_count = 1;
while ( abs_code > top_of_range ) {
   bit_count++;
   top_of_range = ( ( top_of_range + 1 ) * 2 ) - 1;
}
 if ( bit_count < 3 )
   OutputBits( output_file, bit_count + 1, 3 );
else
   OutputBits( output_file, bit_count + 5, 4 );
 if ( code > 0 )
   OutputBits( output_file, code, bit_count );
else
   OutputBits( output_file, code + top_of_range, bit_count );
}
```

Number of Bits	Binary Code
0	00
1	010
2	011
3	1000
4	1001
5	1010
6	1011
7	1100
8	1101
9	1110
10	1111

Figure 11-13. The coding for number of bits.

As if this prefix code didn't complicate things enough, OutputCode() has an additional thing to worry about: run-length encoding. Since it doesn't make sense to have a number of bits equal to zero, that value is actually used to encode a run of zeros. The number of consecutive zeros is encoded as a four-bit number immediately following a bit count of zero. Note that the four-bit number encodes runs of length 1 to 16, not 0 to 15 as might be first suspected. This is done since there is no reason to waste a code on a run length of zero.

To properly encode runs of zeros, OutputCode tracks the current run length. Anytime OutputCode() is called to send out a value of zero, the routine actually just increments the run-length counter, then returns.

The routine will finally be able to output the length of a run when one of two things happens. First, the run length can actually reach sixteen. This is the longest run we can encode, which means it will flush the counter with a run output. The other situation is when OutputCode() is called to send a non-zero code, and the run-length counter is zero. This means a run has just concluded, and it is time to output it.

The final complication in this routine is the encoding of normal numbers. As was shown in the earlier figure, these have an unusual format, with each code encoding a range of negative numbers, then a range of positive numbers, with a gap in between.

OutputCode() first determines how many bits are going to be needed to encode the code by sitting in a loop checking to see if the output code falls in the appropriate range. When it finds the correct range, it encodes the number, using a different offset for negative and positive numbers.

File Expansion. Once the file-compression algorithm is understood, file expansion is relatively easy to follow. The expansion routine first reads in the quality number from the file and uses it to initialize the matrix data. It then sits in a loop, reading in 8-by-8 DCT blocks. The routine that reads the DCT data also takes it out of the zig-zag sequence, storing it in row normal fashion, then dequantizing it. At that point, it is run through the inverse DCT procedure, which returns a block of pixel data. Once an entire strip of pixel data has been read in, it is written to the uncompressed output file.

Note that the expansion routine uses an array of pointers to redirect the output of the inverse DCT to the PixelStrip array. This array has to be set up before every inverse DCT is called so the data is directed to the correct point in the pixel strip. The pixel strip is a matrix 8 rows deep and 320 columns wide.

```c
void ExpandFile( BIT_FILE *input, FILE *output,
                 int argc, char *argv[] )
{
    int row;
    int col;
    int i;
    int input_array[ N ][ N ];
    unsigned char *output_array[ N ];
    int quality;

    quality = (int) InputBits( input, 8 );
    Initialize( quality );
    for ( row = 0 ; row < ROWS ; row += N ) {
        for ( col = 0 ; col < COLS ; col += N ) {
            for ( i = 0 ; i < N ; i++ )
                output_array[ i ] = PixelStrip[ i ] + col;
            ReadDCTData( input, input_array );
            InverseDCT( input_array, output_array );
        }
        WritePixelStrip( output, PixelStrip );
    }
}
```

ReadDCTData(). This routine reads in DCT codes from the InputCode routine, dequantizes them, then stores them in the correct location. The codes read back in have been stored in the zig-zag sequence, so they have to be redirected to their appropriate locations in the 8-by-8 block. This is accomplished with a simple table lookup.

```
void ReadDCTData( input_file, input_data )
BIT_FILE *input_file;
int input_data[ N ][ N ];
{
    int i;
    int row;
    int col;

    for ( i = 0 ; i < ( N * N ) ; i++ ) {
        row = ZigZag[ i ].row;
        col = ZigZag[ i ].col;
        input_data[ row ][ col ] = InputCode( input_file ) *
                            Quantum[ row ][ col ];
    }
}
```

Input DCT Codes. Reading in the DCT codes is somewhat less complicated than writing them out, but a number of factors still need to be taken into account. First, we read in the first two bits of the bit count code. If the two bits have a value of zero, it means that a run of zeros is being encoded with this value. The zero count is read in using the next four bits and stored in the global run-length indicator.

The global run-length indicator is stored in the InputRunLength variable, and it is checked every time the InputCode routine is called. If the value in this variable is non-zero, we are still returning a run of zeros. When this is the case, the run-length indicator is decremented, and a zero is returned to the calling program.

In the event that the first two bits aren't zero, we are working with a normal bit count code. Either two or three more bits are read in to compose the rest of the code, which yields the correct bit count. We can then read in the encoded amplitude of the DCT variable by reading in that bit count.

Once that value is loaded in, we need to convert it to a normal number from the specially encoded form it is in, which is relatively simple. Finally, the correct number is returned to the calling routine for dequantization and processing.

```
int InputCode( input_file )
BIT_FILE *input_file;
{
    int bit_count;
    int result;

    if ( InputRunLength > 0 ) {
        InputRunLength--;
        return( 0 );
    }
    bit_count = (int) InputBits( input_file, 2 );
    if ( bit_count == 0 ) {
        InputRunLength = (int) InputBits( input_file, 4 );
        return( 0 );
    }
    if ( bit_count == 1 )
        bit_count = (int) InputBits( input_file, 1 ) + 1;
    else
        bit_count = (int) InputBits( input_file, 2 ) +
                    ( bit_count << 2 ) - 5;
    result = (int) InputBits( input_file, bit_count );
    if ( result & ( 1 << ( bit_count - 1 ) ) )
        return( result );
    return( result - ( 1 << bit_count ) + 1 );
}
```

The Inverse DCT. The Inverse DCT is performed using the exact reverse of the operations performed in the DCT. First, the DCT values in the N-by-N matrix are multiplied by the cosine transform matrix. The result of this transformation is stored in a temporary N-by-N matrix of doubles. This matrix is then multiplied by the transposed cosine transform matrix. The result of this multiplication is rounded, scaled to the correct unsigned character range of zero to 255, then stored in the output block of pixels.

```
void InverseDCT( int input[ N ][ N ], unsigned char *output[ N ] )
{
    double temp[ N ][ N ];
    double temp1;
    int i;
    int j;
    int k;

/* MatrixMultiply( temp, input, C ); */
    for ( i = 0 ; i < N ; i++ ) {
        for ( j = 0 ; j < N ; j++ ) {
            temp[ i ][ j ] = 0.0;
            for ( k = 0 ; k < N ; k++ )
                temp[ i ][ j ] += input[ i ][ k ] * C[ k ][ j ];
        }
    }

/* MatrixMultiply( output, Ct, temp ); */
    for ( i = 0 ; i < N ; i++ ) {
        for ( j = 0 ; j < N ; j++ ) {
            temp1 = 0.0;
            for ( k = 0 ; k < N ; k++ )
                temp1 += Ct[ i ][ k ] * temp[ k ][ j ];
            temp1 += 128.0;
            if ( temp1 < 0 )
                output[ i ][ j ] = 0;
            else if ( temp1 > 255 )
                output[ i ][ j ] = 255;
            else
                output[ i ][ j ] = ROUND( temp1 );
        }
    }
}
```

The Complete Code Listing

The complete listing of DCT.C follows.

```
/*********************** Start of DCT.C ***********************
*
* This is the DCT module, which implements a graphics compression
* program based on the discrete cosine transform. It needs to be
* linked with the standard support routines.
*
*/

#include <stdio.h>
#include <stdlib.h>
#include <math.h>
#include "bitio.h"
#include "errhand.h"

/*
* A few parameters can be adjusted to modify the compression
* algorithm. The first two define the number of rows and columns in
* the grey-scale image. The last one, 'N,' defines the DCT block size.
*/
#define ROWS    200
#define COLS    320
#define N       8

/*
* This macro is used to ensure correct rounding of integer values.
*/
#define ROUND( a )      ( ( (a) < 0 ) ? (int) ( (a) - 0.5 ) : \
                                        (int) ( (a) + 0.5 ) )

char *CompressionName = "DCT compression";
char *Usage           = "infile outfile [quality]\nQuality from 0-25";
```

```
/*
 * Function prototypes for both ANSI and K&R.
 */
#ifdef __STDC__

void Initialize( int quality );
void ReadPixelStrip( FILE *input, unsigned char strip[ N ][ COLS ] );
int InputCode( BIT_FILE *input );
void ReadDCTData( BIT_FILE *input, int input_data[ N ][ N ] );
void OutputCode( BIT_FILE *output_file, int code );
void WriteDCTData( BIT_FILE *output_file, int output_data[ N ][ N ] );
void WritePixelStrip( FILE *output, unsigned char strip[ N ][ COLS ] );
void ForwardDCT( unsigned char *input[ N ], int output[ N ][ N ] );
void InverseDCT( int input[ N ][ N ], unsigned char *output[ N ] );
void CompressFile( FILE *input, BIT_FILE *output,
                   int argc, char *argv[] );
void ExpandFile( BIT_FILE *input, FILE *output, int argc, char *argv[] );

#else

void Initialize();
void ReadPixelStrip();
int InputCode();
void ReadDCTData();
void OutputCode();
void WriteDCTData();
void WritePixelStrip();
void ForwardDCT();
void InverseDCT();
void CompressFile();
void ExpandFile();

#endif

/*
 * Global data used at various places in the program.
 */
```

```
unsigned char PixelStrip[ N ][ COLS ];
double C[ N ][ N ];
double Ct[ N ][ N ];
int InputRunLength;
int OutputRunLength;
int Quantum[ N ][ N ];

struct zigzag {
    int row;
    int col;
} ZigZag[ N * N ] =
{
{0, 0},
{0, 1}, {1, 0},
{2, 0}, {1, 1}, {0, 2},
{0, 3}, {1, 2}, {2, 1}, {3, 0},
{4, 0}, {3, 1}, {2, 2}, {1, 3}, {0, 4},
{0, 5}, {1, 4}, {2, 3}, {3, 2}, {4, 1}, {5, 0},
{6, 0}, {5, 1}, {4, 2}, {3, 3}, {2, 4}, {1, 5}, {0, 6},
{0, 7}, {1, 6}, {2, 5}, {3, 4}, {4, 3}, {5, 2}, {6, 1}, {7, 0},
{7, 1}, {6, 2}, {5, 3}, {4, 4}, {3, 5}, {2, 6}, {1, 7},
{2, 7}, {3, 6}, {4, 5}, {5, 4}, {6, 3}, {7, 2},
{7, 3}, {6, 4}, {5, 5}, {4, 6}, {3, 7},
{4, 7}, {5, 6}, {6, 5}, {7, 4},
{7, 5}, {6, 6}, {5, 7},
{6, 7}, {7, 6},
{7, 7}
};

/*
 * The initialization routine has the job of setting up the cosine
 * transform matrix, as well as its transposed value. These two matrices
 * are used when calculating both the DCT and its inverse. In addition,
 * the quantization matrix is set up based on the quality parameter
 * passed to this routine. The two run-length parameters are both
 * set to zero.
 */
```

```
void Initialize( quality )
int quality;
{
    int i;
    int j;
    double pi = atan( 1.0 ) * 4.0;

    for ( i = 0 ; i < N ; i++ )
      for ( j = 0 ; j < N ; j++ )
        Quantum[ i ][ j ] = 1 + ( ( 1 + i + j ) * quality );
    OutputRunLength = 0;
    InputRunLength = 0;
    for ( j = 0 ; j < N ; j++ ) {
      C[ 0 ][ j ] = 1.0 / sqrt( (double) N );
      Ct[ j ][ 0 ] = C[ 0 ][ j ];
    }
    for ( i = 1 ; i < N ; i++ ) {
      for ( j = 0 ; j < N ; j++ ) {
        C[ i ][ j ] = sqrt( 2.0 / N ) *
                      cos( pi * ( 2 * j + 1 ) * i / ( 2.0 * N ) );
        Ct[ j ][ i ] = C[ i ][ j ];
      }
    }
}


/*
 * This routine is called when compressing a grey-scale file. It reads
 * in a strip that is N (usually eight) rows deep and COLS (usually 320)
 * columns wide. This strip is then repeatedly processed, a block at a
 * time, by the forward DCT routine.
 */
void ReadPixelStrip( input, strip )
FILE *input;
unsigned char strip[ N ][ COLS ];
{
    int row;
    int col;
```

```
    int c;
    for ( row = 0 ; row < N ; row++ )
      for ( col = 0 ; col < COLS ; col++ ) {
        c = getc( input );
        if ( c == EOF )
          fatal_error( "Error reading input grey scale file" );
        strip[ row ][ col ] = (unsigned char) c;
      }
}
/*
* This routine reads in a DCT code from the compressed file. The code
* consists of two components, a bit count, and an encoded value. The
* bit count is encoded as a prefix code with the following binary
* values:
*
*          Number of Bits              Binary Code
*                0                          00
*                1                          010
*                2                          011
*                3                          1000
*                4                          1001
*                5                          1010
*                6                          1011
*                7                          1100
*                8                          1101
*                9                          1110
*               10                          1111
```

```
 *
 * A bit count of zero is followed by a four-bit number telling how many
 * zeros are in the encoded run. A value of one through ten indicates a
 * code value follows, which takes up that many bits. The encoding of
 * values into this system has the following characteristics:
 *
 *              Bit Count                  Amplitudes
 *                 1                          -1, 1
 *                 2                      -3 to -2, 2 to 3
 *                 3                      -7 to -4, 4 to 7
 *                 4                     -15 to -8, 8 to 15
 *                 5                    -31 to -16, 16 to 31
 *                 6                    -63 to -32, 32 to 64
 *                 7                   -127 to -64, 64 to 127
 *                 8                 -255 to -128, 128 to 255
 *                 9                 -511 to -256, 256 to 511
 *                10               -1023 to -512, 512 to 1023
 *
 */

int InputCode( input_file )
BIT_FILE *input_file;
{
   int bit_count;
   int result;

   if ( InputRunLength > 0 ) {
     InputRunLength--;
     return( 0 );
   }
   bit_count = (int) InputBits( input_file, 2 );
   if ( bit_count == 0 ) {
     InputRunLength = (int) InputBits( input_file, 4 );
     return( 0 );
   }
   if ( bit_count == 1 )
     bit_count = (int) InputBits( input_file, 1 ) + 1;
```

```
    else
      bit_count = (int) InputBits( input_file, 2 ) +
                        ( bit_count << 2 ) - 5;
    result = (int) InputBits( input_file, bit_count );
    if ( result & ( 1 << ( bit_count - 1 ) ) )
      return( result );
    return( result - ( 1 << bit_count ) + 1 );
}


/*
 * This routine reads in a block of encoded DCT data from a compressed
 * file. The routine reorders it in row major format and dequantizes it
 * using the quantization matrix.
 */

void ReadDCTData( input_file, input_data )
BIT_FILE *input_file;
int input_data[ N ][ N ];
{
    int i;
    int row;
    int col;

    for ( i = 0 ; i < ( N * N ) ; i++ ) {
      row = ZigZag[ i ].row;
      col = ZigZag[ i ].col;
      input_data[ row ][ col ] = InputCode( input_file ) *
                                 Quantum[ row ][ col ];
    }
}


/*
 * This routine outputs a code to the compressed DCT file. For specs
 * on the exact format, see the comments that go with InputCode, shown
 * earlier in this file.
 */
```

```
void OutputCode( output_file, code ) BIT_FILE *output_file;
int code;
{
   int top_of_range;
   int abs_code;
   int bit_count;

   if ( code == 0 ) {
      OutputRunLength++;
      return;
   }
   if ( OutputRunLength != 0 ) {
      while ( OutputRunLength > 0 ) {
         OutputBits( output_file, 0L, 2 );
         if ( OutputRunLength <= 16 ) {
             OutputBits( output_file,
                        (unsigned long) (OutputRunLength - 1 ), 4 );
             OutputRunLength = 0;
      } else {
         OutputBits( output_file, 15L, 4 );
         OutputRunLength -= 16;
      }
   }
}
if ( code < 0 )
   abs_code = -code;
else
   abs_code = code;
top_of_range = 1;
bit_count = 1;
while ( abs_code > top_of_range ) {
   bit_count++;
   top_of_range = ( ( top_of_range + 1 ) * 2 ) - 1;
```

```
    }
    if ( bit_count < 3 )
        OutputBits( output_file, (unsigned long) ( bit_count + 1 ), 3 );
    else
        OutputBits( output_file, (unsigned long) ( bit_count + 5 ), 4 );
    if ( code > 0 )
      OutputBits( output_file, (unsigned long) code, bit_count );
    else
      OutputBits( output_file, (unsigned long) ( code + top_of_range ) ,
                  bit_count );
}


/*
* This routine takes DCT data, puts it in zigzag order, quantizes
* it, and outputs the code.
*/

void WriteDCTData( output_file, output_data )
BIT_FILE *output_file;
int output_data[ N ][ N ];
{
    int i;
    int row;
    int col;
    double result;

    for ( i = 0 ; i < ( N * N ) ; i++ ) {
      row = ZigZag[ i ].row;
      col = ZigZag[ i ].col;
      result = output_data[ row ][ col ] / Quantum[ row ][ col ];
      OutputCode( output_file, ROUND( result ) );
    }
}
```

```
/*
 * This routine writes out a strip of pixel data to a GS format file.
 */

void WritePixelStrip( output, strip )
FILE *output;
unsigned char strip[ N ][ COLS ];
{
    int row;
    int col;

    for ( row = 0 ; row < N ; row++ )
      for ( col = 0 ; col < COLS ; col++ )
        putc( strip[ row ][ col ], output ); }

/*
 * The Forward DCT routine implements the matrix function:
 *
 *              DCT = C * pixels * Ct
 */

void ForwardDCT( input, output )
unsigned char *input[ N ];
int output[ N ][ N ];
{
    double temp[ N ][ N ];
    double temp1;
    int i;
    int j;
    int k;

/* MatrixMultiply( temp, input, Ct ); */
    for ( i = 0 ; i < N ; i++ ) {
      for ( j = 0 ; j < N ; j++ ) {
        temp[ i ][ j ] = 0.0;
        for ( k = 0 ; k < N ; k++ )
```

```
                 temp[ i ][ j ] += ( (int) input [ i ][ k ] - 128 ) *
                                Ct[ k ][ j ];
        }
   }

/* MatrixMultiply( output, C, temp ); */
    for ( i = 0 ; i < N ; i++ ) {
      for ( j = 0 ; j < N ; j++ ) {
         temp1 = 0.0;
         for ( k = 0 ; k < N ; k++ )
           temp1 += C[ i ][ k ] * temp[ k ][ j ];
         output[ i ][ j ] = ROUND( temp1 );
      }
   }
}


/*
 * The Inverse DCT routine implements the matrix function:
 *
 *              pixels = C * DCT * Ct
 */

void InverseDCT( input, output )
int input[ N ][ N ];
unsigned char *output[ N ];
{
   double temp[ N ][ N ];
   double temp1;
   int i;
   int j;
   int k;

/* MatrixMultiply( temp, input, C ); */
    for ( i = 0 ; i < N ; i++ ) {
      for ( j = 0 ; j < N ; j++ ) {
         temp[ i ][ j ] = 0.0;
         for ( k = 0 ; k < N ; k++ )
           temp[ i ][ j ] += input[ i ][ k ] * C[ k ][ j ];
```

```
      }
   }


/* MatrixMultiply( output, Ct, temp ); */
   for ( i = 0 ; i < N ; i++ ) {
     for ( j = 0 ; j < N ; j++ ) {
       temp1 = 0.0;
       for ( k = 0 ; k < N ; k++ )
         temp1 += Ct[ i ][ k ] * temp[ k ][ j ];
       temp1 += 128.0;
       if ( temp1 < 0 )
         output[ i ][ j ] = 0;
       else if ( temp1 > 255 )
         output[ i ][ j ] = 255;
       else
         output[ i ][ j ] = (unsigned char) ROUND( temp1 );
     }
   }
}


/*
 * This is the main compression routine. By the time it gets called,
 * the input and output files have been properly opened, so all it has to
 * do is the compression. Note that the compression routine expects an
 * additional parameter, the quality value, ranging from 0 to 25.
 */

void CompressFile( input, output, argc, argv )
FILE *input;
BIT_FILE *output;
int argc;
char *argv[];
{
   int row;
   int col;
   int i;
   unsigned char *input_array[ N ];
```

```
    int output_array[ N ][ N ];
    int quality;

    if ( argc-- > 0 )
       quality = atoi( argv[ 0 ] );
    else
       quality = 3;
    if ( quality < 0 || quality > 50 )
       fatal_error( "Illegal quality factor of %d\n", quality );
    printf( "Using quality factor of %d\n", quality );
    Initialize( quality );
    OutputBits( output, (unsigned long) quality, 8 );
    for ( row = 0 ; row < ROWS ; row += N ) {
       ReadPixelStrip( input, PixelStrip );
       for ( col = 0 ; col < COLS ; col += N ) {
          for ( i = 0 ; i < N ; i++ )
             input_array[ i ] = PixelStrip[ i ] + col;
          ForwardDCT( input_array, output_array );
          WriteDCTData( output, output_array );
       }
    }
    OutputCode( output, 1 );
    while ( argc-- > 0 )
       printf( "Unused argument: %s\n", *argv++ );
}

/*
 * The expansion routine reads in the compressed data from the DCT file,
 * then writes out the decompressed grey-scale file.
 */

void ExpandFile( input, output, argc, argv )
BIT_FILE *input;
FILE *output;
int argc;
char *argv[];
{
```

```
    int row;
    int col;
    int i;
    int input_array[ N ][ N ];
    unsigned char *output_array[ N ];
    int quality;

    quality = (int) InputBits( input, 8 );
    printf( "\rUsing quality factor of %d\n", quality );
    Initialize( quality );
    for ( row = 0 ; row < ROWS ; row += N ) {
      for ( col = 0 ; col < COLS ; col += N ) {
        for ( i = 0 ; i < N ; i++ )
          output_array[ i ] = PixelStrip[ i ] + col;
        ReadDCTData( input, input_array );
        InverseDCT( input_array, output_array );
      }
      WritePixelStrip( output, PixelStrip );
    }
    while ( argc-- > 0 )
      printf( "Unused argument: %s\n", *argv++ );
}
/*********************** End of DCT.C ****************************/
```

Support Programs

The two support programs used in this chapter are GS.C, used to display "non-format" grey-scale files, and GSDIFF.C, used to display the differences between two files and to print the rms value of the error. They follow.

```
/************************ Start of GS.C *************************
*
* This is the GS program, which displays grey-scale files on the
* IBM VGA adaptor. It assumes that the grey-scale values run from
* zero to 255, and scales them down to a range of zero to sixty-three,
* so they will be displayed properly on the VGA.
```

```
 *
 * This program can be called with a list of files, and will display them
 * in consecutive order, which is useful for trying to measure visual
 * differences in compressed files.
 *
 * This program writes directly to video memory, which should work
 * properly on most VGA adaptors. In the event that it doesn't, the
 * constant USE_BIOS can be turned on, and the code will use BIOS calls
 * to write pixels instead. This will be somewhat slower, but should work
 * on every VGA adaptor.
 *
 * Note that the use of far pointers means this program should probably
 * be compiled without using the strict ANSI option of your compiler.
 */

#include <stdio.h>
#include <stdlib.h>
#include <dos.h>
#include <conio.h>

main( int argc, char *argv[] )
{
    union REGS rin;
    union REGS rout;
    int i;
    FILE *file;
    char far *video;

    if ( argc < 2 ) {
        printf( "Usage: gs file\n\n" );
        exit( 1 );
    }
    rin.h.ah = 0;
    rin.h.al = 0x13;
    int86( 0x10, &rin, &rout );
    rin.h.ah = 0x10;
    rin.h.al = 0x10;
```

```
    for ( i = 0 ; i < 64 ; i++ ) {
        rin.h.dh =  (unsigned char) i;
        rin.h.ch =  (unsigned char) i;
        rin.h.cl =  (unsigned char) i;
        rin.x.bx =  i;
        int86( 0x10, &rin, &rout );
    }
    rin.h.ah = 0x10;
    rin.h.al = 0x1b;
    rin.x.cx = 256;
    rin.x.bx = 0;
    int86( 0x10, &rin, &rout );

    argv++;
    while ( --argc > 0 ) {
        file = fopen( *argv++, "rb" );
        if ( file == NULL ) {
            putc( 7, stdout );
            break;
        }
        video = (char far *) 0xA0000000L;
        rin.h.ah = 0x0c;
        rin.h.bh = 0;
        for ( rin.x.dx = 0 ; rin.x.dx < 200 ; rin.x.dx++ ) {
            for ( rin.x.cx = 0 ; rin.x.cx < 320 ; rin.x.cx++ ) {
#ifdef USE_BIOS
                rin.h.al = (unsigned char) ( getc( file ) >> 2);
                int86( 0x10, &rin, &rout );
#else
                *video++ = (char) ( getc( file ) >> 2);
#endif
            }
        }
        fclose( file );
        getch();
    }
    rin.h.ah = 0;
```

```
    rin.h.al = 3;
    int86( 0x10, &rin, &rout );
    return 0;
}


/*********************** End of GS.C ****************************/

/************************ Start of GSDIFF.C ************************
 *
 * This is the GSDIFF program, which displays the differences between
 * two grey-scale files on the IBM VGA adaptor. It assumes that the
 * grey-scale values run from zero to 255, and scales them down to a
 * range of zero to sixty-three, so they will be displayed properly on
 * the VGA.
 *
 * This program writes directly to video memory, which should work
 * properly on most VGA adaptors. In the event that it doesn't, the
 * constant USE_BIOS can be turned on, and the code will use BIOS calls
 * to write pixels instead. This will be somewhat slower, but should work
 * on every VGA adaptor.
 *
 * While this program is writing out to the display, it is also keeping a
 * running total of the error differences. When the program is
 * complete, it prints out the RMS error. If the -B switch is turned
 * on, the program operates in batch mode, and doesn't display the
 * differences. It just computes and prints the rms error value.
 *
 * Note that the use of far pointers means this program should probably
 * be compiled without using the strict ANSI option of your compiler.
 */

#include <stdio.h>
#include <stdlib.h>
#include <string>
#include <dos.h>
#include <conio.h>
#include <math.h>
```

```
main( int argc, char *argv[] )
{
    union REGS rin;
    union REGS rout;
    int i;
    FILE *file1;
    FILE *file2;
    int diff;
    int c1;
    int c2;
    char far *video;
    double error;
    int batch;

    if ( argc < 3 ) {
        printf( "Usage: gsdiff file1 file2 [-B]\n\n" );
        exit( 1 );
    }
    file1 = fopen( argv[ 1 ], "rb" );
    file2 = fopen( argv[ 2 ], "rb" );
    if ( file1 == NULL || file2 == NULL ) {
        printf( "Could not open file!\n" );
        exit( 1 );
    }
    batch = 0;
    if ( argc > 3 )
        if ( strcmp( argv[ 3 ], "-b" ) == 0 ||
            strcmp( argv[ 3 ], "-B" ) == 0 )
            batch = 1;
    if ( !batch ) {
        rin.h.ah = 0;
        rin.h.al = 0x13;
        int86( 0x10, &rin, &rout );
        rin.h.ah = 0x10;
        rin.h.al = 0x10;
```

```
    for ( i = 0 ; i < 64 ; i++ ) {
        rin.h.dh =  (unsigned char) i;
        rin.h.ch =  (unsigned char) i;
        rin.h.cl =  (unsigned char) i;
        rin.x.bx =  i;
        int86( 0x10, &rin, &rout );
    }
    rin.h.ah = 0x10;
    rin.h.al = 0x1b;
    rin.x.cx = 256;
    rin.x.bx = 0;
    int86( 0x10, &rin, &rout );
}
error = 0.0;
video = (char far *) 0xA0000000L;
rin.h.ah = 0x0c;
rin.h.bh = 0;
for ( rin.x.dx = 0 ; rin.x.dx < 200 ; rin.x.dx++ ) {
    for ( rin.x.cx = 0 ; rin.x.cx < 320 ; rin.x.cx++ ) {
        c1 = getc( file1 );
        c2 = getc( file2 );
        diff = c1 - c2;
        error += diff*diff;
        if ( diff < 0 )
            diff *= -1;
        if ( diff > 63 )
            diff = 63;
        if ( !batch ) {
#ifdef USE_BIOS
            rin.h.al = diff;
            int86( 0x10, &rin, &rout );
#else
            *video++ = diff;
#endif
        }
    }
}
```

```
  fclose( file1 );
  fclose( file2 );
  if ( !batch ) {
    getch();
    rin.h.ah = 0;
    rin.h.al = 3;
    int86( 0x10, &rin, &rout );
  }
  error /= 320.0 * 200.0;
  printf( "RMS error between %s and %s is %lf\n",
    argv[ 1 ], argv[ 2 ], sqrt( error ) );
    return 0;
  }
/*************************** End of GSDIFF.C ***************************/
```

Some Compression Results

The disk included with this book contains five grey-scale files to experiment with. Some of the results of compressing these files using the DCT program is shown in figure 11-13.

On most of the images, compression quality figures of five or lower produce a slight loss of resolution, but no significant loss of picture quality. Once the quality factor gets above five, visible artifacts of the compression process start to become visible as "blocking" of the image.

File	Quality	Starting Size	Compressed Size	Ratio	RMS Error
CHEETAH.GS	1	64000	27809	57%	4.3
CHEETAH.GS	2	64000	18367	72%	6.9
CHEETAH.GS	3	64000	14084	78%	8.6
CHEETAH.GS	4	64000	11731	82%	9.9
CHEETAH.GS	5	64000	10232	85%	10.9
CHEETAH.GS	10	64000	7167	89%	13.6
CHEETAH.GS	15	64000	6074	91%	15.2
CHEETAH.GS	25	64000	5094	93%	17.4
CLOWN.GS	1	64000	20835	68%	3.7
CLOWN.GS	2	64000	14243	78%	5.6
CLOWN.GS	3	64000	11323	83%	6.9
CLOWN.GS	4	64000	9674	85%	7.9
CLOWN.GS	5	64000	8636	87%	8.6
CLOWN.GS	10	64000	6355	91%	10.9
CLOWN.GS	15	64000	5513	92%	12.3
CLOWN.GS	25	64000	4811	93%	14.1
LISAW.GS	1	64000	10650	84%	2.3
LISAW.GS	3	64000	6971	90%	3.2
LISAW.GS	5	64000	5941	91%	3.7
LISAW.GS	10	64000	4968	93%	4.7
LISAW.GS	25	64000	4170	94%	6.6
ROSE.GS	1	64000	19425	70%	3.6
ROSE.GS	3	64000	10452	84%	6.7
ROSE.GS	5	64000	8170	88%	8.4
ROSE.GS	10	64000	6277	91%	10.7
ROSE.GS	25	64000	4807	93%	14.3
MOUSE.GS	1	64000	9265	86%	2.1
MOUSE.GS	3	64000	6403	90%	3.0
MOUSE.GS	5	64000	5651	92%	3.5
MOUSE.GS	10	64000	4917	93%	4.5
MOUSE.GS	25	64000	4337	94%	6.3

Figure 11-13. Compression results

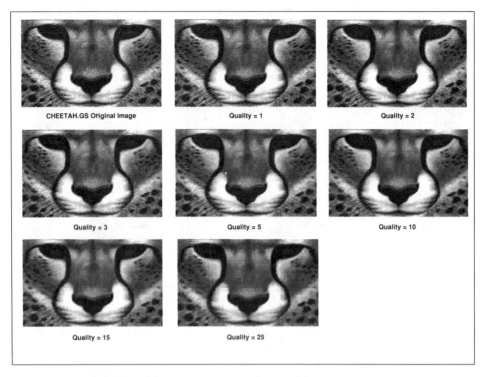

CHEETAH.GS Original Image   Quality = 1   Quality = 2

Quality = 3   Quality = 5   Quality = 10

Quality = 15   Quality = 25

Figure 11-14. CHEETAH.GS after a compression cycle.

Figure 11-14 shows a few images of CHEETAH.GS after going through a compression cycle. The first few images look fairly good. In fact, it is hard to spot much of a difference. Viewing the images one immediately after the other using GS.EXE will clearly show that there have been changes, but they are not glaring differences. At quality 5, close inspection shows a few areas where the compression is clearly starting to cause picture quality to slip. The images with quality factors 10, 15, and 20 show clear degradation.

The compression results achieved from these experiments are quite impressive. In most cases, images can be compressed up to about 85 percent without losing much picture quality. Better compression than this could be expected from the JPEG algorithm, since it adds a Huffman coding stage which DCT.C lacks.

CHAPTER 12

An Archiving Package

Programmers and users are perhaps most frequently exposed directly to data compression through the use of an archiving program. In the MS-DOS world, the use of archiving packages is ubiquitous, with the distribution of some packages fast approaching the saturation point. Programs such as PKZIP and ARJ that are distributed through non-commercial channels tend to blanket the world of "power users", with new releases getting world-wide distribution in a matter of only days.

Because data compression is a competitive field, these programs tend to have very good performance characteristics, having both high throughput and tight compression ratios. They tend to do their jobs well.

But for the programmer, these data-compression programs are sorely lacking in one respect: their handling of source code. While it's nice to be able to invoke PAK or ARC from the MS-DOS command line, that doesn't help the programmer who wants to compress all of the on-line help screens in his new spreadsheet program. It would be somewhat impractical for his program to have to spawn a copy of PKUNZIP every time a new help screen needed to be accessed.

This chapter presents a solution to such dilemmas by showing you how to create a simple, stripped down version of an archiving program. While space limitations in the book prevent this program from being a match for commercial programs, a good programmer armed with the techniques found in this book should be able to enhance this program to make it as useful as commercial equivalents.

CAR and CARMAN

This chapter deals with two topics: Compressed Archive files and the program used to maintain them. Compressed archive files conventionally have a file extension of ".CAR," and will be referred to as CAR files. The CAR file Manager will be named CARMAN.

CARMAN is a stand alone program designed to manipulate CAR files. It has a fairly simple set of commands, and runs using command-line mode. CARMAN's real strength lies in either its extension with more powerful compression techniques or more detailed file data, or the inclusion of portions of its code into other programs.

The CARMAN Command Set. Running CARMAN with no arguments gives a brief help screen showing the usage of the program, as shown in Figure 12-1.

```
CARMAN 1.0 : CARMAN Compressed ARchive MANager
Usage: carman command car-file [file ...]
Commands:
    a: Add files to a CAR archive (replace if present)
    x: Extract files from a CAR archive
    r: Replace files in a CAR archive
    d: Delete files from a CAR archive
    p: Print files on standard output
    l: List contents of a CAR archive
    t: Test files in a CAR archive
```

Figure 12-1. The CARMAN Help Screen

Every CARMAN operation has two basic requirements. First, it must have a single letter command and, second, it must have the name of a CAR file. A brief synopsis of the commands follows.

Add files: This command is used to add new files to an archive, which may or may not already exist. Wild cards on the command line will be expanded under MS-DOS. Full path names can be used to specify input files, but CAR will strip the path components before storing the files. If the CAR file already exists, and a file to be added already exists in the archive, the new version will replace the old.

Xtract files: This command extracts files from the archive and stores them in the current directory. If no file names are listed on the command line, all files are extracted from the archive.

Replace files: This command attempts to replace all of the named archive files with a new version from the current directory. If a specified file exists in the archive but not in the current directory, a warning message is printed.

Delete files: The named files are deleted from the CAR file.

Print files: The specified files are copied to stdout. If no files are named, all files will be extracted.

Test files: The specified files are tested to be sure they can be properly extracted, and that the resulting CRC value will be correct.

List files: The statistics for the specified files are listed on stdout. If no file names are specified, all files are listed. A typical listing is shown next.

Filename	Original Size	Compressed Size	Ratio	CRC-32	Method
buildcrc.c	6995	3891	45%	d04954fe	LZSS
checkcrc.c	5964	3574	41%	1a364b88	LZSS
carman.c	62214	23187	63%	a9bd559e	LZSS
io.c	2369	1162	51%	37f575ac	LZSS

Figure 12-2. CARMAN List Command Output

As can be seen from this listing, the compression method employed in CARMAN is LZSS, with the compression code being nearly identical to that shown in Chapter 8. Files that could not be compressed to less than their original size will instead be stored in uncompressed format.

While LZSS does not offer the tightest compression possible, it does provide adequate performance. In addition, it has one unique advantage: its expansion speed will meet or exceed that of nearly any compression program available. So applications that need to decompress frequently may find LZSS to be the algorithm of choice.

The CAR File. The structure of a CAR file is very simple: it simply consists of a sequential list of file header blocks followed by file data. This sequence repeats indefinitely until a special header with a null file name is encountered. An illustration of this structure is shown in Figure 12-3.

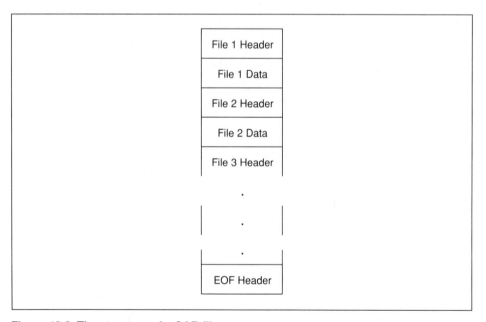

Figure 12-3. The structure of a CAR file.

A sequential structure like this has both advantages and disadvantages. The sequential nature of the data means that both searches through and updates of the archive are not done using a random access method. Instead, linear searches and copies are used. Even worse, any time files in the archive are modified, it means the entire archive has to be copied from the original to a new version of the file. These disadvantages are outweighed by the simplicity this technique offers. Good reliable code can easily be written to support this storage method. In fact, most popular archiving programs use a nearly identical format.

The Header. In the CAR format, the header for each file contains everything we know about the file. Thus, selecting what goes in the header and what doesn't is fairly important. CARMAN uses a fairly stripped down set of information in the header file, with a C structure as follows:

```
typedef struct header {
    char file_name[ FILENAME_MAX ];
    char compression_method;
    unsigned long original_size;
    unsigned long compressed_size;
    unsigned long original_crc;
    unsigned long header_crc;
} HEADER;
```

Most of the information in the header is self explanatory, particularly in terms of how it is used inside a C program. The place where the header information gets a little confusing is in the process of storing or reading it to/from a CAR file.

Storing the Header. To make CAR files portable across different systems and architectures, you need to take care when writing data to files. Conventionally, if we were to write this structure out to a file, we might use a line of code that looks like this:

```
fwrite( header, sizeof( HEADER ), 1, outfile );
```

This writes a binary image of the header data directly out to the file, so that can be easily read in using an equivalent fread() statement.

There are two potential problems that crop up when writing data out this way. The first relates to the packing of structures. Different C compilers will pack structure elements in different fashions. For example, we have a single char element as the second element of the header array shown above. Since the next element is a long integer, an MS-DOS compiler might put in three bytes of padding so that the long element is aligned on a four-byte boundary. Generally, this is done to generate faster, more efficient code. (Many CPUs tend to work better with data aligned on certain boundaries.) A different compiler on a different machine might not insert any padding, or might use an eight-byte boundary.

When structures are packed differently, we can no longer count on portability between binary files generated using fwrite() calls such as the one shown above. However, it would seem that this would be a relatively easy problem to overcome. Instead of writing out the structure as a single entity, we could just store it one element at a time, which would guarantee that no packing bytes were inadvertently added to our output.

This solution runs afoul of our second portability problem. Unfortunately, we cannot be sure that different computers will store identical data elements using the same structure. For example, a long integer with the hex value 0x12345678L would be stored in the following manner on an Intel 8086 machine:

Address	Value
0000	78
0001	56
0002	34
0003	12

The same long integer stored on a machine based on the Motorola 68000 architecture would have the bytes stored in exactly the reverse order! These differences result from decisions the hardware designers made long ago, for better or worse, and we all have to live with the consequences. In this case, the consequence is a problem with binary file interchange.

The solution is to take control of the binary file format at the lowest level. Instead of trying to write out short and long integers in one fell swoop, we write them out a byte at a time, using the ordering that we select. This way we should be able to store and retrieve data items so that our CAR files can be ported across various systems without worrying about incompatibilities.

When reading and writing the headers, you would first pack and unpack the short and long integer data in the header file into a character array, using a pair of utility routines. We arbitrarily pack the data with the least significant bytes first, although it could just as easily be done in the other order. The routines that do the packing follow.

```
void PackUnsignedData( number_of_bytes, number, buffer )
int number_of_bytes;
unsigned long number;
unsigned char *buffer;
{
   while ( number_of_bytes-- > 0 ) {
     *buffer++ = ( unsigned char ) number & 0xff;
     number >>= 8;
   }
}


unsigned long UnpackUnsignedData( number_of_bytes, buffer )
int number_of_bytes;
unsigned char *buffer;
{
   unsigned long result;
   int shift_count;

   result = 0;
   shift_count = 0;
   while ( number_of_bytes-- > 0 ) {
     result |= (unsigned long) *buffer++ << shift_count;
     shift_count += 8;
   }
   return( result );
}
```

Given these packing and unpacking routines, reading and storing the header files is simple. The process is accomplished for the file I/O using an intermediate character array. The actual header data is packed and unpacked to and from the array.

```
void WriteFileHeader()
{
  unsigned char header_data[ 17 ];
  int i;

  for ( i = 0 ; ; ) {
    putc( Header.file_name[ i ], OutputCarFile );
    if ( Header.file_name[ i++ ] == '\0' )
      break;
  }
  Header.header_crc = CalculateBlockCRC32( i, CRC_MASK,
                                                Header.file_name );
  PackUnsignedData( 1, (long)
                       Header.compression_method, header_data + 0 );
  PackUnsignedData( 4, Header.original_size, header_data + 1 );
  PackUnsignedData( 4, Header.compressed_size, header_data + 5 );
  PackUnsignedData( 4, Header.original_crc, header_data + 9 );
  Header.header_crc = CalculateBlockCRC32( 13, Header.header_crc,
           header_data );
  Header.header_crc ^= CRC_MASK;
  PackUnsignedData( 4, Header.header_crc, header_data + 13 );
  fwrite( header_data, 1, 17, OutputCarFile );
}
```

The routine to write the file header out to the CAR file is somewhat simpler than the routine to read the same data, since it doesn't have to check for some of the possible error conditions. The first part of a header consists of the name of the compressed file, stored with a null terminator character. No special care needs to be taken when writing out the file name, since eight-bit ASCII characters are portable across all of the systems toward which CARMAN is targeted.

The remaining elements of the header are packed, one by one, into a character array using the PackUnsignedData() routine. Once they have all been properly packed, they can be written out with a call to fwrite(), with everything being in a known state.

The Header CRC. One of the header elements written out by WriteFileHeader() is called "header_crc." The header CRC is a 32-bit number generated using the data in the header structure, and used as a checksum. The CRC is generated using the CCITT-32 formula, which is the same formula used by many other archiving programs, such as PKZIP and ARJ. It provides us with a reasonably high probability of detecting errors in the header.

The reason for creating a CRC checksum for the header data is to provide an additional check for validity of a CAR file. If for some reason one of the data elements in the header file was inadvertently modified, it could lead to to disastrous results either during decompression, or later when attempting to use erroneous file data.

```
int ReadFileHeader()
{
    unsigned char header_data[ 17 ];
    unsigned long header_crc;
    int i;
    int c;

    for ( i = 0 ; ; ) {
        c = getc( InputCarFile );
        Header.file_name[ i ] = (char) c;
        if ( c == '\0' )
            break;
        if ( ++i == FILENAME_MAX )
            FatalError( "File name exceeded maximum in header" );
    }
    if ( i == 0 )
        return( 0 );
    header_crc = CalculateBlockCRC32( i + 1, CRC_MASK, Header.file_name );
    fread( header_data, 1, 17, InputCarFile );
```

```
Header.compression_method= (char)
                           UnpackUnsignedData( 1, header_data + 0 );
Header.original_size      = UnpackUnsignedData( 4, header_data + 1 );
Header.compressed_size    = UnpackUnsignedData( 4, header_data + 5 );
Header.original_crc       = UnpackUnsignedData( 4, header_data + 9 );
Header.header_crc         = UnpackUnsignedData( 4, header_data + 13 );
header_crc = CalculateBlockCRC32( 13, header_crc, header_data );
header_crc ^= CRC_MASK;
if ( Header.header_crc != header_crc )
   FatalError( "Header checksum error for file %s", Header.file_name );
return( 1 );
}
```

Reading the file header is essentially the reverse procedure of writing it out—with a couple of twists. During the process of reading in the file name, we need to check for a couple of different possibilities. First, if this is the last header file in a CAR file, it will have a file name length of 0. If this is the case, we immediately return with a failure indication, so the calling routine will know that we have reached the end of the input CAR file.

A second possibility is that the file name may exceed the storage allocated for in the header structure. In that case, a fatal error exit is taken.

After all of the header data has been read in, we perform one last validity check by comparing the calculated CRC for the header file with the CRC that was stored in the CAR file. In case of a mismatch, we once again take the fatal error exit.

Command-Line Processing. Once we have the ability to read in a header from a CAR file, we have the capability to list the archive. A simple loop like this would be enough to do it:

```
while ( ReadFileHeader() != 0 ) {
   ListCarFileEntry();
   fseek( input, header.compressed_size, SEEK_CUR );
}
```

All that is needed to skip over all of the compressed data for a given file is the fseek() statement, since we know the size of the compressed data. This is the mechanism used to work our way through the CAR file when performing any type of processing. We start with the very first file, and work our way from header to header, processing each file as needed. At no time does CARMAN ever back up through an input archive, or try to seek ahead past the next file.

Now that we have the ability to start doing something with the CAR file, it is time to start putting the other pieces of the program together. The next logical step is to start adding the ability to handle the command line.

There are three components to the CARMAN command line. First, the command is one of seven single letters discussed previously. Second is the name of the CAR file. Finally comes the optional list of file names. An initial call to ParseArguments() checks for the validity of the first command, and performs some checking on the next two.

```c
int ParseArguments( argc, argv )
int argc;
char *argv[];
{
    int command;

    if ( argc < 3 || strlen( argv[ 1 ] ) > 1 )
        UsageExit();
    switch( command = toupper( argv[ 1 ][ 0 ] ) ) {
    case 'X' :
        fprintf( stderr, "Extracting files\n" );
        break;
    case 'R' :
        fprintf( stderr, "Replacing files\n" );
        break;
    case 'P' :
        fprintf( stderr, "Print files to stdout\n" );
        break;
    case 'T' :
```

```
    fprintf( stderr, "Testing integrity of files\n" );
    break;
  case 'L' :
    fprintf( stderr, "Listing archive contents\n" );
    break;
  case 'A' :
    if ( argc <= 3 )
      UsageExit();
    fprintf( stderr, "Adding/replacing files to archive\n" );
    break;
  case 'D' :
    if ( argc <= 3 )
      UsageExit();
    fprintf( stderr, "Deleting files from archive\n" );
    break;
  default  :
    UsageExit();
  };
  return( command );
}
```

The first step in parsing the command line is to make sure that there are at least three arguments on the command line: the command name (CARMAN), a single letter command, and a CAR file name. The next step is to check the command letter for validity, to be sure it is one of the legally defined CARMAN commands. As the command letter is determined, a short message is printed to indicate that CARMAN has acknowledged the command. Finally, for two particular cases, CARMAN insists that specific file names be included on the command line. For most of the CARMAN commands, specifying no file names on the command line is defined as the equivalent of using the wildcard argument "*", (or "*.*", the MS-DOS equivalent). That means that "CARMAN l backup.car" will list all the files in the backup.car archive.

For the Add and Delete commands, this default mode of operation is probably a little too dangerous, so it results in an error message. If the user wants to add every file in the current directory to a CAR file, it will be necessary to specify "*" or "*.*" on the command line, which should not be too much of an inconvenience.

Generating the File List

One of the basic requirements of CARMAN is that it be able to handle lists of files, so that it can perform operations on select groups of files. Every one of the seven CARMAN commands accepts a list of files as an argument, so we need to have a general purpose way to build and manage a list of files. The list function should also be able to accommodate at least some level of wild card pattern matching as well.

Wild card matching needs to be done a little differently under MS-DOS and UNIX. First of all, there are actually two types of wild card matching taking place in CARMAN. File specifications on the command line with the 'Add' command, including wild cards, specify external files that are going to be added to the CAR file. File specifications for all of the other commands refer to files stored inside the CAR file. Thus we have to handle these two types of file lists using slightly different methods.

To complicate matters further, UNIX and MS-DOS differ significantly in the way their command lines handle wild card file specifications. Under either operating system, if we want to add all the C files in a directory to an archive, we would type a similar command:

```
carman a c_files.car *.c
```

Under UNIX, the command interpreter, or shell program, expands the list of wild card file names before the program ever sees it. This means that by the time CARMAN is invoked, it is presented with a command line that might look something like this:

```
carman a c_files.car test.c io.c foo.c bar.c
```

This is one of the nice features of UNIX; an application program doesn't have to worry about wild card expansion of files from the command line because the shell takes care of the work.

Under MS-DOS, matters are a little more complicated. Wild card expansion is thought of as being the province of an application program, not the command-line interpreter. So code that builds the file name list has to perform the expansion manually using C run-time library functions. Even worse, the function names and structure definitions used to expand wild card listings have not been standardized among compiler vendors, so that each new compiler needs a slightly different implementation.

In CARMAN, the list of file names is found in an array called FileList[]. FileList is an array of character pointers which is set up via a routine called BuildFileList(). BuildFileList() is called right after the command line is parsed, and is passed a list of command-line arguments, along with a count.

BuildFileList() normally just copies the arguments passed to it into the FileList[] array. If there are no command-line arguments, FileList[0] is set to '*', so that all file names in the archive will be matched as they are processed. This has the effect of converting a command like "CARMAN L TEST.CAR" to "CARMAN L TEST.CAR *".

BuildFileList() changes its mode of operation if the user has specified that the command is 'A,' to add files, and the operating system is MS-DOS. Under these circumstances, a special routine is called to expand a potential wild-card file specification into a list of file names, with the results all being stored in the FileList[].

```
void BuildFileList( argc, argv, command )
int argc;
char *argv[];
int command;
{
    int i;
    int count;

    count = 0;
    if ( argc == 0 )
        FileList[ count++ ] = "*";
    else {
```

```
        for ( i = 0 ; i < argc ; i++ ) {
#ifdef MSDOS
            if ( command == 'A' )
                count = ExpandAndMassageMSDOSFileNames (count, argv[ i ]);
            else
                MassageMSDOSFileName( count++, argv[ i ] );
#endif
#ifndef MSDOS
        FileList[ count ] = malloc( strlen( argv[ i ] ) + 2 );
        if ( FileList[ count ] == NULL )
            FatalError( "Ran out of memory storing file names" );
        strcpy( FileList[ count++ ], argv[ i ] );
#endif
        if ( count > 99 )
            FatalError( "Too many file names" );
        }
    }
    FileList[ count ] = NULL;
}
```

In addition, a special routine called MassageMSDOSFileName() is called to normalize all MS-DOS file names. MS-DOS has a couple of complications in its file system. First of all, file names are case insensitive, meaning that "FOO.BAR" and "foo.bar" both refer to the same file, despite the fact that their names are different. Secondly, the 8+3 file naming convention means that "FOO" and "FOO." both refer to the same file, even though one has a trailing '.' character and the other doesn't.

MassageMSDOSFileName() gets around this problem by performing two operations on file names. First of all, uppercase characters in file names on the command line are all converted to lowercase, to avoid ambiguities created by case mismatches. Secondly, any file that doesn't have an extension or a '.' in the name has a '.' character appended to the end of its name. Note that if the file name contains a '*' or '?' character, meaning it is a wild card, the '.' character is not appended to a file name with no extension.

Note that not all MS-DOS C compilers will define the manifest constant MSDOS. If your compiler doesn't, you may need to edit the source files for CARMAN.C.

```c
void MassageMSDOSFileName( count, file )
int count;
char *file;
{
    int i;
    char *p;

    FileList[ count ] = malloc( strlen( file ) + 2 );
    if ( FileList[ count ] == NULL )
        FatalError( "Ran out of memory storing file names" );
    strcpy( FileList[ count ], file );
    for ( i = 0 ; FileList[ count ][ i ] != '\0' ; i++ )
        FileList[ count ][ i ] = tolower( FileList[ count ][ i ] );
    if ( strpbrk( FileList[ count ], "*?" ) == NULL ) {
        p = strrchr( FileList[ count ], '\\' );
        if ( p == NULL )
            p = FileList[ count ];
        if ( strrchr( p, '.' ) == NULL )
            strcat( FileList[ count ], "." );
    }
}


int ExpandAndMassageMSDOSFileNames( count, wild_name )
int count;
char *wild_name;
{
    int done;
    DIR_STRUCT file_info_block
    char *leading_path;
    char *file_name;
```

```
char *p;

leading_path = malloc( strlen( wild_name ) + 1 );
file_name = malloc( strlen( wild_name ) + 13 );
if ( leading_path == NULL || file_name == NULL )
   FatalError( "Ran out of memory storing file names" );
strcpy( leading_path, wild_name );
     p = strrchr( leading_path, '\\' );
if ( p != NULL )
     p[ 1 ] = '\0';
else {
     p = strrchr( leading_path, ':' );
   if ( p != NULL )
        p[ 1 ] = '\0';
   else
        leading_path[ 0 ] = '\0';
}
done = FIND_FIRST( wild_name, &file_info_block, 0);
while ( !done ) {
   strcpy( file_name, leading_path );
   strcat( file_name, file_info_block.DIR_FILE_NAME );
   MassageMSDOSFileName( count++, file_name );
   done = FINDNEXT( &file_info_block );
   if ( count > 99 )
     FatalError( "Too many file names" );
}
free( leading_path );
free( file_name );
return( count );
}
```

The code shown here for expanding wild cards works with most popular MS-DOS compilers. Conditional complication is used to define the macros in slightly different ways depending on which compiler is being used. Check the complete listing at the end of this chapter for details on how this is accomplished.

Opening the Archive Files. The final step before you can begin processing the CAR file is opening the input and output CAR files. This routine is complicated by several possible conditions. In general, a routine that modifies the archive will have both an input and an output CAR file. This includes the 'Add', 'Replace', and 'Delete' commands. These commands operate by reading in and processing the CAR file while copying files to the output file.

The remaining processing commands don't actually modify the input CAR file, so they don't have to open an OutputFile. In addition, if the command is to 'Add' files to the archive, an input file may not exist, in which case a new one has to be created. The OpenArchiveFiles() command manages all these possibilities.

```c
void OpenArchiveFiles( name, command )
char *name;
int command;
{
    char *s;
    int i;

    strncpy( CarFileName, name, FILENAME_MAX - 1 );
    CarFileName[ FILENAME_MAX - 1 ] = '\0';
    InputCarFile = fopen( CarFileName, "rb" );
    if ( InputCarFile == NULL ) {
#ifdef MSDOS
        s = strrchr( CarFileName, '\\' );
#else /* UNIX */
        s = strrchr( CarFileName, '/' );
#endif
        if ( s == NULL )
            s = CarFileName;
        if ( strrchr( s, '.' ) == NULL )
            if ( strlen( CarFileName ) < ( FILENAME_MAX - 4 ) ) {
                strcat( CarFileName, ".car" );
                InputCarFile = fopen( CarFileName, "rb" );
            }
    }
```

```
if ( InputCarFile == NULL && command != 'A' )
   FatalError( "Can't open archive '%s'", CarFileName );
if ( command == 'A' || command == 'R' || command == 'D' ) {
   strcpy( TempFileName, CarFileName );
   s = strrchr( TempFileName, '.' );
   if ( s == NULL )
      s = TempFileName + strlen( TempFileName );
   for ( i = 0 ; i < 10 ; i++ ) {
      sprintf( s, ".$$%d", i );
      if ( ( OutputCarFile = fopen( TempFileName, "r" ) ) == NULL )
         break;
      fclose( OutputCarFile );
      OutputCarFile = NULL;
   }
   if (i == 10)
      FatalError( "Can't open temporary file %s", TempFileName );
   OutputCarFile = fopen( TempFileName, "wb" );
   if ( OutputCarFile == NULL )
      FatalError( "Can't open temporary file %s", TempFileName );
};
if ( InputCarFile != NULL )
   setvbuf( InputCarFile, NULL, _IOFBF, 8192 );
if ( OutputCarFile != NULL )
   setvbuf( OutputCarFile, NULL, _IOFBF, 8192 );
}
```

When an output file is created, it will be the file that eventually gets a copy of all the selected files from the input archive. Once all that processing is over, the input file can be deleted and the output file can be renamed to have the correct name. However, while CARMAN is still processing, the output file has to have a different name. In this case, we create a temporary file name based on the name of the CAR file. We do a limited amount of checking to try and create a name that isn't already in use.

One additional feature that CARMAN develops in this routine is the ability to automatically attempt to add a file extension to the archive name. If the input file name does not include an extension, OpenArchiveFiles() first tries to open it normally. If the file cannot be opened, OpenArchiveFiles() tries again with the ".car" extension appended to the file name. This lets the user type a command like "CARMAN L FILES" when the correct command might really be "CARMAN L FILES.CAR".

Finally, note that both files have big buffers set up using the setvbuf() command. This helps throughput, particularly when performing bulk copies of compressed files from the input archive to the output CAR file.

The Main Processing Loop

With these steps out of the way, CARMAN is ready to begin processing in earnest. The main processing loop is found in the routine called ProcessAllFilesInInputCar(). It sits in a big loop, finding files in the input CAR file, checking to see if they match up with any of the names in the file list, then deciding what to do based on the command.

Before entering the main processing loop, CARMAN checks to see if the command given was to 'Add' files to the CAR file. If it was, these files all need to be inserted into the output CAR file before anything else happens. This is done in a routine called AddFileListToArchive(). This routine attempts to add every file name that was specified in the command line to the output CAR file.

```
int AddFileListToArchive
( )
{
    int i;
    int j;
    int skip;
    char *s;
    FILE *input_text_file;

    for ( i = 0 ; FileList[ i ] != NULL ; i++ ) {
        input_text_file = fopen( FileList[ i ], "rb" );
        if ( input_text_file == NULL )
            FatalError( "Could not open %s to add to CAR file",
                                                    FileList[ i ] );
```

```
#ifdef MSDOS
        s = strrchr( FileList[ i ], '\\' );
        if ( s == NULL )
            s = strrchr( FileList[ i ], ':' );
#endif
#ifndef MSDOS /* Must be UNIX */
        s = strrchr( FileList[ i ], '/' );
#endif
        if ( s != NULL )
            s++;
        else
            s = FileList[ i ];
        skip = 0;
        for ( j = 0 ; j < i ; j++ )
            if ( strcmp( s, FileList[ j ] ) == 0 ) {
                fprintf( stderr, "Duplicate file name: %s", FileList[ i ] );
                fprintf( stderr, " Skipping this file...\n" );
                skip = 1;
                break;
            }
        if ( s != FileList[ i ] ) {
            for ( j = 0 ; s[ j ] != '\0' ; j++ )
                FileList[ i ][ j ] = s[ j ];
            FileList[ i ][ j ] = '\0';
        }
        if ( !skip ) {
            strcpy( Header.file_name, FileList[ i ] );
            Insert( input_text_file, "Adding" );
        } else
            fclose( input_text_file );
    }
```

```
    return( i );
}
```

Adding files to the archive has to take care of several things in order to accomplish its goal. First, it has to use the full path name specified on the command line to try to open the file to be added. Once the file is opened, however, the file name needs to be stripped of its path and drive component. CARMAN stores file names only, not leading drive or path definitions. Once the file name has been stripped down, a search is made to be sure that this is not a duplicate file name. Adding two files with the same name to a CARMAN file would be a bad idea. Finally, if everything went well, the Insert() routine is called to compress the file and place it in the output CAR file.

Once any new files have been added, CARMAN enters the main processing loop, where most of the real work takes place. The main processing loop is fairly simple in structure. It simply reads in a file header from the input file, then checks to see if the file appears in the FileList, saving the answer. Next, it enters a switch, and then performs processing on the input file based on the command type. Each command makes a different decision on what to do based on whether or not the file name appeared in the file list.

Two commands used in the main processing loop require a small amount of setup. The 'Test' and 'Print' commands actually act just like the 'Xtract' command, except that they direct their output to the null device and stdout, respectively. These output destinations are set up before the loop is entered.

```
int ProcessAllFilesInInputCar( command, count )
int command;
int count;
{
    int matched;
    FILE *input_text_file;
    FILE *output_destination;

    if ( command == 'P' )
        output_destination = stdout;
    else if ( command == 'T' )
```

```
#ifdef MSDOS
    output_destination = fopen( "NUL", "wb" );
#else
    output_destination = fopen( "/dev/null", "wb" );
#endif
  else
    output_destination = NULL;
/*
* This is the loop where it all happens. I read in the header for
* each file in the input CAR, then see if it matches any of the file
* and wild card specifications in the FileList created earlier. That
* information, combined with the command, tells me what I need to
* know in order to process the file. Note that if the 'Addfiles' command
* is being executed, the InputCarFile will be NULL, so this loop
* can be safely skipped.
*/
  while ( InputCarFile != NULL && ReadFileHeader() != 0 ) {
    matched = SearchFileList( Header.file_name );
    switch ( command ) {
      case 'D' :
        if ( matched ) {
          SkipOverFileFromInputCar();
          count++;
        } else
          CopyFileFromInputCar();
        break;
      case 'A' :
        if ( matched )
          SkipOverFileFromInputCar();
        else
          CopyFileFromInputCar();
        break;
      case 'L' :
        if ( matched ) {
          ListCarFileEntry();
          count++;
        }
```

```
          SkipOverFileFromInputCar();
          break;
      case 'P' :
      case 'X' :
      case 'T' :
        if ( matched ) {
           Extract( output_destination );
           count++;
        } else
           SkipOverFileFromInputCar();
        break;
      case 'R' :
        if ( matched ) {
           input_text_file = fopen( Header.file_name, "rb" );
           if ( input_text_file == NULL ) {
              fprintf( stderr, "Could not find %s", Header.file_name );
              fprintf( stderr, " for replacement, skipping\n" );
              CopyFileFromInputCar();
           } else {
              SkipOverFileFromInputCar();
              Insert( input_text_file, "Replacing" );
              count++;
              fclose( input_text_file );
           }
        } else
           CopyFileFromInputCar();
        break;
    }
  }
  return( count );
}
```

The processing loop starts off by reading in the next available header file from the input CAR file. If we are at the end of file, this operation returns a 0 and we exit. Otherwise, we call SearchFileList(), which looks for a match of the file name in the

FileList[] array, including wild card matches. The result of that search is stored in the match variable, at which point the switch statement is started. The actions taken in the switch depend on the command give on the command line:

Delete :   If match is true, it means the user wants to delete this file from the CAR archive. In this case, the file is skipped over with a call to SkipOverFileFromInputCar(). Otherwise, the file is copied to the output CAR file with a call to CopyFileFromInputCar().

Add: If match is true, it means that one of the files that was added to the output CAR file at the start of the program also appears in input CAR file. When this is the case, we have to skip over the file, since it has been superseded. If no match is found, the file is copied to the output CAR file.

List: If a match is found, the file statistics are listed on stdout. No output file is being created by this command, so after it is listed, it is automatically skipped.

Print: If a match is found, it means this file has to be extracted to one of the
Test: possible destinations. For the Print command, it goes to stdout. For Test,
Xtract: it goes to the null devices, and for Xtract, to a file that is created with the appropriate name. If no match was found, the file is skipped.

Replace: If a match is found, it means we need to replace the version of the file found in the archive with a file of the same name in the current directory. If that file is found, it is Inserted into the output file, and the current input file is skipped. If no match is found, or the file cannot be opened, the file in the input CAR file is copied to the output CAR file.

Once all of these operations are complete, a count of matched files is returned to the calling routine, for display when the program exits.

Skipping/Copying Input File. The main processing loop only has one of three choices to take to go past the current file in the input CAR file. The first two are the skip and copy routines. One of these copies the current file in the Input CAR to the output CAR file. The second routine skips over the file and moves on to the next header.

The skip operation was discussed previously, and is quite simple, since we have the exact size in bytes of the compressed file stored in the header. All the program has to do is advance that number of bytes forward in the input file. Once this is done, the file is lost to the output file, so this is only done when the file is to be Deleted or Replaced (including replacement with an Add command).

```
void SkipOverFileFromInputCar()
{
    fseek( InputCarFile, Header.compressed_size, SEEK_CUR );
}

void CopyFileFromInputCar()
{
  char buffer[ 256 ];
  unsigned int count;

  WriteFileHeader();
  while ( Header.compressed_size != 0 ) {
    if ( Header.compressed_size < 256 )
      count = (int) Header.compressed_size;
    else
      count = 256;
    if ( fread( buffer, 1, count, InputCarFile ) != count )
      FatalError( "Error reading input file %s", Header.file_name );
    Header.compressed_size -= count;
    if ( fwrite( buffer, 1, count, OutputCarFile) != count )
      FatalError( "Error writing to output CAR file" );
  }
}
```

Copying the file from the input CAR file to the output CAR file is the "normal" mode of operation, where the contents of the input file are not lost. This is only marginally more complicated than the skip routine. All we need to do here is read in the predetermined number of bytes a block at a time, and write them out to the output file, checking for errors along the way.

Once the copy is complete, the input file pointer is left pointing at the next file header in the input CAR file, and the program is ready to start back at the top of the loop.

File Insertion. The Insertion routine is called to insert an external file into the output CAR file. The insertion routine makes a first attempt to compress the file using the LZSS compression routine. If that routine fails, a straight storage routine is called instead. Since we don't know what the size of the compressed file will be until after the compression actually takes place, Insert() has to back up and rewrite the header after the compression is finally successful. In addition, the compression method is stored in the header file as well. A compression method of 1 is used for normal storage, 2 for LZSS compression. Clearly it would be relatively simple to add new forms of compression by adding new numbers to the table. All that would be needed then is additional code in the Extract() routine to support the new compression method.

```
void Insert( input_text_file, operation )
FILE *input_text_file;
char *operation;
{
    long saved_position_of_header;
    long saved_position_of_file;

    fprintf( stderr, "%s %-20s", operation, Header.file_name );
    saved_position_of_header = ftell( OutputCarFile );
    Header.compression_method = 2;
    WriteFileHeader();
    saved_position_of_file = ftell(OutputCarFile);
    fseek( input_text_file, 0L, SEEK_END );
    Header.original_size = ftell( input_text_file );
    fseek( input_text_file, 0L, SEEK_SET );
```

```
if ( !LZSSCompress( input_text_file ) ) {
    Header.compression_method = 1;
    fseek( OutputCarFile, saved_position_of_file, SEEK_SET );
    rewind( input_text_file );
    Store( input_text_file );
}
fclose( input_text_file );
fseek( OutputCarFile, saved_position_of_header, SEEK_SET );
WriteFileHeader();
fseek( OutputCarFile, 0L, SEEK_END );
printf( " %d%%\n", RatioInPercent( Header.compressed_size,
                                  Header.original_size ) );
}
```

File Extraction. The extraction routine in some ways is simpler than the Insert() routine. It doesn't have to deal with the possibility that the LZSS compression routine failed to compress. Instead, it just calls the appropriate routine based on the compression method stored in the header file. However, it does have a few extra jobs to deal with.

First of all, Extract can be called with a predefined destination FILE pointer. This occurs when the Print or Test commands are being executed. Print just extracts to stdout, and Test extracts to the null device, or the "bit bucket". When this is the case, Extract() doesn't have to open a file to store the output.

In the case where Extract() is being called based on the Xtract command, it has to open the output file, check to make sure that goes okay, then close the file after the expansion takes place.

In all cases, Extract() has to check the CRC of the output file after the expansion routine has completed. When using the Test command, this is the way CARMAN verifies the integrity of the CAR file.

```
void Extract( destination )
FILE *destination;
{
    FILE *output_text_file;
    unsigned long crc;
```

```c
int error;

fprintf( stderr, "%-20s ", Header.file_name );
error = 0;
if ( destination == NULL ) {
   if ( ( output_text_file = fopen(Header.file_name, "wb")
                                                  ) == NULL ) {
      fprintf( stderr, "Can't open %s\n", Header.file_name );
      fprintf( stderr, "Not extracted\n" );
      SkipOverFileFromInputCar();
      return;
   }
} else
   output_text_file = destination;
switch( Header.compression_method ) {
   case 1 :
      crc = Unstore( output_text_file );
      break;
   case 2 :
      crc = LZSSExpand( output_text_file );
      break;
   default :
      fprintf( stderr, "Unknown method: %c\n",
               Header.compression_method );
      SkipOverFileFromInputCar();
      error = 1;
      crc = Header.original_crc;
      break;
}
if ( crc != Header.original_crc ) {
      fprintf( stderr, "CRC error reading data\n" );
      error = 1;
}
if ( destination == NULL ) {
   fclose( output_text_file );
   if ( error )
#ifdef __STDC__
```

```
                remove( Header.file_name );
  #else
                unlink( Header.file_name );
  #endif
  }
  if ( !error )
    fprintf( stderr, " OK\n" );
}
```

Cleanup. The final job left to CARMAN after making its way through the main processing loop is to clean up the workspace used by the program. The first step is to write out the special EOF header to the output CAR file. This is done using a dedicated routine called WriteEndOfCarHeader(), which simply writes a zero length file name to the header file.

Next, the output CAR file is closed and checked for errors. At this point, the output CAR file has been completely processed and is ready to replace the input file. In order to do this, the input file is deleted, and the output file is renamed to have the original archive name. This takes slightly different code under UNIX than MS-DOS, but it is relatively straightforward.

The Code

A complete listing of the CARMAN program follows, including sections that have only been lightly touched on in this chapter. The LZSS compression code is nearly identical to that shown earlier in Chapter 8, with a slightly modified I/O system.

Programmers wishing to compile this under MS-DOS are advised to pay close attention to those portions of the code that are surrounded by #ifdef MSDOS sections. These portions may need slight modifications to work with different MSDOS compilers, but the modifications should only consist of renamed functions and structures. The actual flow of control inside the program should be identical.

```
/*********************** Start of CARMAN.C ***********************
*
* This is the main program for the simple Compressed Archive Manager.
* This program can be used to add, delete, extract, or list the files
```

```
 * in a CAR archive. The code here should run under standard ANSI
 * compilers under MS-DOS (with ANSI mode selected) or K&R compilers
 * under UNIX. The code uses an LZSS compression algorithm identical to
 * that used earlier in the book.
 */

#include <stdio.h>
#include <stdlib.h>
#include <string.h>
#include <ctype.h>
#ifdef __STDC__
#include <stdarg.h>
#else
#include <varargs.h>
#endif

#ifdef __STDC__
    /* All Borland C/C++ versions */
    #ifdef __TURBOC__
      #define MSDOS 1
      #include <io.h>
      #include (dir.h>
      #define DIR_STRUCT struct ffblk
      #define FIND_FIRST(n, d, a ) findfirst( n, d, a )
      #define FIND_NEXT findnext
      #define DIR_FILE_NAME ff_name
#endif
    /*Microsoft, Watcom, Zortech */
#if defined( M__I86 ) || defined ( __ZTC__ ) || defined ( __TSC__ )
    #define MSDOS 1
    #include <dos.h>
    #define DIR_STRUCT struct find_t
    #define FIND_FIRST( n, d, a) _dos_findfirst( n, a, d )
    #define FIND_NEXT _dos_findnext
    #define DIR_FILE_NAME name
  #endif
```

```
#endif
/*
* A few constants used throughout the program.
*/

#define BASE_HEADER_SIZE 19
#define CRC_MASK 0xFFFFFFFFL
#define CRC32_POLYNOMIAL 0xEDB88320L

/*
* The only data structure used inside the CAR file is the header block.
* Each file is preceded by a header, stored in a portable format.
* The header is read into and out of the structure defined below.
* The CAR file is structured as a series of header/data sequences, with
* the EOF being denoted as a header with a file name length of 0. Note
* that the length of each header will vary depending on the length of
* the file name.
*/
#ifndef FILENAME_MAX
#define FILENAME_MAX 128
#endif

typedef struct header {
    char file_name[ FILENAME_MAX ];
    char compression_method;
    unsigned long original_size;
    unsigned long compressed_size;
    unsigned long original_crc;
    unsigned long header_crc;
} HEADER;

/*
* Local function prototypes
*/

#ifdef __STDC__
```

```
void FatalError( char *message, ... );
void BuildCRCTable( void );
unsigned long CalculateBlockCRC32( unsigned int count, unsigned long crc,
                                                        void *buffer );
unsigned long UpdateCharacterCRC32( unsigned long crc, int c );
int ParseArguments( int argc, char *argv[] );
void UsageExit( void );
void OpenArchiveFiles( char *name, int command );
void BuildFileList( int argc, char *argv[], int command );
int ExpandAndMassageMSDOSFileNames( int count, char *wild_name );
void MassageMSDOSFileName( int count, char *file );
int AddFileListToArchive( void );
int ProcessAllFilesInInputCar( int command, int count );
int SearchFileList( char *file_name );
int WildCardMatch( char *s1, char *s2 );
void SkipOverFileFromInputCar( void );
void CopyFileFromInputCar( void );
void PrintListTitles( void );
void ListCarFileEntry( void );
int RatioInPercent( unsigned long compressed, unsigned long original );
int ReadFileHeader( void );
unsigned long UnpackUnsignedData( int number_of_bytes,
                                            unsigned char *buffer );
void WriteFileHeader( void );
void PackUnsignedData( int number_of_bytes, unsigned long number,
                                            unsigned char *buffer );
void WriteEndOfCarHeader( void );
void Insert( FILE *input_text_file, char *operation );
void Extract( FILE *destination );
int Store( FILE *input_text_file );
unsigned long Unstore( FILE *destination );
int LZSSCompress( FILE *input_text_file );
unsigned long LZSSExpand( FILE *destination );

#else

void FatalError();
```

```
void BuildCRCTable();
unsigned long CalculateBlockCRC32();
unsigned long UpdateCharacterCRC32();
int ParseArguments();
void UsageExit();
void OpenArchiveFiles();
void BuildFileList();
int ExpandAndMassageMSDOSFileNames();
void MassageMSDOSFileName();
int AddFileListToArchive();
int ProcessAllFilesInInputCar();
int SearchFileList();
int WildCardMatch();
void SkipOverFileFromInputCar();
void CopyFileFromInputCar();
void PrintListTitles();
void ListCarFileEntry();
int RatioInPercent();
int ReadFileHeader();
unsigned long UnpackUnsignedData();
void WriteFileHeader();
void PackUnsignedData();
void WriteEndOfCarHeader();
void Insert();
void Extract();
int Store();
unsigned long Unstore();
int LZSSCompress();
unsigned long LZSSExpand();

#endif

/*
 * All global variables are defined here.
 */

char *TempFileName[ FILENAME_MAX ]; /* The output archive is first    */
```

```
                                    /* opened with a temporary name   */

FILE *InputCarFile;                 /* The input CAR file.  This file */
                                    /* may not exist for 'A' commands */

char CarFileName[ FILENAME_MAX ];   /* Name of the CAR file, defined  */
                                    /* on the command line            */

FILE *OutputCarFile;                /* The output CAR, only exists for*/
                                    /* the 'A' and 'R' operations     */

HEADER Header;                      /* The Header block for the file  */
                                    /* presently being operated on    */

char *FileList[ 100 ];              /* The list of file names passed  */
                                    /* on the command line            */

unsigned long Ccitt32Table[ 256 ]; /* This array holds the CRC        */
                                    /* table used to calculate the 32 */
                                    /* bit CRC values                 */

/*
 * This is the main program for processing CAR commands. Most of the
 * major work involved here has been delegated to other functions.
 * This routine first parses the command line, then opens up the input
 * and possibly the output archive. It then builds a list of files
 * to be processed by the current command. If the command was 'A', all
 * of the files are immediately added to the output archives. Finally,
 * the main processing loop is called. It scans through the entire
 * archive, taking action on each file as necessary. Once that is
 * complete, all that is left to do is optionally delete the input file,
 * then rename the output file to have the correct CAR file name.
 */

int main( argc, argv )
int argc;
char *argv[];
```

```
{
    int command;
    int count;

    setbuf( stdout, NULL );
    setbuf( stderr, NULL );
    fprintf( stderr, "CARMAN 1.0 : " );
    BuildCRCTable();
    command = ParseArguments( argc, argv );
    fprintf( stderr, "\n" );
    OpenArchiveFiles( argv[ 2 ], command );
    BuildFileList( argc - 3, argv + 3, command );
    if ( command == 'A' )
        count = AddFileListToArchive();
    else
        count = 0;
    if ( command == 'L' )
        PrintListTitles();
    count = ProcessAllFilesInInputCar( command, count );
    if ( OutputCarFile != NULL && count != 0 ) {
        WriteEndOfCarHeader();
        if ( ferror( OutputCarFile ) || fclose( OutputCarFile ) == EOF )
            FatalError( "Can't write" );

#ifdef __STDC__
    remove( CarFileName );
    rename(TempFileName, CarFileName );
#else
        unlink( CarFileName );
        link( TempFileName, CarFileName );
        unlink( TempFileName );
#endif
```

```
  }
  if ( command != 'P' )
    printf( "\n%d file%s\n", count, ( count == 1 ) ? "" : "s" );
  else
    fprintf( stderr, "\n%d file%s\n", count,
                                    ( count == 1 ) ? '' : "s" );
  return( 0 );
}


/*
 * FatalError provides a short way for us to exit the program when
 * something bad happens, as well as printing a diagnostic message.
 * If an output CAR file has been opened, it is deleted as well,
 * which cleans up most of the traces of our work here. Note that
 * K&R compilers handle variable length argument lists differently
 * than ANSI compilers, so we have two different entries for the
 * routines.
 */

#ifdef __STDC__

void FatalError( char *fmt, ... )
{
   va_list args;

   va_start( args, fmt );
#else

void FatalError( va_alist )
va_dcl
{
   va_list args;
   char *fmt;

   va_start( args );
   fmt = va_arg( args, char * );
#endif
```

```
  putc( '\n', stderr );
  vfprintf( stderr, fmt, args );
  putc( '\n', stderr );
  va_end( args );
  if ( OutputCarFile != NULL )
    fclose( OutputCarFile );
#ifdef __STDC__
      remove( TempFileName );
#else
    unlink( TempFileName );
#endif
  exit( 1 );
}


/*
 * This routine simply builds the coefficient table used to calculate
 * 32-bit CRC values throughout this program. The 256-long word table
 * has to be set up once when the program starts. Alternatively, the
 * values could be hard-coded in, which would offer a miniscule
 * improvement in overall performance of the program.
 */

void BuildCRCTable()
{
  int i;
  int j;
  unsigned long value;

  for ( i = 0; i <= 255 ; i++ ) {
    value = i;
    for ( j = 8 ; j > 0; j-- ) {
      if ( value & 1 )
        value = ( value >> 1 ) ^ CRC32_POLYNOMIAL;
      else
        value >>= 1;
    }
    Ccitt32Table[ i ] = value;
```

```
      }
    }


    /*
     * This is the routine used to calculate the 32-bit CRC of a block of
     * data. This is done by processing the input buffer using the
     * coefficient table that was created when the program was initialized.
     * This routine takes an input value as a seed, so that a running
     * calculation of the CRC can be used as blocks are read and written.
     */

    unsigned long CalculateBlockCRC32( count, crc, buffer )
    unsigned int count;
    unsigned long crc;
    void *buffer;
    {
        unsigned char *p = (unsigned char *) buffer;
        unsigned long temp1;
        unsigned long temp2;

        while ( count-- != 0 ) {
          temp1 = ( crc >> 8 ) & 0x00FFFFFFL;
          temp2 = Ccitt32Table[ ( (int) crc ^ *p++ ) & 0xff ];
          crc = temp1 ^ temp2;
        }
        return( crc );
    }


    /*
     * If I/O is being done on a byte-by-byte basis, as is the case with the
     * LZSS code, it is easier to calculate the CRC of a byte at a time
     * instead of a block at a time. This routine performs that function,
     * once again taking a CRC value as input, so that this can be used to
     * perform on the fly calculations. In situations where performance is
     * critical, this routine could easily be recoded as a macro.
     */
    unsigned long UpdateCharacterCRC32( crc, c )
    unsigned long crc;
```

```
int c;
{
    unsigned long temp1;
    unsigned long temp2;

    temp1 = ( crc >> 8 ) & 0x00FFFFFFL;
    temp2 = Ccitt32Table[ ( (int) crc ^ c ) & 0xff ];
    crc = temp1 ^ temp2;
    return( crc );
}

/*
 * When CARMAN first starts up, it calls this routine to parse the
 * command line. We look for several things here. If any of the
 * conditions needed to run CARMAN is not met, the routine opts for
 * the usage printout exit. The first thing to be sure of is that
 * the command line has at least three arguments, which should be
 * the "CARMAN", a single character command, and an CAR archive name.
 * After that, we check to be sure that the command name is a valid
 * letter, and incidentally print out a short message based on it.
 * Both the Addfiles and Delete commands require that some file names
 * be listed as well, so a check is made for additional arguments when
 * each of those arguments is encountered. Finally, the command itself
 * is returned to main(), for use later in processing the command.
 */

int ParseArguments( argc, argv )
int argc;
char *argv[];
{
    int command;

    if ( argc < 3 || strlen( argv[ 1 ] ) > 1 )
        UsageExit();
    switch( command = toupper( argv[ 1 ][ 0 ] ) ) {
        case 'X' :
            fprintf( stderr, "Extracting files\n" );
```

```
        break;
      case 'R' :
        fprintf( stderr, "Replacing files\n" );
        break;
      case 'P' :
        fprintf( stderr, "Print files to stdout\n" );
        break;
      case 'T' :
        fprintf( stderr, "Testing integrity of files\n" );
        break;
      case 'L' :
        fprintf( stderr, "Listing archive contents\n" );
        break;
      case 'A' :
        if ( argc <= 3 )
          UsageExit();
        fprintf( stderr, "Adding/replacing files to archive\n" );
        break;
      case 'D' :
        if ( argc <= 3 )
          UsageExit();
        fprintf( stderr, "Deleting files from archive\n" );
        break;
      default  :
        UsageExit();
    };
    return( command );
}


/*
 * UsageExit just provides a universal point of egress for those
 * times when there appears to be a problem on the command line.
 * This routine prints a short help message then exits back to the OS.
 */

void UsageExit()
{
    fputs( "CARMAN - Compressed ARchive MANager\n", stderr );
```

```
    fputs( "Usage: carman command car-file [file ...]\n", stderr );
    fputs( "Commands:\n", stderr );
    fputs( " a: Add files to a CAR archive (replace if present)\n",
                                                        stderr );
    fputs( " x: Extract files from a CAR archive\n", stderr );
    fputs( " r: Replace files in a CAR archive\n", stderr );
    fputs( " d: Delete files from a CAR archive\n", stderr );
    fputs( " p: Print files on standard output\n", stderr );
    fputs( " l: List contents of a CAR archive\n", stderr );
    fputs( " t: Test files in a CAR archive\n", stderr );
    fputs( "\n", stderr );
    exit( 1 );
}


/*
 * After the command line has been parsed, main() has enough information
 * to intelligently open the input and output CAR archive files. The
 * name should have been specified on the command line, and passed to
 * this routine by main(). As a convenience to the user, if the CAR
 * suffix is left off the archive, this routine will add it on.
 * There is one legitimate excuse for not being able to open the input
 * file, which is if this is the 'Addfiles' command. There may not be
 * an input archive when that command is called, in which case a failure
 * is tolerated. Once the input file has been opened, an output file
 * may have to be opened as well. The 'Addfiles', 'Delete', and
 * 'Replace' commands all modify the CAR archive, which means the input
 * CAR file is going to be processed and copied to the output. Initially,
 * the output CAR file gets a temporary name. It will be renamed later
 * after the input has been processed.
 *
 * Since we will probably be doing lots of bulk copies from the input
 * CAR file to the output CAR file, it makes sense to allocate big
 * buffers for the files. This is done with the two calls to setvbuf()
 * right before the routine exits.
 *
 */
void OpenArchiveFiles( name, command )
```

```
char *name;
int command;
{
   char *s;
   int i;

   strncpy( CarFileName, name, FILENAME_MAX - 1 );
   CarFileName[ FILENAME_MAX - 1 ] = '\0';
   InputCarFile = fopen( CarFileName, "rb" );
   if ( InputCarFile == NULL ) {
#ifdef MSDOS
        s = strrchr( CarFileName, '\\' );
#else /* UNIX */
        s = strrchr( CarFileName, '/' );
#endif
      if ( s == NULL )
        s = CarFileName;
      if ( strrchr( s, '.' ) == NULL )
        if ( strlen( CarFileName ) < ( FILENAME_MAX - 4 ) ) {
           strcat( CarFileName, ".car" );
           InputCarFile = fopen( CarFileName, "rb" );
        }
   }
   if ( InputCarFile == NULL && command != 'A' )
     FatalError( "Can't open archive '%s'", CarFileName );
   if ( command == 'A' || command == 'R' || command == 'D' ) {
     strcpy( TempFileName, CarFileName );
     s = strrchr( TempFileName, '.');
     if ( s == NULL )
       s = TempFileName + strlen( TempFileName );
     for ( i = 0 ; i < 10 ; i++ ) {
       sprintf( s, ".$$%d", i );
       if ( ( OutputCarFile = fopen( TempFileName, "r" ) ) == NULL )
         break;
       fclose( OutputCarFile );
       OutputCarFile = NULL;
     }
```

```
    if ( i == 10 )
       FatalError( "Can't open temporary file %s", TempFileName ) ;
    OutputCarFile = fopen( TempFileName, "wb" );
    if ( OutputCarFile == NULL )
       FatalError( "Can't open temporary file %s", TempFileName );
  }
  if ( InputCarFile != NULL )
    setvbuf( InputCarFile, NULL, _IOFBF, 8192 );
  if ( OutputCarFile != NULL )
    setvbuf( OutputCarFile, NULL, _IOFBF, 8192 );
}


/** Most of the commands given here take one or more file names as
 * arguments. The list of files given on the command line needs to be
 * processed here and put into a list that can easily be manipulated by
 * other parts of the program. That processing is done here. An array
 * called FileList is created, which will have a series of pointers to
 * file names. If no file names were listed on the command line, which
 * could be the case for commands like 'List' or 'Extract', a single
 * file name of '*' is put on the start of the list. Since '*' is the
 * ultimate wild card, matching everything, we don't have to have special
 * processing anywhere else for an empty file list. The file names here
 * are also massaged a bit further for MS-DOS file names. Under MS-DOS,
 * case is not significant in file names. This means that CARMAN
 * shouldn't get confused by thinking 'foo.c' and 'FOO.C' are two
 * different files. To avoid this, all MS-DOS file names are converted
 * here to lower case. Additionally, any file name without an extension
 * is forced to end with a period, for similar reasons. This ensures that
 * CARMAN knows 'FOO' and 'FOO.' are the same file. Note that I don't
 * want to do this for wild card specifications. Finally, there is the
 * problem of MS-DOS wild card file names. When using the 'Add' command,
 * wild cards on the command line need to be expanded into real file
 * names, then undergo the additional processing mentioned earlier. This
 * is done with a call to a function that is MS-DOS specific. None of
 * this special processing is done under UNIX, where case is significant,
 * and wild cards are expanded by the shell.
 */
```

```
void BuildFileList( argc, argv, command )
int argc;
char *argv[];
int command;
{
    int i;
    int count;

    count = 0;
    if ( argc == 0 )
        FileList[ count++ ] = "*";
    else {
        for ( i = 0 ; i < argc ; i++ ) {
#ifdef MSDOS
            if ( command == 'A' )
                count = ExpandAndMassageMSDOSFileNames( count, argv[ i ] );
            else
                MassageMSDOSFileName( count++, argv[ i ] );
#endif
#ifndef __MSDOS__
            FileList[ count ] = malloc( strlen( argv[ i ] ) + 2 );
            if ( FileList[ count ] == NULL )
                FatalError( "Ran out of memory storing file names" );
            strcpy( FileList[ count++ ], argv[ i ] );
#endif
        if ( count > 99 )
            FatalError( "Too many file names" );
        }
    }
    FileList[ count ] = NULL;
}

/*
 * Under MS-DOS, wildcards on the command line are not expanded to
 * a list of file names, so it is up to application programs to do the
 * expansion themselves. This routine takes care of that, by using
 * the findfirst and findnext routines. Unfortunately, each MS-DOS
```

```
 * compiler  maker has implemented this function slightly differently, so
 * this may need to be modified for your particular compiler. However,
 * this routine can be replaced with a call to MassageMSDOSFileName(),
 * and the program will work just fine, without the ability to handle
 * wild card file names.
 */
#ifdef MSDOS

#include <dos.h>
#include <dir.h>

int ExpandAndMassageMSDOSFileNames( count, wild_name )
int count;
char *wild_name;
{
   int done;
   DIR_STRUCT file_info_block;
   char *leading_path;
   char *file_name;
   char *p;

   leading_path = malloc( strlen( wild_name ) + 1 );
   file_name = malloc( strlen( wild_name ) + 13 );
   if ( leading_path == NULL || file_name == NULL )
     FatalError( "Ran out of memory storing file names" );
   strcpy( leading_path, wild_name );
   p = strrchr( leading_path, '\\' );
   if ( p != NULL )
     p[ 1 ] = '\0';
   else {
     p = strrchr( leading_path, ':' );
     if ( p != NULL )
       p[ 1 ] = '\0';
     else
       leading_path[ 0 ] = '\0';
   }
```

```
   done = FIND_FIRST( wild_name, &file_info_block, 0 );
   while ( !done ) {
      strcpy( file_name, leading_path );
      strcat( file_name, file_info_block.DIR_FILE_NAME );
      MassageMSDOSFileName( count++, file_name );
      done = FIND_NEXT( &file_info_block );
      if ( count > 99 )
        FatalError( "Too many file names" );
   }
   free( leading_path );
   free( file_name );
   return( count );
}
/*
 * As was discussed earlier, this routine is called to perform a small
 * amount of normalization on file names. Under MS_DOS, case is not
 * significant in file names. In order to avoid confusion later, we force
 * all file names to be all lower case, so we can't accidentally add two
 * files with the same name to a CAR archive. Likewise, we need to
 * prevent confusion between files that end in a period, and the same
 * file without the terminal period. We fix this by always forcing the
 * file name to end in a period.
 */

void MassageMSDOSFileName( count, file )
int count;
char *file;
{
   int i;
   char *p;

   FileList[ count ] = malloc( strlen( file ) + 2 );
   if ( FileList[ count ] == NULL )
      FatalError( "Ran out of memory storing file names" );
   strcpy( FileList[ count ], file );
   for ( i = 0 ; FileList[ count ][ i ] != '\0' ; i++ )
      FileList[ count ][ i ] = (char)
```

```
              tolower(FileList[ count ][ i ];
   if ( strpbrk( FileList[ count ], "*?" ) == NULL ) {
     p = strrchr( FileList[ count ], '\\' );
     if ( p == NULL )
       p = FileList[ count ];
     if ( strrchr( p, '.' ) == NULL )
       strcat( FileList[ count ], "." );
   }
}

#endif

/*
 * Once all of the argument processing is done, the main() procedure
 * checks to see if the command is 'Addfiles'. If it is, it calls
 * this procedure to add all of the listed files to the output buffer
 * before any other processing is done. That is taken care of right
 * here. This routine basically does three jobs before calling the
 * Insert() routine, where the compression actually takes place. First,
 * it tries to open the file, which ought to work. Second, it strips the
 * leading drive and path information from the file, since we don't keep
 * that information in the archive. Finally, it checks to see if the
 * resulting name is one that has already been added to the archive.
 * If it has, the file is skipped so that we don't end up with an
 * invalid archive.
 */

int AddFileListToArchive()
{
    int i;
    int j;
    int skip;
    char *s;
    FILE *input_text_file;

    for ( i = 0 ; FileList[ i ] != NULL ; i++ ) {
        input_text_file = fopen( FileList[ i ], "rb" );
```

```
    if ( input_text_file == NULL )
        FatalError( "Could not open %s to add to CAR file",
                    FileList[ i ] );
#ifdef MSDOS
    s = strrchr( FileList[ i ], '\\' );
    if ( s == NULL )
        s = strrchr( FileList[ i ], ':' );
#endif
#ifndef MSDOS /* Must be UNIX */
    s = strrchr( FileList[ i ], '/' );
#endif
    if ( s != NULL )
        s++;
    else
        s = FileList[ i ];
    skip = 0;
    for ( j = 0 ; j < i ; j++ )
        if ( strcmp( s, FileList[ j ] ) == 0 ) {
            fprintf( stderr, "Duplicate file name: %s", FileList[ i ] );
            fprintf( stderr, " Skipping this file...\n" );
            skip = 1;
            break;
        }
    if ( s != FileList[ i ] ) {
        for ( j = 0 ; s[ j ] != '\0' ; j++ )
            FileList[ i ][ j ] = s[ j ];
        FileList[ i ][ j ] = '\0';
    }
    if ( !skip ) {
        strcpy( Header.file_name, FileList[ i ] );
        Insert( input_text_file, "Adding" );
    } else
        fclose( input_text_file );
    }
    return( i );
}
```

```
/*
 * This is the main loop where all the serious work done by this
 * program takes place. Essentially, this routine starts at the
 * beginning of the input CAR file, and processes every file in
 * the CAR. Depending on what command is being executed, that might
 * mean expanding the file, copying it to standard output,
 * adding it to the output CAR, or skipping over it completely.
 */

int ProcessAllFilesInInputCar( command, count )
int command;
int count;
{
    int matched;
    FILE *input_text_file;
    FILE *output_destination;

    if ( command == 'P' )
        output_destination = stdout;
    else if ( command == 'T' )
#ifdef MSDOS
        output_destination = fopen( "NUL", "wb" );
#else
        output_destination = fopen( "/dev/null", "wb" );
#endif
    else
        output_destination = NULL;
/*
 * This is the loop where it all happens. I read in the header for
 * each file in the input CAR, then see if it matches any of the file
 * and wildcard specifications in the FileList created earlier. That
 * information, combined with the command, tells me what I need to
 * know in order to process the file. Note that if the 'Addfiles' command
 * is being executed, the InputCarFile will be NULL, so this loop
 * can be safely skipped.
 */
    while ( InputCarFile != NULL && ReadFileHeader() != 0 ) {
```

```
matched = SearchFileList( Header.file_name );
switch ( command ) {
   case 'D' :
      if ( matched ) {
         SkipOverFileFromInputCar();
         count++;
      } else
         CopyFileFromInputCar();
      break;
   case 'A' :
      if ( matched )
         SkipOverFileFromInputCar();
      else
         CopyFileFromInputCar();
      break;
   case 'L' :
      if ( matched ) {
         ListCarFileEntry();
         count++;
      }
      SkipOverFileFromInputCar();
      break;
   case 'P' :
   case 'X' :
   case 'T' :
      if ( matched ) {
         Extract( output_destination );
         count++;
      } else
         SkipOverFileFromInputCar();
      break;
   case 'R' :
      if ( matched ) {
         input_text_file = fopen( Header.file_name, "rb" );
         if ( input_text_file == NULL ) {
            fprintf( stderr, "Could not find %s", Header.file_name );
            fprintf( stderr, " for replacement, skipping\n" );
```

```
            CopyFileFromInputCar();
         } else {
            SkipOverFileFromInputCar();
            Insert( input_text_file, "Replacing" );
            count++;
            fclose( input_text_file );
         }
      } else
         CopyFileFromInputCar();
      break;
   }
  }
  return( count );
}



/*
 * This routine looks through the entire list of arguments to see if
 * there is a match with the file name currently in the header. As each
 * new file in InputCarFile is encountered in the main processing loop,
 * this routine is called to determine if it has an appearance anywhere
 * in the FileList[] array. The results is used to in the main loop
 * to determine what action to take. For example, if the command were
 * the 'Delete' command, the match result would determine whether to
 * copy the file form the InputCarFile to the OutputCarFile, or skip
 * over it.
 *
 * The actual work in this routine is really performed by the
 * WildCardMatch() routine which checks the file name against one of the
 * names in the FileList[] array. Since most of the commands can use
 * wild cards to specify file names inside the CAR file, we need a
 * special comparison routine.
 */

int SearchFileList( file_name )
char *file_name;
```

```
{
  int i;

  for ( i = 0 ; FileList[ i ] != NULL ; i++ ) {
    if ( WildCardMatch( file_name, FileList[ i ] ) )
      return( 1 );
  }
  return( 0 );
}


/*
 * WildCardMatch() compares string to wild_string, looking for a match.
 * Wild card characters supported are only '*' and '?', where '*'
 * represents a string of any length, including 0, and '?' represents any
 * single character.
 */

int WildCardMatch( string, wild_string )
char *string;
char *wild_string;
{
  for ( ; ; ) {
    if ( *wild_string == '*' ) {
      wild_string++;
      for ( ; ; ) {
        while ( *string != '\0' && *string != *wild_string )
          string++;
        if ( WildCardMatch( string, wild_string ) )
          return( 1 );
        else if ( *string == '\0' )
          return( 0 );
        else
          string++;
      }
    } else if ( *wild_string == '?' ) {
      wild_string++;
      if ( *string++ == '\0' )
```

```
        return( 0 );
    } else {
      if ( *string != *wild_string )
        return( 0 );
      if ( *string == '\0' )
        return( 1 );
      string++;
      wild_string++;
    }
  }
}

/*
 * When the main processing loop reads in a header, it checks to see
 * if it is going to copy that file either to the OutputCarFile or expand
 * it. If neither is going to happen, we need to skip past this file and
 * go on to the next header. This can be done by seeking past the
 * compressed file. Since the compressed size is stored in the header
 * information, it is easy to do. Note that this routine assumes that the
 * file pointer has not been modified since the header was read in. This
 * means it should be located at the first byte of the compressed data.
 */

void SkipOverFileFromInputCar()
{
    fseek( InputCarFile, Header.compressed_size, SEEK_CUR );
}

/*
 * When performing an operation that modifies the input CAR file,
 * compressed files will frequently need to be copied from the input CAR
 * file to the output CAR file. This routine does that using simple
 * repeated block copy operations. Since it is writing directly to the
 * output CAR file, the first thing it needs to do is write out the
 * current Header so that the CAR file will be properly structured.
 * Following that, the compressed file is copied one block at a time to
 * the output. When this routine completes, the input file pointer is
```

```
 * positioned at the next header in the input CAR file, and the output
 * file pointer is positioned at the EOF position in the output file.
 * This is the proper place for the next record to begin.
 */

void CopyFileFromInputCar()
{
   char buffer[ 256 ];
   int count;

   WriteFileHeader();
   while ( Header.compressed_size != 0 ) {
      if ( Header.compressed_size < 256 )
        count = (int) Header.compressed_size;
      else
        count = 256;
      if ( fread( buffer, 1, count, InputCarFile ) != count )
        FatalError( "Error reading input file %s", Header.file_name );
      Header.compressed_size -= count;
      if ( fwrite( buffer, 1, count, OutputCarFile) != count )
        FatalError( "Error writing to output CAR file" );
   }
}


/*
 * When the operation requested by the user is 'List', this routine is
 * called to print out the column headers. List output goes to standard
 * output, unlike most of the other messages in this program, which go
 * to stderr.
 */

void PrintListTitles()
{
   printf( "\n" );
   printf( "                    Original  Compressed\n" );
   printf( "Filename    Size   Size        Ratio CRC-32 Method\n" );
   printf( "————————    ————   —————       ————— —————— ———————\n" );
```

```
}

/*
 * When the List command is given, the main loop reads in each header
 * block, then tests to see if the file name in the header block matches
 * one of the file names (including wildcards) in the FileList. If it is,
 * this routine is called to print out the information on the file.
 */

void ListCarFileEntry()
{
    static char *methods[] = {
        "Stored",
        "LZSS"
    };

printf( "%-20s %10lu  %10lu   %4d%%   %08lx   %s\n",
        Header.file_name,
        Header.original_size,
        Header.compressed_size,
        RatioInPercent( Header.compressed_size, Header.original_size ),
        Header.original_crc,
        methods[ Header.compression_method - 1 ] );
}

/*
 * The compression figure used in this book is calculated here. The value
 * is scaled so that a file that has just been stored has a compression
 * ratio of 0%, while one that has been shrunk down to nothing would have
 * a ratio of 100%.
 */

int RatioInPercent( compressed, original )
unsigned long compressed;
unsigned long original;
{
    int result;
```

```
  if ( original == 0 )
    return( 0 );
  result = (int) ( ( 100L * compressed ) / original );
  return( 100 - result );
}


/*
 * This routine is where all the information about the next file in
 * the archive is read in. The data is read into the global Header
 * structure. To preserve portability of CAR files across systems,
 * the data in each file header is packed into an unsigned char array
 * before it is written out to the file. To read this data back in
 * to the Header structure, we first read it into another unsigned
 * character array, then employ an unpacking routine to convert that
 * data into ints and longs. This helps us avoid problems with
 * big/little endian conflicts, as well as incompatibilities in structure
 * packing, which show up even between different compilers targetted for
 * the same architecture.
 *
 * To avoid causing any additional confusion, the data members for the
 * header structure are at least stored in exactly the same order as
 * they appear in the structure definition. The primary difference is
 * that the entire file name character array is not stored, which would
 * waste a lot of space. Instead, we just store the number of characters
 * in the name, including the null termination character. The file name
 * serves the additional purpose of identifying the end of the CAR file
 * with a file name length of 0 bytes.
 */

int ReadFileHeader()
{
  unsigned char header_data[ 17 ];
  unsigned long header_crc;
  int i;
  int c;
```

```
  for ( i = 0 ; ; ) {
    c = getc( InputCarFile );
    Header.file_name[ i ] = (char) c;
    if ( c == '\0' )
      break;
    if ( ++i == FILENAME_MAX )
      FatalError( "File name exceeded maximum in header" );
  }
  if ( i == 0 )
    return( 0 );
  header_crc = CalculateBlockCRC32( i + 1, CRC_MASK, Header.file_name );
  fread( header_data, 1, 17, InputCarFile );
  Header.compression_method = (char)
                               UnpackUnsignedData( 1, header_data + 0 );
  Header.original_size     = UnpackUnsignedData( 4, header_data + 1 );
  Header.compressed_size   = UnpackUnsignedData( 4, header_data + 5 );
  Header.original_crc      = UnpackUnsignedData( 4, header_data + 9 );
  Header.header_crc        = UnpackUnsignedData( 4, header_data + 13 );
  header_crc = CalculateBlockCRC32( 13, header_crc, header_data );
  header_crc ^= CRC_MASK;
  if ( Header.header_crc != header_crc )
    FatalError( "Header checksum error for file %s", Header.file_name );
  return( 1 );
}


/*
 * This routine is used to transform packed characters into unsigned
 * integers. Its only purpose is to convert packed character data
 * into integers and longs.
 */

unsigned long UnpackUnsignedData( number_of_bytes, buffer )
int number_of_bytes;
unsigned char *buffer;
{
  unsigned long result;
  int shift_count;
```

```
    result = 0;
    shift_count = 0;
    while ( number_of_bytes-- > 0 ) {
        result |= (unsigned long) *buffer++ << shift_count;
        shift_count += 8;
    }
    return( result );
}


/*
 * This routine is called to write out the current Global header block
 * to the output CAR file. It employs the same packing mechanism
 * discussed earlier. This routine also calculates the CRC of the
 * header, which is sometimes not necessary.
 */

void WriteFileHeader()
{
    unsigned char header_data[ 17 ];
    int i;

    for ( i = 0 ; ; ) {
        putc( Header.file_name[ i ], OutputCarFile );
        if ( Header.file_name[ i++ ] == '\0' )
            break;
    }
    Header.header_crc = CalculateBlockCRC32( i, CRC_MASK,
                                             Header.file_name );
    PackUnsignedData( 1, (long)
                         Header.compression_method, header_data + 0 );
    PackUnsignedData( 4, Header.original_size,      header_data + 1 );
    PackUnsignedData( 4, Header.compressed_size,    header_data + 5 );
    PackUnsignedData( 4, Header.original_crc,       header_data + 9 );
    Header.header_crc = CalculateBlockCRC32( 13, Header.header_crc,
                                             header_data );
    Header.header_crc ^= CRC_MASK;
```

```
   PackUnsignedData( 4, Header.header_crc, header_data + 13 );
   fwrite( header_data, 1, 17, OutputCarFile );
}


/*
 * This is the routine used to pack integers and longs into a character
 * array. The character array is what eventually gets written out to the
 * CAR file. The data is always written out with the least significant
 * bytes of the integers or long integers going first.
 */

void PackUnsignedData( number_of_bytes, number, buffer )
int number_of_bytes;
unsigned long number;
unsigned char *buffer;
{
   while ( number_of_bytes-- > 0 ) {
     *buffer++ = ( unsigned char ) number & 0xff;
     number >>= 8;
   }
}


/*
 * The last header in a CAR file is defined by the fact that it has
 * a file name length of zero. Since the file name is the
 * first element to be written out, we can create the final header
 * by just writing out a null termination character. This technique
 * saves a little bit of space.
 */

void WriteEndOfCarHeader()
{
   fputc( 0, OutputCarFile );
}
```

```
/*
 * This is the routine called by the main processing loop and the
 * Addfiles routine. It takes an input file and writes the header and
 * file data to the Output CAR file. There are several complications that
 * the routine has to deal with. First of all, the header information
 * it gets when it first starts is incomplete. For instance, we don't
 * know how many bytes the file will take up when it is compressed.
 * Because of this, the position of the header is stored, and the
 * incomplete copy is written out. After the compression routine finishes,
 * the header is now complete. In order to put the correct header into
 * the output CAR file, this routine seeks back in the file to the
 * original header position and rewrites it.
 *
 * The second complication lies in the fact that some files are not very
 * compressible. In fact, for some files the LZSS algorithm may actually
 * cause the file to expand. In these cases, the compression routine
 * gives up and passes a failure code back to Insert(). When this
 * happens, the routine has to seek back to the start of the file, rewind
 * the input file, and store it instead of compressing it. Because of
 * this, the starting position of the file in the output CAR file is also
 * stored when the routine starts up.
 */

void Insert( input_text_file, operation )
FILE *input_text_file;
char *operation;
{
    long saved_position_of_header;
    long saved_position_of_file;

    fprintf( stderr, "%s %-20s", operation, Header.file_name );
    saved_position_of_header = ftell( OutputCarFile );
    Header.compression_method = 2;
    WriteFileHeader();
    saved_position_of_file = ftell(OutputCarFile);
    fseek( input_text_file, 0L, SEEK_END );
```

```
    Header.original_size = ftell( input_text_file );
    fseek( input_text_file, 0L, SEEK_SET );
    if ( !LZSSCompress( input_text_file ) ) {
      Header.compression_method = 1;
      fseek( OutputCarFile, saved_position_of_file, SEEK_SET );
      rewind( input_text_file );
      Store( input_text_file );
    }
    fclose( input_text_file );
    fseek( OutputCarFile, saved_position_of_header, SEEK_SET );
    WriteFileHeader();
    fseek( OutputCarFile, 0L, SEEK_END );
    printf( " %d%%\n", RatioInPercent( Header.compressed_size,
                                       Header.original_size ) );
}


/*
 * The Extract routine can be called for one of three reasons. If the
 * file in the CAR is truly being extracted, Extract() is called with
 * no destination specified. In this case, the Extract routine opens the
 * file specified in the header and either unstores or decompresses the
 * file from the CAR file. If the archive is being tested for veracity,
 * the destination file will have been opened up earlier and specified as
 * the null device. Finally, the 'Print' option may have been selected,
 * in which case the destination file will be extracted to stdout.
 */

void Extract( destination )
FILE *destination;
{
  FILE *output_text_file;
  unsigned long crc;
  int error;

  fprintf( stderr, "%-20s ", Header.file_name );
  error = 0;
  if ( destination == NULL ) {
```

```
    if ( ( output_text_file = fopen(Header.file_name, "wb")
                                                 ) == NULL ) {
      fprintf( stderr, "Can't open %s\n", Header.file_name );
      fprintf( stderr, "Not extracted\n" );
      SkipOverFileFromInputCar();
      return;
    }
  } else
    output_text_file = destination;
  switch( Header.compression_method ) {
    case 1 :
      crc = Unstore( output_text_file );
      break;
    case 2 :
      crc = LZSSExpand( output_text_file );
      break;
    default :
      fprintf( stderr, "Unknown method: %c\n",
        Header.compression_method );
      SkipOverFileFromInputCar();
      error = 1;
      crc = Header.original_crc;
      break;
  }
  if ( crc != Header.original_crc ) {
    fprintf( stderr, "CRC error reading data\n" );
    error = 1;

  }
  if ( destination == NULL ) {
      fclose( output_text_file );
      if ( error )
#ifdef __STDC__
      remove( Header.file_name );
#else
      unlink( Header.file_name );
#endif
```

```
    }
    if ( !error )
      fprintf( stderr, " OK\n" );
}


/*
 * The CAR manager program is capable of handling many different forms of
 * compression. All the compression program has to do is obey a few
 * simple rules. First of all, the compression routine is required
 * to calculate the 32-bit CRC of the uncompressed data, and store the
 * result in the file Header, so it can be written out by the Insert()
 * routine. The expansion routine calculates the CRC of the file it
 * creates, and returns it to Extract() for a check against the Header
 * value. Second, the compression routine is required to quit if its
 * output is going to exceed the length of the input file. It needs to
 * quit *before* the output length passes the input, or problems will
 * result. The compression routine is required to return a true or false
 * value indicating whether or not the compression was a success. And
 * finally, the expansion routine is expected to leave the file pointer
 * to the Input CAR file positioned at the first byte of the next file
 * header. This means it has to read in all the bytes of the compressed
 * data, no more or less.
 *
 * All these things are relatively easy to accomplish for Store() and
 * Unstore(), since they do no compression or expansion.
 *
 */

int Store( input_text_file )
FILE *input_text_file;
{
    unsigned int n;
    char buffer[ 256 ];
    int pacifier;

    pacifier = 0;
    Header.original_crc = CRC_MASK;
```

```
   while ( ( n = fread( buffer, 1, 256, input_text_file ) ) != 0 ) {
      fwrite( buffer, 1, n, OutputCarFile );
      Header.original_crc = CalculateBlockCRC32( n, Header.original_crc,
                                                               buffer );

      if ( ( ++pacifier & 15 ) == 0 )
         putc( '.', stderr );
   }
   Header.compressed_size = Header.original_size;
   Header.original_crc ^= CRC_MASK;
   return( 1 );
}

unsigned long Unstore( destination )
FILE *destination;
{
   unsigned long crc;
   unsigned int count;
   unsigned char buffer[ 256 ];
   int pacifier;

   pacifier = 0;
   crc = CRC_MASK;
   while ( Header.original_size != 0 ) {
      if ( Header.original_size > 256 )
         count = 256;
      else
         count = (int) Header.original_size;
      if ( fread( buffer, 1, count, InputCarFile ) != count )
         FatalError( "Can't read from input CAR file" );
      if ( fwrite( buffer, 1, count, destination ) != count ) {
         fprintf( stderr, "Error writing to output file" );
         return( ~Header.original_crc );
      }
      crc = CalculateBlockCRC32( count, crc, buffer );
      if ( destination != stdout && ( pacifier++ & 15 ) == 0 )
         putc( '.', stderr );
      Header.original_size -= count;
   }
```

```
    return( crc ^ CRC_MASK );
}


/*
 * The second set of compression routines is found here. These
 * routines implement LZSS compression and expansion using 12-bit
 * index pointers and 4-bit match lengths. These values were
 * specifically chosen because they allow for "blocked I/O". Because
 * of their values, we can pack match/length pairs into pairs of
 * bytes, with characters that don't have matches going into single
 * bytes. This helps increase I/O since single bit input and
 * output does not have to be employed. Other than this single change,
 * this code is identical to the LZSS code used earlier in the book.
 */


/*
 * Various constants used to define the compression parameters. The
 * INDEX_BIT_COUNT tells how many bits we allocate to indices into the
 * text window. This directly determines the WINDOW_SIZE. The
 * LENGTH_BIT_COUNT tells how many bits we allocate for the length of
 * an encode phrase. This determines the size of the look ahead buffer.
 * The TREE_ROOT is a special node in the tree that always points to
 * the root node of the binary phrase tree. END_OF_STREAM is a special
 * index used to flag the fact that the file has been completely
 * encoded, and there is no more data. UNUSED is the null index for
 * the tree. MOD_WINDOW() is a macro used to perform arithmetic on tree
 * indices.
 *
 */


#define INDEX_BIT_COUNT      12
#define LENGTH_BIT_COUNT     4
#define WINDOW_SIZE          ( 1 << INDEX_BIT_COUNT )
#define RAW_LOOK_AHEAD_SIZE  ( 1 << LENGTH_BIT_COUNT )
#define BREAK_EVEN           ( ( 1 + INDEX_BIT_COUNT + LENGTH_BIT_COUNT )\
                               / 9 )
#define LOOK_AHEAD_SIZE      ( RAW_LOOK_AHEAD_SIZE + BREAK_EVEN )
```

```
#define TREE_ROOT         WINDOW_SIZE
#define END_OF_STREAM     0
#define UNUSED            0
#define MOD_WINDOW( a )   ( ( a ) & ( WINDOW_SIZE - 1 ) )

/*
 * These are the two global data structures used in this program.
 * The window[] array is exactly that, the window of previously seen
 * text, as well as the current look ahead text. The tree[] structure
 * contains the binary tree of all of the strings in the window sorted
 * in order.
 */
unsigned char window[ WINDOW_SIZE ];

struct {
    int parent;
    int smaller_child;
    int larger_child;
} tree[ WINDOW_SIZE + 1 ];

/*
 * Function prototypes for both ANSI C compilers and their K&R brethren.
 */

#ifdef __STDC__

void InitTree( int r );
void ContractNode( int old_node, int new_node );
void ReplaceNode( int old_node, int new_node );
int FindNextNode( int node );
void DeleteString( int p );
int AddString( int new_node, int *match_position );
void InitOutputBuffer( void );
int FlushOutputBuffer( void );
int OutputChar( int data );
int OutputPair( int position, int length );
void InitInputBuffer( void );
```

```
int InputBit( void );


#else

void InitTree();
void ContractNode();
void ReplaceNode();
int FindNextNode();
void DeleteString();
int AddString();
void InitOutputBuffer();
int FlushOutputBuffer();
int OutputChar();
int OutputPair();
void InitInputBuffer();
int InputBit();

#endif

void InitTree( r )
int r;
{
  int i;

  for ( i = 0 ; i < ( WINDOW_SIZE + 1 ) ; i++ ) {
    tree[ i ].parent = UNUSED;
    tree[ i ].larger_child = UNUSED;
    tree[ i ].smaller_child = UNUSED;
  }
  tree[ TREE_ROOT ].larger_child = r;
  tree[ r ].parent = TREE_ROOT;
```

```
   tree[ r ].larger_child = UNUSED;
   tree[ r ].smaller_child = UNUSED;
}


/*
 * This routine is used when a node is being deleted. The link to
 * its descendant is broken by pulling the descendant in to overlay
 * the existing link.
 */
void ContractNode( old_node, new_node )
int old_node;
int new_node;
{
   tree[ new_node ].parent = tree[ old_node ].parent;
   if ( tree[ tree[ old_node ].parent ].larger_child == old_node )
     tree[ tree[ old_node ].parent ].larger_child = new_node;
   else
     tree[ tree[ old_node ].parent ].smaller_child = new_node;
   tree[ old_node ].parent = UNUSED;
}


/*
 * This routine is also used when a node is being deleted. However,
 * in this case, it is being replaced by a node that was not previously
 * in the tree.
 */
void ReplaceNode( old_node, new_node )
int old_node;
int new_node;
{
   int parent;

   parent = tree[ old_node ].parent;
   if ( tree[ parent ].smaller_child == old_node )
     tree[ parent ].smaller_child = new_node;
   else
     tree[ parent ].larger_child = new_node;
```

```
  tree[ new_node ] = tree[ old_node ];
  tree[ tree[ new_node ].smaller_child ].parent = new_node;
  tree[ tree[ new_node ].larger_child ].parent = new_node;
  tree[ old_node ].parent = UNUSED;
}

/*
 * This routine is used to find the next smallest node after the node
 * argument. It assumes that the node has a smaller child. We find
 * the next smallest child by going to the smaller_child node, then
 * going to the end of the larger_child descendant chain.
 */
int FindNextNode( node )
int node;
{
  int next;

  next = tree[ node ].smaller_child;
  while ( tree[ next ].larger_child != UNUSED )
    next = tree[ next ].larger_child;
  return( next );
}

/*
 * This routine performs the classic binary tree deletion algorithm.
 * If the node to be deleted has a null link in either direction, we
 * just pull the non-null link up one to replace the existing link.
 * If both links exist, we instead delete the next link in order, which
 * is guaranteed to have a null link, then replace the node to be deleted
 * with the next link.
 */
void DeleteString( p )
int p;
{
  int  replacement;

  if ( tree[ p ].parent == UNUSED )
```

```
    return;
  if ( tree[ p ].larger_child == UNUSED )
    ContractNode( p, tree[ p ].smaller_child );
  else if ( tree[ p ].smaller_child == UNUSED )
    ContractNode( p, tree[ p ].larger_child );
  else {
    replacement = FindNextNode( p );
    DeleteString( replacement );
    ReplaceNode( p, replacement );
  }
}


/*
 * This is where most of the work done by the encoder takes place. This
 * routine is responsible for adding the new node to the binary tree.
 * It also has to find the best match among all the existing nodes in
 * the tree, and return that to the calling routine. To make matters
 * even more complicated, if the new_node has a duplicate in the tree,
 * the old_node is deleted, for reasons of efficiency.
 */

int AddString( new_node, match_position )
int new_node;
int *match_position;
{
  int i;
  int test_node;
  int delta;
  int match_length;
  int *child;

  if ( new_node == END_OF_STREAM )
    return( 0 );
  test_node = tree[ TREE_ROOT ].larger_child;
  match_length = 0;
  for ( ; ; ) {
    for ( i = 0 ; i < LOOK_AHEAD_SIZE ; i++ ) {
```

```
        delta =window[ MOD_WINDOW( new_node + i ) ] -
               window[ MOD_WINDOW( test_node + i ) ];
        if ( delta != 0 )
          break;
      }
      if ( i >= match_length ) {
        match_length = i;
        *match_position = test_node;
        if ( match_length >= LOOK_AHEAD_SIZE ) {
          ReplaceNode( test_node, new_node );
          return( match_length );
        }
      }
      if ( delta >= 0 )
        child = &tree[ test_node ].larger_child;
      else
        child = &tree[ test_node ].smaller_child;
      if ( *child == UNUSED ) {
        *child = new_node;
        tree[ new_node ].parent = test_node;
        tree[ new_node ].larger_child = UNUSED;
        tree[ new_node ].smaller_child = UNUSED;
        return( match_length );
      }
      test_node = *child;
    }
}

/*
 * This section of code and data makes up the blocked I/O portion of the
 * program. Every token output consists of a single flag bit, followed
 * by either a single character or a index/length pair. The flag bits
 * are stored in the first byte of a buffer array, and the characters
 * and index/length pairs are stored sequentially in the remaining
 * positions in the array. After every eight output operations, the
 * first character of the array is full of flag bits, so the remaining
```

```
* bytes stored in the array can be output. This can be done with a
* single fwrite() operation, making for greater efficiency.
*
* All that is needed to implement this is a few routines, plus three
* data objects, which follow below. The buffer has the flag bits
* packed into its first character, with the remainder consisting of
* the characters and index/length pairs, appearing in the order they
* were output. The FlagBitMask is used to indicate where the next
* flag bit will go when packed into DataBuffer[ 0 ]. Finally, the
* BufferOffset is used to indicate where the next token will be stored
* in the buffer.
*/

char DataBuffer[ 17 ];
int FlagBitMask;
int BufferOffset;

/*
* To initialize the output buffer, we set the FlagBitMask to the first
* bit position, can clear DataBuffer[0], which will hold all the
* Flag bits. Finally, the BufferOffset is set to 1, which is where the
* first character or index/length pair will go.
*/

void InitOutputBuffer()
{
    DataBuffer[ 0 ] = 0;
    FlagBitMask = 1;
    BufferOffset = 1;
}

/*
* This routine is called during one of two different situations. First,
* it can potentially be called right after a character or a length/index
* pair is added to the DataBuffer[]. If the position of the bit in the
* FlagBitMask indicates that it is full, the output routine calls this
```

```
* routine to flush data into the output file, and reset the output
* variables to their initial state. The other time this routine is
* called is when the compression routine is ready to exit. If there is
* any data in the buffer at that time, it needs to be flushed.
*
* Note that this routine checks carefully to be sure that it doesn't
* ever write out more data than was in the original uncompressed file.
* It returns a 0 if this happens, which filters back to the compression
* program, so that it can abort if this happens.
*
*/

int FlushOutputBuffer()
{
    if ( BufferOffset == 1 )
        return( 1 );
    Header.compressed_size += BufferOffset;
    if ( ( Header.compressed_size ) >= Header.original_size )
        return( 0 );
    if ( fwrite( DataBuffer, 1, BufferOffset, OutputCarFile )
         !=BufferOffset )
         FatalError( "Error writing compressed data to CAR file" );
    InitOutputBuffer();
    return( 1 );
}

/*
* This routine adds a single character to the output buffer. In this
* case, the flag bit is set, indicating that the next character is an
* uncompressed byte. After setting the flag and storing the byte,
* the flag bit is shifted over, and checked. If it turns out that all
* eight bits in the flag bit character are used up, then we have to
* flush the buffer and reinitialize the data. Note that if the
* FlushOutputBuffer() routine detects that the output has grown larger
* than the input, it returns a 0 back to the calling routine.
*/

int OutputChar( data )
```

```
int data;
{
  DataBuffer[ BufferOffset++ ] = (char) data;
  DataBuffer[ 0 ] |= FlagBitMask;
  FlagBitMask <<= 1;
  if ( FlagBitMask == 0x100 )
    return( FlushOutputBuffer() );
  else
    return( 1 );
}


/*
* This routine is called to output a 12-bit position pointer and a 4-bit
* length. The 4-bit length is shifted to the top four bits of the first
* of two DataBuffer[] characters. The lower four bits contain the upper
* four bits of the 12-bit position index. The next of the two DataBuffer
* characters gets the lower eight bits of the position index. After
* all that work to store those 16 bits, the FlagBitMask is shifted over,
* and checked to see if we have used up all our bits. If we have,
* the output buffer is flushed, and the output data elements are reset.
* If the FlushOutputBuffer routine detects that the output file has
* grown too large, it passes and error return back via this routine,
* so that it can abort.
*/

int OutputPair( position, length )
int position;
int length;
{
  DataBuffer[ BufferOffset ] = (char) ( length << 4 );
  DataBuffer[ BufferOffset++ ] |= ( position >> 8 );
  DataBuffer[ BufferOffset++ ] = (char) ( position & 0xff );
  FlagBitMask <<= 1;
  if ( FlagBitMask == 0x100 )
    return( FlushOutputBuffer() );
  else
    return( 1 );
```

```
}

/*
 * The input process uses the same data structures as the blocked output
 * routines, but it is somewhat simpler, in that it doesn't actually have
 * to read in a whole block of data at once. Instead, it just reads in
 * a single character full of flag bits into DataBuffer[0], and passes
 * individual bits back to the Expansion program when asked for them.
 * The expansion program is left to its own devices for reading in the
 * characters, indices, and match lengths. They can be read in
 * sequentially using normal file I/O.
 */
void InitInputBuffer()
{
    FlagBitMask = 1;
    DataBuffer[ 0 ] = (char) getc( InputCarFile );
}

/*
 * When the Expansion program wants a flag bit, it calls this routine.
 * This routine has to keep track of whether or not it has run out of
 * flag bits. If it has, it has to go back and reinitialize so as to
 * have a fresh set.
 */

int InputBit()
{
    if ( FlagBitMask == 0x100 )
        InitInputBuffer();
    FlagBitMask <<= 1;
    return( DataBuffer[ 0 ] & ( FlagBitMask >> 1 ) );
}

/*
 * This is the compression routine. It has to first load up the look
 * ahead buffer, then go into the main compression loop. The main loop
 * decides whether to output a single character or an index/length
```

```
*  token that defines a phrase. Once the character or phrase has been
*  sent out, another loop has to run. The second loop reads in new
*  characters, deletes the strings that are overwritten by the new
*  character, then adds the strings that are created by the new
*  character. While running it has the additional responsibility of
*  creating the checksum of the input data, and checking for when the
*  output data grows too large. The program returns a success or failure
*  indicator. It also has to update the original_crc and compressed_size
*  elements in Header data structure.
*
*/


int LZSSCompress( input_text_file )
FILE *input_text_file;
{
    int i;
    int c;
    int look_ahead_bytes;
    int current_position;
    int replace_count;
    int match_length;
    int match_position;

    Header.compressed_size = 0;
    Header.original_crc = CRC_MASK;
    InitOutputBuffer();

    current_position = 1;
    for ( i = 0 ; i < LOOK_AHEAD_SIZE ; i++ ) {
        if ( ( c = getc( input_text_file ) ) == EOF )
            break;
        window[ current_position + i ] = (unsigned char) c;
        Header.original_crc = UpdateCharacterCRC32( Header.original_crc, c );
    }
    look_ahead_bytes = i;
    InitTree( current_position );
    match_length = 0;
```

```
match_position = 0;
while ( look_ahead_bytes > 0 ) {
  if ( match_length > look_ahead_bytes )
    match_length = look_ahead_bytes;
  if ( match_length <= BREAK_EVEN ) {
    replace_count = 1;
    if ( !OutputChar( window[ current_position ] ) )
      return( 0 );
  } else {
    if ( !OutputPair( match_position, match_length -
                                ( BREAK_EVEN + 1 ) ) )
      return( 0 );
    replace_count = match_length;
  }
  for ( i = 0 ; i < replace_count ; i++ ) {
    DeleteString( MOD_WINDOW( current_position + LOOK_AHEAD_SIZE ) );
    if ( ( c = getc( input_text_file ) ) == EOF ) {
      look_ahead_bytes--;
    } else {
      Header.original_crc =
        UpdateCharacterCRC32( Header.original_crc, c );
      window[ MOD_WINDOW( current_position + LOOK_AHEAD_SIZE ) ] =
        (unsigned char) c;
    }
    current_position = MOD_WINDOW( current_position + 1 );
    if ( current_position == 0 )
      putc( '.', stderr );
    if ( look_ahead_bytes )
      match_length = AddString( current_position, &match_position );
  }
};
Header.original_crc ^= CRC_MASK;
return( FlushOutputBuffer() );
}
```

```
/*
 * This is the expansion routine for the LZSS algorithm. All it has to do
 * is read in flag bits, decide whether to read in a character or a
 * index/length pair, and take the appropriate action. It is responsible
 * for keeping track of the crc of the output data, and must return it
 * to the calling routine, for verification.
 */

unsigned long LZSSExpand( output )
FILE *output;
{
    int i;
    int current_position;
    int c;
    int match_length;
    int match_position;
    unsigned long crc;
    unsigned long output_count;

    output_count = 0;
    crc = CRC_MASK;
    InitInputBuffer();
    current_position = 1;
    while ( output_count < Header.original_size ) {
        if ( InputBit() ) {
            c = getc( InputCarFile );
            putc( c, output );
            output_count++;
            crc = UpdateCharacterCRC32( crc, c );
            window[ current_position ] = (unsigned char) c;
            current_position = MOD_WINDOW( current_position + 1 );
            if ( current_position == 0 && output != stdout )
                putc( '.', stderr );
        } else {
            match_length = getc( InputCarFile );
            match_position = getc( InputCarFile );
            match_position |= ( match_length & 0xf ) << 8;
```

```
        match_length >>= 4; match_length += BREAK_EVEN;
        output_count += match_length + 1;
        for ( i = 0 ; i <= match_length ; i++ ) {
          c = window[ MOD_WINDOW( match_position + i ) ];
          putc( c, output );
          crc = UpdateCharacterCRC32( crc, c );
          window[ current_position ] = (unsigned char) c;
          current_position = MOD_WINDOW( current_position + 1 );
          if ( current_position == 0 && output != stdout )
            putc( '.', stderr );
        }
      }
    }
    return( crc ^ CRC_MASK );
}
/*************************** End of CARMAN>C ***************************/
```

Appendix A:
Statistics for Compression
Programs

This appendix gives statistics for some of the compression programs found in this book. The data sets used to test the compression where identical to the ones I used when judging the 1991 *Dr. Dobb's Journal* Data Compression Contest. The results of that contest can be found in the November 1991 issue of *Dr. Dobb's Journal*.

The compression and expansion speeds given here should be taken with a grain of salt. First of all, no attempt was made to optimize these programs. Secondly, some variation will be seen depending on what compiler was used to build the executable. Most of the executables were built using Borland C++ 2.0, but in a few cases, expanded memory requirements led me to use Zortech C++ 3.0 with either the 286 or 386 DOS Extender.

| | Compression Ratios | | |
	Graphics	Executables	Text Files	Overall
HUFF.C Chapter 3 Huffman Coding	27.22	24.79	40.38	31.04
AHUFF.C Chapter 4 Adaptive Huffman	32.59	26.69	40.72	33.27
ARITH.C Chapter 5 Arithmetic Coding	27.78	25.25	40.81	31.51
ARITHN.C Chapter 6 Order = 1	61.66	44.74	59.60	54.49

	Compression Ratios continued			
	Graphics	Executables	Text Files	Overall
ARITHN.C Chapter 6 (1) Order = 2	59.85	50.47	68.43	59.37
ARITHN.C Chapter 6 (1) Order = 3	58.51	51.55	71.86	60.67
LZSS.C Chapter 8 Index/Length = 12/4	43.45	41.44	58.83	48.22
LZSS.C Chapter 8 Index/Length = 13/4	44.57	42.56	60.91	49.69
LZSS.C Chapter 8 (3) Index/Length = 14/4	44.71	42.32	61.10	49.70
LZSS.C Chapter 8 Index/Length = 12/3	42.83	40.38	57.27	47.10
LZSS.C Chapter 8 Index/Length = 12/5	43.91	42.31	59.21	48.81
LZSS.C Chapter 8 Index/Length = 12/8	40.60	39.60	54.67	45.29
LZW15V.C Chapter 9 15 bit variable LZW	48.44	36.15	58.28	47.31
LZW15V.C Chapter 9 14 bit variable LZW	48.23	36.27	57.76	47.11
LZW15V.C Chapter 9 13 bit variable LZW	47.76	36.34	56.71	46.65
LZW15V.C Chapter 9 12 bit variable LZW	46.78	36.61	54.82	45.81
LZW12.C Chapter 9 12 bit fixed LZW	20.61	15.07	50.32	29.20

	Compression Rates			
	Graphics	**Executables**	**Text Files**	**Overall**
HUFF.C Chapter 3 Huffman Coding	15273	13306	13353	13835
AHUFF.C Chapter 4 Adaptive Huffman	7553	6200	7523	7028
ARITH.C Chapter 5 Arithmetic Coding	4616	4667	4474	4584
ARITHN.C Chapter 6 Order = 1	804	395	953	702
ARITHN.C Chapter 6 (1) Order = 2	929	462	1158	834
ARITHN.C Chapter 6 (1) Order = 3	975	483	1206	871
LZSS.C Chapter 8 Index/Length = 12/4	3657	4159	3165	3671
LZSS.C Chapter 8 Index/Length = 13/4	3268	3853	2839	3336
LZSS.C Chapter 8 (3) Index/Length = 14/4	3082	3832	2563	3180
LZSS.C Chapter 8 Index/Length = 12/3	4093	4392	3594	4027
LZSS.C Chapter 8 Index/Length = 12/5	2942	3764	2773	3194
LZSS.C Chapter 8 Index/Length = 12/8	1831	1460	2411	1899
LZW15V.C Chapter 9 15 bit variable LZW	14913	11744	13332	13140

	Compression Rates continued			
	Graphics	Executables	Text Files	Overall
LZW15V.C Chapter 9 14 bit variable LZW	14850	11332	12783	12769
LZW15V.C Chapter 9 13 bit variable LZW	14256	10904	12241	12257
LZW15V.C Chapter 9 12 bit variable LZW	13669	10320	11432	11591
LZW12.C Chapter 9 12 bit fixed LZW	13106	11057	14379	12786
	Expansion Rates			
	Graphics	Executables	Text Files	Overall
HUFF.C Chapter 3 Huffman Coding	12428	10892	12560	11891
AHUFF.C Chapter 4 Adaptive Huffman	7366	6141	7755	7041
ARITH.C Chapter 5 Arithmetic Coding	2320	2205	2074	2188
ARITHN.C Chapter 6 Order = 1	793	405	944	700
ARITHN.C Chapter 6 (1) Order = 2	905	472	1136	824
ARITHN.C Chapter 6 (1) Order = 3	946	492	1173	855
LZSS.C Chapter 8 Index/Length = 12/4	18622	16526	17424	17394
LZSS.C Chapter 8 Index/Length = 13/4	18899	16716	17798	17673

	Expansion Rates continued			
	Graphics	**Executables**	**Text Files**	**Overall**
LZSS.C Chapter 8 (3) Index/Length = 14/4	30334	25120	27120	27196
LZSS.C Chapter 8 Index/Length = 12/3	18248	16572	16756	17074
LZSS.C Chapter 8 Index/Length = 12/5	18680	16674	17266	17409
LZSS.C Chapter 8 Index/Length = 12/8	18113	16230	16673	16879
LZW15V.C Chapter 9 15 bit variable LZW	15167	11986	13077	13206
LZW15V.C Chapter 9 14 bit variable LZW	14942	11804	12911	13018
LZW15V.C Chapter 9 13 bit variable LZW	14445	11462	12495	12609
LZW15V.C Chapter 9 12 bit variable LZW	13567	10893	11608	11845
LZW12.C Chapter 9 12 bit fixed LZW	15326	13978	15705	14950

Notes:
(1) Built with Zortech's 286 DOS Extender, so as to access all available extended memory. Higher order models can use megabytes of memory.

(2) Built with Zortech's 386 DOS Extender. One of the arrays in the program was larger than 64K, and this was an easy way to rebuild the code without using MS-DOS based "huge" pointers.

Appendix B:
Test Programs

One of the problems I noticed when testing data compression programs for the *Dr. Dobb's* programming contest of 1991 was that of inadequate testing. Many of the programs I was given failed on several of the test files in our compression database.

After good design, the best weapon to use against these kind of errors is exhaustive testing. I have a test program I use under MS-DOS, named CHURN, which can apply a compression program to every file on a disk volume, performing both compression, decompression, then comparing the input to the output. This has proven very helpful to me when testing the software in this book.

The MS-DOS version of the program is given below. Instructions on how to use this program are found in the program listing.

```
/*************************START OF CHURN.C************************
*
* This is a utility program used to test compression/decompression
* programs for accuracy, speed, and compression ratios. CHURN is
* called with three arguments. The first is a root directory. CHURN
* will attempt to compress and then decompress every file in and under
* the specified root directory. The next parameter on the command
* line is the compression command. CHURN needs to compress the input
* file to a file called TEST.CMP. The compression command tells CHURN
* how to to do this. CHURN will execute the compression command by
* passing the command line to DOS using the system() function call.
* It attempts to insert the file name into the compression command by
* calling sprintf(), with the file name as an argument. This means that
* if the compression command has a %s anywhere in it, the name of the
* input file should be substituted for it. Finally, the third argument
* on the command line should be the command CHURN needs to spawn to
* decompress TEST.CMP to TEST.OUT.
```

THE DATA COMPRESSION BOOK

```
 *
 * An example of how this works using programs created in this book
 * would look like this:
 *
 * CHURN C:\ "LZSS-C %%s test.cmp" "LZSS-E test.cmp test.out"
 *
 * The doubled up % symbols are there to defeat variable substitution
 * under some command-line interpreters, such as 4DOS.
 *
 * A more complicated example testing PKZIP might look like this:
 *
 * CHURN C:\ "TEST %%s" "PKUNZIP TEST.CMP"
 *
 * where TEST.BAT had two lines that look like this:
 *
 * COPY %1 TEST.OUT
 * PKZIP -M TEST.CMP TEST.OUT
 *
 * CHURN stores a summary of compression in a file called CHURN.LOG. This
 * file could be used for further analysis by other programs.
 *
 * To abort this program while it is running, don't start pounding away
 * on the BREAK or CTRL-C keys. They will just get absorbed by the
 * compression program. Instead, hit a single key, which will be detected
 * by CHURN, and used as an abort signal.
 */

#include <stdio.h>
#include <stdlib.h>
#include <string.h>
#include <time.h>
#include <process.h>
#include <conio.h>
#include <dos.h>

/*
 * The findfirst and findnext functions operate nearly identically
```

```
 * under TurboC and MSC. The only difference is that the functions
 * names, structures, and structure elements all have different names.
 * I just create macros for these things and redefine them appropriately
 * here.
 */


#ifdef __TURBOC__

#include <dir.h>
#define FILE_INFO               struct ffblk
#define FIND_FIRST( name, info ) findfirst( ( name ), ( info ),
                                                       FA_DIREC )
#define FIND_NEXT( info )       findnext( ( info ) )
#define FILE_IS_DIR( info )     ( ( info ).ff_attrib & FA_DIREC )
#define FILE_NAME( info )       ( ( info ).ff_name )

#else

#define MSDOS 1
#define FILE_INFO               struct find_t
#define FIND_FIRST( name, info ) _dos_findfirst( ( name ), _A_SUBDIR,
                                                       ( info ) )
#define FIND_NEXT( info )       _dos_findnext( ( info ) )
#define FILE_IS_DIR( info )     ( ( info ).attrib & _A_SUBDIR )
#define FILE_NAME( info )       ( ( info ).name )

#endif

/*
 * Some global variables.
 */

int total_files;
int total_passed;
int total_failed;
char *compress_command;
char *expand_command;
```

```
FILE *input;
FILE *output;
FILE *compressed;
FILE *log_file;

/*
 * Declarations for global routines.
 */

void churn_files( char *path );
int file_is_already_compressed( char *name );
void close_all_the_files( void );
int compress( char *file_name );
void usage_exit( void );


/*
 * main() doesn't have to do a whole lot in this program. It
 * reads in the command line to determine what the root directory
 * to start looking at is, then it initializes the total byte counts
 * and the start time. It can then call churn_files(), which does all
 * the work, then report on the statistics resulting from churn_files.
 */

void main( int argc, char *argv[] )
{
    time_t start_time;
    time_t stop_time;
    char root_dir[ 81 ];

    if ( argc != 4 )
        usage_exit();
    strcpy( root_dir, argv[ 1 ] );
    if ( root_dir[ strlen( root_dir ) - 1 ] != '\\' )
        strcat( root_dir, "\\" );
    compress_command = argv[ 2 ];
    expand_command = argv[ 3 ];
```

```
setbuf( stdout, NULL );
setbuf( stderr, NULL );
total_files = 0;
total_passed = 0;
total_failed = 0;
log_file = fopen( "CHURN.LOG", "w" );
if ( log_file == NULL ) {
  printf( "Couldn't open the log file!\n" );
  exit( 1 );
}
fprintf( log_file, "                              "
    "Original Packed\n" );
fprintf( log_file, "          File Name    "
    " Size Size Ratio   Result\n" );
fprintf( log_file, "——————————————    "
    "———— ———— —— ——\n" );
time( &start_time );
churn_files( root_dir );
time( &stop_time );
fprintf( log_file, "\nTotal elapsed time: %f seconds\n",
    difftime( stop_time, start_time ) );
fprintf( log_file, "Total files: %d\n", total_files );
fprintf( log_file, "Total passed: %d\n", total_passed );
fprintf( log_file, "Total failed: %d\n", total_failed );
}


/*
* churn_files() is a routine that sits in a loop looking at
* files in the directory specified by its single argument, "path".
* As each file is looked at, one of three things happens. If it
* is a normal file, and has a compressed extension name, like ".ZIP",
* the file is ignored. If it is a normal file, and doesn't have a
* compressed extension name, it is compressed and decompressed by
* another routine. Finally, if the file is a subdirectory,
* churn_files() is called recursively with the file name as its
* path argument. This is one of those rare routines where recursion
* provides a way to truly simplify the task at hand.
```

```
*/

void churn_files( char *path )
{
    FILE_INFO file_info;
    int result;
    char full_name[ 81 ];

    strcpy( full_name, path );
    strcat( full_name, "*.*" );
    result = FIND_FIRST( full_name, &file_info );

    while ( result == 0 ) {
        if ( kbhit() ) {
            getch();
            exit(0);
        }
        if ( FILE_IS_DIR( file_info ) ) {
            if ( FILE_NAME( file_info )[ 0 ] != '.' ) {
                strcpy( full_name, path );
                strcat( full_name, FILE_NAME( file_info) );
                strcat( full_name, "\\" );
                churn_files( full_name );
            }
        } else {
            strcpy( full_name, path );
            strcat( full_name, FILE_NAME( file_info ) );
            if ( !file_is_already_compressed( full_name ) ) {
                fprintf( stderr, "Testing %s\n", full_name );
                if ( !compress( full_name ) )
                    fprintf( stderr, "Comparison failed!\n" );
            }
        }
        result = FIND_NEXT( &file_info );
    }
}
```

```
/*
 * The job of this routine is simply to check on the file
 * whose name is passed as an argument. The file extension is compared
 * against a list of standard extensions that are commonly used on
 * compressed files. If it matches one of these names, we assume it is
 * compressed and return a TRUE, otherwise FALSE is returned.
 *
 * Note that when checking a compression routine for accuracy, it is
 * probably a good idea to stub out this routine. Trying to compress
 * "uncompressible" files is a very good exercise for a compression
 * program. It is probably not a good idea when checking compression
 * ratios, however.
 */

int file_is_already_compressed( char *name )
{
    char *extension;
    static char *matches[]={ "ZIP", "ICE", "LZH", "ARC", "GIF", "PAK",
                             "ARJ", NULL };
    int i;

    extension=strchr( name, '.' );
    if ( extension++ == NULL )
       return( 0 );
    i = 0;
    while ( matches[ i ] != NULL )
        if ( strcmp( extension, matches[ i++ ] ) == 0 )
           return( 1 );
    return( 0 );
}



/*
 * This is the routine that does the majority of the work for
 * this program. It takes a file whose name is passed here. It first
 * compresses, then decompresses that file. It then compares the file
 * to the decompressed output, and reports on the results.
```

```
*/

int compress( char *file_name )
{
    long new_size;
    long old_size;
    int c;
    char command[ 132 ];

    printf( "%s\n", file_name );
    fprintf( log_file, "%-40s ", file_name );
    sprintf( command, compress_command, file_name );
    system( command );
    sprintf( command, expand_command, file_name );
    system( command );

    input = fopen( file_name, "rb" );
    output = fopen( "TEST.OUT", "rb" );
    compressed = fopen( "TEST.CMP", "rb" );

    total_files++;
    if ( input == NULL || output == NULL || compressed == NULL ) {
        total_failed++;
        close_all_the_files();
        fprintf( log_file, "Failed, couldn't open file!\n" );
        return( 0 );
    }

    fseek( input, 0L, SEEK_END );
    old_size = ftell( input );
    fseek( input, 0L, SEEK_SET );
    fseek( compressed, 0L, SEEK_END );
    new_size = ftell( compressed );

    fprintf( log_file, " %8ld %8ld ", old_size, new_size );
    if ( old_size == 0L )
        old_size = 1L;
```

```
    fprintf( log_file, "%4ld%% ",
      100L - ( ( 100L * new_size ) / old_size ) );
    do {
      c = getc( input );
      if ( getc( output ) != c ) {
        fprintf( log_file, "Failed\n" );
        total_failed++;
        close_all_the_files();
        return( 0 );
      }
    }
    while ( c != EOF );
    fprintf( log_file, "Passed\n" );
    close_all_the_files();
    total_passed++;
    return( 1 );
}

void close_all_the_files()
{
    if ( input != NULL )
      fclose( input );
    if ( output != NULL )
      fclose( output );
    if ( compressed != NULL )
      fclose( compressed );
}

/*
 * This routine is used to print out basic instructions for the use
 * of CHURN, and then exit.
 */

void usage_exit( void )
{
    char *usage = "CHURN 1.0. Usage: CHURN root-dir \"compress "
                  "command\" \"expand command\n"
```

```
                    "\n"
                    "CHURN is used to test compression programs. "
                    "It does this by compressing\n"
                    "then expanding all of the files in and under "
                    "the specified root dir.\n"
                    "\n"
                    "For each file it finds, CHURN first executes "
                    "the compress command to create a\n"
                    "compressed file called TEST.CMP. It then "
                    "executes the expand command to\n"
                    "create a file called TEST.OUT. CHURN then "
                    "compares the two file to make sure\n"
                    "the compression cycle worked properly.\n"
                    "\n"
                    "The file name to be compressed will be "
                    "inserted into the  compress command\n"
                    "using sprintf, with any %%s argument being "
                    "substituted with the name of the\n"
                    "file being compressed. Note that the "
                    "compress and expand commands should be\n"
                    "enclosed in double quotes so that multiple "
                    "words can be included in the\n"
                    "printf( " commands.\n"
                    "\n"
                    "Note that you may have to double the %% "
                    "character on your command line to get\n"
                    "around argument substitution under some "
                    "command processors. Finally, note that\n"
                    "CHURN executes the compression program "
                    "using a system() function call, so\n"
                    "batch files can be used to execute complex\n"
                    "compression sequences.\n"
                    "\n"
                    "Example: CHURN C:\\ \"LZSS-C %%%%s TEST.CMP\"
                    "\"LZSS-C TEST.CMP TEST.OUT\"";
    puts( usage );
    exit( 1 );
}
```

Glossary

Adaptive compression, Adaptive modeling

Data compression techniques that use a model can either use a fixed model for the entire stream they are processing, or modify the model as the stream is processed. Techniques that modify the model as it is processed are said to use adaptive modeling. An example of an adaptive compression technique would be LZW compression.

ADPCM

Adaptive Differential Pulse Code Modulation. Standard PCM encoding is a common technique for encoding audio data. Telephone conversations and audio CDs both use conventional PCM. PCM samples a waveform at uniform steps and encodes the level of the waveform. DPCM is Differential Pulse Code Modulation. DPCM doesn't encode the level, it instead encodes the difference from the last sample. ADPCM takes that a step further, and modifies the coding of the difference depending on the state of the waveform. PCM encoding in telephone systems uses 64 K bits per second. ADPCM can reduce that rate to 32 or even 16 K bits per second with relatively little reduction in voice quality.

Alphabet

An Alphabet is the set of all of the possible symbols that may appear in a message. For example, when compressing ASCII text files, the Alphabet would probably consist of characters 0x00 through 0x7f.

Archive

An archive is a volume or file containing one or more files that may or may not have been compressed. An archive is typically used as a convenient way to store or transport files. Programs such as ARC and PKZip compress files before placing them into archives.

Arithmetic coding

Traditional coding techniques such as ASCII or Huffman coding encode symbols into unique patterns of bits. Arithmetic coding instead takes an entire text and encodes it as a single floating point number less than 1 and greater than or equal to 0. Arithmetic coding can more efficiently encode texts by eliminating the quantization effects of other coding techniques.

ARC, MS-DOS program

ARC is a commercial archiving program created by System Enhancement Associates, of Wayne, N.J. ARC was one of the earliest compression/archive utilities to achieve wide popularity in the desktop computing world, beginning in the mid-1980s.

ARJ, MS-DOS program

ARJ is a commercial archiving program created by Robert Jung. ARJ is free of charge for individual use, but commercial users must pay a license fee. ARJ is also supplied with ANSI C source code for extracting files from ARJ archives that may be distributed without restrictions.

Block Coding

Compression of images is frequently done by coding smaller blocks of the image independent of one another. For example, the JPEG algorithm uses an 8-by-8 block size when compressing graphics.

CCITT

CCITT is the International Telegraph and Telephone Consultative Committee. This standards organization is responsible for the sanctioning of many compression and transmission methods in use today, including several PCM and ADPCM techniques, FAX transmission, and the evolving JPEG and MPEG standards.

Codes, (en)coding

Symbols that are to be stored or manipulated by a computer are converted to codes. This process is referred to as coding. ASCII and EBCDIC are two of the most common methods of coding written text. Data compression can occur if more efficient methods of coding, such as Huffman coding, are used.

COMPACT, UNIX program

COMPACT is a UNIX program that used Dynamic Huffman coding to compress files. It generally fell out of use in favor of the COMPRESS program.

COMPRESS, UNIX program

COMPRESS is a UNIX program that uses an LZW implementation to compress files. COMPRESS has found widespread use in the UNIX community, and is available in the public domain. It has recently been thought that COMPRESS may infringe on a Unisys patent, which may curtail its use and distribution.

Compression ratios

Compression ratios are used to describe the difference between a file and a compressed copy of itself. There are several different ways of expressing this number. One common method is a ratio between input and output, as in "a 4:1 compression ratio." Another popular method is to express the difference between the files as a percentage ranging from 0% to 100% (or greater, if the compression failed to actually reduce the size of the file). Some people invert this scale, using 100% as the "best" compression ratio. Occasionally, you still see the ratio of compressed to plain files expressed as "bits per byte."

CRC, Cyclical Redundancy Check

A CRC is a number generated by applying a formula to a block of data, generally for use as a checksum. A good CRC formula should generate a different number for as many different error conditions as possible. The CRC formula referred to in this book is the commonly used 32-bit CCITT-specified formula.

Discrete Cosine Transform

The DCT is used in the JPEG image compression method. The DCT is similar to the Fourier Transform, in that it transforms a set of data from the the spatial domain to the frequency domain and back again. Once a photographic image is transformed by the DCT into a set of frequency information, it can be effectively compressed using "lossy" techniques. Expanding the same image involves converting the frequency information back to spatial information.

Dictionary, adaptive/static

Macro substitution methods use a dictionary to compress data. A string of symbols is encoded as a pointer into a dictionary. An adaptive method, such as LZ77, is continually modifying its dictionary. A static dictionary will compress an entire stream using the same dictionary.

Entropy, Information content

Entropy is a measure of the amount of information in an object. The concept of "absolute entropy" remains elusive. In general, entropy is calculated with respect to a given model. Entropy can be expressed in bits. In this form it is generally referred to as "information content."

Escape code

An Escape code is a special symbol used to 'escape' from the current context. In data compression, escape codes are frequently used when a symbol, not found in the current dictionary of symbols, needs to be encoded. The Escape code tells the decoder to change to a different context, where the symbol can be properly coded.

Freeware

Freeware is a term applied to software that is distributed without charge and may be used freely by anyone. It is distinguished from Public Domain software by virtue of the fact that the owner of the software retains the copyright to the work. Retaining the copyright allows the owner to restrain or control any modification or redistribution of the package. Software distributed by the Free Software Foundation, such as the EMACS editor, is generally referred to as freeware.

Group 3 FAX

Group 3 FAX is a CCITT standard for transmission of facsimile data. It can compress black and white images using a combination of differential, run length, and Huffman coding.

Huffman coding

Huffman is a method of encoding symbols that varies the length of the symbol in proportion to its information content. Symbols with a low probability of appearance are encoded with a code using may bits. Symbols with a high probability of appearance are represented with a code using fewer bits. Huffman codes can be properly decoded because they obey the prefix property, which means no code can be a prefix of another code. Huffman coding was first described in a seminal paper by D.A. Huffman in 1952.

Information theory

Information theory is the study of the storage, processing, and transmission of information. This branch of science is generally acknowledged as having been created by Claude Shannon at Bell Labs shortly after World War II.

ISO

ISO is the International Standards Organization. ISO is one of the bodies (along with the CCITT) involved in the JPEG and MPEG standardization efforts.

JPEG

JPEG stands for the Joint Photographic Experts Group. It is referred as a "joint" group because this committee is sanctioned by the CCITT and the ISO, two prominent international standards groups. JPEG refers both to the committee and their work in progress—a compression standard that will define a method for compressing photographic images. Images compressed with the JPEG algorithm undergo a "lossy" compression. The amount of compression can be varied, with a result loss or gain in resolution. As of this writing, the JPEG standard appears to be in the final stage of the release process.

Most of the JPEG-like algorithms in use today rely on powerful dedicated processors to perform compression and decompression. Software-only techniques on general purpose desktop processors are still fairly slow. JPEG compression can achieve impressive compression ratios, reducing the storage required by images to less than 10% of the size of the original with only very slight loss of resolution. By sacrificing more resolution, you can compress images to 95% or more using JPEG.

LHarc

LHarc is a freeware compression program authored by Haruyasu Yoshizaki. It uses the LZSS variant of LZ77 compression, followed by a Dynamic Huffman postprocessing stage. The freeware status of this program, combined with the availability of source code, have made this a popular program.

Linear Predictive Coding

LPC is a coding technique that transmits voice data using a model of the vocal tract.

Lossless

Lossless compression is used to compress a text stream so that it can be expanded into an identical copy of the stream. This type of compression is normally required for data files.

Lossy

Lossy compression refers to a compression technique where the compressed stream cannot be expanded into an exact copy of the input. Lossy compression can be used on digitally stored representations of analog phenomena, such as graphics images and stored audio samples. The ability to sacrifice small amounts of resolution allows lossy algorithms to compress files to significantly smaller ratios. Lossy compression is sometimes referred to as "noisy" compression.

LZW, LZSS, LZ-77, LZ-78

Jacob Ziv and Abraham Lempel published a pair of papers in 1977 and 1978 that described two different dictionary-based compression techniques. LZ77 substituted strings from a fixed-size window into previously seen text. LZ78 builds up a phrase dictionary from previously seen text, with no limit on how far back a phrase may have appeared. These papers spurred a flurry of activity by other researchers who refined these techniques, resulting in compression algorithms that were superior to earlier statistical-based Huffman coding. Dictionary methods are widely-used today in V.42*bis* modems, in software such as LHarc, ARJ, and PKZIP, and in QIC magnetic tape drives.

Model

Compression algorithms generally maintain a "model," which is a set of accumulated statistics describing the state of the encoder. For example, in a simple compression program, the model may be a count of the frequency of every symbol in an input file.

MPEG

MPEG stands for Moving Pictures Experts Group. Like JPEG, MPEG refers to both a group and the standard that the group is developing. MPEG is a committee sanctioned by the ISO to work on the digital transmission of broadcast quality full motion video and sound. The goal of the MPEG group is to be able to send a high-quality picture and stereo soundtrack through a 1.5 Mbps channel. The MPEG has drafted a standard which is presently under review.

Nyquist Rate:

The rate that analog signal of frequency f has to be sampled at in order to be accurately reproduced. Harry Nyquist determined that this rate has to be greater than 2*f.

Order (in re. model)

The order of a model refers to how many previous symbols are taken into consideration when encoding. For example, an order-0 model ignores all previous symbols when determining what code to use for a given symbol. So even if the previous character in a file was 'q', the probability of a 'u' in an order-0 model will not go up. An order-1 model would take note of the 'q' and greatly increase the probability for the 'u'.

Phrase

A phrase is a string of symbols of an arbitrary length. When programming in C, the term "string" can usually be substituted for phrase.

PKZIP

PKZIP is a popular desktop compression/archiving program. PKZIP is distributed via shareware channels by PKWare, Glendale, WI. This program uses several different dictionary-based compression algorithms to compress input files. It has achieved enough popularity in the MS-DOS world to be accepted as a "standard", although the source code for the program remains proprietary.

p X 64

p x 64 refers to the CCITT standard regarding digital transmission of audiovisual information, commonly referred to as videoconferencing. ISDN communications networks allocate bandwidth in 64K bit/second "chunks". The 'p' in p X 64 refers the notion that a video transmission channel will be allocated a certain number of 64 Kbps channels. The quality of transmission will be affected by the magnitude of p. Videoconferencing can be done with p as low as 1 or 2, but transmission of motion is severely restricted. As p grows, higher quality transmission becomes possible.

Run Length Encoding

Run Length Encoding, or RLE, is a simple technique used to compress runs of identical symbols in a data stream. Typically RLE encodes a run of symbols as a symbol and a count. The simplicity of RLE and ease of implementation result in its frequent appearance in compression programs, although its performance is relatively poor.

Shannon Fano coding

Shannon Fano coding is a coding technique developed in the early 1950s which attempted to minimize the number of bits used in a message when the probabilities of symbols in the message were known. Shannon Fano coding has generally been superseded by Huffman coding, which produces provably optimum code sets, resulting in marginally better performance than Shannon Fano codes.

Shannon, Claude

Claude Shannon is known as the father of information theory for his work done in the 1940s and 1950s. Shannon defined the concept of "information content" and entropy as it relates to data. Shannon is also an ardent student of the art of juggling, both by man and machine.

Shareware

Shareware refers to an increasingly common method of software distribution. Shareware is based on a "try before you buy" concept. The user of a shareware program is authorized by the creator to try the program for a limited amount of time. After the evaluation period is over, the user is expected to "register" the program if it will continue being used. Registration generally consists of a payment in return for improved documentation, support, and other considerations.

While shareware is a decidedly ad hoc concept, some standardization in the industry is being attempted by the Association for Shareware Professionals. The ASP has established a set of guidelines for authors of shareware defining various standards for distribution and support.

While not part of the shareware definition, most shareware programs also have a significantly lower price than their commercial counterparts. Many consumers mistakenly feel that shareware is "free," an idea being battled by the ASP.

SQ, MS-DOS compression program

One of the earliest desktop compression programs was SQ, and its counterpart USQ. These two programs implemented a simple order 0 Huffman compression algorithm. They were first developed for the CP/M operating system, and were ported to MS-DOS soon after its release. SQ did not perform file archiving, so it was frequently combined with LU, a program that combined files into a library.

The appearance of ARC as a shareware program soon drove SQ into obscurity. ARC not only offered superior compression performance with its LZW algorithm, it also combined the compression and librarian functions into a single program. This let users compress groups of files and move them into a single archive in one operation.

Static model

A static model is one that does not change while a stream of symbols is compressed. An example of this would be a simple order-0 Huffman code compression program. The classic implementation of this program counts all of the different characters in a file during a first pass. This data is used to then build a Huffman coding tree, which constitutes the static model. A second pass is then made over the data to perform the actual compression.

Symbols

In data compression terminology, a symbol is an atomic unit of information. General purpose compression programs frequently compress streams of bytes, where the byte is the same thing as the symbol. However, a symbol could just as easily be a floating point number, or a spoken word, etc.

TAR, UNIX program

TAR is a standard UNIX program used to create archives. It takes a group of files and combines them into a single file or volume. TAR does not perform any compression of the files. UNIX archives are frequently created by using TAR to pack a group of files together, then using COMPRESS to perform the data compression. The resulting file is referred to as being in "TAR.Z" format.

Token

An arbitrary object used to encode something else. In dictionary-based compression, a token is an object that can be used to decode a phrase.

Welch, Terry

Terry Welch took the LZ78 data compression algorithm and refined it into a "Technique for High-Performance Data Compression". His patent on the LZW algorithm is now controlled by Unisys.

Ziv & Lempel

Jacob Ziv and Abraham Lempel are two Israeli information theorists who published the seminal papers on dictionary-based data compression in 1977 and 1978.

Bibliography

Bell, Timothy C., Cleary, John G., Witten, Ian H, (1990) *Text Compression*, Prentice Hall, Englewood Cliffs NJ.

Embree, Paul M., and Kimble, Bruce, (1991), *C Language Algorithms for Digital Signal Processing*, Prentice Hall, Englewood Cliffs, NJ.

Fiala, Edward R., and Greene, Daniel H., "Data compression with finite windows," *Communications of the ACM*, Volume 32, Number 4, April 1989, pages 490-505.

Huffman, D. A., "A method for the construction of minimum-redundancy codes," *Proceedings of the IRE*, Volume 40, Number 9, September 1952, pages 1098-1101.

Jain, Anil K., Farrelle, Paul M., and Algazi, V. Ralph, (1984) *Image Data Compression, Digital Image Processing Techniques*, Academic Press, pages 171-226

Karl, John H., *An Introduction to Digital Signal Processing*, Academic Press, 1989.

Monsour, Robert A., and Whiting, Douglas L., "Data Compression Breaks Through to Disk Memory Technology," *Computer Technology Review*, Volume 11, Number 6, May 1991, pp 39-45

Nelson, Mark, "LZW Data Compression," *Dr. Dobb's Journal*, Volume 14, Number 10, October 1989, pp 29-37

Ramabadran, Tenkasi V., and Gaitonde, Sunil S., "A Tutorial on CRC Computations," *IEEE Micro*, August 1988, pp. 62-75.

Storer, J.A., (1988) *Data Compression*, Computer Science Press, Rockville, MD

Wallace, Gregory K., "The JPEG Still Picture Compression Standard," *Communications of the ACM*, Volume 34, Number 4, April 199, pp 31-44.

Welch, Terry, "A Technique for High-Performance Data Compression," *IEEE Computer*, Volume 17, Number 6, June 1984, pages 8-19.

Witten, Ian H., Neal, Radford M., and Cleary, John G., "Arithmetic Coding for Data Compression," *Communications of the ACM*, Volume 30, Number 6, June 1987, pages 520-540.

Ziv, J., and Lempel, A., "A universal algorithm for sequential data compression," *IEEE Transactions on Information Theory*, Volume 23, Number 3, May 1977, pages 337-343.

Ziv, J., and Lempel, "A., Compression of individual sequences via variable-rate coding," *IEEE Transactions on Information Theory*, Volume 24, Number 5, September 1978, pages 530-536.

Other Resources

An excellent resource for programmers wanting to learn more about Data Compression is the IBM Programming Forum on Compuserve. To open a Compuserve account, call their customer service department at 1-800-848-8990. Some files of interest presently on in the Data Compression Library of that forum include:

AR002.EXE   A   straightforward compression/archive program, with
                commented C source.

ARJ220.EXE   The ARJ compression program. ARJ is free for non-
UNARJ220.EXE   commercial use, and includes UNARJ.C, which can be
                freely distributed and incorporated in other products.

CMPPAS.EXE   LZSS and LZARI compression programs in Turbo Pascal.

COMPR.TXT   A paper by Haruhiko Okumura discussing the state of the
                  art in Japanese shareware compression programs,
                  notably LHarc.

LHA213.EXE   The LHarc compression program, freeware, with C and
LHASRC.EXE   assembly source.

LZCOMP.EXE   C source for LZSS, LZHUF, and LZSS algorithms.

PAK251.EXE   Shareware compresson program, supports multiple formats.

PKZ110.EXE   The well known PKZIP shareware archive/compression
                  package.

ZOO210.EXE   The UNIX archiving package. Public Domain.

Afterword

When writing about data compression, I am haunted by the idea that many of the techniques discussed in this book have been patented by their inventors or others. The knowledge that a data compression algorithm can effectively be taken out of the hands of programmers through the use of so-called "intellectual property" law seems contrary to the basic principles that led me and many others into this profession.

I have yet to see any evidence that applying patents to software advances the art or protects the rights of inventors. Several companies continue to collect royalties on patents long after their inventors have moved onto bigger and better thing with other companies. Have the patent-holders done anything notable other than collect royalties? Have they advanced the art of computer science?

Making a software product into a commercial success requires innovation, good design, high-quality documentation, and listening to customers. These are things that nobody can steal from you. On the other hand, a mountain of patents can't keep you from letting these things slip away through inattention or complacency. This lesson seems to be lost on those who traffic in intellectual property "portfolios."

What can you do? First, don't patent your own work, and discourage your peers from doing so. Work on improving your products, not erecting legal obstacles to competition. Secondly, lobby for change. This means change within your company, those you do business with, and most importantly, within the federal government. Write to your congressman and your senator. Write to the ACM. Write to the House Subcommittee on Intellectual Property. And finally, you can join me by becoming a member of the League for Programming Freedom. Write for more information:

> League For Programming Freedom
> 1 Kendall Square #143
> P.O. Box 9171
> Cambridge, MA 02139

Index

A

Adaptive
  arithmetic coding 170
  coding 82–83, 351–353
  compression 220–225, 221
  models 21, 22, 169–176
Adaptive Differential Pulse Code Modulation
  (ADPCM 346
Adaptive Huffman coding 11, 81–99
Adaptive PCM 12
AHUFF.C 109
Analog data 24
Analog-to-digital converter (ADC) 316
ANSI
  C 7
  standard 47
  standard XJ11.34 6
ARC 26, 227–230, 409
Archive program 12
Archiving 409–488
ARITH-1.C 176
ARITH-N.C 178, 185, 188, 188–218
ARITH.C 134, 148–165
ARITH1.C 172
ARITH1E.C 175, 178
Arithmetic coding 11, 18, 19, 123–
  131, 170, 369
ARJ 27, 228, 409
ARJ 2.10 325

B

Bell 179
BILL GATES message 124
Binary tree support routines 262–265
BITIO.C 38–42, 42, 101
BITIO.H 39, 41, 55

BIX 324
Block coding 360
Blocking 408
BMP format 348
Borland C++ 2.0 489
Borland C++ program 5
Buzzwords 13

C

C program 4–5
CAR 409–428
  file structure 412–413
  header 413–425
CARMAN 409–428
  command line 419
  command set 410–412
  list command 411
CARMAN.C 438–488
CCITT 231, 311, 353
CCITT-32 formula 417
Central Point Software 228
CHURN test program 495
CHURN.C 495
Cleary, John 176, 179
CloseInputBitFile() 40
CloseOutputBitFile() 40
Coding 14, 14–15, 17–19
COMPAND.C 340, 341–345
Companding 336–345
Companding codec 338
COMPRESS program
  compression ratio 303
  hashing function 292
  LZ78 284
  LZW 12, 285
  public release of 227
  versus COMPACT 26

O R D E R   F O R M

To Order: Return this form with your payment to M&T Books, 411 Borel Avenue, Suite 100, San Mateo, CA 94402 or **call toll-free 1-800-533-4372 (in California, call 1-800-356-2002).**

ITEM #	DESCRIPTION	DISK	PRICE

Subtotal	
CA residents add sales tax ___%	
Add $4.50 per item for shipping and handling	
TOTAL	

CARD NO.

Charge my:

❑ **Visa**   SIGNATURE   EXP. DATE

❑ **MasterCard**

❑ **AmExpress**   NAME

                    ADDRESS

❑ **Check enclosed,**   CITY

payable to

M&T Books.   STATE   ZIP

M&T GUARANTEE: If your are not satisfied with your order for any reason, return it to us within 25 days of receipt for a full refund. Note: Refunds on disks apply only when returned with book within guarantee period. Disks damaged in transit or defective will be promptly replaced, but cannot be exchanged for a disk from a different title.

8049

Tell us what you think and we'll send you a free M&T Books catalog

It is our goal at M&T Books to produce the best technical books available. But you can help us make our books even better by letting us know what you think about this particular title.Please take a moment to fill out this card and mail it to us. Your opinion is appreciated.

Tell us about yourself

Name _____

Company _____

Address _____

City _____

State/Zip _____

Title of this book?

_____

Where did you purchase this book?

☐ Bookstore
☐ Catalog
☐ Direct Mail
☐ Magazine Ad
☐ Postcard Pack
☐ Other

Why did you choose this book?

☐ Recommended
☐ Read book review
☐ Read ad/catalog copy
☐ Responded to a special offer
☐ M&T Books' reputation
☐ Price
☐ Nice Cover

How would you rate the overall content of this book?

☐ Excellent
☐ Good
☐ Fair
☐ Poor

Why?

_____

_____

What chapters did you find valuable?

_____

_____

_____

What did you find least useful?

_____

_____

_____

What topic(s) would you add to future editions of this book?

_____

_____

_____

What other titles would you like to see M&T Books publish?

_____

_____

_____

Which format do you prefer for the optional disk?

☐ 5.25"   ☐ 3.5"

Any other comments?

_____

_____

☐ Check here for
M&T Books Catalog

M&T BOOKS